CCNA®
Cisco Certified Network Associate
Review Guide

Todd Lammle

WILEY
Wiley Publishing, Inc.

Senior Acquisitions Editor: Jeff Kellum
Development Editor: Kathi Duggan
Technical Editors: Troy McMillan and Dax Michelson
Production Editor: Christine O'Connor
Copy Editor: Kathy Grider-Carlyle
Editorial Manager: Pete Gaughan
Production Manager: Tim Tate
Vice President and Executive Group Publisher: Richard Swadley
Vice President and Publisher: Neil Edde
Media Project Manager 1: Laura Moss-Hollister
Media Associate Producer: Marilyn Hummel
Media Quality Assurance: Doug Kuhn
Book Designer: Happenstance Type-O-Rama
Compositor: Craig Woods, Happenstance Type-O-Rama
Proofreader: Louise Watson, Word One New York
Indexer: Robert Swanson
Project Coordinator, Cover: Katherine Crocker
Cover Designer: Ryan Sneed

ISBN: 978-1-118-06346-0
ISBN: 978-1-118-11361-5 (ebk.)
ISBN: 978-1-118-11360-8 (ebk.)
ISBN: 978-1-118-11362-2 (ebk.)

Dear Reader,

Thank you for choosing *CCNA: Cisco Certified Network Associate Review Guide*. This book is part of a family of premium-quality Sybex books, all of which are written by outstanding authors who combine practical experience with a gift for teaching.

Sybex was founded in 1976. More than 30 years later, we're still committed to producing consistently exceptional books. With each of our titles, we're working hard to set a new standard for the industry. From the paper we print on, to the authors we work with, our goal is to bring you the best books available.

I hope you see all that reflected in these pages. I'd be very interested to hear your comments and get your feedback on how we're doing. Feel free to let me know what you think about this or any other Sybex book by sending me an email at nedde@wiley.com. If you think you've found a technical error in this book, please visit http://sybex.custhelp.com. Customer feedback is critical to our efforts at Sybex.

Best regards,

Neil Edde
Vice President and Publisher
Sybex, an Imprint of Wiley

Acknowledgments

To my best editor, Kathi Duggan: You came in and helped me knock this out with great enthusiasm. Thank you!

Thanks to Jeff Kellum, who always keeps me working hard and makes sure I am headed in the right direction. This is no easy task for Jeff!

And thanks to Christine O'Connor, who somehow made sense of my work and helped me put it together in a great, easy-to-study format.

And as always, Troy McMillian was instrumental in helping me put this book together, as well as tech editing it.

Thank you all!

About the Author

Todd Lammle   CCSI, CCNA/CCNP/CCSP, MCSE, CEH/CHFI, FCC RF Licensed, is the authority on Cisco Certification internetworking. He is a world-renowned author, speaker, trainer, and consultant. Todd has over 30 years of experience working with LANs, WANs, and large licensed and unlicensed wireless networks. He is president of GlobalNet Training and Consulting, Inc., a network integration and training firm based in Dallas, Texas. You can reach him through GlobalNet Training Solutions, Inc. at www.globalnettc.com or through his online forum at www.lammle.com.

Contents at a Glance

Introduction   *xiii*

Chapter 1   Describe How a Network Works   1

Chapter 2   Configure, Verify, and Troubleshoot a Switch with
                VLANs and Interswitch Communications   57

Chapter 3   Implement an IP Addressing Scheme and IP Services
                to Meet Network Requirements in a Medium-Sized
                Enterprise Branch Office Network   119

Chapter 4   Configure, Verify, and Troubleshoot Basic Router
                Operation and Routing on Cisco Devices   153

Chapter 5   Explain and Select the Appropriate Administrative
                Tasks Required for a WLAN   235

Chapter 6   Identify Security Threats to a Network and Describe
                General Methods to Mitigate Those Threats   255

Chapter 7   Implement, Verify, and Troubleshoot NAT and ACLs
                in a Medium-Sized Enterprise Branch Office Network   269

Chapter 8   Implement and Verify WAN Links   299

Appendix   About the Companion CD   325

Index   *329*

Contents

Introduction   *xiii*

Chapter   1   Describe How a Network Works   **1**

Describe the Purpose and Functions of Various
    Network Devices   2
Use the OSI and TCP/IP Models and Their Associated
    Protocols to Explain How Data Flows in a Network   8
Describe Common Networked Applications, Including
    Web Applications   10
Describe the Purpose and Basic Operation of the Protocols
    in the OSI and TCP Models   15
Describe the Impact of Applications (Voice over IP and
    Video over IP) on a Network   19
Interpret Network Diagrams   23
Determine the Path between Two Hosts across a Network   31
Describe the Components Required for Network and
    Internet Communications   35
Identify and Correct Common Network Problems at
    Layers 1, 2, 3, and 7 Using a Layered Model Approach   39
Differentiate between LAN/WAN Operation and Features   42
Review Questions   54
Answers to Review Questions   56

**Chapter   2   Configure, Verify, and Troubleshoot a Switch
with VLANs and Interswitch Communications**   **57**

Select the Appropriate Media, Cables, Ports, and Connectors
    to Connect Switches to Other Network Devices and Hosts   59
Explain the Technology and Media Access Control Method
    for Ethernet Networks   62
Explain Network Segmentation and Basic Traffic
    Management Concepts   67
Explain Basic Switching Concepts and the Operation
    of Cisco Switches   69
Perform and Verify Initial Switch Configuration Tasks,
    Including Remote Access Management   74
Verify Network Status and Switch Operation Using Basic
    Utilities (Including ping, traceroute, Telnet, SSH, arp, and
    ipconfig) and *SHOW* and *DEBUG* Commands   77
Identify, Prescribe, and Resolve Common Switched Network
    Media Issues, Configuration Issues, Auto Negotiation, and
    Switch Hardware Failures   83
Describe Enhanced Switching Technologies (Including
    VTP, RSTP, VLAN, PVSTP, and 802.1q)   84

Describe How VLANs Create Logically Separate Networks
and the Need for Routing between Them   88
Configure, Verify, and Troubleshoot VLANs   92
Configure, Verify, and Troubleshoot Trunking on Cisco Switches 95
Configure, Verify, and Troubleshoot InterVLAN Routing   99
Configure, Verify, and Troubleshoot VTP   103
Configure, Verify, and Troubleshoot RSTP Operation   109
Interpret the Output of Various *SHOW* and *DEBUG*
Commands to Verify the Operational Status of a Cisco
Switched Network   111
Implement Basic Switch Security (Including Port
Security, Trunk Access, Management VLAN Other
Than VLAN 1, Etc.)   111
Review Questions   114
Answers to Review Questions   118

**Chapter   3   Implement an IP Addressing Scheme and
IP Services to Meet Network Requirements in a
Medium-Sized Enterprise Branch Office Network   119**

Describe the Operation and Benefits of Using Private and
Public IP Addressing   121
Explain the Operation and Benefits of Using DHCP and DNS 124
Configure, Verify, and Troubleshoot DHCP and DNS
Operation on a Router (Including CLI/SDM)   124
Implement Static and Dynamic Addressing Services for Hosts
in a LAN Environment   127
Calculate and Apply an Addressing Scheme, Including
VLSM IP Addressing Design, to a Network   132
Determine the Appropriate Classless Addressing Scheme
Using VLSM and Summarization to Satisfy Addressing
Requirements in a LAN/WAN Environment   134
Describe the Technological Requirements for Running IPv6
in Conjunction with IPv4 (Including Protocols, Dual Stack,
Tunneling, Etc.)   142
Describe IPv6 Addresses   145
Identify and Correct Common Problems Associated
with IP Addressing and Host Configurations   149
Review Questions   150
Answer to Review Questions   152

**Chapter   4   Configure, Verify, and Troubleshoot Basic Router
Operation and Routing on Cisco Devices   153**

Describe Basic Routing Concepts (Including Packet
Forwarding and the Router Lookup Process)   155

Describe the Operation of Cisco Routers (Including the
   Router Bootup Process, POST, and Router Components)   158
Select the Appropriate Media, Cables, Ports, and Connectors
   to Connect Routers to Other Network Devices and Hosts   160
Configure, Verify, and Troubleshoot RIPv2   162
Access and Utilize the Router to Set Basic Parameters
   (Including CLI/SDM)   165
Connect, Configure, and Verify the Operational Status
   of a Device Interface   175
Verify Device Configuration and Network Connectivity
   Using ping, traceroute, Telnet, SSH, or Other Utilities   189
Perform and Verify Routing Configuration Tasks for a Static
   or Default Route Given Specific Routing Requirements   189
Manage IOS Configuration Files (Including Save, Edit,
   Upgrade, and Restore)   192
Manage Cisco IOS   196
Compare and Contrast Methods of Routing and
   Routing Protocols   200
Configure, Verify, and Troubleshoot OSPF   202
Configure, Verify, and Troubleshoot EIGRP   211
Verify Network Connectivity (Including Using ping,
   traceroute, and Telnet or SSH)   216
Troubleshoot Routing Issues   216
Verify Router Hardware and Software Operation Using
   the *show* and *debug* Commands   221
Implement Basic Router Security   227
Review Questions   231
Answers to Review Questions   233

**Chapter   5   Explain and Select the Appropriate Administrative
Tasks Required for a WLAN   235**

Describe Standards Associated with Wireless Media
   (Including IEEE, Wi-Fi Alliance, and ITU/FCC)   236
Identify and Describe the Purpose of the Components in a
   Small Wireless Network (Including SSID, BSS, and ESS)   243
Identify the Basic Parameters to Configure on a Wireless
   Network to Ensure That Devices Connect to the Correct
   Access Point   246
Compare and Contrast Wireless Security Features and
   Capabilities of WPA Security (Including Open, WEP,
   and WPA-1/2)   248
Identify Common Issues with Implementing Wireless
   Networks (Including Interfaces and Misconfigurations)   251
Review Questions   252
Answers to Review Questions   254

**Chapter   6   Identify Security Threats to a Network and Describe
                    General Methods to Mitigate Those Threats   255**

Describe Today's Increasing Network Security Threats and
    Explain the Need to Implement a Comprehensive Security
    Policy to Mitigate the Threats   256
Explain General Methods to Mitigate Common Security
    Threats to Network Devices, Hosts, and Applications   260
Describe the Functions of Common Security Appliances
    and Applications   261
Describe Security Recommended Practices, Including Initial
    Steps to Secure Network Devices   264
Review Questions   266
Answers to Review Questions   268

**Chapter   7   Implement, Verify, and Troubleshoot NAT
                    and ACLs in a Medium-Sized Enterprise Branch
                    Office Network   269**

Describe the Purpose and Types of ACLs   270
Configure and Apply ACLs Based on Network Filtering
    Requirements (Including CLI/SDM)   270
Configure and Apply ACLs to Limit Telnet and SSH Access
    to the Router Using (Including SDM/CLI)   283
Verify and Monitor ACLs in a Network Environment   285
Troubleshoot ACL Issues   288
Explain the Basic Operation of NAT   288
Configure NAT for Given Network Requirements
    Using (Including CLI/SDM)   290
Troubleshoot NAT Issues   293
Review Questions   295
Answers to Review Questions   297

Chapter   8   Implement and Verify WAN Links   299

Describe Different Methods for Connecting to a WAN   300
Configure and Verify a Basic WAN Serial Connection   301
Configure and Verify Frame Relay on Cisco Routers   304
Troubleshoot WAN Implementation Issues   310
Describe VPN Technology (Including Importance,
    Benefits, Role, Impact, and Components)   314
Configure and Verify a PPP Connection between
    Cisco Routers   315
Review Questions   319
Answers to Review Questions   323

Appendix   About the Companion CD   325

Index   *329*

Introduction

Welcome to the exciting world of Cisco certification! You picked up this book because you want something better—namely, a better job with more satisfaction. Rest assured that you made a good decision. Cisco certification can help you get your first networking job, or more money and a promotion if you are already in the field.

Cisco certification can also improve your understanding of the internetworking of more than just Cisco products. By studying the material in this book, you will develop a complete understanding of networking and how different network topologies work together to form a network. This is beneficial to every networking job and is the reason Cisco certification is in such high demand, even at companies with few Cisco devices.

Cisco is the king of routing and switching, the Microsoft of the internetworking world. The Cisco certifications reach beyond the popular certifications, such as the MCSE, to provide you with an indispensable factor in understanding today's network—insight into the Cisco world of internetworking. By deciding that you want to become Cisco certified, you are saying that you want to be the best—the best at routing and the best at switching. This book will lead you in that direction.

What Is CCNA Certification?

The CCNA certification was the first in the new line of Cisco certifications and was the precursor to all current Cisco certifications. Now you can become a Cisco Certified Network Associate for the meager cost of this book and either one exam or two exams However, the CCNA exams are extremely hard and cover a lot of material, so you have to really know your stuff. Taking a Cisco class or spending months getting hands-on experience is not out of the norm.

Once you have your CCNA certification, you don't have to stop there. You can continue your studies and achieve a higher certification, called the Cisco Certified Network Professional (CCNP). Someone with a CCNP certification has all the skills and knowledge he or she needs to attempt the Routing and Switching CCIE lab. Just becoming a CCNA can land you the job you've dreamed about.

This book covers everything CCNA related. For up-to-date information on Todd Lammle Cisco Authorized CCNA, CCNP, CCSP, CCVP, and CCIE bootcamps, please see www.lammle.com and/or www.globalnettc.com.

Is This Book For You?

CCNA: Cisco Certified Network Associate Review Guide is designed to be a succinct, portable exam review guide that can be used in conjunction with a more complete study guide such as the *CCNA: Cisco Certified Network Associate Study Guide, 7th Edition* or *CCNA: Cisco Certified Network Associate Deluxe Study Guide, 6th Edition* (Sybex, 2011), Todd Lammle Video Series, and a CBT courseware, and a classroom/lab environment. It can also be used as an exam review for those who don't feel the need for more extensive test preparation. It isn't my goal to give away the answers, but rather to identify those topics on which you can expect to be tested and to provide sufficient coverage of those topics.

Perhaps you've been working with information technologies for years. The thought of paying lots of money for a specialized IT exam-preparation course probably doesn't sound appealing. What can they teach you that you don't already know, right? Be careful, though—many experienced network administrators have walked confidently into the test center only to sheepishly walk out of it after failing an IT exam. After you've finished reading this book, you should have a clear idea of how your understanding of the technologies involved matches up with the expectations of the CCNA test makers.

Perhaps you're relatively new to the world of IT, drawn to it by the promise of challenging work and higher salaries. You've just waded through an 800-page study guide or taken a week-long class at a local training center. That is a lot of information to keep track of, isn't it? Well, by organizing this book according to Cisco's exam objectives, and by breaking up the information into concise, manageable pieces, we've created what we think is the handiest exam review guide available. Throw it in your briefcase and carry it to work with you. As you read the book, you'll be able to quickly identify those areas you know best and those that require a more in-depth review.

How Is This Book Organized?

This book is organized according to the official objectives list prepared by Cisco for the CCNA exam. The chapters correspond with the eight broad objective categories:

Chapter 1: Describe How a Network Works

Chapter 2: Configure, Verify, and Troubleshoot a Switch with VLANs and Interswitch Communications

Chapter 3: Implement an IP Addressing Scheme and IP Services to Meet Network Requirements in a Medium-Size Enterprise Branch Office Network

Chapter 4: Configure, Verify, and Troubleshoot Basic Router Operation and Routing on Cisco Devices

Chapter 5: Explain and Select the Appropriate Administrative Tasks Required for a WLAN

Chapter 6: Identify Security Threats to a Network and Describe General Methods to Mitigate Those Threats

Chapter 7: Implement, Verify, and Troubleshoot NAT and ACLs in a Medium-Sized Enterprise Branch Office Network

Chapter 8: Implement and Verify WAN Links

Within each chapter, the individual exam objectives are addressed. Each section of a chapter covers one exam objective. For each objective, the critical information is first presented, and then there are several Exam Essentials for each exam objective. Additionally, each chapter ends with a section of Review Questions. Here is a closer look at each of these components:

Exam Objectives   The individual exam objective sections present the greatest level of detail on information that is relevant to the CCNA exam. This is the place to start if you're unfamiliar with or uncertain about the technical issues related to the objective.

Exam Essentials   Here you are given a short list of topics that you should explore fully before taking the exam. Included in the Exam Essentials areas are notations of the key information you should take out of the exam objective section.

Review Questions   This section ends every chapter and provides 10 questions to help you gauge your mastery of the chapter.

On the CD

We've included several testing features on the CD that accompanies this book. These tools will help you retain vital exam content as well as prepare you to sit for the actual exams:

Two CCNA Practice Exams   The CD contains the Sybex Test Engine, with two exclusive CCNA bonus practice exams. Using this custom test engine, you can identify weak areas up front and then develop a solid studying strategy using each of these robust testing features. Our thorough readme file will walk you through the quick, easy installation process.

Electronic Flashcards   You'll find flashcard questions on the CD for on-the-go review. These are short questions and answers, just like the flashcards you probably used to study in school.

Glossary of Terms in PDF   The CD contains a very useful Glossary of Terms in PDF (Adobe Acrobat) format, so you can easily read it on any computer. If you have to travel and brush up on any key terms, and you have a laptop with a CD drive, you can do so with this useful resource.

Tips for Taking Your CCNA Exam

The CCNA exam contains about 55 questions or more, to be completed in about 90 minutes or less. This can change per exam. You must get a score of about 85 percent to pass this exam, but again, each exam can be different.

Many questions on the exam have answer choices that at first glance look identical—especially the syntax questions! Remember to read through the choices carefully, because close doesn't cut it. If you get commands in the wrong order or forget just one character, you'll get the question wrong. So, to practice, do the hands-on exercises at the end of the chapters in this book over and over again until they feel natural to you.

Also, never forget that the right answer is the Cisco answer. In many cases, more than one appropriate answer is presented, but the *correct* answer is the one that Cisco recommends. The exam always tells you to pick one, two, or three answers (never "choose all that apply").

The CCNA 640-802 exam includes the following test formats:

- Multiple-choice single answer
- Multiple-choice multiple answer
- Drag-and-drop
- Fill-in-the-blank
- Router simulations

Here are some general tips for exam success:

- Arrive early at the exam center, so you can relax and review your study materials.
- Read the questions *carefully*. Don't jump to conclusions. Make sure you're clear about *exactly* what each question asks.
- When answering multiple-choice questions that you're not sure about, use the process of elimination to get rid of the obviously incorrect answers first. Doing this greatly improves your odds if you need to make an educated guess.
- You can no longer move forward and backward through the Cisco exams—so double-check your answer before clicking Next, because *you can't change your mind*.

After you complete an exam, you'll get immediate, online notification of your pass or fail status, a printed Examination Score Report that indicates your pass or fail status, and your exam results by section. (The test administrator will give you the printed score report.) Test scores are automatically forwarded to Cisco within five working days after you take the test, so you don't need to send your score to them. If you pass the exam, you'll receive confirmation from Cisco, typically within two to four weeks.

The CCNA Exam Objectives

Cisco has posted eight categories with specific objectives within each category. As mentioned previously, these exam objectives form the outline for this book. Following are Cisco's objectives for the CCNA exam:

 Exam objectives are subject to change at any time without prior notice and at Cisco's sole discretion. Please visit the CCNA page of Cisco's website (www.cisco.com) for the most current listing of exam objectives.

Describe how a network works

- Describe the purpose and functions of various network devices
- Select the components required to meet a network specification
- Use the OSI and TCP/IP models and their associated protocols to explain how data flows in a network
- Describe common networked applications, including web applications
- Describe the purpose and basic operation of the protocols in the OSI and TCP models
- Describe the impact of applications (Voice over IP and Video over IP) on a network
- Interpret network diagrams
- Determine the path between two hosts across a network
- Describe the components required for network and Internet communications
- Identify and correct common network problems at layers 1, 2, 3, and 7 using a layered model approach
- Differentiate between LAN/WAN operation and features

Configure, verify, and troubleshoot a switch with VLANs and interswitch communications

- Select the appropriate media, cables, ports, and connectors to connect switches to other network devices and hosts
- Explain the technology and media access control method for Ethernet networks
- Explain network segmentation and basic traffic management concepts
- Explain basic switching concepts and the operation of Cisco switches
- Perform and verify initial switch configuration tasks, including remote access management
- Verify network status and switch operation using basic utilities (including ping, traceroute, Telnet, SSH, arp, and ipconfig) and SHOW and DEBUG commands
- Identify, prescribe, and resolve common switched network media issues, configuration issues, auto negotiation, and switch hardware failures
- Describe enhanced switching technologies (including VTP, RSTP, VLAN, PVSTP, and 802.1q)
- Describe how VLANs create logically separate networks and the need for routing between them
- Configure, verify, and troubleshoot VLANs
- Configure, verify, and troubleshoot trunking on Cisco switches
- Configure, verify, and troubleshoot interVLAN routing
- Configure, verify, and troubleshoot VTP

- Configure, verify, and troubleshoot RSTP operation
- Interpret the output of various Show and Debug commands to verify the operational status of a Cisco switched network
- Implement basic switch security (including port security, trunk access, management VLAN other than VLAN 1, etc.)

Implement an IP addressing scheme and IP Services to meet network requirements in a medium-size Enterprise branch office network

- Describe the operation and benefits of using private and public IP addressing
- Explain the operation and benefits of using DHCP and DNS
- Configure, verify, and troubleshoot DHCP and DNS operation on a router (including CLI/SDM)
- Implement static and dynamic addressing services for hosts in a LAN environment
- Calculate and apply an addressing scheme, including VLSM IP addressing design, to a network
- Determine the appropriate classless addressing scheme using VLSM and summarization to satisfy addressing requirements in a LAN/WAN environment
- Describe the technological requirements for running IPv6 in conjunction with IPv4 (including protocols, dual stack, tunneling, etc.)
- Describe IPv6 addresses
- Identify and correct common problems associated with IP addressing and host configurations

Configure, verify, and troubleshoot basic router operation and routing on Cisco devices

- Describe basic routing concepts (including packet forwarding and the router lookup process)
- Describe the operation of Cisco routers (including the router bootup process, POST, and router components)
- Select the appropriate media, cables, ports, and connectors to connect routers to other network devices and hosts
- Configure, verify, and troubleshoot RIPv2
- Access and utilize the router to set basic parameters (including CLI/SDM)
- Connect, configure, and verify the operational status of a device interface
- Verify device configuration and network connectivity using ping, traceroute, Telnet, SSH, or other utilities
- Perform and verify routing configuration tasks for a static or default route given specific routing requirements

- Manage IOS configuration files. (including save, edit, upgrade, and restore)
- Manage Cisco IOS
- Compare and contrast methods of routing and routing protocols
- Configure, verify, and troubleshoot OSPF
- Configure, verify, and troubleshoot EIGRP
- Verify network connectivity (including using ping, traceroute, and telnet or SSH)
- Troubleshoot routing issues
- Verify router hardware and software operation using the SHOW and DEBUG commands
- Implement basic router security

Explain and select the appropriate administrative tasks required for a WLAN

- Describe standards associated with wireless media (including IEEE WI-FI Alliance and ITU/FCC)
- Identify and describe the purpose of the components in a small wireless network (including SSID, BSS, and ESS)
- Identify the basic parameters to configure on a wireless network to ensure that devices connect to the correct access point
- Compare and contrast wireless security features and capabilities of WPA security (including open, WEP, and WPA-1/2)
- Identify common issues with implementing wireless networks (including interfaces and misconfigurations)

Identify security threats to a network and describe general methods to mitigate those threats

- Describe today's increasing network security threats and explain the need to implement a comprehensive security policy to mitigate the threats
- Explain general methods to mitigate common security threats to network devices, hosts, and applications
- Describe the functions of common security appliances and applications
- Describe security recommended practices, including initial steps to secure network devices

Implement, verify, and troubleshoot NAT and ACLs in a medium-size Enterprise branch office network

- Describe the purpose and types of ACLs
- Configure and apply ACLs based on network filtering requirements (including CLI/SDM)
- Configure and apply ACLs to limit Telnet and SSH access to the router using (including SDM/CLI)
- Verify and monitor ACLs in a network environment

- Troubleshoot ACL issues
- Explain the basic operation of NAT
- Configure NAT for given network requirements using (including CLI/SDM)
- Troubleshoot NAT issues

Implement and verify WAN links

- Describe different methods for connecting to a WAN
- Configure and verify a basic WAN serial connection
- Configure and verify Frame Relay on Cisco routers
- Troubleshoot WAN implementation issues
- Describe VPN technology (including importance, benefits, role, impact, components)
- Configure and verify a PPP connection between Cisco routers

Describe How a Network Works

THE CISCO CCNA EXAM OBJECTIVES COVERED IN THIS CHAPTER INCLUDE THE FOLLOWING:

✓ Describe the purpose and functions of various network devices.

✓ Select the components required to meet a network specification.

✓ Use the OSI and TCP/IP models and their associated protocols to explain how data flows in a network.

✓ Describe common networked applications, including web applications.

✓ Describe the purpose and basic operation of the protocols in the OSI and TCP models.

✓ Describe the impact of applications (Voice over IP and Video over IP) on a network.

✓ Interpret network diagrams.

✓ Determine the path between two hosts across a network.

✓ Describe the components required for network and Internet communications.

✓ Identify and correct common network problems at layers 1, 2, 3, and 7 using a layered model approach.

✓ Differentiate between LAN/WAN operation and features.

In this chapter, we will review the basics of internetworking. First, we will examine what an internetwork is; next, we will look at the Open Systems Interconnection (OSI) model and review each part. We will also review the difference between TCP and UDP with regard to VoIP and video streaming. Our review will also include PDU encapsulation, TCP/IP troubleshooting, Ethernet, and WAN connections.

Describe the Purpose and Functions of Various Network Devices

It is likely that at some point you'll have to break up one large network into a bunch of smaller ones because user response will have dwindled to a slow crawl as the network grows and grows. With all that growth, your LAN's traffic congestion will have reached epic proportions. The best way to handle this will be to break up your large network into several smaller networks—something called *network segmentation*.

You can do this by using devices like *routers*, *switches*, and *bridges*. Figure 1.1 displays a network that's been segmented with a switch so each network segment connected to the switch is a separate collision domain. But make note of the fact that this network is still one broadcast domain.

Keep in mind that the hub used in Figure 1.1 just extended the one collision domain from the switch port. Here's a list of some of the things that commonly cause LAN traffic congestion:

- Too many hosts in a broadcast domain
- Broadcast storms
- Multicasting
- Low bandwidth
- Adding hubs for connectivity to the network

Routers are used to connect networks together and route packets of data from one network to another. Cisco became the de facto standard of routers because of its high-quality router products, great selection, and fantastic service. Routers, by default, break up a *broadcast domain*—the set of all devices on a network segment that hear all the broadcasts sent on that segment. Figure 1.2 shows a router in a little network that creates an internetwork and breaks up broadcast domains.

FIGURE 1.1 A switch can replace the hub, breaking up collision domains.

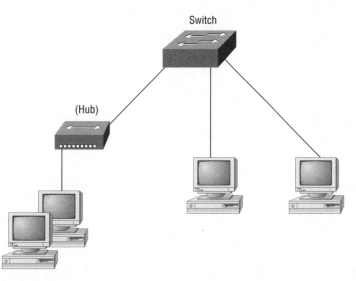

FIGURE 1.2 Routers create an internetwork.

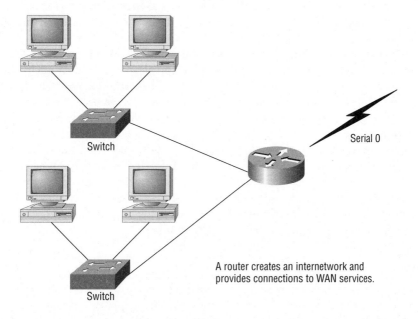

A router creates an internetwork and provides connections to WAN services.

The network in Figure 1.2 shows that each host is connected to its own collision domain, and the router has created two broadcast domains—and don't forget that the router provides connections to WAN services as well. The router uses something called a *serial interface* for WAN connections—specifically, a V.35 physical interface on a Cisco router.

Breaking up a broadcast domain is important because when a host or server sends a network broadcast, every device on the network must read and process that broadcast—unless you have a router. When the router's interface receives this broadcast, it can respond by discarding the broadcast without forwarding it to other networks. Even though routers are known for breaking up broadcast domains by default, it's important to remember that they break up collision domains as well.

Here are two advantages of using routers in your network:

- They don't forward broadcasts by default.
- They can filter the network based on layer 3 (Network layer) information (such as an IP address).

Four router functions in your network can be listed as follows:

- Packet switching
- Packet filtering
- Internetwork communication
- Path selection

Routers are actually layer 3 switches (we'll talk about layers later in this chapter). Unlike layer 2 switches, which forward or filter frames, routers (layer 3 switches) use logical addressing and provide what is called *packet switching*. When routers connect two or more networks together and use logical addressing (IP or IPv6), this is called an *internetwork*. Last, routers use a *routing table* (map of the internetwork) to make path selections and to forward packets to remote networks.

Conversely, switches don't break up broadcast domains to create internetworks. The main purpose of a switch is to optimize a LAN's performance and provide more bandwidth for its users. And switches don't forward packets to other networks as routers do. Instead, they only "switch" frames from one port to another within the switched network.

By default, switches break up *collision domains*. This is an Ethernet term used to describe a network scenario wherein one particular device sends a packet on a network segment, forcing every other device on that same segment to pay attention to it. At the same time, a different device tries to transmit, leading to a collision, after which both devices must retransmit, one at a time, which is not very efficient. This situation is typically found in a hub environment where each host segment connects to a hub that represents only one collision domain and only one broadcast domain. By contrast, each and every port on a switch represents its own collision domain.

 Switches create separate collision domains but a single broadcast domain. Routers provide a separate broadcast domain for each interface.

The term *bridging* was introduced before routers, switches, and hubs were implemented, so it's pretty common to hear people referring to bridges as switches. That's because bridges and switches basically do the same thing: they break up collision domains on a LAN. (In reality, you cannot buy a physical bridge these days; you can buy only LAN switches, but they use bridging technologies, so Cisco still calls them multiport bridges.)

A switch is basically a multiple-port bridge with greatly enhanced management capabilities and features. Also, while bridges may have up to 16 ports, switches can have hundreds!

 You would use a switch/bridge in a network to reduce collisions within broadcast domains and to increase the number of collision domains in your network. Doing this provides more bandwidth for users. Keep in mind that using hubs in your network can contribute to congestion on your Ethernet network. As always, plan your network design carefully!

Exam Essentials

Understand the difference between a hub, a bridge, a switch, and a router.   Hubs create one collision domain and one broadcast domain. Bridges break up collision domains but create one large broadcast domain. They use hardware addresses to filter the network. Switches are really just multiple-port bridges with more intelligence. They break up collision domains but create one large broadcast domain by default. Switches use hardware addresses to filter the network. Routers break up broadcast domains (and collision domains) and use logical addressing to filter the network.

Identify the functions and advantages of routers.   Routers perform packet switching, filtering, and path selection; and they facilitate internetwork communication. One advantage of routers is that they reduce broadcast traffic.

Remember the possible causes of LAN traffic congestion.   Too many hosts in a broadcast domain, broadcast storms, multicasting, and low bandwidth are all possible causes of LAN traffic congestion.

Understand the difference between a collision domain and a broadcast domain.   Collision domain is an Ethernet term used to describe a network collection of devices in which one particular device sends a packet on a network segment, forcing every other device on that same segment to pay attention to it. On a broadcast domain, a set of all devices on a network segment hears all broadcasts sent on that segment.

Select the Components Required to Meet a Network Specification

As mentioned in the previous objective, routers, bridges, and switches are used in an internetwork.

Figure 1.3 shows how a network would look with all these internetwork devices in place. Remember that the router will not only break up broadcast domains for every LAN interface, but it will also break up collision domains.

FIGURE 1.3 Internetworking devices

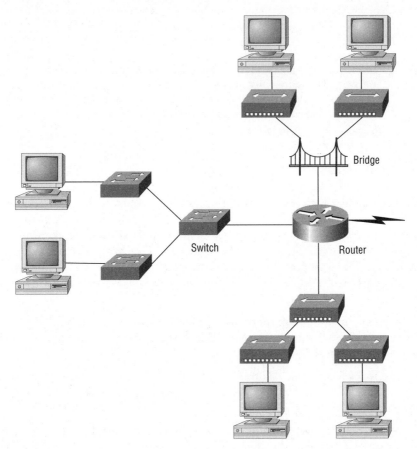

When you looked at Figure 1.3, you may have noticed that the router is at center stage and that it connects each physical network together. This type of layout is necessary because of the older technologies involved—bridges and hubs.

On the top internetwork in Figure 1.3, you'll notice that a bridge was used to connect the hubs to a router. The bridge breaks up collision domains, but all the hosts connected to both hubs are still crammed into the same broadcast domain. Also, the bridge created only two collision domains, so each device connected to a hub is in the same collision domain as every other device connected to that same hub. This is still better than having one collision domain for all hosts.

Also, notice that the three hubs at the bottom are connected to the router, creating one collision domain and one broadcast domain. This makes the bridged network work much better.

> Although bridges/switches are used to segment networks, they will not isolate broadcast or multicast packets.

In Figure 1.3, the best network connected to the router is the LAN switch network on the left. This is because each port on that switch breaks up collision domains. But it's not all good—all devices are still in the same broadcast domain. Do you remember why this can be a really bad thing? Because all devices must listen to all broadcasts transmitted, that's why. If your broadcast domains are too large, users have less bandwidth and are required to process more broadcasts, and network response time will slow to an unacceptable level.

Once you have only switches in your network, things change a lot! Figure 1.4 shows the network that is typically found today.

FIGURE 1.4   Switched networks creating an internetwork

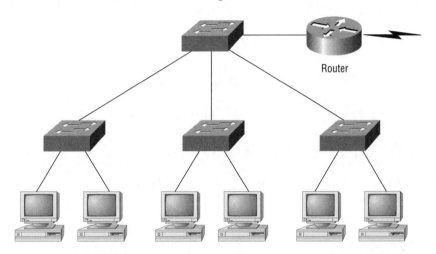

Here, the LAN switches are placed at the center of the network world so that the routers are connecting only logical networks together. If this kind of setup is implemented, virtual LANs (VLANs) are created. But it is really important to understand that even though you have a switched network, you still need a router to provide your inter-VLAN communication, or internetworking.

Obviously, the best network is one that's correctly configured to meet the business requirements of the company it serves. LAN switches with routers, correctly placed in the network, are the best network design. This book will help you understand the basics of routers and switches, so you can make tight, informed decisions on a case-by-case basis.

Let's go back to Figure 1.3. Looking at the figure, how many collision domains and broadcast domains are in this internetwork? Hopefully, you answered nine collision domains and three broadcast domains. The broadcast domains are definitely the easiest to see because only routers break up broadcast domains by default. Because there are three connections, that gives you three broadcast domains. The all-hub network is one collision domain; the bridge network equals three collision domains. Add in the switch network of five collision domains—one for each switch port—and you've got a total of nine collision domains.

So now that you've reviewed internetworking and the various devices in an internetwork, it's time to head into internetworking models.

Exam Essentials

Understand which devices create a LAN and which separate and connect LANs.   Switches and bridges are used to create LANs. While they do separate collision domains, they do not create separate LANs (collision domain and LAN are not the same concept). Routers are used to separate LANs and connect LANs (broadcast domains).

Understand the difference between a hub, a bridge, a switch, and a router.   Hubs create one collision domain and one broadcast domain. Bridges break up collision domains but create one large broadcast domain. They use hardware addresses to filter the network. Switches are really just multiple-port bridges with more intelligence. They break up collision domains but create one large broadcast domain by default. Switches use hardware addresses to filter the network. Routers break up broadcast domains (and collision domains) and use logical addressing to filter the network.

Use the OSI and TCP/IP Models and Their Associated Protocols to Explain How Data Flows in a Network

The Department of Defense (DoD) model is basically a condensed version of the OSI model—it's composed of the following four (instead of seven) layers:

- Process/Application layer
- Host-to-Host layer
- Internet layer
- Network Access layer

Figure 1.5 shows a comparison of the DoD model and the OSI reference model. As you can see, the two are similar in concept, but each has a different number of layers with different names.

 When the different protocols in the IP stack are discussed, the layers of the OSI and DoD models are interchangeable. In other words, the Internet layer and the Network layer describe the same thing, as do the Host-to-Host layer and the Transport layer.

A vast array of protocols combine at the DoD model's *Process/Application layer* to integrate the various activities and duties spanning the focus of the OSI's corresponding top three layers (Application, Presentation, and Session). We'll be looking closely at those protocols in the next part of this chapter. The Process/Application layer defines protocols for node-to-node application communication and controls user-interface specifications.

FIGURE 1.5   The DoD and OSI models

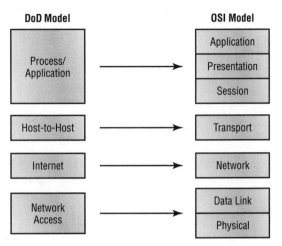

The *Host-to-Host layer* parallels the functions of the OSI's Transport layer, defining protocols for setting up the level of transmission service for applications. It tackles issues such as creating reliable end-to-end communication and ensuring the error-free delivery of data. It handles packet sequencing and maintains data integrity.

The *Internet layer* corresponds to the OSI's Network layer, designating the protocols relating to the logical transmission of packets over the entire network. It addresses the hosts by giving them an IP (Internet Protocol) address, and it handles the routing of packets among multiple networks.

At the bottom of the DoD model, the *Network Access layer* monitors the data exchange between the host and the network. The equivalent of the Data Link and Physical layers of the OSI model, the Network Access layer oversees hardware addressing and defines protocols for the physical transmission of data.

The DoD and OSI models are alike in design and concept and have similar functions in similar layers. Figure 1.6 shows the TCP/IP protocol suite and how its protocols relate to the DoD model layers.

In the following sections, we will look at the different protocols in more detail, starting with the Process/Application layer protocols.

Exam Essentials

Remember that the OSI/DoD model is a layered approach.   Functions are divided into layers, and the layers are bound together. This allows layers to operate transparently to each other—that is, changes in one layer should not impact other layers.

Remember the layers of the OSI and DoD models and how they are related.   The OSI was created after the DoD model and closely resembles the DoD model. The OSI Application, Presentation, and Session layers are contained in one layer of the DoD model: the Process/Application layer. The Transport layer is equivalent to the Host-to-Host layer of the DoD model, and the Network layer parallels the Internet layer.

FIGURE 1.6   The TCP/IP protocol suite

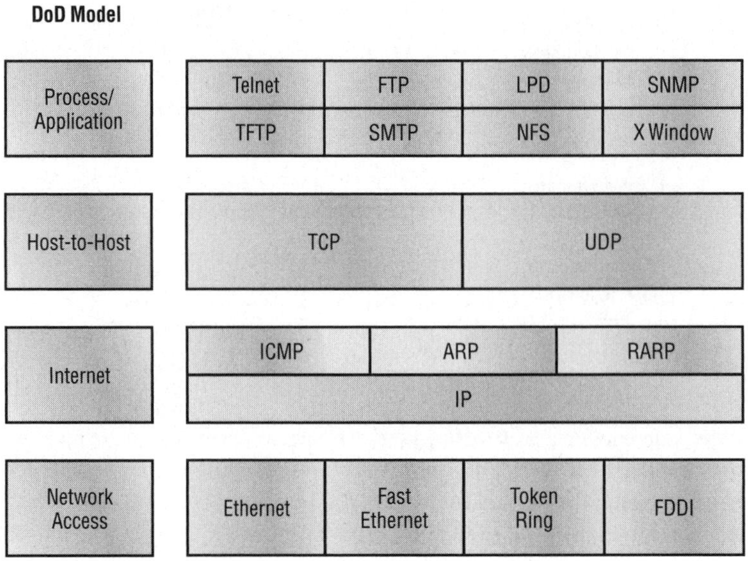

DoD Model

| Process/
Application | Telnet | FTP | LPD | SNMP |
| | TFTP | SMTP | NFS | X Window |

| Host-to-Host | TCP | | UDP | |

| Internet | ICMP | ARP | | RARP |
| | IP | | | |

| Network
Access | Ethernet | Fast
Ethernet | Token
Ring | FDDI |

Describe Common Networked Applications, Including Web Applications

In this section, I'll describe the different applications and services typically used in IP networks. The following protocols and applications are covered in this section:

- Telnet
- FTP
- TFTP
- NFS
- SMTP
- LPD
- X Window
- SNMP
- DNS
- DHCP/BootP

Telnet

Telnet is the chameleon of protocols—its specialty is terminal emulation. It allows a user on a remote client machine, called the *Telnet client*, to access the resources of another machine, the *Telnet server*. The client machine appears as though it were a dumb terminal directly attached to the local network, which allows the Telnet client to run programs on the Telnet server. This projection is actually a software image—a virtual terminal that can interact with the chosen remote host.

Users begin a Telnet session by running the Telnet client software and then logging into the Telnet server.

The problem with Telnet is that all data, even login data, is sent in cleartext. This can be a security risk. If you are having problems Telnetting into a device, you should verify that both the transmitting and receiving devices have Telnet services enabled. Lastly, by default, Cisco devices allow five simultaneous Telnet sessions.

File Transfer Protocol (FTP)

File Transfer Protocol (FTP) is the protocol that actually lets you transfer files, and it can accomplish this between any two machines using it. But FTP isn't just a protocol; it's also a program. Operating as a protocol, FTP is used by applications. As a program, it's employed by users to perform file tasks by hand. FTP also allows for access to both directories and files and can accomplish certain types of directory operations, such as relocating into different ones. FTP teams up with Telnet to transparently log you in to the FTP server and then provides for the transfer of files.

Accessing a host through FTP is only the first step, though. Users must then be subjected to an authentication login that's probably secured with passwords and usernames implemented by system administrators to restrict access. You can get around this somewhat by adopting the username *anonymous*—although what you'll gain access to will be limited.

Trivial File Transfer Protocol (TFTP)

Trivial File Transfer Protocol (TFTP) is the stripped-down, stock version of FTP, but it's the protocol of choice if you know exactly what you want and where to find it. Plus, it's easy to use and fast! It doesn't give you the abundance of functions that FTP does, though. TFTP has no directory-browsing abilities—it can do nothing but send and receive files. This compact little protocol also skimps in the data department, sending much smaller blocks of data than FTP sends, and there's no authentication as with FTP, so it's insecure. Few sites support it because of the inherent security risks.

Network File System (NFS)

Network File System (NFS) is a jewel of a protocol specializing in file sharing. It allows two different types of file systems to interoperate. It works like this: Suppose that the NFS server software is running on an NT server and the NFS client software is running on a Unix host. NFS allows for a portion of the RAM on the NT server to transparently store Unix files, which can, in turn, be used by Unix users. Even though the NT file system and Unix file system are unlike—they have different case sensitivity, filename lengths, security, and so on—both Unix users and NT users can access that same file with their normal file systems, in their normal way.

Simple Mail Transfer Protocol (SMTP)

Simple Mail Transfer Protocol (SMTP) allows us to send email and uses a spooled, or *queued*, method of mail delivery. Once a message has been sent to a destination, the message is spooled to a device—usually a disk. The server software at the destination regularly checks the queue for messages. When it detects them, it proceeds to deliver them to their destination. SMTP is used to send mail; POP3 is used to receive mail.

Line Printer Daemon (LPD)

The Line Printer Daemon (LPD) protocol is designed for printer sharing. The LPD, along with the *Line Printer (LPR)* program, allows print jobs to be spooled and sent to the network's printers using TCP/IP.

X Window

Designed for client/server operations, *X Window* defines a protocol for writing client/server applications based on a graphical user interface (GUI). The idea is to allow a program, called a *client*, to run on one computer and have it display things through an X Window server on another computer.

Simple Network Management Protocol (SNMP)

Simple Network Management Protocol (SNMP) collects and manipulates valuable network information. It gathers data by polling the devices on the network from a management station at fixed or random intervals, requiring them to disclose certain information. When all is well, SNMP receives something called a *baseline*—a report delimiting the operational traits of a healthy network. This protocol can also stand as a watchdog over the network, quickly notifying managers of any sudden turn of events. These network watchdogs are called *agents*, and when aberrations occur, agents send an alert called a *trap* to the management station.

Domain Name Service (DNS)

Domain Name Service (DNS) resolves hostnames—specifically, Internet names, such as www.lammle.com. You don't have to use DNS—you can just type in the IP address of any device with which you want to communicate. An IP address identifies hosts on a network as well as on the Internet. However, DNS was designed to make our lives easier. Think about what would happen if you wanted to move your web page to a different service provider. The IP address would change, and no one would know what the new one was. DNS allows you to use a domain name to specify an IP address. You can change the IP address as often as you want, and no one will know the difference.

DNS is used to resolve a *fully qualified domain name (FQDN)*—for example, www.lammle .com or todd.lammle.com. An FQDN is a hierarchy that can logically locate a system based on its domain identifier.

If you want to resolve the name *todd*, you either must type in the FQDN of **todd.lammle .com** or have a device such as a PC or router add the suffix for you. For example, on a Cisco router, you can use the command ip domain-name lammle.com to append each request with the lammle.com domain. If you don't do that, you'll have to type in the FQDN to get DNS to resolve the name.

Dynamic Host Configuration Protocol (DHCP)/Bootstrap Protocol (BootP)

Dynamic Host Configuration Protocol (DHCP) assigns IP addresses to hosts. It allows easier administration and works well in small to even very large network environments. All types of hardware can be used as a DHCP server, including a Cisco router.

DHCP differs from BootP in that BootP assigns an IP address to a host, but the host's hardware address must be entered manually in a BootP table. You can think of DHCP as a dynamic BootP. But remember that BootP is also used to send an operating system from which a host can boot. DHCP can't do that.

But there is a lot of information a DHCP server can provide to a host when the host is requesting an IP address from the DHCP server. Here's a list of the information a DHCP server can provide:

- IP address
- Subnet mask
- Domain name
- Default gateway (routers)
- DNS server address
- WINS server address

A DHCP server can provide even more information than this, but the items in the list are the most common.

A client that sends out a DHCP Discover message in order to receive an IP address sends out a broadcast at both layer 2 and layer 3.

- The layer 2 broadcast is all *F*s in hex, which looks like this: FF:FF:FF:FF:FF:FF.
- The layer 3 broadcast is 255.255.255.255, which means all networks and all hosts.

How does a router perform when it receives the broadcast mentioned previously? Although you can configure a router to forward this broadcast to a DHCP server when received, the router will discard this packet by default.

DHCP is connectionless, which means it uses User Datagram Protocol (UDP) at the Transport layer, also known as the Host-to-Host layer, which we'll talk about next.

Figure 1.7 shows the process of a client/server relationship using a DHCP connection.

FIGURE 1.7   DHCP client four-step process

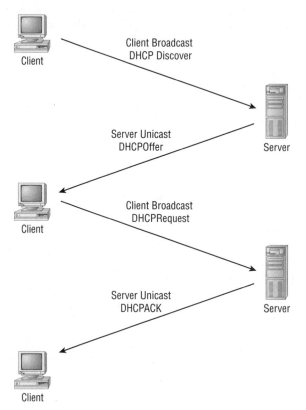

The following is the four-step process a client takes to receive an IP address from a DHCP server:

1. The DHCP client broadcasts a DHCP Discover message looking for a DHCP server (port 67).

2. The DHCP server that received the DHCP Discover message sends a unicast DHCP Offer message back to the host.

3. The client then broadcasts to the server a DHCP Request message asking for the offered IP address and possibly other information.

4. The server finalizes the exchange with a unicast DHCP Acknowledgment message.

DHCP Conflicts

A DHCP address conflict occurs when two hosts use the same IP address. This sounds bad because it is. Thankfully, the issue won't even need to be discussed after everyone starts using IPv6.

During IP address assignment, a DHCP server checks for conflicts using the ping program to test the availability of the address before it is assigned from the pool. If no host replies, then the DHCP server assumes that the IP address is not already allocated. This helps the server know that it is providing a good address, but what about the host? To provide extra protection against the all-so-terrible IP conflict issue, the host can broadcast for its own address.

A host uses something called a gratuitous ARP to help avoid a possible duplicate address. The DHCP client sends an ARP broadcast out on the local LAN or VLAN using its newly assigned address to solve conflicts before they occur.

So, if an IP address conflict is detected, the address is removed from the DHCP pool (scope), and it is all-so-important to remember that the address will not be assigned to a host until the administrator resolves the conflict by hand.

Exam Essentials

Remember the Process/Application layer protocols.   Telnet is a terminal emulation program that allows you to log in to a remote host and run programs. File Transfer Protocol (FTP) is a connection-oriented service that allows you to transfer files. Trivial FTP (TFTP) is a connectionless file transfer program. Simple Mail Transfer Protocol (SMTP) is a send-mail program.

Understand DNS and DHCP.   *Domain Name Service (DNS)* resolves hostnames—specifically, Internet names, such as www.lammle.com. You don't have to use DNS; you can just type in the IP address of any device with which you want to communicate. An IP address identifies hosts on a network and the Internet as well. *Dynamic Host Configuration Protocol (DHCP)* assigns IP addresses to hosts. It allows easier administration and works well in small to even very large network environments.

Understand DHCP conflict resolution issues.   A DHCP server will use the ping program to verify that an IP address from a scope will not cause a conflict with another host. A DHCP host will use gratuitous ARP to verify that once it has an IP address from a DHCP server no other host has this address. If a conflict does occur, it is important to understand that an administrator must resolve the conflict by hand on the server.

Describe the Purpose and Basic Operation of the Protocols in the OSI and TCP Models

When networks first came into being, computers typically could communicate only with computers from the same manufacturer. For example, companies ran either a complete DECnet solution or an IBM solution—not both together. In the late 1970s, the *Open Systems Interconnection (OSI) reference model* was created by the International Organization for Standardization (ISO) to break this barrier.

The OSI model was meant to help vendors create interoperable network devices and software in the form of protocols so that different vendor networks could work with each other. Like world peace, it'll probably never happen completely, but it's still a great goal.

In the following section, I am going to explain the layered approach and how you can use this approach to help troubleshoot your internetworks.

The Layered Approach

A *reference model* is a conceptual blueprint of how communications should take place. It addresses all the processes required for effective communication and divides these processes into logical groupings called *layers*. When a communication system is designed in this manner, it's known as *layered architecture*.

Software developers can use a reference model to understand computer communication processes and see what types of functions need to be accomplished on any one layer. If they are developing a protocol for a certain layer, all they need to concern themselves with is that specific layer's functions, not those of any other layer. Another layer and protocol will handle the other functions. The technical term for this idea is *binding*. The communication processes that are related to each other are bound, or grouped together, at a particular layer.

Advantages of Reference Models

The OSI model is hierarchical, and the same benefits and advantages can apply to any layered model. The primary purpose of all such models, especially the OSI model, is to allow different vendors' networks to interoperate.

Advantages of using the OSI layered model include, but are not limited to, the following:

- It divides the network communication process into smaller and simpler components, thereby aiding in component development, design, and troubleshooting.

- It allows multiple-vendor development through the standardization of network components.

- It encourages industry standardization by defining what functions occur at each layer of the model.

- It allows various types of network hardware and software to communicate.

- It prevents changes in one layer from affecting other layers, so it does not hamper development.

The OSI Reference Model

One of the greatest functions of the OSI specifications is to assist in data transfer between disparate hosts—meaning, for example, that they enable us to transfer data between a Unix host and a PC or a Mac.

The OSI isn't a physical model, though. It's a set of guidelines that application developers can use to create and implement applications that run on a network. It also provides a framework for creating and implementing networking standards, devices, and internetworking schemes.

The OSI has seven different layers, divided into two groups. The top three layers define how the applications within the end stations will communicate with each other and with users. The bottom four layers define how data is transmitted from end to end. Figure 1.8 shows the three upper layers and their functions, and Figure 1.9 shows the four lower layers and their functions.

FIGURE 1.8   The upper layers

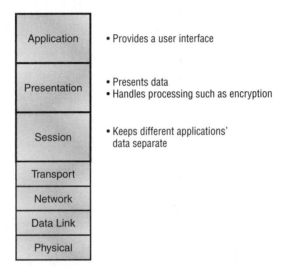

When you study Figure 1.8, understand that the user interfaces with the computer at the Application layer and also that the upper layers are responsible for applications communicating between hosts. Remember that none of the upper layers knows anything about networking or network addresses. That's the responsibility of the four bottom layers.

In Figure 1.9, you can see that the four bottom layers are what actually define how data is transferred through a physical wire or through switches and routers. These bottom layers also determine how to rebuild a data stream from a transmitting host to a destination host's application.

The following network devices operate at all seven layers of the OSI model:

- Network management stations (NMSs)

- Web and application servers

- Gateways (not default gateways)

- Network hosts

Basically, the ISO is pretty much the Emily Post of the network protocol world. Just as Mrs. Post wrote the book setting the standards—or protocols—for human social interaction, the ISO developed the OSI reference model as the precedent and guide for an open network protocol set. Defining the etiquette of communication models, it remains today the most popular means of comparison for protocol suites.

FIGURE 1.9   The lower layers

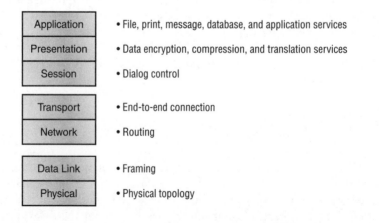

Transport	• Provides reliable or unreliable delivery • Performs error correction before retransmit
Network	• Provides logical addressing, which routers use for path determination
Data Link	• Combines packets into bytes and bytes into frames • Provides access to media using MAC address • Performs error detection, not correction
Physical	• Moves bits between devices • Specifies voltage, wire speed, and pin-out of cables

The OSI reference model has seven layers:

- Application layer (layer 7)

- Presentation layer (layer 6)

- Session layer (layer 5)

- Transport layer (layer 4)

- Network layer (layer 3)

- Data Link layer (layer 2)

- Physical layer (layer 1)

Figure 1.10 shows a summary of the functions defined at each layer of the OSI model. With this in hand, you're ready to explore each layer's function in detail.

In the next section, we'll delve deeper into TCP and UDP that reside at the Transport layer.

FIGURE 1.10   Layer functions

Application	• File, print, message, database, and application services
Presentation	• Data encryption, compression, and translation services
Session	• Dialog control
Transport	• End-to-end connection
Network	• Routing
Data Link	• Framing
Physical	• Physical topology

Exam Essentials

Understand the advantages of using layered models.   The OSI model is hierarchical, and the same benefits and advantages can apply to any layered model. The primary purpose of all such models, especially the OSI model, is to allow different vendors' networks to inter-operate. Remember that the OSI/DoD model is a layered approach.

Functions are divided into layers, and the layers are bound together. This allows layers to oper-ate transparently to each other—that is, changes in one layer should not impact other layers.

Define the OSI layers, understand the function of each, and describe how devices and net-working protocols can be mapped to each layer.   You must remember the seven layers of the OSI model and what function each layer provides. The Application, Presentation, and Session layers are upper layers and are responsible for communicating from a user interface to an application. The Transport layer provides segmentation, sequencing, and virtual cir-cuits. The Network layer provides logical network addressing and routing through an inter-network. The Data Link layer provides framing and placing data on the network medium. The Physical layer is responsible for taking 1s and 0s and encoding them into a digital sig-nal for transmission on the network segment.

Remember the layers of the OSI model.   The OSI model has seven (7) layers; starting at the top, they are as follows:

7. Application

6. Presentation

5. Session

4. Transport

3. Network

2. Data Link

1. Physical

Describe the Impact of Applications (Voice over IP and Video over IP) on a Network

The main purpose of the Host-to-Host layer is to shield the upper-layer applications from the complexities of the network. This layer says to the upper layer, "Just give me your data stream, with any instructions, and I'll begin the process of getting your information ready to send."

The following sections describe the two protocols at this layer:

- Transmission Control Protocol (TCP)
- User Datagram Protocol (UDP)

By understanding how TCP and UDP work, you can interpret the impact of applications on networks when using Voice and Video over IP.

Transmission Control Protocol (TCP)

Transmission Control Protocol (TCP) takes large blocks of information from an application and breaks them into segments. It numbers and sequences each segment so that the destination's TCP stack can put the segments back into the order the application intended. After these segments are sent, TCP (on the transmitting host) waits for an acknowledgment of the receiving end's TCP virtual circuit session, retransmitting those that aren't acknowledged.

Before a transmitting host starts to send segments down the model, the sender's TCP stack contacts the destination's TCP stack to establish a connection. What is created is known as a *virtual circuit*. This type of communication is called *connection-oriented*. During this initial handshake, the two TCP layers also agree on the amount of information that's going to be sent before the recipient's TCP sends back an acknowledgment. With everything agreed upon in advance, the path is paved for reliable communication to take place.

TCP is a full-duplex, connection-oriented, reliable, and accurate protocol, but establishing all these terms and conditions, in addition to error checking, is no small task. TCP is very complicated and, not surprisingly, costly in terms of network overhead—and because today's networks are much more reliable than those of yore, this added reliability is often unnecessary.

TCP Segment Format

Because the upper layers just send a data stream to the protocols in the Transport layers, I'll demonstrate how TCP segments a data stream and prepares it for the Internet layer. When the Internet layer receives the data stream, it routes the segments as packets through an internetwork. The segments are handed to the receiving host's Host-to-Host layer protocol, which rebuilds the data stream to hand to the upper-layer applications or protocols.

Figure 1.11 shows the TCP segment format. The figure shows the different fields within the TCP header.

The TCP header is 20 bytes long, or up to 24 bytes with options. To read more detail regarding the TCP header, please see my *CCNA Cisco Certified Network Associate Study Guide, 7th Edition* (Sybex, 2011).

User Datagram Protocol (UDP)

If you were to compare the *User Datagram Protocol (UDP)* with TCP, the former is basically the scaled-down economy model that's sometimes referred to as a *thin protocol*. Like a thin person on a park bench, a thin protocol doesn't take up a lot of room—or in this case, much bandwidth on a network.

FIGURE 1.11   TCP segment format

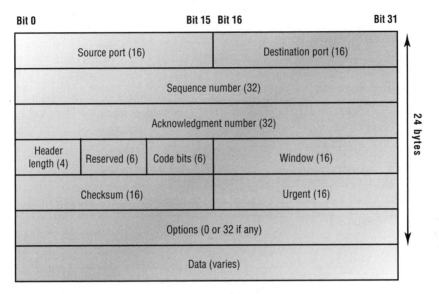

UDP doesn't offer all the bells and whistles of TCP either, but it does do a fabulous job of transporting information that doesn't require reliable delivery—and it does so using far fewer network resources. (UDP is covered thoroughly in Request for Comments 768.)

There are some situations in which it would definitely be wise for developers to opt for UDP rather than TCP. Remember the watchdog SNMP up there at the Process/Application layer? SNMP monitors the network, sending intermittent messages and a fairly steady flow of status updates and alerts, especially when running on a large network. The cost in overhead to establish, maintain, and close a TCP connection for each one of those little messages would reduce what would be an otherwise healthy, efficient network to a dammed-up bog in no time!

Another circumstance calling for UDP over TCP is when reliability is already handled at the Process/Application layer. Network File System (NFS) handles its own reliability issues, making the use of TCP both impractical and redundant. But ultimately, it's up to the application developer to decide whether to use UDP or TCP, not the user who wants to transfer data faster.

UDP does *not* sequence the segments and does not care in which order the segments arrive at the destination. But after that, UDP sends the segments off and forgets about them. It doesn't follow through, check up on them, or even allow for an acknowledgment of safe arrival—complete abandonment. Because of this, it's referred to as an unreliable protocol. This does not mean that UDP is ineffective, only that it doesn't handle issues of reliability.

Further, UDP doesn't create a virtual circuit, nor does it contact the destination before delivering information to it. Because of this, it's also considered a *connectionless* protocol. Because UDP assumes that the application will use its own reliability method, it doesn't use any. This gives an application developer a choice when running the Internet Protocol stack: TCP for reliability or UDP for faster transfers.

So if you're using Voice over IP (VoIP), for example, you really need to understand UDP, because if the segments arrive out of order (very common in IP networks), they'll just be passed up to the next OSI (DoD) layer in whatever order they're received, resulting in some seriously garbled data. On the other hand, TCP sequences the segments so they get put back together in exactly the right order—something that UDP just can't do.

UDP Segment Format

Figure 1.12 clearly illustrates UDP's markedly low overhead as compared to TCP's hungry usage. Look at the figure carefully—UDP doesn't use windowing or provide for acknowledgments in the UDP header.

FIGURE 1.12   The UDP segment

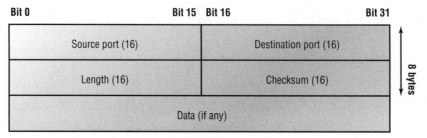

For a more detailed discussion on the UDP header, please see my *CCNA Cisco Certified Network Associate Study Guide, 7th Edition* (Sybex, 2011).

Key Concepts of Host-to-Host Protocols

Because you've seen both a connection-oriented (TCP) and connectionless (UDP) protocol in action, summarizing the two here would be helpful. Table 1.1 highlights some of the key concepts that you should keep in mind regarding these two protocols. You should memorize this table.

TABLE 1.1   Key Features of TCP and UDP

TCP	UDP
Sequenced	Unsequenced
Reliable	Unreliable
Connection-oriented	Connectionless
Virtual circuit	Low overhead
Acknowledgments	No acknowledgment
Windowing flow control	No windowing or flow control

Should your Voice or Video application use TCP or UDP? Because most of the applications use UDP due to time sensitivity, it is critical that you understand how to implement QoS on switch ports in order to provide priority to time sensitive data, such as voice and video. This objective wants you to simply understand the difference between TCP and UDP. It is not asking you how to configure QoS.

Exam Essentials

Remember the Host-to-Host layer protocols.   Transmission Control Protocol (TCP) is a connection-oriented protocol that provides reliable network service by using acknowledgments and flow control. User Datagram Protocol (UDP) is a connectionless protocol that provides low overhead and is considered unreliable.

Remember the Internet layer protocols.   Internet Protocol (IP) is a connectionless protocol that provides network address and routing through an internetwork. Address Resolution Protocol (ARP) finds a hardware address from a known IP address. Reverse ARP (RARP) finds an IP address from a known hardware address. Internet Control Message Protocol (ICMP) provides diagnostics and destination unreachable messages.

Remember the difference between connection-oriented and connectionless network services.   Connection-oriented services use acknowledgments and flow control to create a reliable session. More overhead is used than in a connectionless network service. Connectionless services are used to send data with no acknowledgments or flow control. This is considered unreliable.

Remember that Voice and Video mostly use UDP.   When you understand the difference between UDP and TCP, you can also understand why most application developers choose UDP: because time is of the essence, especially when connecting to phones. Plus, Cisco considers that most networks are much better today and can handle the UDP traffic better; however, you still need to implement a QoS strategy in order to achieve the desired results.

Interpret Network Diagrams

The best way to look at, build, and troubleshoot network diagrams is to use CDP. *Cisco Discovery Protocol (CDP)* is a proprietary protocol designed by Cisco to help administrators collect information about both locally attached and remote devices. By using CDP, you can gather hardware and protocol information about neighbor devices, which is useful info for troubleshooting and documenting the network.

In the following sections, I am going to discuss the CDP timer and CDP commands used to verify your network.

Getting CDP Timers and Holdtime Information

The show cdp command (sh cdp for short) gives you information about two CDP global parameters that can be configured on Cisco devices:

- *CDP timer* is how often CDP packets are transmitted out all active interfaces.
- *CDP holdtime* is the amount of time that the device will hold packets received from neighbor devices.

Both Cisco routers and Cisco switches use the same parameters.

For this section, I used my 2811. In the example, it will have the hostname of Corp, and it will have four serial connections to routers named R1, R2, and R3 (there are two connections to R1) and one Fast Ethernet connection to a 1242 access point with a hostname of just ap.

The output on the Corp router looks like this:

```
Corp#sh cdp
Global CDP information:
        Sending CDP packets every 60 seconds
        Sending a holdtime value of 180 seconds
        Sending CDPv2 advertisements is enabled
```

Use the global commands cdp holdtime and cdp timer to configure the CDP holdtime and timer on a router:

```
Corp(config)#cdp ?
  advertise-v2     CDP sends version-2 advertisements
  holdtime         Specify the holdtime (in sec) to be sent in packets
  log              Log messages generated by CDP
  run              Enable CDP
  source-interface Insert the interface's IP in all CDP packets
  timer            Specify rate (in sec) at which CDP packets are sent  run
Corp(config)#cdp holdtime ?
  <10-255> Length  of time (in sec) that receiver must keep this packet
Corp(config)#cdp timer ?
  <5-254>  Rate at which CDP packets are sent (in sec)
```

You can turn off CDP completely with the no cdp run command from the global configuration mode of a router. To turn CDP off or on for an interface, use the no cdp enable and cdp enable commands. Be patient—we'll work through these commands shortly.

Gathering Neighbor Information

The show cdp neighbor command (sh cdp nei for short) delivers information about directly connected devices. It's important to remember that CDP packets aren't passed through a Cisco switch and that you see only what's directly attached. So this means that if your router is connected to a switch, you won't see any of the devices hooked up to that switch.

The following output shows the show cdp neighbor command used on my ISR router:

```
Corp#sh cdp neighbors
Capability Codes: R - Router, T - Trans Bridge, B - Source Route Bridge
                  S - Switch, H - Host, I - IGMP, r - Repeater
Device ID   Local Intrfce   Holdtme   Capability  Platform   Port ID
ap          Fas 0/1           165        T I      AIR-AP124  Fas 0
R2          Ser 0/1/0         140       R S I     2801       Ser 0/2/0
R3          Ser 0/0/1         157       R S I     1841       Ser 0/0/1
R1          Ser 0/2/0         154       R S I     1841       Ser 0/0/1
R1          Ser 0/0/0         154       R S I     1841       Ser 0/0/0
Corp#
```

Okay, I am displaying an output from a directly connected console cable to the Corp ISR router, and the router is directly connected to four devices. The Corp router has two connections to the R1 router. The device ID shows the configured hostname of the connected device, the local interface is our interface, and the port ID is the remote devices' directly connected interface. All you get to view are directly connected devices.

Table 1.2 summarizes the information displayed by the show cdp neighbor command for each device.

TABLE 1.2   Output of the show cdp neighbor Command

Field	Description
Device ID	The hostname of the device directly connected
Local Interface	The port or interface on which you are receiving the CDP packet
Holdtime	The amount of time the router will hold the information before discarding it if no more CDP packets are received
Capability	The capability of the neighbor, such as the router, switch, or repeater. The capability codes are listed at the top of the command output.
Platform	The type of Cisco device directly connected. In the previous output, a 1240AP is connected off of F0/1, a 2801 off of S0/1/0, an 1841 off of s0/0/0, another 1841 off of s0/2/0, and one last 1841 router off of s0/0/0.
Port ID	The neighbor device's port or interface on which the CDP packets are multicast

It is imperative that you have the ability to look at the output of a show cdp neighbors command and decipher the neighbor's device (capability—i.e., router or switch), model number (platform), your port connecting to that device (local interface), and the port of the neighbor connecting to you (port ID).

Another command that'll deliver the goods on neighbor information is the show cdp neighbors detail command (show cdp nei de for short). This command can be run on both routers and switches, and it displays detailed information about each device connected to the device on which you're running the command. Check out this router output for an example:

```
Corp#sh cdp neighbors detail
-------------------------
Device ID: ap
Entry address(es): 10.1.1.2
Platform: cisco AIR-AP1242AG-A-K9 , Capabilities: Trans-Bridge IGMP
Interface: FastEthernet0/1, Port ID (outgoing port): FastEthernet0
Holdtime : 122 sec

Version :
Cisco IOS Software, C1240 Software (C1240-K9W7-M), Version 12.3(8)JEA,
    RELEASE SOFTWARE (fc2)
Technical Support: http://www.cisco.com/techsupport
Copyright (c) 1986-2006 by Cisco Systems, Inc.
Compiled Wed 23-Aug-06 16:45 by kellythw

advertisement version: 2
Duplex: full
Power drawn: 15.000 Watts
-------------------------
Device ID: R2
Entry address(es):
  IP address: 10.4.4.2
Platform: Cisco 2801, Capabilities: Router Switch IGMP
Interface: Serial0/1/0, Port ID (outgoing port): Serial0/2/0
Holdtime : 135 sec

Version :
Cisco IOS Software, 2801 Software (C2801-ADVENTERPRISEK9-M),
    Experimental Version 12.4(20050525:193634) [jezhao-ani 145]
Copyright (c) 1986-2005 by Cisco Systems, Inc.
```

```
Compiled Fri 27-May-05 23:53 by jezhao

advertisement version: 2
VTP Management Domain: ''
------------------------
Device ID: R3
Entry address(es):
  IP address: 10.5.5.1
Platform: Cisco 1841, Capabilities: Router Switch IGMP
Interface: Serial0/0/1, Port ID (outgoing port): Serial0/0/1
Holdtime : 152 sec

Version :
Cisco IOS Software, 1841 Software (C1841-IPBASE-M), Version 12.4(1c),
    RELEASE SOFTWARE (fc1)
Technical Support: http://www.cisco.com/techsupport
Copyright (c) 1986-2005 by Cisco Systems, Inc.
Compiled Tue 25-Oct-05 17:10 by evmiller

advertisement version: 2
VTP Management Domain: ''
------------------------
[output cut]
Corp#
```

First, the hostnames and IP addresses of all directly connected devices are displayed. In addition to the same information displayed by the show cdp neighbor command (see Table 1.2), the show cdp neighbor detail command displays the IOS version of the neighbor device.

Remember that you can see only the IP addresses of directly connected devices.

The show cdp entry * command displays the same information as the show cdp neighbor details command. Here's an example of the router output using the show cdp entry * command:

```
Corp#sh cdp entry *
------------------------
Device ID: ap
Entry address(es):
Platform: cisco AIR-AP1242AG-A-K9 , Capabilities: Trans-Bridge IGMP
```

```
Interface: FastEthernet0/1, Port ID (outgoing port): FastEthernet0
Holdtime : 160 sec

Version :
Cisco IOS Software, C1240 Software (C1240-K9W7-M), Version 12.3(8)JEA,
    RELEASE SOFTWARE (fc2)
Technical Support: http://www.cisco.com/techsupport
Copyright (c) 1986-2006 by Cisco Systems, Inc.
Compiled Wed 23-Aug-06 16:45 by kellythw

advertisement version: 2
Duplex: full
Power drawn: 15.000 Watts
------------------------
Device ID: R2
Entry address(es):
  IP address: 10.4.4.2
Platform: Cisco 2801, Capabilities: Router Switch IGMP
  --More--
```
[output cut]

Although the show cdp neighbors detail and show cdp entry * commands are very similar, the show cdp entry * command allows you to display only one line of output for each directly connected neighbor, whereas the show cdp neighbor detail command does not.

Documenting a Network Topology Using CDP

As the title of this section implies, I'm going to show you how to document a sample network by using CDP. You'll learn to determine the appropriate router types, interface types, and IP addresses of various interfaces using only CDP commands and the show running-config command. You can only console into the Lab_A router to document the network. You'll have to assign any remote routers the next IP address in each range. You can use Figure 1.13 to complete the documentation.

In this output, you can see that you have a router with four interfaces: two FastEthernet and two Serial. First, determine the IP addresses of each interface by using the show running-config command:

```
Lab_A#sh running-config
Building configuration...

Current configuration : 960 bytes
!
```

```
version 12.2
service timestamps debug uptime
service timestamps log uptime
no service password-encryption
!
hostname Lab_A
!
ip subnet-zero
!
!
interface FastEthernet0/0
 ip address 192.168.21.1 255.255.255.0
 duplex auto
!
interface FastEthernet0/1
 ip address 192.168.18.1 255.255.255.0
 duplex auto
!
interface Serial0/0
ip address 192.168.23.1 255.255.255.0
!
interface Serial0/1
ip address 192.168.28.1 255.255.255.0
!
ip classless
!
line con 0
line aux 0
line vty 0 4
!
end
```

Now that this step is completed, you can write down the IP addresses of the Lab_A router's four interfaces. Next, you need to determine the type of device on the other end of each of these interfaces. It's easy to do this—just use the show cdp neighbors command:

```
Lab_A#sh cdp neighbors
Capability Codes: R - Router, T - Trans Bridge, B - Source Route Bridge
S - Switch, H - Host, I - IGMP, r - Repeater
Device ID    Local Intrfce    Holdtme    Capability Platform  Port ID
Lab_B        Fas 0/0          178        R          2501      E0
```

Lab_C	Fas 0/1	137	R	2621	Fa0/0
Lab_D	Ser 0/0	178	R	2514	S1
Lab_E	Ser 0/1	137	R	2620	S0/1
Lab_A#					

FIGURE 1.13   Documenting a network topology using CDP

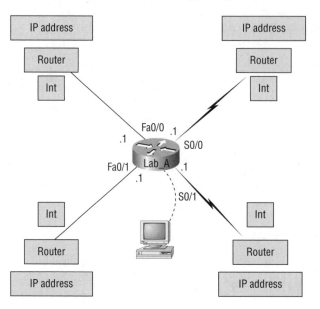

You've got a good deal of information now. By using both the show running-config and show cdp neighbors commands, you know about all the IP addresses of the Lab_A router, plus the types of routers connected to each of the Lab_A router's links, and all the interfaces of the remote routers.

By using all the information gathered from show running-config and show cdp neighbors, you can create the topology in Figure 1.14.

If you needed to, you also could've used the show cdp neighbors detail command to view the neighbor's IP addresses. But because you know the IP addresses of each link on the Lab_A router, you already know what the next available IP address is going to be.

Exam Essentials

Understand when to use CDP.   Cisco Discovery Protocol can be used to help you document as well as troubleshoot your network.

Remember what the output from the various show cdp neighbors commands provides.   The show cdp neighbors command provides the following information: device ID, local interface, holdtime, capability, platform, and port ID (remote interface). The show cdp neighbors detail and show cdp entry * commands provide everything the show cdp neighbors provides, plus the IP address of each directly connected neighbor and the IOS version.

FIGURE 1.14   Network topology documented

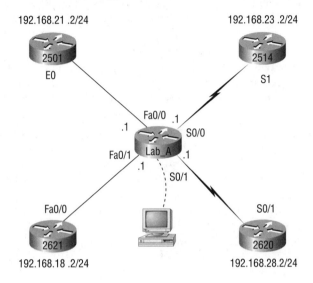

Determine the Path between Two Hosts across a Network

Once you create an internetwork by connecting your WANs and LANs to a router, you'll need to configure logical network addresses, such as IP addresses, to all hosts on the internetwork so that they can communicate across that internetwork.

The term *routing* is used for taking a packet from one device and sending it through the network to another device on a different network. Routers don't really care about hosts—they only care about networks and the best path to each network. The logical network address of the destination host is used to get packets to a network through a routed network, and then the hardware address of the host is used to deliver the packet from a router to the correct destination host.

If your network has no routers, then it should be apparent that you are not routing. Routers route traffic to all the networks in your internetwork. To be able to route packets, a router must know, at a minimum, the following:

- Destination address

- Neighbor routers from which it can learn about remote networks

- Possible routes to all remote networks

- The best route to each remote network

- How to maintain and verify routing information

The router learns about remote networks from neighbor routers or from an administrator. The router then builds a routing table (a map of the internetwork) that describes how to find the remote networks. If a network is directly connected, then the router already knows how to get to it.

If a network isn't directly connected to the router, the router must use one of two ways to learn how to get to the remote network: *static routing*, meaning that someone must hand-type all network locations into the routing table, or something called *dynamic routing*. In dynamic routing, a protocol on one router communicates with the same protocol running on neighbor routers. The routers then update each other about all the networks they know about and place this information into the routing table. If a change occurs in the network, the dynamic routing protocols automatically inform all routers about the event. If static routing is used, the administrator is responsible for updating all changes by hand into all routers. Typically, in a large network, a combination of both dynamic and static routing is used.

Before we jump into the IP routing process, let's take a look at a simple example that demonstrates how a router uses the routing table to route packets out of an interface. We'll be going into a more detailed study of the process in the next section.

Figure 1.15 shows a simple two-router network. Lab_A has one serial interface and three LAN interfaces.

FIGURE 1.15   A simple routing example

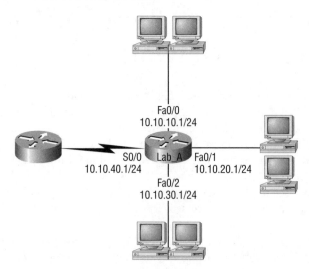

By looking at Figure 1.15, you can see which interface Lab_A will use to forward an IP datagram to a host with an IP address of 10.10.10.10.

By using the command show ip route, you can see the routing table (map of the internetwork) that Lab_A uses to make forwarding decisions:

```
Lab_A#sh ip route
[output cut]
Gateway of last resort is not set
C       10.10.10.0/24 is directly connected, FastEthernet0/0
C       10.10.20.0/24 is directly connected, FastEthernet0/1
C       10.10.30.0/24 is directly connected, FastEthernet0/2
C       10.10.40.0/24 is directly connected, Serial 0/0
```

The C in the routing table output means that the networks listed are "directly connected," and until you add a routing protocol—something like RIP, EIGRP, or the like—to the routers in your internetwork (or use static routes), you'll have only directly connected networks in your routing table.

> RIP and EIGRP are routing protocols and are covered in Chapters 8 and 9 of my *CCNA Cisco Certified Network Associate Study Guide, 7th Edition* (Sybex, 2011).

So let's get back to the original question: By looking at the figure and the output of the routing table, can you tell what IP will do with a received packet that has a destination IP address of 10.10.10.10? The router will packet-switch the packet to interface FastEthernet 0/0, and this interface will frame the packet and then send it out on the network segment.

Based on the output of the next routing table, which interface will a packet with a destination address of 10.10.10.14 be forwarded from?

```
Lab_A#sh ip route
[output cut]
Gateway of last resort is not set
C       10.10.10.16/28 is directly connected, FastEthernet0/0
C       10.10.10.8/29 is directly connected, FastEthernet0/1
C       10.10.10.4/30 is directly connected, FastEthernet0/2
C       10.10.10.0/30 is directly connected, Serial 0/0
```

First, you can see that the network is subnetted and each interface has a different mask. If you can't subnet, you just can't answer this question. The address 10.10.10.14 would be a host in the 10.10.10.8/29 subnet connected to the FastEthernet0/1 interface. If you don't understand or are struggling, just go back and reread Chapter 4 of the *CCNA Cisco Certified Network Associate Study Guide, 7th Edition*—this should make perfect sense to you afterward.

You really need to make sure you understand IP routing because it's super-important. This section is going to test your understanding of the IP routing process by having you look at a figure and answer a very basic IP routing question.

Figure 1.16 shows a LAN connected to RouterA, which is, in turn, connected via a WAN link to RouterB. RouterB has a LAN connected with an HTTP server attached. How does a frame from HostA get to the HTTP server?

FIGURE 1.16 IP routing example

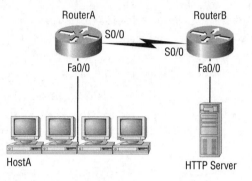

The critical information you need to glean from this figure is exactly how IP routing will occur in this example.

1. The destination address of a frame, from HostA, will be the MAC address of the F0/0 interface of the RouterA router.

2. The destination address of a packet will be the IP address of the network interface card (NIC) of the HTTP server.

3. The destination port number in the segment header will have a value of 80.

That example was a pretty simple one, and it was also to the point. One thing to remember is that if multiple hosts are communicating to the server using HTTP, they must all use a different source port number. That is how the server keeps the data separated at the Transport layer.

Exam Essentials

Understand the basic IP routing process.   You need to remember that the frame changes at each hop but that the packet is never changed or manipulated in any way until it reaches the destination device.

Understand that MAC addresses are always local.   A MAC (hardware) address will only be used on a local LAN. It will never pass a router's interface.

Understand that a frame carries a packet to only two places.   A frame uses MAC (hardware) addresses to send a packet on a LAN. The frame will take the packet to either a host on the LAN or a router's interface if the packet is destined for a remote network.

Describe the Components Required for Network and Internet Communications

When a host transmits data across a network to another device, the data goes through *encapsulation*: It is wrapped with protocol information at each layer of the OSI model. Each layer communicates only with its peer layer on the receiving device.

To communicate and exchange information, each layer uses *Protocol Data Units (PDUs)*. These units hold the control information attached to the data at each layer of the model. They are usually attached to the header in front of the data field, but they can also be in the trailer, or end, of it.

Each PDU attaches to the data by encapsulating it at each layer of the OSI model, and each has a specific name, depending on the information provided in each header. This PDU information is read only by the peer layer on the receiving device. After it's read, it's stripped off and the data is then handed to the next layer up.

Figure 1.17 shows the PDUs and how they attach control information to each layer. This figure demonstrates how the upper-layer user data is converted for transmission on the network. The data stream is then handed down to the Transport layer, which sets up a virtual circuit to the receiving device by sending over a sync packet. Next, the data stream is broken into smaller pieces, and a Transport layer header (a PDU) is created and attached to the header of the data field; now the piece of data is called a *segment*. Each segment is sequenced so the data stream can be put back together on the receiving side exactly as it was transmitted.

FIGURE 1.17   Data encapsulation

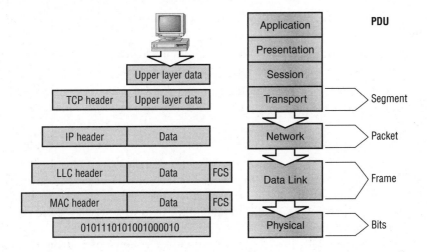

Each segment is then handed to the Network layer for network addressing and routing through the internetwork. Logical addressing (for example, IP) is used to get each segment to the correct network. The Network layer protocol adds a control header to the segment handed down from the Transport layer, creating what is called a *packet* or *datagram*. Remember that the Transport and Network layers work together to rebuild a data stream on a receiving host, but it's not part of their work to place their PDUs on a local network segment—which is the only way to get the information to a router or host.

The Data Link layer is responsible for taking packets from the Network layer and placing them on the network medium (cable or wireless). The Data Link layer encapsulates each packet in a *frame*, and the frame's header carries the hardware address of the source and destination hosts. If the destination device is on a remote network, then the frame is sent to a router to be routed through an internetwork. Once it gets to the destination network, a new frame is used to get the packet to the destination host.

To put this frame on the network, it must first be put into a digital signal. Because a frame is really a logical group of 1s and 0s, the Physical layer is responsible for encoding these digits into a digital signal, which is read by devices on the same local network. The receiving devices will synchronize on the digital signal and extract (decode) the 1s and 0s from the digital signal. At this point, the devices build the frames, run a CRC, and then check their answer against the answer in the frame's FCS field. If it matches, the packet is pulled from the frame and what's left of the frame is discarded. This process is called *de-encapsulation*. The packet is handed to the Network layer, where the address is checked. If the address matches, the segment is pulled from the packet and what's left of the packet is discarded. The segment is processed at the Transport layer, which rebuilds the data stream and acknowledges to the transmitting station that it received each piece. It then happily hands the data stream to the upper-layer application.

At a transmitting device, the data encapsulation method works like this:

1. User information is converted to data for transmission on the network.

2. Data is converted to segments and a reliable connection is set up between the transmitting and receiving hosts.

3. Segments are converted to packets or datagrams, and a logical address is placed in the header so each packet can be routed through an internetwork.

4. Packets or datagrams are converted to frames for transmission on the local network. Hardware (Ethernet) addresses are used to uniquely identify hosts on a local network segment.

5. Frames are converted to bits, and a digital encoding and clocking scheme is used.

Figure 1.18 illustrates these concepts in more detail, using the layer addressing.

Remember that a data stream is handed down from the upper layer to the Transport layer. As technicians, we really don't care who generates the data stream because that's really a programmer's problem. Our job is to rebuild the data stream reliably and hand it to the upper layers on the receiving device.

Before discussing Figure 1.18 any further, let's discuss port numbers and make sure you understand them. The Transport layer uses port numbers to define both the virtual circuit and the upper-layer process, as you can see from Figure 1.19.

FIGURE 1.18   PDU and layer addressing

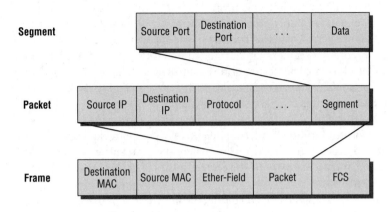

Bit   1011011100011110000

FIGURE 1.19   Port numbers at the Transport layer

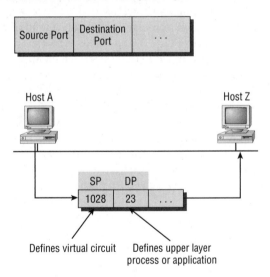

The Transport layer takes the data stream, makes segments out of it, and establishes a reliable session by creating a virtual circuit. It then sequences (numbers) each segment and uses acknowledgments and flow control. If you're using TCP, the virtual circuit is defined by the source port number. Remember, the host just makes this up starting at port number 1024 (0 through 1023 are reserved for well-known port numbers). The destination port number defines the upper-layer process (application) that the data stream is handed to when the data stream is reliably rebuilt on the receiving host.

Now that you understand port numbers and how they are used at the Transport layer, let's go back to Figure 1.18. Once the Transport layer header information is added to the piece of data, it becomes a segment and is handed down to the Network layer along with the destination IP address. (The destination IP address was handed down from the upper layers to the Transport layer with the data stream, and it was discovered through a name-resolution method at the upper layers—probably DNS.)

The Network layer adds a header and adds the logical addressing (IP addresses) to the front of each segment. Once the header is added to the segment, the PDU is called a packet. The packet has a protocol field that describes where the segment came from (either UDP or TCP) so it can hand the segment to the correct protocol at the Transport layer when it reaches the receiving host.

The Network layer is responsible for finding the destination hardware address that dictates where the packet should be sent on the local network. It does this by using the Address Resolution Protocol (ARP). IP at the Network layer looks at the destination IP address and compares that address to its own source IP address and subnet mask. If it turns out to be a local network request, the hardware address of the local host is requested via an ARP request. If the packet is destined for a remote host, IP will look for the IP address of the default gateway (router) instead.

The packet, along with the destination hardware address of either the local host or default gateway, is then handed down to the Data Link layer. The Data Link layer will add a header to the front of the packet and the piece of data then becomes a frame. (It is called a frame because both a header and a trailer are added to the packet, which makes the data resemble bookends or a frame, if you will.) This is shown in Figure 1.19. The frame uses an Ether-Type field to describe which protocol the packet came from at the Network layer. Now a CRC is run on the frame, and the answer to the CRC is placed in the FCS field found in the trailer of the frame.

The frame is now ready to be handed down, one bit at a time, to the Physical layer, which will use bit timing rules to encode the data in a digital signal. Every device on the network segment will synchronize itself with the clock and extract the 1s and 0s from the digital signal and build a frame. After the frame is rebuilt, a CRC is run to make sure that the frame is okay. If everything turns out to be all good, the hosts will check the destination address to see if the frame is for them.

Exam Essentials

Remember the steps of the encapsulation method.   The encapsulation method is data, segment, packet, frames, and bits.

Remember the Transport port numbers that are reserved.   Hosts can create a session to another host by using any number from 1024 to 65535. Ports 0 through 1023 are well known port numbers and are reserved.

Identify and Correct Common Network Problems at Layers 1, 2, 3, and 7 Using a Layered Model Approach

Troubleshooting IP addressing is obviously an important skill because running into trouble somewhere along the way is pretty much a sure thing—and it's going to happen to you. Because of this nasty fact, it will be great when you can save the day because you can figure out (diagnose) the problem and fix it on an IP network whether you're at work or at home!

This is where I'm going to show you the "Cisco way" of troubleshooting IP addressing. Let's go over the troubleshooting steps that Cisco uses first. These steps are pretty simple, but they are important nonetheless. Pretend that you're at a customer host, and they're complaining that their host cannot communicate with a server, which just happens to be on a remote network. Here are the four troubleshooting steps that Cisco recommends:

1. Open a DOS window and ping 127.0.0.1. This is the diagnostic or loopback address, and if you get a successful ping, your IP stack is then considered to be initialized. If it fails, then you have an IP stack failure and need to reinstall TCP/IP on the host.

2. From the DOS window, ping the IP address of the local host. If that's successful, then your network interface card (NIC) is functioning. If it fails, then there is a problem with the NIC card. Success does not mean that a cable is plugged into the NIC, only that the IP protocol stack on the host can communicate with the NIC.

3. From the DOS window, ping the default gateway (router). If the ping works, it means that the NIC is plugged into the network and can communicate on the local network. It also means the default router is responding and configured with the proper IP address on its local interface. If it fails, then you have a local physical network problem that could be happening anywhere from the NIC to the router.

4. If steps 1 through 3 were successful, try to ping the remote server. If that works, then you know that you have IP communication between the local host and the remote server. You also know that the remote physical network is working.

If the user still can't communicate with the server after steps 1 through 4 are successful, then you probably have some type of name resolution problem and need to check your Domain Name Service (DNS) settings. But if the ping to the remote server fails, then you know you have some type of remote physical network problem and need to go to the server and work through steps 1 through 3 until you find the snag.

Once you've gone through all these steps, what do you do if you find a problem? How do you go about fixing an IP address configuration error? Let's move on and discuss how to determine the IP address problems and how to fix them.

Let's use Figure 1.20 as an example of your basic IP trouble—poor Sally can't log in to the Windows server. You could call the Microsoft team to tell them their server is a pile of junk that's causing all of your problems, but that is probably not such a great idea. First, you should double-check your network instead.

FIGURE 1.20   Basic IP troubleshooting

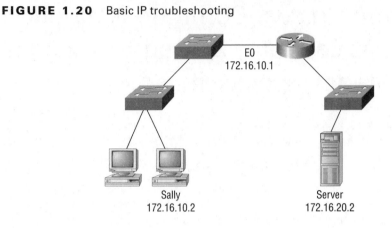

Sally
172.16.10.2

Server
172.16.20.2

Okay, let's get started by going over the troubleshooting steps that Cisco follows. They're pretty simple, but important nonetheless. Pretend that you're with a customer and they're complaining that their host can't communicate with a server that just happens to be on a remote network. Here are the four troubleshooting steps Cisco recommends:

1. Open a DOS window and ping 127.0.0.1. This is the diagnostic, or *loopback*, address, and if you get a successful ping, your IP stack is considered to be initialized. If it fails, then you have an IP stack failure and need to reinstall TCP/IP on the host.

```
C:\>ping 127.0.0.1
Pinging 127.0.0.1 with 32 bytes of data:
Reply from 127.0.0.1: bytes=32 time<1ms TTL=128
Reply from 127.0.0.1: bytes=32 time<1ms TTL=128
Reply from 127.0.0.1: bytes=32 time<1ms TTL=128
Reply from 127.0.0.1: bytes=32 time<1ms TTL=128
Ping statistics for 127.0.0.1:
    Packets: Sent = 4, Received = 4, Lost = 0 (0% loss),
Approximate round trip times in milli-seconds:
    Minimum = 0ms, Maximum = 0ms, Average = 0ms
```

2. From the DOS window, ping the IP address of the local host. If that's successful, your NIC is functioning. If it fails, there is a problem with the NIC. Success here doesn't mean that a cable is plugged into the NIC, only that the IP protocol stack on the host can communicate to the NIC (via the LAN driver).

```
C:\>ping 172.16.10.2
Pinging 172.16.10.2 with 32 bytes of data:
Reply from 172.16.10.2: bytes=32 time<1ms TTL=128
Reply from 172.16.10.2: bytes=32 time<1ms TTL=128
```

```
Reply from 172.16.10.2: bytes=32 time<1ms TTL=128
Reply from 172.16.10.2: bytes=32 time<1ms TTL=128
Ping statistics for 172.16.10.2:
    Packets: Sent = 4, Received = 4, Lost = 0 (0% loss),
Approximate round trip times in milli-seconds:
    Minimum = 0ms, Maximum = 0ms, Average = 0ms
```

3. From the DOS window, ping the default gateway (router). If the ping works, it means that the NIC is plugged into the network and can communicate on the local network. If it fails, you have a local physical network problem that could be anywhere from the NIC to the router.

```
C:\>ping 172.16.10.1
Pinging 172.16.10.1 with 32 bytes of data:
Reply from 172.16.10.1: bytes=32 time<1ms TTL=128
Reply from 172.16.10.1: bytes=32 time<1ms TTL=128
Reply from 172.16.10.1: bytes=32 time<1ms TTL=128
Reply from 172.16.10.1: bytes=32 time<1ms TTL=128
Ping statistics for 172.16.10.1:
    Packets: Sent = 4, Received = 4, Lost = 0 (0% loss),
Approximate round trip times in milli-seconds:
    Minimum = 0ms, Maximum = 0ms, Average = 0ms
```

4. If steps 1 through 3 were successful, try to ping the remote server. If that works, then you know that you have IP communication between the local host and the remote server. You also know that the remote physical network is working.

```
C:\>ping 172.16.20.2
Pinging 172.16.20.2 with 32 bytes of data:
Reply from 172.16.20.2: bytes=32 time<1ms TTL=128
Reply from 172.16.20.2: bytes=32 time<1ms TTL=128
Reply from 172.16.20.2: bytes=32 time<1ms TTL=128
Reply from 172.16.20.2: bytes=32 time<1ms TTL=128
Ping statistics for 172.16.20.2:
    Packets: Sent = 4, Received = 4, Lost = 0 (0% loss),
Approximate round trip times in milli-seconds:
    Minimum = 0ms, Maximum = 0ms, Average = 0ms
```

If the user still can't communicate with the server after steps 1 through 4 are successful, you probably have some type of name resolution problem and need to check your DNS settings. But if the ping to the remote server fails, then you know you have some type of remote physical network problem and need to go to the server and work through steps 1 through 3 until you find the snag.

Before we move on to determining IP address problems and how to fix them, let's review some basic DOS commands that you can use to help troubleshoot your network from both a PC and a Cisco router (the commands might do the same thing, but they are implemented differently).

Packet InterNet Groper (ping)   Uses ICMP echo request and replies to test if a node IP stack is initialized and alive on the network.

traceroute   Displays the list of routers on a path to a network destination by using TTL time-outs and ICMP error messages. This command will not work from a DOS prompt.

tracert   Same command as `traceroute`, but it's a Microsoft Windows command and will not work on a Cisco router.

arp -a   Displays IP-to-MAC address mappings on a Windows PC.

show ip arp   Same command as `arp -a`, but displays the ARP table on a Cisco router. Like the commands `traceroute` and `tracert`, they are not interchangeable between DOS and Cisco.

ipconfig /all   Used only from a DOS prompt, shows you the PC network configuration.

For more details about troubleshooting IP address problems, see the *CCNA Cisco Certified Network Associate Study Guide, 7th Edition* (Sybex, 2011).

Exam Essentials

Remember how to test your local stack.   You can ping 127.0.0.1 to test that the IP protocol is initialized on your system.

Understand how to test IP on your local host.   To verify that IP is communicating on your host, you need to ping your IP address. Open a DOS prompt and use the `ipconfig` command to find your IP address. This will verify that your host is communicating from IP to your LAN driver.

Understand how to verify that your host is communicating on the local network.   The best way to verify that your host is communicating on the local network is to ping your default gateway.

Differentiate between LAN/WAN Operation and Features

Layer 2 switching is considered hardware-based bridging because it uses specialized hardware called an *application-specific integrated circuit (ASIC)*. ASICs can run up to gigabit speeds with very low latency rates.

Latency is the time measured from when a frame enters a port to the time it exits a port.

Bridges and switches read each frame as it passes through the network. The layer 2 device then puts the source hardware address in a filter table and keeps track of the port on which the frame was received. This information (logged in the bridge's or switch's filter table) is what helps the machine determine the location of the specific sending device. Figure 1.21 shows a switch in an internetwork.

FIGURE 1.21   A switch in an internetwork

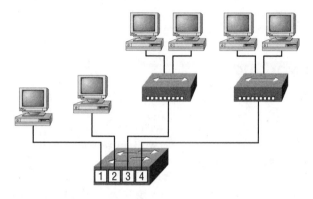

Each segment has its own collision domain.
All segments are in the same broadcast domain.

The real estate business is all about location, location, location, and it's the same for both layer 2 and layer 3 devices. Although both need to be able to negotiate the network, it's crucial to remember that they're concerned with very different parts of it. Primarily, layer 3 machines (such as routers) need to locate specific networks, whereas layer 2 machines (switches and bridges) need to eventually locate specific devices. So, networks are to routers as individual devices are to switches and bridges. And routing tables that "map" the internetwork are for routers as filter tables that "map" individual devices are for switches and bridges.

After a filter table is built on the layer 2 device, it will forward frames only to the segment where the destination hardware address is located. If the destination device is on the same segment as the frame, the layer 2 device will block the frame from going to any other segments. If the destination is on a different segment, the frame can be transmitted only to that segment. This is called *transparent bridging*.

When a switch interface receives a frame with a destination hardware address that isn't found in the device's filter table, it will forward the frame to all connected segments except for the source port. If the unknown device that was sent the "mystery frame" replies to this forwarding action, the switch updates its filter table regarding that device's location. But in the event the destination address of the transmitting frame is a broadcast address, the switch will forward all broadcasts to every connected segment by default.

All devices that the broadcast is forwarded to are considered to be in the same broadcast domain. This can be a problem; layer 2 devices propagate layer 2 broadcast storms that choke performance, and the only way to stop a broadcast storm from propagating through an internetwork is with a layer 3 device—a router.

The biggest benefit of using switches instead of hubs in your internetwork is that each switch port is actually its own collision domain. (Conversely, a hub creates one large collision domain.) But even armed with a switch, you still can't break up broadcast domains. Neither switches nor bridges will do that. They'll typically simply forward all broadcasts instead.

Another benefit of LAN switching over hub-centered implementations is that each device on every segment plugged into a switch can transmit simultaneously—at least, they can as long as there is only one host on each port and a hub isn't plugged into a switch port. As you might have guessed, hubs allow only one device per network segment to communicate at a time.

Ethernet Networking

Ethernet is a contention-based media access method that allows all hosts on a network to share the same bandwidth of a link. Ethernet is popular because it's readily scalable, meaning that it's comparatively easy to integrate new technologies, such as upgrading from Fast Ethernet to Gigabit Ethernet, into an existing network infrastructure. It's also relatively simple to implement in the first place, and with it, troubleshooting is reasonably straightforward. Ethernet uses both Data Link and Physical layer specifications, and this chapter will give you both the Data Link layer and Physical layer information you need to effectively implement, troubleshoot, and maintain an Ethernet network.

Collision Domain

As mentioned in earlier in this chapter, the term *collision domain* is an Ethernet term that refers to a particular network scenario wherein one device sends a packet out on a network segment, thereby forcing every other device on that same physical network segment to pay attention to it. This can be bad because if two devices on one physical segment transmit at the same time, a collision event—a situation where each device's digital signals interfere with another on the wire—occurs and forces the devices to retransmit later. Collisions can have a dramatically negative effect on network performance, so they're definitely something you want to avoid.

This type of situation is typically found in a hub environment where each host segment connects to a hub that represents only one collision domain and one broadcast domain. This begs a question that was discussed earlier: What's a broadcast domain?

Broadcast Domain

Here's the written definition: a *broadcast domain* refers to a group of devices on a network segment that hear all the broadcasts sent on that network segment.

Even though a broadcast domain is typically a boundary delimited by physical media like switches and routers, it can also reference a logical division of a network segment where all hosts can reach each other via a Data Link layer (hardware address) broadcast.

That's the basic story, so now let's take a look at a collision detection mechanism used in half-duplex Ethernet.

CSMA/CD

Ethernet networking uses *Carrier Sense Multiple Access with Collision Detection (CSMA/CD)*, a protocol that helps devices share the bandwidth evenly without having two devices transmit at the same time on the network medium. CSMA/CD was created to overcome the problem of those collisions that occur when packets are transmitted simultaneously from different nodes. And trust me—good collision management is crucial, because when a node transmits in a CSMA/CD network, all the other nodes on the network receive and examine that transmission. Only bridges and routers can effectively prevent a transmission from propagating throughout the entire network.

So, how does the CSMA/CD protocol work? Let's start by taking a look at Figure 1.22.

FIGURE 1.22   CSMA/CD

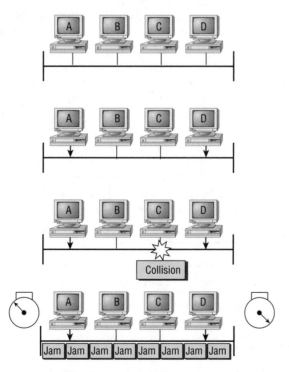

Carrier Sense Multiple Access with Collision Detection (CSMA/CD)

When a host wants to transmit over the network, it first checks for the presence of a digital signal on the wire. If all is clear (no other host is transmitting), the host will then proceed with its transmission. But it doesn't stop there. The transmitting host constantly monitors the wire to make sure that no other hosts begin transmitting. If the host detects another signal on the wire, it sends out an extended jam signal that causes all nodes on the segment to stop sending data (think busy signal). The nodes respond to that jam signal by waiting a while before attempting to transmit again. Backoff algorithms determine when the colliding stations can retransmit. If collisions keep occurring after 15 tries, the nodes attempting to transmit will then time out.

In the following sections, I am going to cover Ethernet in detail at both the Data Link layer (layer 2) and the Physical layer (layer 1).

Half-Duplex and Full-Duplex Ethernet

Half-duplex Ethernet is defined in the original 802.3 Ethernet; Cisco says it uses only one wire pair with a digital signal running in both directions on the wire. Certainly, the IEEE specifications discuss the process of half-duplex somewhat differently, but what Cisco is talking about is a general sense of what is happening here with Ethernet.

It also uses the CSMA/CD protocol to help prevent collisions and to permit retransmitting if a collision does occur. If a hub is attached to a switch, it must operate in half-duplex mode because the end stations must be able to detect collisions. Half-duplex Ethernet— typically 10BaseT—is only about 30 to 40 percent efficient as Cisco sees it because a large 10BaseT network will usually only give you 3 to 4Mbps, at most.

But full-duplex Ethernet uses two pairs of wires instead of one wire pair like half-duplex. And full-duplex uses a point-to-point connection between the transmitter of the transmitting device and the receiver of the receiving device. This means that with full-duplex data transfer, you get a faster data transfer than with half-duplex. And because the transmitted data is sent on a different set of wires than the received data, no collisions will occur.

The reason that you don't need to worry about collisions is because now it's like there is a freeway with multiple lanes instead of the single-lane road provided by half-duplex. Full-duplex Ethernet is supposed to offer 100 percent efficiency in both directions—for example, you can get 20Mbps with a 10Mbps Ethernet running full-duplex or 200Mbps for Fast Ethernet. But this rate is something known as an aggregate rate, which translates as "you're supposed to get" 100 percent efficiency. There are no guarantees in networking, as in life.

Full-duplex Ethernet can be used in five situations:

- With a connection from a switch to a host
- With a connection from a switch to a switch
- With a connection from a host to a host
- With a connection from a switch to a router
- With a connection from a router to a router

 Full-duplex Ethernet requires a point-to-point connection when only two nodes are present. You can run full-duplex with just about any device except a hub.

Now, if it's capable of all that speed, why wouldn't it deliver? Well, when a full-duplex Ethernet port is powered on, it first connects to the remote end and then negotiates with the other end of the Fast Ethernet link. This is called an *auto-detect mechanism*. This mechanism first decides on the exchange capability, which means that it checks to see if it can run at 10 or 100Mbps. It then checks to see if it can run full-duplex, and if it can't, it will run half-duplex.

Remember that half-duplex Ethernet shares a collision domain and provides a lower effective throughput than full-duplex Ethernet, which typically has a private collision domain and a higher effective throughput.

Last, remember these important points:

- There are no collisions in full-duplex mode.
- A dedicated switch port is required for each full-duplex node.
- The host network card and the switch port must be capable of operating in full-duplex mode.

Ethernet at the Data Link Layer

Ethernet at the Data Link layer is responsible for Ethernet addressing, commonly referred to as hardware addressing or MAC addressing. Ethernet is also responsible for framing packets received from the Network layer and preparing them for transmission on the local network through the Ethernet contention-based media access method.

Ethernet Addressing

Here's where we get into how Ethernet addressing works. It uses the *Media Access Control (MAC)* address burned into each and every Ethernet network interface card (NIC). The MAC, or hardware, address is a 48-bit (6-byte) address written in a hexadecimal format.

Figure 1.23 shows the 48-bit MAC addresses and how the bits are divided.

FIGURE 1.23   Ethernet addressing using MAC addresses

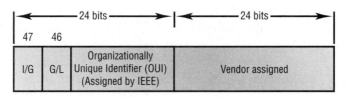

The *organizationally unique identifier (OUI)* is assigned by the IEEE to an organization. It's composed of 24 bits, or 3 bytes. The organization, in turn, assigns a globally administered address (24 bits, or 3 bytes) that is unique (supposedly, again—no guarantees) to each and every adapter it manufactures. Look closely at the figure. The high-order bit is the

Individual/Group (I/G) bit. When it has a value of 0, you can assume that the address is the MAC address of a device and may well appear in the source portion of the MAC header. When it is a 1, you can assume that the address represents either a broadcast or multicast address in Ethernet or a broadcast or functional address in Token Ring and FDDI.

The next bit is the global/local bit, or just G/L bit (also known as U/L, where *U* means *universal*). When set to 0, this bit represents a globally administered address (as by the IEEE). When the bit is a 1, it represents a locally governed and administered address. The low-order 24 bits of an Ethernet address represent a locally administered or manufacturer-assigned code. This portion commonly starts with 24 0s for the first card made and continues in order until there are 24 1s for the last (16,777,216th) card made. You'll find that many manufacturers use these same six hex digits as the last six characters of their serial number on the same card.

Defining WAN Terms

Before you run out and order a WAN service type from a provider, it would be a really good idea to understand the following terms that service providers typically use:

Customer premises equipment (CPE)   *Customer premises equipment (CPE)* is equipment that's owned by the subscriber and located on the subscriber's premises.

Demarcation point   The *demarcation point* is the precise spot where the service provider's responsibility ends and the CPE begins. It's generally a device in a telecommunications closet owned and installed by the telecommunications company (telco). It's your responsibility to cable (extended demarc) from this box to the CPE, which is usually a connection to a CSU/DSU or ISDN interface.

Local loop   The *local loop* connects the demarc to the closest switching office, which is called a central office.

Central office (CO)   This point connects the customer's network to the provider's switching network. Good to know is that a *central office (CO)* is sometimes referred to as a *point of presence (POP)*.

Toll network   The *toll network* is a trunk line inside a WAN provider's network. This network is a collection of switches and facilities owned by the ISP.

Definitely familiarize yourself with these terms because they're crucial to understanding WAN technologies.

WAN Connection Types

As you're probably aware, a WAN can use a number of different connection types, and I'm going to introduce you to each of the various types of WAN connections you'll find on the market today. Figure 1.24 shows the different WAN connection types that can be used to connect your LANs together (DTE) over a DCE network.

FIGURE 1.24   WAN connection types

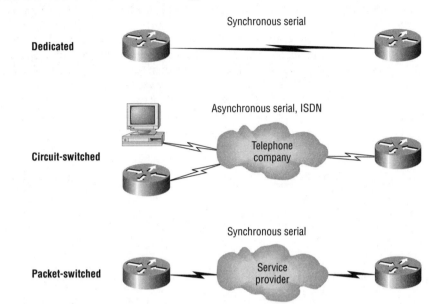

Here's a list explaining the different WAN connection types:

Leased Lines   These are usually referred to as a *point-to-point* or dedicated connection. A *leased line* is a preestablished WAN communications path that goes from the CPE through the DCE switch, then over to the CPE of the remote site. The CPE enables DTE networks to communicate at any time with no cumbersome setup procedures to muddle through before transmitting data. When you've got plenty of cash, this is really the way to go because it uses synchronous serial lines up to 45Mbps. HDLC and PPP encapsulations are frequently used on leased lines. We'll go over them in detail in a bit.

Circuit Switching   When you hear the term *circuit switching*, think phone call. The big advantage is cost—you only pay for the time you actually use. No data can transfer before an end-to-end connection is established. Circuit switching uses dial-up modems or ISDN and is used for low-bandwidth data transfers. You're probably thinking, "Modems? Did he say modems? Aren't those only in museums by now?" After all, with all the wireless technologies available, who would use a modem these days? Well, some people do have ISDN, and it still is viable (and I do suppose someone does use a modem now and then), but circuit switching can be used in some of the newer WAN technologies as well.

Packet Switching   This is a WAN switching method that allows you to share bandwidth with other companies to save money. *Packet switching* can be thought of as a network that's designed to look like a leased line yet charges you more like circuit switching. But lower cost isn't always better—there's definitely a downside: If you need to transfer data constantly, just forget about this option. Instead, get yourself a leased line. Packet switching will work for you only if your data transfers are the bursty type—not continuous. Frame Relay and X.25 are packet-switching technologies with speeds that can range from 56Kbps up to T3 (45Mbps).

> *MultiProtocol Label Switching (MPLS)* uses a combination of both circuit switching and packet switching, but it's out of this book's scope. Even so, after you pass your CCNA exam, it would be well worth your time to look into MPLS, so I'll briefly talk about MPLS shortly.

WAN Support

Basically, Cisco supports only HDLC, PPP, and Frame Relay on its serial interfaces, and you can see this with the `encapsulation ?` command from any serial interface (your output may vary depending on the IOS version you are running):

```
Corp#config t
Corp(config)#int s0/0/0
Corp(config-if)#encapsulation ?
  atm-dxi      ATM-DXI encapsulation
  frame-relay  Frame Relay networks
  hdlc         Serial HDLC synchronous
  lapb         LAPB (X.25 Level 2)
  ppp          Point-to-Point protocol
  smds         Switched Megabit Data Service (SMDS)
  x25          X.25
```

If I had other types of interfaces on my router, I would have other encapsulation options, such as ISDN or ADSL. And remember, you can't configure Ethernet or Token Ring encapsulation on a serial interface.

Next, I'm going to define the most prominently known WAN protocols used today: Frame Relay, ISDN, LAPB, LAPD, HDLC, PPP, PPPoE, Cable, DSL, MPLS, and ATM. Just so you know, the only WAN protocols you'll usually find configured on a serial interface are HDLC, PPP, and Frame Relay—but who said we're stuck with using only serial interfaces for wide area connections?

Frame Relay A packet-switched technology that made its debut in the early 1990s, *Frame Relay* is a high-performance Data Link and Physical layer specification. It's pretty much a successor to X.25, except that much of the technology in X.25 used to compensate for physical errors (noisy lines) has been eliminated. An upside to Frame Relay is that it can be more cost effective than point-to-point links, plus it typically runs at speeds of 64Kbps up to 45Mbps (T3). Another Frame Relay benefit is that it provides features for dynamic bandwidth allocation and congestion control.

ISDN *Integrated Services Digital Network (ISDN)* is a set of digital services that transmits voice and data over existing phone lines. ISDN offers a cost-effective solution for remote users who need a higher-speed connection than analog dial-up links can give them, and it's also a good choice to use as a backup link for other types of links like Frame Relay or T1 connections.

LAPB *Link Access Procedure, Balanced (LAPB)* was created to be a connection-oriented protocol at the Data Link layer for use with X.25, but it can also be used as a simple data link transport. A not-so-good characteristic of LAPB is that it tends to create a tremendous amount of overhead due to its strict time-out and windowing techniques.

LAPD *Link Access Procedure, D-Channel (LAPD)* is used with ISDN at the Data Link layer (layer 2) as a protocol for the D (signaling) channel. LAPD was derived from the Link Access Procedure, Balanced (LAPB) protocol and is designed primarily to satisfy the signaling requirements of ISDN basic access.

HDLC *High-Level Data-Link Control (HDLC)* was derived from Synchronous Data Link Control (SDLC), which was created by IBM as a Data Link connection protocol. HDLC works at the Data Link layer and creates very little overhead compared to LAPB.

It wasn't intended to encapsulate multiple Network layer protocols across the same link—the HDLC header doesn't contain any identification about the type of protocol being carried inside the HDLC encapsulation. Because of this, each vendor that uses HDLC has its own way of identifying the Network layer protocol, meaning each vendor's HDLC is proprietary with regard to its specific equipment.

PPP *Point-to-Point Protocol (PPP)* is a pretty famous, industry-standard protocol. Because all multiprotocol versions of HDLC are proprietary, PPP can be used to create point-to-point links between different vendors' equipment. It uses a Network Control Protocol field in the Data Link header to identify the Network layer protocol and allows authentication and multilink connections to be run over asynchronous and synchronous links.

PPPoE *Point-to-Point Protocol over Ethernet* encapsulates PPP frames in Ethernet frames and is usually used in conjunction with ADSL services. It gives you a lot of the familiar PPP features such as authentication, encryption, and compression, but there's a downside—it has a lower maximum transmission unit (MTU) than standard Ethernet does, and if your firewall isn't solidly configured, this little attribute can really give you some grief.

Still somewhat popular in the United States, the main feature of PPPoE is that it adds a direct connection to Ethernet interfaces while providing DSL support as well. It's often used by many hosts on a shared Ethernet interface for opening PPP sessions to various destinations via at least one bridging modem.

In a modern HFC network, typically 500 to 2,000 active data subscribers are connected to a certain cable network segment, all sharing the upstream and downstream bandwidth. (*Hybrid fibre-coaxial*, or HFC, is a telecommunications industry term for a network that incorporates both optical fiber and coaxial cable to create a broadband network.) The actual bandwidth for Internet service over a cable TV (CATV) line can be up to about 27Mbps on the download path to the subscriber, with about 2.5Mbps of bandwidth on the upload path. Typically, users get an access speed from 256Kbps to 6Mbps. This data rate varies greatly throughout the United States.

DSL   *Digital Subscriber Line* is a technology used by traditional telephone companies to deliver advanced services (high-speed data and sometimes video) over twisted-pair copper telephone wires. It typically has lower data-carrying capacity than HFC networks, and data speeds can be range limited by line lengths and quality. Digital subscriber line is not a complete end-to-end solution but rather a Physical layer transmission technology like dial-up, cable, or wireless. DSL connections are deployed in the last mile of a local telephone network—the local loop. The connection is set up between a pair of modems on either end of a copper wire that is run between the CPE and the Digital Subscriber Line Access Multiplexer (DSLAM). A *DSLAM* is the device located at the provider's CO and concentrates connections from multiple DSL subscribers.

MPLS   *MultiProtocol Label Switching (MPLS)* is a data-carrying mechanism that emulates some properties of a circuit-switched network over a packet-switched network. MPLS is a switching mechanism that imposes labels (numbers) on packets and then uses those labels to forward packets. The labels are assigned on the edge of the MPLS of the network, and forwarding inside the MPLS network is done solely based on labels. Labels usually correspond to a path to layer 3 destination addresses (equal to IP destination-based routing). MPLS was designed to support forwarding of protocols other than TCP/IP. Because of this, label switching within the network is performed the same regardless of the layer 3 protocol. In larger networks, the result of MPLS labeling is that only the edge routers perform a routing lookup. All the core routers forward packets based on the labels, which makes forwarding the packets through the service provider network faster. (Most companies are replacing their Frame Relay networks with MPLS today).

ATM   Asynchronous Transfer Mode (ATM) was created for time-sensitive traffic, providing simultaneous transmission of voice, video, and data. ATM uses cells that are a fixed 53 bytes long instead of packets. It also can use isochronous clocking (external clocking) to help the data move faster. Typically, if you are running Frame Relay today, you will be running Frame Relay over ATM.

Exam Essentials

Understand half-duplex technology.   Half-duplex only uses one wire pair at a time to both transmit and receive. Hubs can run only half-duplex.

Understand full-duplex technology.   Full-duplex devices use both wire pairs, so they can both transmit and receive at the same time. Hubs cannot run full-duplex. You must have a switch to run full-duplex on your PC.

Describe the operation of Carrier Sense Multiple Access with Collision Detection (CSMA/CD).   CSMA/CD is a protocol that helps devices share the bandwidth evenly without having two devices transmit at the same time on the network medium. Although it does not eliminate collisions, it helps to greatly reduce them, which reduces retransmissions, resulting in a more efficient transmission of data for all devices.

Know the differences between leased lines, circuit switching, and packet switching.   A leased line is a dedicated connection, a circuit-switched connection is like a phone call and can be on or off, and packet switching is essentially a connection that looks like a leased line but is priced more like a circuit-switched connection.

Understand the different WAN protocols.   Pay particular attention to HDLC, Frame Relay, and PPP. HDLC is the default encapsulation on Cisco routers. PPP provides an industry-standard way of encapsulating multiple routed protocols across a link and must be used when connecting equipment from multiple vendors. Frame relay is a packet-switched technology that can offer cost advantages over leased lines but has more complex configuration options.

Review Questions

1. How does a router respond when an interface receives a broadcast?

   A. The router forwards the broadcast out all ports.

   B. The router reads the data and responds accordingly to the request.

   C. The router discards the broadcast.

   D. The router forwards it to only the Ethernet LANs.

2. You want to implement a mechanism that automates the IP configuration, including IP address, subnet mask, default gateway, and DNS information. Which protocol will you use to accomplish this?

   A. SMTP

   B. SNMP

   C. DHCP

   D. ARP

3. What does a DHCP host use to verify that a duplicate IP address has not been received by the DHCP server?

   A. Ping

   B. ARP

   C. Gratuitous ping

   D. RARP

   E. Gratuitous ARP

4. Which of the following describe the DHCP Discover message? (Choose two.)

   A. It uses FF:FF:FF:FF:FF:FF as a layer 2 broadcast.

   B. It uses UDP as the Transport layer protocol.

   C. It uses TCP as the Transport layer protocol.

   D. It does not use a layer 2 destination address.

5. What are two characteristics of Telnet? (Choose two.)

   A. It sends data in cleartext format.

   B. It is a protocol designed and used only by Cisco routers.

   C. It is more secure than using Secure Shell (SSH).

   D. You must purchase Telnet from Microsoft.

   E. It requires that the destination device be configured to support Telnet services and connections.

6. If you are running a VoIP application and a UDP segment is received out of order, what does IP do with this segment?

    A. Rejects the packet

    B. Accepts the packet and hands it up to the next layer in the order it was received

    C. Accepts the packet and hands it up to the next layer in the order it was supposed to be received

    D. Broadcasts the packet

7. Which of the following are TCP/IP protocols used at the Application layer of the OSI model? (Choose three.)

    A. IP

    B. TCP

    C. Telnet

    D. FTP

    E. TFTP

8. When data is encapsulated, which is the correct order?

    A. Data, frame, packet, segment, bit

    B. Segment, data, packet, frame, bit

    C. Data, segment, packet, frame, bit

    D. Data, segment, frame, packet, bit

9. Which two statements about a reliable connection-oriented data transfer are true?

    A. Receiving hosts acknowledge receipt of data.

    B. When buffers are full, packets are discarded and are not retransmitted.

    C. Windowing is used to provide flow control and unacknowledged data segments.

    D. If the transmitting host's timer expires before receipt of an acknowledgment, the transmitting host drops the virtual circuit.

10. Which of the following describe router functions? (Choose four.)

    A. Packet switching

    B. Collision prevention

    C. Packet filtering

    D. Broadcast domain enlargement

    E. Internetwork communication

    F. Broadcast forwarding

    G. Path selection

Answers to Review Questions

1. C. Routers will discard any broadcast by default, unless configured to forward to a specific destination.

2. C. Dynamic Host Configuration Protocol (DHCP) is used to provide IP information to hosts on your network. DHCP can provide a lot of information, but the most common is IP address, subnet mask, default gateway, and DNS information.

3. E. To verify that a DHCP host has not received a duplicate IP address from a DHCP server, the host will send out an ARP request using its own IP address; this is called a gratuitous ARP.

4. A, B. A client that sends out a DHCP Discover message in order to receive an IP address sends out a broadcast at both layer 2 and layer 3. The layer 2 broadcast is all Fs in hex, or FF:FF:FF:FF:FF:FF. The layer 3 broadcast is 255.255.255.255, which means all networks and all hosts. DHCP is connectionless, which means it uses User Datagram Protocol (UDP) at the Transport layer, also called the Host-to-Host layer.

5. A, E. Telnet has been around as long as networking, and there is no cost to implement Telnet services on your network. However, all data is sent in a cleartext format and both the sending and receiving devices must have Telnet services running.

6. B. UDP does not have sequencing, so it will hand the segment up in the order it was received.

7. C, D, E. Telnet, File Transfer Protocol (FTP), and Trivial FTP (TFTP) are all Application layer protocols. IP is a Network layer protocol. Transmission Control Protocol (TCP) is a Transport layer protocol.

8. C. The encapsulation method is data, segment, packet, frame, bit.

9. A, C. When a virtual circuit is created, windowing is used for flow control and acknowledgment of data.

10. A, C, E, G. Routers provide packet switching, packet filtering, internetwork communication, and path selection.

Chapter

2

Configure, Verify, and Troubleshoot a Switch with VLANs and Interswitch Communications

THE CISCO CCNA EXAM OBJECTIVES COVERED IN THIS CHAPTER INCLUDE THE FOLLOWING:

- ✓ Select the appropriate media, cables, ports, and connectors to connect switches to other network devices and hosts.

- ✓ Explain the technology and media access control method for Ethernet networks.

- ✓ Explain network segmentation and basic traffic management concepts.

- ✓ Explain basic switching concepts and the operation of Cisco switches.

- ✓ Perform and verify initial switch configuration tasks, including remote access management.

- ✓ Verify network status and switch operation using basic utilities (including ping, traceroute, Telnet, SSH, arp, and ipconfig) and SHOW and DEBUG commands.

- ✓ Identify, prescribe, and resolve common switched network media issues, configuration issues, auto negotiation, and switch hardware failures.

- ✓ Describe enhanced switching technologies (including VTP, RSTP, VLAN, PVSTP, and 802.1q).

✓ Describe how VLANs create logically separate networks and the need for routing between them.

✓ Configure, verify, and troubleshoot VLANs.

✓ Configure, verify, and troubleshoot trunking on Cisco switches.

✓ Configure, verify, and troubleshoot interVLAN routing.

✓ Configure, verify, and troubleshoot VTP.

✓ Configure, verify, and troubleshoot RSTP operation.

✓ Interpret the output of various Show and Debug commands to verify the operational status of a Cisco switched network.

✓ Implement basic switch security (including port security, trunk access, management VLAN other than VLAN 1, etc.).

When Cisco discusses switching, they're talking about layer 2 switching unless they say otherwise. *Layer 2 switching* is the process of using the hardware address of devices on a LAN to segment a network.

Because you've got the basic ideas down, I am going to focus on the particulars of layer 2 switching and nail down how it works.

Select the Appropriate Media, Cables, Ports, and Connectors to Connect Switches to Other Network Devices and Hosts

Ethernet cabling is an important discussion, especially if you are planning to take the Cisco exams. Three types of Ethernet cables are available:

- Straight-through cable
- Crossover cable
- Rolled cable

We will look at each of these types in the following sections.

Straight-Through Cable

The *straight-through cable* is used to connect

- Host to switch or hub
- Router to switch or hub

Four wires are used in straight-through cable to connect Ethernet devices. It is relatively simple to create this type; Figure 2.1 shows the four wires used in a straight-through Ethernet cable.

Notice that only pins 1, 2, 3, and 6 are used. Just connect 1 to 1, 2 to 2, 3 to 3, and 6 to 6, and you'll be up and networking in no time. However, remember that this would be an Ethernet-only cable and wouldn't work with voice, Token Ring, ISDN, and so on.

FIGURE 2.1   Straight-through Ethernet cable

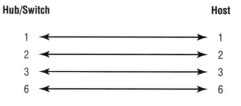

Crossover Cable

The *crossover cable* can be used to connect the following:

- Switch to switch
- Hub to hub
- Host to host
- Hub to switch
- Router direct to host

The same four wires are used in this cable as in the straight-through cable; you just connect different pins together. Figure 2.2 shows how the four wires are used in a crossover Ethernet cable.

FIGURE 2.2   Crossover Ethernet cable

Notice that instead of connecting 1 to 1, 2 to 2, and so on, here you connect pins 1 to 3 and 2 to 6 on each side of the cable.

Rolled Cable

Although *rolled cable* isn't used to connect any Ethernet connections, you can use a rolled Ethernet cable to connect a host to a router console serial communication (com) port.

If you have a Cisco router or switch, you would use this cable to connect your PC running HyperTerminal to the Cisco hardware. Eight wires are used in this cable to connect serial devices, although not all eight are used to send information, just as in Ethernet networking. Figure 2.3 shows the eight wires used in a rolled cable.

FIGURE 2.3 Rolled Ethernet cable

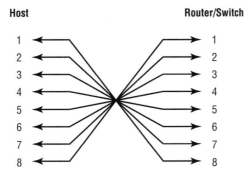

These are probably the easiest cables to make because you just cut the end off on one side of a straight-through cable, turn it over, and put it back on (with a new connector, of course).

We've looked at the most popular various RJ45 unshielded twisted pair (UTP) cables. Keeping this in mind, what cable is used between the switches in Figure 2.4?

FIGURE 2.4 RJ45 UTP

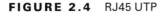
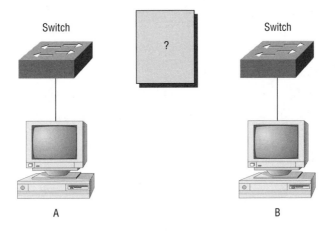

In order for Host A to ping Host B, you need a crossover cable to connect the two switches. What types of cables are used in the network shown in Figure 2.5?

In Figure 2.5, a variety of cables are in use. For the connection between the switches, you'd obviously use a crossover cable as you saw in Figure 2.2. The trouble is, a console connection that uses a rolled cable is in use. Plus, the connection from the router to the switch is a straight-through cable, as is true for the hosts to the switches. Keep in mind that if a serial connection were in use (which it isn't), it would be a V.35 that could be used to connect to a WAN.

Exam Essentials

Remember the types of Ethernet cabling and when you would use them.   The three types
of cables that can be created from an Ethernet cable are straight-through (to connect a PC's
or a router's Ethernet interface to a hub or switch), crossover (to connect hub to hub, hub to
switch, switch to switch, or PC to PC), and rolled (for a console connection from a PC to a
router or switch).

FIGURE 2.5   RJ45 UTP

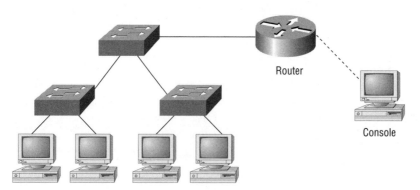

Explain the Technology and Media Access Control Method for Ethernet Networks

Ethernet is a contention media access method that allows all hosts on a network to share
the same bandwidth of a link. Ethernet is popular because it's readily scalable, meaning
that it's comparatively easy to integrate new technologies, such as Fast Ethernet and Gigabit
Ethernet, into an existing network infrastructure. It's also relatively simple to implement
in the first place, and with it, troubleshooting is reasonably straightforward. Ethernet uses
both Data Link and Physical layer specifications, and this section of the chapter will give
you both the Data Link layer and Physical layer information you need to effectively implement, troubleshoot, and maintain an Ethernet network.

Ethernet networking uses *Carrier Sense Multiple Access with Collision Detection
(CSMA/CD)*, a protocol that helps devices share the bandwidth evenly without having two
devices transmit at the same time on the network medium. CSMA/CD was created to overcome the problem of those collisions that occur when packets are transmitted simultaneously from different nodes. And trust me—good collision management is crucial, because

when a node transmits in a CSMA/CD network, all the other nodes on the network receive and examine that transmission. Only bridges and routers can effectively prevent a transmission from propagating throughout the entire network.

So, how does the CSMA/CD protocol work? Let's start by taking a look at Figure 2.6.

FIGURE 2.6   CSMA/CD

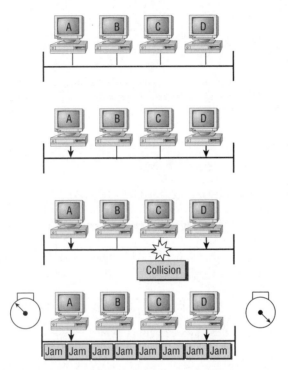

Carrier Sense Multiple Access with Collision Detection (CSMA/CD)

When a host wants to transmit over the network, it first checks for the presence of a digital signal on the wire. If all is clear (no other host is transmitting), the host will then proceed with its transmission—but it doesn't stop there. The transmitting host constantly monitors the wire to make sure no other hosts begin transmitting. If the host detects another signal on the wire, it sends out an extended jam signal that causes all nodes on the segment to stop sending data (think busy signal). The nodes respond to that jam signal by waiting a while before attempting to transmit again. Backoff algorithms determine when the colliding stations can retransmit. If collisions keep occurring after 15 tries, the nodes attempting to transmit will then time out. Pretty clean!

When a collision occurs on an Ethernet LAN, the following happens:

- A jam signal informs all devices that a collision occurred.

- The collision invokes a random backoff algorithm.

- Each device on the Ethernet segment stops transmitting for a short time until the timers expire.

- All hosts have equal priority to transmit after the timers have expired.

  The following are the effects of having a CSMA/CD network sustaining heavy collisions:

- Delay

- Low throughput

- Congestion

For more information and detail on Ethernet, please refer to Chapter 2 in my *CCNA Cisco Certified Network Associate Study Guide, 7th Edition* (Sybex, 2011).

Ethernet at the Physical Layer

Ethernet was first implemented by a group called DIX (Digital, Intel, and Xerox). They created and implemented the first Ethernet LAN specification, which the IEEE used to create the IEEE 802.3 Committee. This was a 10Mbps network that ran on coax and then eventually twisted-pair and fiber physical media.

The IEEE extended the 802.3 Committee to two new committees known as 802.3u (Fast Ethernet) and 802.3ab (Gigabit Ethernet on category 5) and then finally 802.3ae (10Gbps over fiber and coax).

Figure 2.7 shows the IEEE 802.3 and original Ethernet Physical layer specifications.

FIGURE 2.7   Ethernet Physical layer specifications

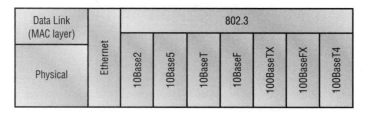

When designing your LAN, it's really important to understand the different types of Ethernet media available to you. Sure, it would be great to run Gigabit Ethernet to each desktop and 10Gbps between switches, and although this might happen one day, justifying the cost of that network today would be pretty difficult. But if you mix and match the different types of Ethernet media methods currently available, you can come up with a cost-effective network solution that works great.

Each Ethernet cable type that is specified by the EIA/TIA has inherent attenuation, which is defined as the loss of signal strength as it travels the length of a cable and is measured in decibels (dB). The cabling used in corporate and home markets is measured in categories. A higher-quality cable will have a higher-rated category and lower attenuation. For example, category 5 is better than category 3 because category 5 cables have more wire twists per foot and, therefore, less crosstalk. Crosstalk is the unwanted signal interference from adjacent pairs in the cable.

Here are the original IEEE 802.3 standards:

10Base2 10Mbps, baseband technology, up to 185 meters in length. Known as *thinnet* and can support up to 30 workstations on a single segment. Uses a physical and logical bus with AUI connectors. The 10 means 10Mbps, *Base* means baseband technology (which is a signaling method for communication on the network), and the 2 means almost 200 meters. 10Base2 Ethernet cards use BNC (British Naval Connector, Bayonet Neill Concelman, or Bayonet Nut Connector) and T-connectors to connect to a network.

10Base5 10Mbps, baseband technology, up to 500 meters in length. Known as *thicknet*. Uses a physical and logical bus with AUI connectors. Up to 2,500 meters with repeaters and 1,024 users for all segments.

10BaseT 10Mbps using category 3 UTP wiring. Unlike with the 10Base2 and 10Base5 networks, each device must connect into a hub or switch, and you can have only one host per segment or wire. Uses an RJ45 connector (8-pin modular connector) with a physical star topology and a logical bus.

Latest Ethernet Standards

Here are the expanded IEEE Ethernet 802.3 standards, starting with Fast Ethernet:

100Base-TX (IEEE 802.3u) 100Base-TX, most commonly known as Fast Ethernet, uses EIA/TIA category 5, 5E, or 6 UTP two-pair wiring. One user per segment; up to 100 meters long. It uses an RJ45 connector with a physical star topology and a logical bus.

100Base-FX (IEEE 802.3u) Uses fiber cabling 62.5/125-micron multimode fiber. Point-to-point topology; up to 412 meters long. It uses ST and SC connectors, which are media-interface connectors.

1000Base-CX (IEEE 802.3z) Copper twisted-pair called twinax (a balanced coaxial pair) that can run only up to 25 meters and uses a special 9-pin connector known as the High-Speed Serial Data Connector (HSSDC).

1000Base-T (IEEE 802.3ab) Category 5, four-pair UTP wiring up to 100 meters long and up to 1Gbps.

1000Base-SX (IEEE 802.3z) The implementation of 1 Gigabit Ethernet running over multimode fiber-optic cable (instead of copper twisted-pair cable) and using short wavelength laser. Multimode fiber (MMF) using 62.5- and 50-micron core; uses an 850 nanometer (nm) laser and can go up to 220 meters with 62.5-micron, 550 meters with 50-micron.

1000Base-LX (IEEE 802.3z) Single-mode fiber that uses a 9-micron core and 1300nm laser and can go from 3 kilometers up to 10 kilometers.

1000Base-ZX (Cisco standard) 1000BaseZX (or 1000Base-ZX) is a Cisco-specified standard for Gigabit Ethernet communication. 1000BaseZX operates on ordinary single-mode fiber-optic link with spans up to 43.5 miles (70km).

10GBase-T   10GBase-T is a standard proposed by the IEEE 802.3ae Committee to provide 10Gbps connections over conventional UTP cables (category 5e, 6, or 7 cables). 10GBase-T allows the conventional RJ45 used for Ethernet LANs. It can support signal transmission at the full 100-meter distance specified for LAN wiring.

The following are all part of the IEEE 802.3ae standard.

10GBase-Short Range (SR)   An implementation of 10 Gigabit Ethernet that uses short-wavelength lasers at 850nm over multimode fiber. It has a maximum transmission distance of between 2 and 300 meters, depending on the size and quality of the fiber.

10GBase-Long Range (LR)   An implementation of 10 Gigabit Ethernet that uses long-wavelength lasers at 1,310nm over single-mode fiber. It also has a maximum transmission distance between 2 meters and 10km, depending on the size and quality of the fiber.

10GBase-Extended Range (ER)   An implementation of 10 Gigabit Ethernet running over single-mode fiber. It uses extra-long-wavelength lasers at 1,550nm. It has the longest transmission distances possible of the 10-Gigabit technologies: anywhere from 2 meters up to 40km, depending on the size and quality of the fiber used.

10GBase-Short Wavelength (SW)   10GBase-SW, as defined by IEEE 802.3ae, is a mode of 10GBase-S for MMF with an 850nm laser transceiver with a bandwidth of 10Gbps. It can support up to 300 meters of cable length. This media type is designed to connect to SONET equipment.

10GBase-Long Wavelength (LW)   10GBase-LW is a mode of 10GBase-L supporting a link length of 10km on standard single-mode fiber (SMF) (G.652). This media type is designed to connect to SONET equipment.

10GBase-Extra Long Wavelength (EW)   10GBase-EW is a mode of 10GBase-E supporting a link length of up to 40km on SMF based on G.652 using optical-wavelength 1,550nm. This media type is designed to connect to SONET equipment.

If you want to implement a network medium that is not susceptible to electromagnetic interference (EMI), fiber-optic cable provides a more secure, long-distance cable that is not susceptible to EMI at high speeds.

Exam Essentials

Identify the IEEE physical standards for Ethernet cabling.   These standards describe the capabilities and physical characteristics of various cable types and include but are not limited to 10Base2, 10Base5, and 10Base T.

Remember the Cisco proprietary 1000Base-ZX.   1000BaseZX (or 1000Base-ZX) is a Cisco-specified standard for Gigabit Ethernet communication. 1000BaseZX operates on ordinary single-mode fiber-optic link with spans up to 43.5 miles (70km).

Remember the distances possible with the latest IEEE 802.3 standards.   1000BaseZX (or 1000Base-ZX) is a Cisco-specified fiber that goes up to 43.5 miles (70km). The 1000Base-LX (long range) can go from 3 kilometers up to 10 kilometers. The ranges are: SX (short range), LX (long range), EX (extended range), and EW (extra long wavelength).

Explain Network Segmentation and Basic Traffic Management Concepts

There are a number of interchangeable terms you can use for "LAN," depending on the context. They include:

- Broadcast domain (in the context of layer 2 versus layer 1 segmentation)

- Subnet or network (in the context of IP networking)

- Data Link (layer 2 in the OSI model)

- VLAN (in the context of creating broadcast domains in switched Ethernet environments)

As mentioned, these terms are roughly equivalent. They are used to describe the simple LAN in different contexts. Why discuss a simple LAN? Well, it is the basis of every internetwork. An internetwork is simply a collection of connected LANs. An individual LAN is created using a variety of devices and techniques, such as routers, switches, and bridges.

These devices connect the hosts on the single LAN to each other, and connect the LAN to the other LANs forming the internetwork.

It's likely that at some point, you'll have to break up one large network into a number of smaller ones because user response has dwindled to a trickle as networks have grown and grown and LAN traffic congestion has reached overwhelming proportions. Congestion is a really big problem. Some possible causes of LAN traffic congestion include:

- Too many hosts in a broadcast domain

- Broadcast storms

- Multicasting

- Low bandwidth

You can help solve the congestion issue by breaking up a large network into a number of smaller networks (otherwise known as *network segmentation)*. Network segmentation is accomplished using *routers, switches,* and *bridges.*

Routers

Routers are used to connect networks together and route packets of data from one network to another. Cisco became the de facto standard of routers because of their high-quality router products, great selection, and fantastic service. Routers, by default, break up a *broadcast domain*, which is the set of all devices on a network segment that hear all broadcasts sent on that segment. Breaking up a broadcast domain is important because when a host or server sends a network broadcast, every device on the network must read and process that broadcast—unless you have a router. When the router's interface receives this broadcast, it can respond by basically saying "Thanks, but no thanks," and discard the broadcast without forwarding it on to other networks. Even though routers are known for breaking up broadcast domains by default, it's important to remember that they also break up collision domains.

Two advantages of using routers in your network:

- They don't forward broadcasts by default.
- They can filter the network based on layer-3 information (i.e., IP address).

Switches

Conversely, switches aren't used to create internetworks; they're employed to add functionality to a LAN. The main purpose of a switch is to make a LAN work better—to optimize its performance—providing more bandwidth for the LAN's users, and switches don't forward packets to other networks as routers do. Instead, they only "switch" frames from one port to another within the switched network.

By default, switches break up *collision domains*. This is an Ethernet term used to describe a network scenario wherein one particular device sends a packet on a network segment, forcing every other device on that same segment to pay attention to it. At the same time, a different device tries to transmit, leading to a collision, after which both devices must retransmit, one at a time. This situation is not good and is very inefficient. It is typically found in a hub environment where each host segment connects to a hub that represents only one collision domain and only one broadcast domain. By contrast, each and every port on a switch represents its own collision domain.

> **NOTE** Switches create separate collision domains, but a single broadcast domain. Routers separate broadcast domains.

Bridges

The term *bridging* was introduced before routers and hubs were implemented, so it's pretty common to hear people referring to bridges as "switches." That's because bridges and switches basically do the same thing—they break up collision domains on a LAN. So, what this means is that a switch is basically just a multiple-port bridge with more brainpower.

Well, that's pretty much it, but there are differences. Switches do provide this function, but they do so with greatly enhanced management ability and features. Plus, most of the time, bridges had only two or four ports. Yes, you could get your hands on a bridge with up to 16 ports, but that's nothing compared to the hundreds available on some switches.

 You would use a bridge in a network to reduce collisions within broadcast domains and to increase the number of collision domains in your network, which provides more bandwidth for users.

Exam Essentials

Understand the different terms used to describe a LAN.   A LAN is basically the same thing as a VLAN, subnet, or network, broadcast domain, or data link. These terms all describe roughly the same concept in different contexts.

Understand which devices create a LAN and which separate and connect LANs.   Switches and bridges are used to create LANs. While they do separate collision domains, they do not create separate LANs (collision domain and LAN are not the same concept). Routers are used to separate LANs and connect LANs (broadcast domains).

Explain Basic Switching Concepts and the Operation of Cisco Switches

Unlike bridges, which use software to create and manage a filter table, switches use application-specific integrated circuits (ASICs) to build and maintain their filter tables. But it's still okay to think of a layer 2 switch as a multiport bridge because their basic reason for being is the same: to break up collision domains.

Layer 2 switching provides the following:

- Hardware-based bridging (ASIC)
- Wire speed
- Low latency
- Low cost

What makes layer 2 switching so efficient is that no modification to the data packet takes place. The device only reads the frame encapsulating the packet, which makes the switching process considerably faster and less error-prone than routing processes are.

If you use layer 2 switching for both workgroup connectivity and network segmentation (breaking up collision domains), you can create a flatter network design with more network segments than you can with traditional routed networks.

Plus, layer 2 switching increases bandwidth for each user because, again, each connection (interface) into the switch is its own collision domain. This feature makes it possible for you to connect multiple devices to each interface.

In the following sections, we will delve deeper into the layer 2 switching technology.

Limitations of Layer 2 Switching

Because layer 2 switching is commonly placed into the same category as bridged networks, people tend to think it has the same hang-ups and issues that bridged networks have. Keep in mind that bridges are good and helpful things if the network is designed correctly and their features and limitations are accommodated. To design well with bridges, these are the two most important considerations:

- The collision domains must be broken up absolutely correctly.

- The right way to create a functional bridged network is to make sure that its users spend 80 percent of their time on the local segment.

Bridged networks break up collision domains, but remember, that network is still one large broadcast domain. Neither layer 2 switches nor bridges break up broadcast domains by default—something that not only limits your network's size and growth potential but also can reduce its overall performance.

Broadcasts and multicasts, along with the slow convergence time of spanning trees, can give you some major grief as your network grows. These are the big reasons that layer 2 switches and bridges cannot completely replace routers (layer 3 devices) in the internetwork.

Bridging versus LAN Switching

It's true—layer 2 switches really are pretty much just bridges that give us a lot more ports, but there are some important differences you should always keep in mind:

- Bridges are software based, while switches are hardware based because they use ASIC chips to help make filtering decisions.

- A switch can be viewed as a multiport bridge.

- There can be only one spanning-tree instance per bridge, while switches can have many. (I'm going to tell you all about spanning trees in a bit.)

- Switches have a higher number of ports than most bridges.

- Both bridges and switches forward layer 2 broadcasts.

- Bridges and switches learn MAC addresses by examining the source address of each frame received.

- Both bridges and switches make forwarding decisions based on layer 2 addresses.

Three Switch Functions at Layer 2

Layer 2 switching has three distinct functions: *address learning, forward/filter decisions*, and *loop avoidance*. (You need to remember these!)

Address Learning   Layer 2 switches and bridges remember the source hardware address of each frame received on an interface, and they enter this information into a MAC database called a *forward/filter table*.

Forward/Filter Decisions   When a frame is received on an interface, the switch looks at the destination hardware address and finds the exit interface in the MAC database. The frame is only forwarded out the specified destination port.

Loop Avoidance   If multiple connections between switches are created for redundancy purposes, network loops can occur. Spanning Tree Protocol (STP) is used to stop network loops while still permitting redundancy.

I'm going to talk about address learning, forward/filtering decisions, and loop avoidance in detail in the next sections.

Address Learning

When a switch is first powered on, the MAC forward/filter table is empty, as shown in Figure 2.8.

FIGURE 2.8   Empty forward/filter table on a switch

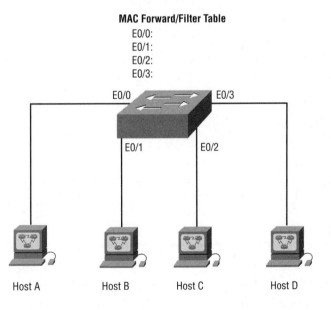

MAC Forward/Filter Table
E0/0:
E0/1:
E0/2:
E0/3:

When a device transmits and an interface receives a frame, the switch places the frame's source address in the MAC forward/filter table, allowing it to remember on which interface the sending device is located. The switch then has no choice but to flood the network with this frame out of every port except the source port because it has no idea where the destination device is actually located.

If a device answers this flooded frame and sends a frame back, then the switch will take the source address from that frame and place that MAC address in its database as well, associating this address with the interface that received the frame. Because the switch now has both of the relevant MAC addresses in its filtering table, the two devices can now make a point-to-point connection. The switch doesn't need to flood the frame as it did the first time because now the frames can and will be forwarded only between the two devices. This is exactly the thing that makes layer 2 switches better than hubs. In a hub network, all frames are forwarded out all ports every time—no matter what. Figure 2.9 shows the processes involved in building a MAC database.

FIGURE 2.9   How switches learn hosts' locations

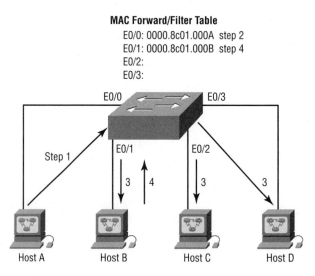

In this figure, you can see four hosts attached to a switch. When the switch is powered on, it has nothing in its MAC address forward/filter table. When the hosts start communicating, the switch places the source hardware address of each frame in the table along with the port to which the frame's address corresponds.

Let me give you an example of how a forward/filter table is populated:

1. Host A sends a frame to Host B. Host A's MAC address is 0000.8c01.000A; Host B's MAC address is 0000.8c01.000B.

2. The switch receives the frame on the E0/0 interface and places the source address in the MAC address table.

3. Because the destination address is not in the MAC database, the frame is forwarded out all interfaces—except the source port.

4. Host B receives the frame and responds to Host A. The switch receives this frame on interface E0/1 and places the source hardware address in the MAC database.

5. Host A and Host B can now make a point-to-point connection and only the two devices will receive the frames. Hosts C and D will not see the frames, nor are their MAC addresses found in the database because they haven't yet sent a frame to the switch.

If Host A and Host B don't communicate to the switch again within a certain amount of time, the switch will flush their entries from the database to keep it as current as possible.

Forward/Filter Decisions

When a frame arrives at a switch interface, the destination hardware address is compared to the forward/filter MAC database. If the destination hardware address is known and listed in the database, the frame is only sent out the correct exit interface. The switch doesn't transmit the frame out any interface except the destination interface. This preserves bandwidth on the other network segments and is called *frame filtering*.

If the destination hardware address is not listed in the MAC database, then the frame is flooded out all active interfaces except the interface on which the frame was received. If a device answers the flooded frame, the MAC database is updated with the device's location (interface).

If a host or server sends a broadcast on the LAN, the switch will flood the frame out all active ports except the source port by default. Remember, the switch creates smaller collision domains, but it's still one large broadcast domain by default.

In Figure 2.10, Host A sends a data frame to Host D. What will the switch do when it receives the frame from Host A?

Because Host A's MAC address is not in the forward/filter table, the switch will add the source address and port to the MAC address table and then forward the frame to Host D. If Host D's MAC address was not in the forward/filter table, the switch would have flooded the frame out all ports except for port Fa0/3.

FIGURE 2.10   Forward/filter table

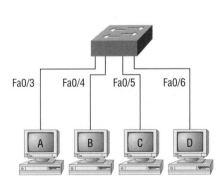

```
Switch#sh mac address-table
Vlan    Mac Address      Ports
----    -----------      -----
   1    0005.dccb.d74b   Fa0/4
   1    000a.f467.9e80   Fa0/5
   1    000a.f467.9e8b   Fa0/6
```

Now let's take a look at the output of a show mac address-table:

```
Switch#sh mac address-table
Vlan    Mac Address     Type        Ports
----    -----------     --------    -----
   1    0005.dccb.d74b  DYNAMIC     Fa0/1
   1    000a.f467.9e80  DYNAMIC     Fa0/3
   1    000a.f467.9e8b  DYNAMIC     Fa0/4
   1    000a.f467.9e8c  DYNAMIC     Fa0/3
   1    0010.7b7f.c2b0  DYNAMIC     Fa0/3
   1    0030.80dc.460b  DYNAMIC     Fa0/3
   1    0030.9492.a5dd  DYNAMIC     Fa0/1
   1    00d0.58ad.05f4  DYNAMIC     Fa0/1
```

Suppose the preceding switch received a frame with the following MAC addresses:

Source MAC: 0005.dccb.d74b

Destination MAC: 000a.f467.9e8c

How will the switch handle this frame? The destination MAC address will be found in the MAC address table and the frame will be forwarded out Fa0/3 only. If the destination MAC address is not found in the forward/filter table, it will forward the frame out all ports of the switch looking for the destination device.

Exam Essentials

Remember the advantages of layer 2 switching.   Switches use an ASIC's chip, which provides fast switching of frames. In addition, each switch builds a MAC address table for forward/filtering decisions, and along with more collision domains, this provides more bandwidth for users.

Remember the three switch functions.   Address learning, forward/filter decisions, and loop avoidance are the functions of a switch.

Remember the command show mac address-table.   The command show mac address-table will show you the forward/filter table used on the LAN switch.

Perform and Verify Initial Switch Configuration Tasks, Including Remote Access Management

I'm going to show you how to start up and configure a Cisco Catalyst switch using the command-line interface (CLI). After you get the basic commands down, I'll show you how to configure virtual LANs (VLANs) plus Inter-Switch Link (ISL), 802.1q routing, and Cisco's Virtual Trunk Protocol (VTP) in the upcoming objectives.

Catalyst Switch Basic Configuration

When you connect switches to each other, remember that first you'll need a crossover cable between the switches; newer switches auto-detect this type of connection, but the CCNA objectives assume no auto-detect mechanisms.

Let's start the configuration by connecting into a switch and setting the administrative functions. We'll also assign an IP address to the switch, but this isn't really necessary to make the network function. The only reason to do that is so we can manage/administer it. Let's use a simple IP scheme like 192.168.10.16/28. This mask should be familiar to you!

Check out the following output:

```
Switch>en
Switch#config t
Enter configuration commands, one per line.  End with CNTL/Z.
Switch(config)#hostname S1
S1(config)#enable secret todd
S1(config)#int F0/1
S1(config-if)#description 1st Connection to Core Switch
S1(config-if)#int F0/2
S1(config-if)#description 2nd Connection to Core Switch
S1(config-if)#int F0/3
S1(config-if)#description Connection to HostA
S1(config-if)#int F0/4
S1(config-if)#description Connection to PhoneA
S1(config-if)#int F0/8
S1(config-if)#description Connection to IVR
S1(config-if)#line console 0
S1(config-line)#password console
S1(config-line)#login
S1(config-line)#exit
S1(config)#line vty 0 ?
  <1-15>  Last Line number
  <cr>
S1(config)#line vty 0 15
S1(config-line)#password telnet
S1(config-line)#login
```

```
S1(config-line)#int vlan 1
S1(config-if)#ip address 192.168.10.17 255.255.255.240
S1(config-if)#no shut
S1(config-if)#exit
S1(config)#banner motd # This is the S1 switch #
S1(config)#exit
S1(config)#ip default-gateway 192.168.10.30
S1#copy run start
Destination filename [startup-config]? [enter]
Building configuration...
[OK]
S1#
```

The first thing to notice about this is that there is no IP address configured on the switch's interfaces. Because all ports on a switch are enabled by default, there's not much to configure. The IP address is configured under a logical interface, called a management domain or VLAN. You would typically use the default VLAN 1 to manage a switched network just as I did here. Also, notice the command ip default-gateway *ip address*, which provides remote management of the switch. This is an important objective.

The rest of the configuration is basically the same as the process you go through for router configuration. Remember, there are no IP addresses on switch interfaces, no routing protocols, and so on. We're performing layer 2 switching at this point, not routing! Also, note that there is no aux port on Cisco switches.

Exam Essentials

Remember how to set an IP address on a switch.   To configure an IP address on a switch, an address is never configured on a switch port, but rather what is called the management VLAN. By default this is VLAN 1. Here is an example of how to set an IP address on a switch using the default VLAN:

```
Switch(config)#int vlan 1
Switch(config-if)#ip address 192.168.10.17 255.255.255.240
Switch(config-if)#no shut
```

Remember how to configure a switch for remote management.   To allow hosts from outside the management VLAN to access the switch for administrative purposes, you need to set a default gateway on the switch. Here is how you would do that:

```
Switch(config)#ip default-gateway 192.168.10.30
```

Verify Network Status and Switch Operation Using Basic Utilities (Including ping, traceroute, Telnet, SSH, arp, and ipconfig) and *SHOW* and *DEBUG* Commands

Let's take a look at some common commands that you can use to help troubleshoot your network from both a PC and a Cisco router (the commands might do the same thing, but they are implemented differently).

Packet InterNet Groper (ping)   Uses ICMP echo requests and replies to test if a node IP stack is initialized and alive on the network.

traceroute   Displays the list of routers on a path to a network destination by using TTL time-outs and ICMP error messages. This command will not work from a DOS prompt.

tracert   Same command as **traceroute**, but it's a Microsoft Windows command and will not work on a Cisco router.

arp -a   Displays IP-to-MAC address mappings on a Windows PC.

show ip arp   Same command as **arp -a**, but displays the ARP table on a Cisco router. Like the commands **traceroute** and **tracert**, they are not interchangeable between DOS and Cisco.

ipconfig /all   Used only from a DOS prompt, shows you the PC network configuration.

Once you've gone through all these steps and used the appropriate DOS commands, what do you do if you find a problem? How do you go about fixing an IP address configuration error? Let's move on and discuss how to determine any IP address problems and how to fix them.

Checking Network Connectivity

You can use the ping and traceroute commands to test connectivity to remote devices, and both of them can be used with many protocols, not just IP.

Using the *Ping* Command

So far, you've seen many examples of pinging devices to test IP connectivity and name resolution using the DNS server. To see all the different protocols that you can use with ping, use the ping ? command like this:

```
Todd#ping ?
  WORD      Ping destination address or hostname
```

```
apollo      Apollo echo
appletalk   Appletalk echo
clns        CLNS echo
decnet      DECnet echo
ip          IP echo
ipx         Novell/IPX echo
srb         srb echo
tag         Tag encapsulated IP echo
vines       Vines echo
xns         XNS echo
<cr>
```

The ping output displays the minimum, average, and maximum times it takes for a Ping packet to find a specified system and return. Here's another example:

```
Todd#ping todd
Translating "todd"...domain server (192.168.0.70)[OK]
Type escape sequence to abort.
Sending 5, 100-byte ICMP Echos to 192.168.0.121, timeout
  is 2 seconds:
!!!!!
Success rate is 100 percent (5/5), round-trip min/avg/max
  = 32/32/32 ms
```

You can see that the DNS server was used to resolve the name, and the device was pinged in 32ms (milliseconds).

 The ping command can be used in user and privileged mode, but not in configuration mode.

Using the *Traceroute* Command

Traceroute (the traceroute command, or trace for short) shows the path a packet takes to get to a remote device. To see the protocols that you can use with traceroute, use the traceroute ? command. Here's an example:

```
Todd#traceroute ?
  WORD        Trace route to destination address or
              hostname
  appletalk   AppleTalk Trace
  clns        ISO CLNS Trace
  ip          IP Trace
  ipx         IPX Trace
```

```
oldvines    Vines Trace (Cisco)
vines       Vines Trace (Banyan)
<cr>
```

The trace command shows the hop or hops that a packet traverses on its way to a remote device. Here's an example:

```
Todd#trace r1
Type escape sequence to abort.
Tracing the route to r1.lammle.com (172.16.10.2)

  1 r1.lammle.com (172.16.10.2) 16 msec *  16 msec
```

You can see that the packet went through only one hop to find the destination.

Do not get confused on the exam. You can't use the tracert command—it's a Windows command. For a router, use the traceroute command!

Verifying Cisco Catalyst Switches

The first thing I like to do with any router or switch is to run through the configurations with a show running-config command. Performing a run-through gives me a really great headshot of each device. However, it's time-consuming and showing you all those configurations would take up a lot of pages in this book. Besides, you can run other commands that will still stock you with really good information.

For example, to verify the IP address set on a switch, you can use the show interface command. Here is the output:

```
S1#sh int vlan 1
Vlan1 is up, line protocol is up
  Hardware is EtherSVI, address is 001b.2b55.7540 (bia 001b.2b55.7540)
  Internet address is 192.168.10.17/28
  MTU 1500 bytes, BW 1000000 Kbit, DLY 10 usec,
     reliability 255/255, txload 1/255, rxload 1/255
  Encapsulation ARPA, loopback not set, reliability 255/255, txload 1/255,
rxload 1/255
  [output cut]
```

Remember that IP addresses aren't needed on a switch. The only reason you would set an IP address, mask, or default gateway is for management purposes.

show mac address-table

I'm sure you remember being shown this command earlier in the chapter. Using it displays the forward filter table, also called a content addressable memory (CAM) table. Here's the output from the S1 switch:

```
S1#sh mac address-table
          Mac Address Table
-------------------------------------------
Vlan    Mac Address        Type       Ports
----    -----------        --------   -----
 All    0100.0ccc.cccc     STATIC     CPU
 All    ffff.ffff.ffff     STATIC     CPU
[output cut]
   1    0002.1762.b235     DYNAMIC    Po1
   1    0009.b79f.c080     DYNAMIC    Po1
   1    000d.29bd.4b87     DYNAMIC    Po1
   1    000d.29bd.4b88     DYNAMIC    Po1
   1    0016.4662.52b4     DYNAMIC    Fa0/4
   1    0016.4677.5eab     DYNAMIC    Po1
   1    001a.2f52.49d8     DYNAMIC    Po1
   1    001a.2fe7.4170     DYNAMIC    Fa0/8
   1    001a.e2ce.ff40     DYNAMIC    Po1
   1    0050.0f02.642a     DYNAMIC    Fa0/3
Total Mac Addresses for this criterion: 31
S1#
```

The switches use what are called *base MAC addresses* that are assigned to the CPU, and the 2960s use 20. From the preceding output, you can see that five MAC addresses are dynamically assigned to EtherChannel port 1. Ports Fa0/3, Fa0/8, and Fa0/4 have only one MAC address assigned, and all ports are assigned to VLAN 1.

Let's take a look at the S2 switch CAM and see what you can find.

```
S2#sh mac address-table
          Mac Address Table
-------------------------------------------

Vlan    Mac Address        Type       Ports
----    -----------        --------   -----
 All    0008.205a.85c0     STATIC     CPU
 All    0100.0ccc.cccc     STATIC     CPU
 All    0100.0ccc.cccd     STATIC     CPU
 All    0100.0cdd.dddd     STATIC     CPU
```

```
[output cut]
    1    0002.1762.b235    DYNAMIC    Fa0/3
    1    000d.29bd.4b80    DYNAMIC    Fa0/1
    1    000d.29bd.4b85    DYNAMIC    Fa0/1
    1    0016.4662.52b4    DYNAMIC    Fa0/1
    1    0016.4677.5eab    DYNAMIC    Fa0/4
    1    001b.2b55.7540    DYNAMIC    Fa0/1
Total Mac Addresses for this criterion: 26
S2#
```

You can see in the preceding output that four MAC addresses are assigned to Fa0/1. Of course, you can also see that there is one connection for each host on ports 3 and 4.

You can set a static MAC address in the MAC address table—but just like setting static MAC port security, that is a ton of work. In case you want to do it, here's how it's done:

```
S1#config t
S1(config)#mac-address-table static aaaa.bbbb.cccc vlan 1 int fa0/5
S1(config)#do show mac address-table
          Mac Address Table
-------------------------------------------

Vlan    Mac Address       Type        Ports
----    -----------       --------    -----
 All    0100.0ccc.cccc    STATIC      CPU
[output cut]
    1    0002.1762.b235    DYNAMIC     Po1
    1    0009.b79f.c080    DYNAMIC     Po1
    1    000d.29bd.4b87    DYNAMIC     Po1
    1    000d.29bd.4b88    DYNAMIC     Po1
    1    0016.4662.52b4    DYNAMIC     Fa0/4
    1    0016.4677.5eab    DYNAMIC     Po1
    1    001a.2f52.49d8    DYNAMIC     Po1
    1    001a.2fe7.4170    DYNAMIC     Fa0/8
    1    001a.e2ce.ff40    DYNAMIC     Po1
    1    0050.0f02.642a    DYNAMIC     Fa0/3
    1    aaaa.bbbb.cccc    STATIC      Fa0/5
Total Mac Addresses for this criterion: 31
S1(config)#
```

You can see that a static MAC address is now assigned permanently to interface Fa0/5, and that it's also assigned to VLAN 1 only.

show spanning-tree

From reading the *CCNA Cisco Certified Network Associate Study Guide, 7th Edition* (Sybex, 2011), you should know that the show spanning-tree command is important. With it, you can see who the root bridge is and what our priorities are set to for each VLAN and your root port.

Understand that Cisco switches run what is called *Per-VLAN Spanning Tree* (PVST), which basically means that each VLAN runs its own instance of the STP protocol. If you enter **show spanning-tree**, you will receive information for each VLAN, starting with VLAN 1. For example, if you have multiple VLANs and you want to see what is up with VLAN 2, you can use the command **show spanning-tree vlan 2**.

Here is an output from the show spanning-tree command from switch S1. Because I am using only VLAN 1, I didn't need to add the VLAN number to the command:

```
S1#sh spanning-tree
VLAN0001
  Spanning tree enabled protocol ieee
  Root ID    Priority    32769
             Address     000d.29bd.4b80
             Cost        3012
             Port        56 (Port-channel1)
             Hello Time   2 sec  Max Age 20 sec  Forward Delay 15 sec

  Bridge ID  Priority    49153  (priority 49152 sys-id-ext 1)
             Address     001b.2b55.7500
             Hello Time   2 sec  Max Age 20 sec  Forward Delay 15 sec
             Aging Time 15
  Uplinkfast enabled


Interface        Role Sts Cost       Prio.Nbr Type
---------------- ---- --- ---------  -------- ----------
Fa0/3            Desg FWD 3100       128.3    Edge Shr
Fa0/4            Desg FWD 3019       128.4    Edge P2p
Fa0/8            Desg FWD 3019       128.8    P2p
Po1              Root FWD 3012       128.56   P2p
```

Because I have only VLAN 1 configured, there's no more output for this command, but if I had more, I would have gotten another page for each VLAN configured on the switch. The default priority is 32768, but there's something called the system ID extension (sys-id-ext), which is the VLAN identifier. The Bridge ID priority is incremented by the number of that VLAN. Because I have only VLAN 1, I incremented by one to 32769.

You must know how to find your root bridge, so if you type in **show spanning-tree** and the bridge is not the root, then look for your root port down in the bottom output. In the preceding example, Po1 is the root port, which connects to the root bridge. Just use the `show cdp neighbors` command to see what is connected to Po1 and you have your root bridge.

Exam Essentials

Understand when you would use the *ping* **command.**   Packet Internet Groper (Ping) uses ICMP echo requests and ICMP echo replies to verify an active IP address on a network.

Understand the main purpose of the spanning tree protocol in a switched LAN.   The main purpose of STP is to prevent switching loops in a network with redundant switched paths.

Remember the command `show spanning-tree`.   You must be familiar with the command `show spanning-tree` and how to determine which switch is the root bridge.

Identify, Prescribe, and Resolve Common Switched Network Media Issues, Configuration Issues, Auto Negotiation, and Switch Hardware Failures

A network port, also called an *RJ-45 port*, connects a computer to a network or VLAN. The connection speed depends on the type of network port. Standard Ethernet can transmit up to 10Mbps; however, it is very common to have Fast Ethernet which can transmit up to 100Mbps. Gigabit Ethernet ports can transmit up to 1,000Mbps. The maximum length of network cable is 328 feet (100 meters).

Twisted-pair is a type of copper cabling that started in telephone communications and now is used in both telephony and most Ethernet networks. A pair of wires forms a circuit that can transmit data. The pair is twisted to provide protection against crosstalk, which is the noise generated by adjacent pairs of wires in the cable.

Common issues with cabling on a switched network include basic switch configuration issues, negotiating both the speed and duplex of a link from a PC to a switch, and the uncommon switch hardware failures.

The most common switch configuration error is not having a port configured into the correct VLAN membership. By using the `show running-config` command or `show vlan` command, you can easily see the port memberships. Always check your VLAN memberships when troubleshooting a switch issue.

At times, you may find a host is not communicating to a switch because of mismatched speed or duplex issues. This is not as much of a problem as it has been in the past because of the better hardware being produced, but it still may show up from time to time. The default on a switch and host is to use 100Mbps full-duplex. If your host or switch port does not support this configuration, you can configure the switch port with the `duplex` and `speed` commands.

The port LED will be green when everything is OK; however, it will be amber if the port is blocked by STP, and it will turn from green to amber when the port experiences errors.

Switches are made pretty resilient today; however, if you boot a switch and the POST completes successfully, the system LED turns green; if the POST fails, it will turn amber. Seeing the amber glow is a very bad thing—typically fatal.

Exam Essentials

Remember to check a switch port's VLAN assignment when plugging in a new host.   If you plug a new host into a switch, then you must verify the VLAN membership of that port. If the membership is different than what is needed for that host, the host will not be able to reach the needed network services, such as a workgroup server.

Remember how the system LED responds when the post test runs.   If you boot a switch and the POST completes successfully, the system LED turns green; if the POST fails, it will turn amber.

Remember how the system LED responds if there are errors on a switch port.   A switch port will turn from green to amber when the port experiences errors.

Describe Enhanced Switching Technologies (Including VTP, RSTP, VLAN, PVSTP, and 802.1q)

The basic goals of *VLAN Trunking Protocol (VTP)* are to manage all configured VLANs across a switched internetwork and to maintain consistency throughout that network. VTP allows you to add, delete, and rename VLANs—this information is then propagated to all other switches in the VTP domain.

Here's a list of some of the cool features VTP has to offer:

- Consistent VLAN configuration across all switches in the network
- VLAN trunking over mixed networks, such as Ethernet to ATM LANE or even FDDI
- Accurate tracking and monitoring of VLANs
- Dynamic reporting of added VLANs to all switches in the VTP domain
- Plug and Play VLAN adding

This is all very nice; but before you can get VTP to manage your VLANs across the network, you have to create a VTP server. All servers that need to share VLAN information must use the same domain name, and a switch can be in only one domain at a time. Basically, this means that a switch can share VTP domain information with other switches only if they're configured into the same VTP domain. You can use a VTP domain if you have more than one switch connected in a network, but if you have all your switches in only one VLAN, you just don't need to use VTP. Do keep in mind that VTP information is sent between switches via only a trunk port.

Switches advertise VTP management domain information as well as a configuration revision number and all known VLANs with any specific parameters. But there's also something called *VTP transparent mode*. In it, you can configure switches to forward VTP information through trunk ports but not to accept information updates or update their VTP databases.

If you've got sneaky users adding switches to your VTP domain behind your back, you can include passwords, but don't forget—every switch must be set up with the same password. As you can imagine, this little snag can be a real hassle administratively.

Switches detect any added VLANs within a VTP advertisement, and then prepare to send information on their trunk ports with the newly defined VLAN in tow. Updates are sent out as revision numbers that consist of the notification plus 1. Anytime a switch sees a higher revision number, it knows the information it's getting is more current, so it will overwrite the existing database with the latest information.

You should know these three requirements for VTP to communicate VLAN information between switches:

- The VTP management domain names of both switches must be set the same.

- One of the switches has to be configured as a VTP server.

- No router is necessary.

Now that you've got that down, we're going to delve deeper in the world of VTP with VTP modes and VTP pruning.

VTP Modes of Operation

Figure 2.11 shows you all three different modes of operation within a VTP domain:

FIGURE 2.11   VTP modes

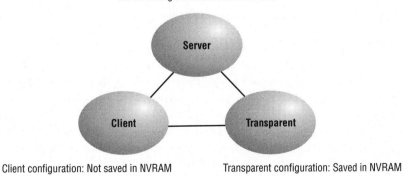

Server configuration: Saved in NVRAM

Client configuration: Not saved in NVRAM   Transparent configuration: Saved in NVRAM

Server This is the default mode for all Catalyst switches. You need at least one server in your VTP domain to propagate VLAN information throughout that domain. It is also important to note that the switch must be in server mode to be able to create, add, and delete VLANs in a VTP domain. VTP information has to be changed in server mode, and any change made to a switch in server mode will be advertised to the entire VTP domain. In VTP server mode, VLAN configurations are saved in NVRAM.

Client In client mode, switches receive information from VTP servers, but they also send and receive updates, so in this way, they behave like VTP servers. The difference is that they can't create, change, or delete VLANs. Plus, none of the ports on a client switch can be added to a new VLAN before the VTP server notifies the client switch of the new VLAN. Also good to know is that VLAN information sent from a VTP server isn't stored in NVRAM, which is important because it means that if the switch is reset or reloaded, the VLAN information will be deleted. Here's a hint: If you want a switch to become a server, first make it a client so it receives all the correct VLAN information, then change it to a server, which is so much easier!

So basically, a switch in VTP client mode will forward VTP summary advertisements and process them. This switch will learn about but won't save the VTP configuration in the running configuration, and it won't save it in NVRAM. Switches that are in VTP client mode will only learn about and pass along VTP information—that's it!

Transparent Switches in transparent mode don't participate in the VTP domain or share its VLAN database, but they'll still forward VTP advertisements through any configured trunk links. They can create, modify, and delete VLANs because they keep their own database—one they keep secret from the other switches. Despite being kept in NVRAM, the VLAN database in transparent mode is actually only locally significant. The whole purpose of transparent mode is to allow remote switches to receive the VLAN database from a VTP server-configured switch through a switch that is not participating in the same VLAN assignments.

VTP only learns about normal-range VLANs, with VLAN IDs 1 to 1005; VLANs with IDs greater than 1005 are called extended-range VLANs, and they're not stored in the VLAN database. The switch must be in VTP transparent mode when you create VLAN IDs from 1006 to 4094, so it would be pretty rare that you'd ever use these VLANs. There is one other thing: VLAN IDs 1 and 1002 to 1005 are automatically created on all switches and can't be removed.

Rapid Spanning-Tree Protocol (RSTP) 802.1w

If you would like to have a good STP configuration running on your switched network (regardless of the brand of switches) and have all the features we just discussed built in and enabled on every switch, then you are in luck. Welcome to the world of Rapid Spanning-Tree Protocol (RSTP)!

Cisco created PortFast, UplinkFast, and BackboneFast to "fix" the holes and liabilities the IEEE 802.1d standard presented. The drawbacks to these enhancements are only that they are Cisco proprietary and need additional configuration. (These are discussed in detail in Chapter 10 of the *CCNA Cisco Certified Network Associate Study Guide, 7th Edition*.)

The new 802.1w standard (RSTP) addresses all these "issues" in one tight package—just turn on RSTP and you're good to go. Importantly, you must make sure that all the switches in your network are running the 802.1w protocol for 802.1w to work properly.

It might come as a surprise, but RSTP actually can interoperate with legacy STP protocols. Just know that the inherently fast convergence ability of 802.1w is lost when it interacts with legacy bridges.

PVST

Cisco switches run what is called Per-VLAN Spanning-Tree (PVST), which basically means that each VLAN runs its own instance of the STP protocol. If you entered **show spanning-tree**, you would receive information for each VLAN, starting with VLAN 1. For example, if you had multiple VLANs, and you wanted to see what's up with VLAN 2, you would use the command show spanning-tree vlan 2.

IEEE 802.1q

Created by the IEEE as a standard method of frame tagging, IEEE 802.1q actually inserts a field into the frame to identify the VLAN. If you're trunking between a Cisco switched link and a different brand of switch, you've got to use 802.1q for the trunk to work.

It works like this: You first designate each port that is going to be a trunk with 802.1q encapsulation. The ports must be assigned a specific VLAN ID, which makes them the native VLAN, in order for them to communicate. The ports that populate the same trunk create a group with this native VLAN, and each port gets tagged with an identification number reflecting that—again, the default is VLAN 1. The native VLAN allows the trunks to carry information that was received without any VLAN identification or frame tag.

The 2960s support only the IEEE 802.1q trunking protocol, but the 3560s will support both the ISL and IEEE methods.

The basic purpose of ISL and 802.1q frame-tagging methods is to provide interswitch VLAN communication. Also, remember that any ISL or 802.1q frame tagging is removed if a frame is forwarded out an access link—tagging is used across trunk links only.

Exam Essentials

Understand the purpose and configuration of VTP.   VTP provides propagation of the VLAN database throughout your switched network. All switches must be in the same VTP domain.

Remember the three VTP modes.   Every Cisco switch defaults to VTP server mode, which allows you to create, delete, and propagate the VLAN database. VTP clients receive VTP summary updates from a server and keep them in RAM, and do not save the VLAN database. Clients also forward VTP summary advertisements to other switches. VTP transparent mode switches have their own VLAN database so they just receive and forward the VTP summary advertisements.

Understand the Rapid Spanning-Tree Protocol.   The 802.1w STP standard (RSTP) addresses all the problems found in the 802.1d STP protocol and is not Cisco proprietary.

This is not enabled on any Cisco switch by default, and if you enable this protocol, you should enable it on all your switches for the fastest convergence times.

Be able to define PVST.   Per-VLAN Spanning-Tree, each VLAN runs its own instance of the STP protocol.

Understand the term *frame tagging*.   Frame tagging refers to VLAN identification; this is what switches use to keep track of all those frames as they're traversing a switch fabric. It's how switches identify which frames belong to which VLANs.

Understand the 802.1q VLAN identification method.   This is a nonproprietary IEEE method of frame tagging. If you're trunking between a Cisco switched link and a different brand of switch, you have to use 802.1q for the trunk to work.

Describe How VLANs Create Logically Separate Networks and the Need for Routing between Them

Figure 2.12 shows how layer 2 switched networks are typically designed—as flat networks. With this configuration, every broadcast packet transmitted is seen by every device on the network, regardless of whether the device needs to receive that data or not.

By default, routers allow broadcasts to occur only within the originating network, while switches forward broadcasts to all segments. It's called a *flat network* because it's one *broadcast domain*, not because the actual design is physically flat. In Figure 2.12, Host A is sending out a broadcast on all ports and all switches are forwarding it—all except the port that originally received it.

FIGURE 2.12   Flat network structure

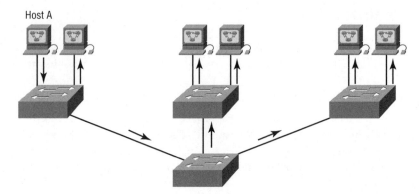

Host A

Now check out Figure 2.13. It depicts a switched network and shows Host A sending a frame with Host D as its destination. What's important is that, as you can see, that frame is only forwarded out the port where Host D is located. This is a huge improvement over the old hub networks, unless having one *collision domain* by default is what you really want—which is probably not the case!

FIGURE 2.13   The benefit of a switched network

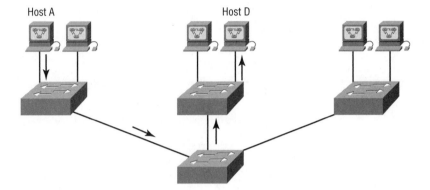

Now you already know that the largest benefit you gain by having a layer 2 switched network is that it creates individual collision domain segments for each device plugged into each port on the switch. This scenario frees us from the Ethernet distance constraints, so now larger networks can be built. But often, each new advance comes with new issues. For instance, the larger the number of users and devices, the more broadcasts and packets each switch must handle.

And here's another issue: security! This one's real trouble because within the typical layer 2 switched internetwork, all users can see all devices by default. You can't stop devices from broadcasting—plus, you can't stop users from trying to respond to broadcasts. This means your security options are dismally limited to placing passwords on your servers and other devices.

But wait—there's hope! That is, if you create a *virtual LAN (VLAN)*. You can solve many of the problems associated with layer 2 switching with VLANs, as you'll soon see.

Here's a short list of ways VLANs simplify network management:

- Network adds, moves, and changes are achieved with ease by just configuring a port into the appropriate VLAN.

- A group of users that need an unusually high level of security can be put into their own VLAN so that users outside of the VLAN can't communicate with them.

- As a logical grouping of users by function, VLANs can be considered independent from their physical or geographic locations.

- VLANs greatly enhance network security.

- VLANs increase the number of broadcast domains while decreasing their size.

To understand how a VLAN looks to a switch, it's helpful to begin by first looking at a traditional network. Figure 2.14 shows how a network was created by using hubs to connect physical LANs to a router.

FIGURE 2.14   Physical LANs connected to a router

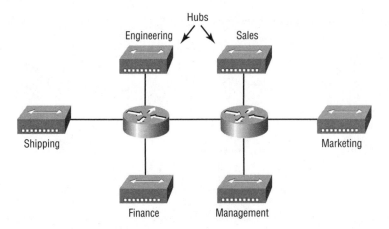

Here, you can see that each network is attached with a hub port to the router (each segment also has its own logical network number even though this isn't obvious from looking at the figure). Each node attached to a particular physical network has to match that network's number in order to be able to communicate on the internetwork. Notice that each department has its own LAN, so if you needed to add new users to—let's say, Sales—you would just plug them into the Sales LAN, and they would automatically be part of the Sales collision and broadcast domain. This design really did work well for many, but there was one major flaw.

What happens if the hub for Sales is full and you need to add another user to the Sales LAN? Or, what do you do if there's no more physical space where the Sales team is located for this new employee? If there happens to be plenty of room in the Finance section of the building, that new Sales team member will just have to sit in the same part of the building as the Finance people, and you'll just plug the poor soul into the hub for Finance.

Doing this obviously makes the new user part of the Finance LAN, which is very bad for many reasons. First and foremost, you now have a major security issue. Because the new Sales employee is a member of the Finance broadcast domain, the newbie can see all the same servers and access all network services that the Finance folks can. Second, for this user to access the Sales network services needed to get his job done, he will have to go through the router to log into the Sales server, which is not exactly efficient.

Now let's look at what a switch accomplishes. Figure 2.15 demonstrates how switches come to the rescue by removing the physical boundary to solve this problem. It also shows how six VLANs (numbered 2 through 7) are used to create a broadcast domain for each department. Each switch port is then administratively assigned a VLAN membership, depending on the host and which broadcast domain it's placed in.

So now, if you need to add another user to the Sales VLAN (VLAN 7), you can just assign the port to VLAN 7 regardless of where the new Sales team member is physically located. Nice! This illustrates one of the sweetest advantages to designing your network with VLANs instead of the old collapsed backbone design. Now, cleanly and simply, each host that needs to be in the Sales VLAN is merely assigned to VLAN 7.

FIGURE 2.15   Switches removing the physical boundary

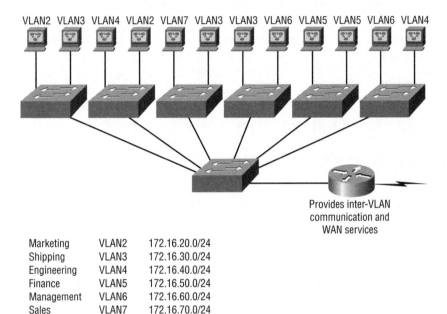

Marketing	VLAN2	172.16.20.0/24
Shipping	VLAN3	172.16.30.0/24
Engineering	VLAN4	172.16.40.0/24
Finance	VLAN5	172.16.50.0/24
Management	VLAN6	172.16.60.0/24
Sales	VLAN7	172.16.70.0/24

Notice that the VLANs were assigned beginning with VLAN number 2. The number is irrelevant, but you might be wondering what happened to VLAN 1? Well that VLAN is an administrative VLAN, and even though it can be used for a workgroup, Cisco recommends that you use it for administrative purposes only. You can't delete or change the name of VLAN 1, and by default, all ports on a switch are members of VLAN 1 until you change them.

Because each VLAN is considered a broadcast domain, it also has to have its own subnet number (refer again to Figure 2.15). If you're also using IPv6, then each VLAN must also be assigned its own IPv6 network number. So you don't get confused, just keep thinking of VLANs as separate subnets or networks.

Looking at Figure 2.15, notice that there are seven VLANs, or broadcast domains, counting VLAN 1. The nodes within each VLAN can communicate with each other but not with anything in a different VLAN because the nodes in any given VLAN "think" that they're actually in a collapsed backbone, as illustrated in Figure 2.14.

So, what handy little tool do you need to enable the hosts to communicate to a node or host on a different VLAN? You guessed it—a router! Those nodes positively need to go through a router, or some other layer 3 device, just as when they're configured for internetwork communication (as shown in Figure 2.14). It works the same way it would if you were trying to connect different physical networks. Communication between VLANs must go through a layer 3 device. So, don't expect mass router extinction anytime soon!

Exam Essentials

Remember what a virtual LAN is and why you'd create one.   Virtual LANs (VLANs) are created on switches to break up layer 2 broadcast domains. Switches only break up collision domains by default, so you can create bridge groups by placing switch ports into VLANs. Each VLAN is a separate broadcast domain and subnet.

Remember that hosts in a VLAN can only communicate with hosts in the same VLAN.   If you have multiple VLANs and need inter-VLAN communication, you must configure a router or buy a more expensive layer 3 switch to provide the routing on the backplane of the switch.

Configure, Verify, and Troubleshoot VLANs

It may come as a surprise to you, but configuring VLANs is actually pretty easy. Figuring out which users you want in each VLAN is not; it's extremely time-consuming. But once you've decided on the number of VLANs you want to create and have established which users you want to belong to each one, it's time to bring your first VLAN into the world.

To configure VLANs on a Cisco Catalyst switch, use the global config vlan command. In the following example, I'm going to demonstrate how to configure VLANs on the S1 switch by creating three VLANs for three different departments—again, remember that VLAN 1 is the native and administrative VLAN by default:

```
S1#config t
S1(config)#vlan ?
  WORD       ISL VLAN IDs 1-4094
  internal   internal VLAN
S1(config)#vlan 2
S1(config-vlan)#name Sales
S1(config-vlan)#vlan 3
S1(config-vlan)#name Marketing
S1(config-vlan)#vlan 4
S1(config-vlan)#name Accounting
S1(config-vlan)#^Z
S1#
```

From the preceding, you can see that you can create VLANs from 2 to 4094. This is only mostly true. As I said, VLANs can really only be created up to 1005, and you can't use, change, rename, or delete VLANs 1 and 1002 through 1005 because they're reserved. The VLAN numbers above that are called extended VLANs and won't be saved in the database unless your switch is set to VTP transparent mode. You won't see these VLAN numbers used too often in production. Here's an example of attempting to set my S1 switch to VLAN 4000 when my switch is set to VTP server mode (the default VTP mode):

```
S1#config t
S1(config)#vlan 4000
S1(config-vlan)#^Z
% Failed to create VLANs 4000
Extended VLAN(s) not allowed in current VTP mode.
%Failed to commit extended VLAN(s) changes.
```

After you create the VLANs that you want, you can use the show vlan command to check them out. But notice that, by default, all ports on the switch are in VLAN 1. To change the VLAN associated with a port, you need to go to each interface and tell it which VLAN to be a part of.

 Remember that a created VLAN is unused until it is assigned to a switch port or ports and that all ports are always assigned in VLAN 1 unless set otherwise.

Once the VLANs are created, verify your configuration with the show vlan command (sh vlan for short):

```
S1#sh vlan
```

VLAN	Name	Status	Ports
1	default	active	Fa0/3, Fa0/4, Fa0/5, Fa0/6
			Fa0/7, Fa0/8, Gi0/1
2	Sales	active	
3	Marketing	active	
4	Accounting	active	

[output cut]

This may seem repetitive, but it's important, and I want you to remember it: You can't change, delete, or rename VLAN 1 because it's the default VLAN and you just can't change that—period. It's the native VLAN of all switches by default, and Cisco recommends that you use it as your administrative VLAN. Basically, any packets that aren't specifically assigned to a different VLAN will be sent down to the native VLAN.

In the preceding S1 output, you can see that ports Fa0/3 through Fa0/8 and the Gi0/1 uplink are all in VLAN 1, but where are ports 1 and 2? Ports 1 and 2 are trunked. Any port that is a trunk port won't show up in the VLAN database. You have to use the show interface trunk command to see your trunked ports.

Assigning Switch Ports to VLANs

You configure a port to belong to a VLAN by assigning a membership mode that specifies the kind of traffic the port carries, plus the number of VLANs to which it can belong. You can configure each port on a switch to be in a specific VLAN (access port) by using the interface switchport command. You can also configure multiple ports at the same time with the interface range command.

Remember that you can configure either static memberships or dynamic memberships on a port. For this book's purpose, I'm only going to cover the static flavor. In the following example, I'll configure interface Fa0/3 to VLAN 3. This is the connection from the S1 switch to a device:

```
S1#config t
S1(config)#int fa0/3
S1(config-if)#switchport ?
  access        Set access mode characteristics of the interface
  backup        Set backup for the interface
  block         Disable forwarding of unknown uni/multi cast addresses
  host          Set port host
  mode          Set trunking mode of the interface
  nonegotiate   Device will not engage in negotiation protocol on this
                interface
  port-security Security related command
  priority      Set appliance 802.1p priority
  protected     Configure an interface to be a protected port
  trunk         Set trunking characteristics of the interface
  voice         Voice appliance attributes
```

You may have noticed some new stuff showing up in the preceding output. You can see the various commands—some that I've already covered, some not. Don't worry; I'm going to cover the access, mode, nonegotiate, trunk, and voice commands very soon in this chapter. Let's start with setting an access port on S1, which is probably the most widely used type of port on production switches that has VLANs configured:

```
S1(config-if)#switchport mode ?
  access   Set trunking mode to ACCESS unconditionally
  dynamic  Set trunking mode to dynamically negotiate access or
trunk mode
  trunk    Set trunking mode to TRUNK unconditionally

S1(config-if)#switchport mode access
S1(config-if)#switchport access vlan 3
```

By starting with the switchport mode access command, you're telling the switch that this is a layer 2 port. You can then assign a VLAN to the port with the switchport access command. Remember, you can choose many ports to configure at the same time if you use the interface range command. The dynamic and trunk commands are used for trunk ports exclusively.

That's it. Well, sort of. If you plugged devices into each VLAN port, they can only talk to other devices in the same VLAN. You want to enable inter-VLAN communication, and you're going to do that, but first you need to learn a bit more about trunking.

Exam Essentials

Remember to check a switch port's VLAN assignment when plugging in a new host.   If you plug a new host into a switch, then you must verify the VLAN membership of that port. If the membership is different from what is needed for that host, the host will not be able to reach the needed network services, such as a workgroup server.

Remember how to set a switch port to a VLAN membership.   By default, all switch ports are members of VLAN 1. In order to change the membership, you must change the port. Here is an example of changing a switch port to VLAN 3:

Switch(config)#**int F0/1**
Switch(config-if)#**switchport access vlan 3**

Configure, Verify, and Troubleshoot Trunking on Cisco Switches

The 2960 switch only runs the IEEE 802.1q encapsulation method. To configure trunking on a Fast Ethernet port, use the interface command trunk [*parameter*]. It's a tad different on the 3560 switch, and I'll show you that in the next section.

The following switch output shows the trunk configuration on interface Fa0/8 as set to trunk on:

S1#**config t**
S1(config)#**int fa0/8**
S1(config-if)#**switchport mode trunk**

The following list describes the different options available when configuring a switch interface:

switchport mode access   I discussed this in the previous section, but this puts the interface (access port) into permanent nontrunking mode and negotiates to convert the link into a nontrunk link. The interface becomes a nontrunk interface regardless of whether the neighboring interface is a trunk interface. The port would be a dedicated layer 2 port.

switchport mode dynamic auto This mode makes the interface able to convert the link to a trunk link. The interface becomes a trunk interface if the neighboring interface is set to trunk or desirable mode. This is now the default switchport mode for all Ethernet interfaces on all new Cisco switches.

switchport mode dynamic desirable This one makes the interface actively attempt to convert the link to a trunk link. The interface becomes a trunk interface if the neighboring interface is set to trunk, desirable, or auto mode. I used to see this mode as the default on some older switches, but not any longer. The default is dynamic auto now.

switchport mode trunk Puts the interface into permanent trunking mode and negotiates to convert the neighboring link into a trunk link. The interface becomes a trunk interface even if the neighboring interface isn't a trunk interface.

switchport nonegotiate Prevents the interface from generating DTP frames. You can use this command only when the interface switchport mode is access or trunk. You must manually configure the neighboring interface as a trunk interface to establish a trunk link.

Dynamic Trunking Protocol (DTP) is used for negotiating trunking on a link between two devices, as well as negotiating the encapsulation type of either 802.1q or ISL. I use the nonegotiate command when I want dedicated trunk ports, no questions asked.

To disable trunking on an interface, use the switchport mode access command, which sets the port back to a dedicated layer 2 switch port.

Trunking with the Cisco Catalyst 3560 Switch

Let's take a look at one more switch—the Cisco Catalyst 3560. The configuration is pretty much the same as it is for a 2960, with the exception that the 3560 can provide layer 3 services and the 2960 can't. Plus, the 3560 can run both the ISL and the IEEE 802.1q trunking encapsulation methods—the 2960 can run only 802.1q. With all this in mind, let's take a quick look at the VLAN encapsulation difference regarding the 3560 switch.

The 3560 has the encapsulation command, which the 2960 switch doesn't:

```
Core(config-if)#switchport trunk encapsulation ?
  dot1q     Interface uses only 802.1q trunking encapsulation
 when trunking
  isl       Interface uses only ISL trunking encapsulation
 when trunking
  negotiate Device will negotiate trunking encapsulation with peer on
            interface
Core(config-if)#switchport trunk encapsulation dot1q
Core(config-if)#switchport mode trunk
```

As you can see, there is the option to add either the IEEE 802.1q (dot1q) encapsulation or the ISL encapsulation to the 3560 switch. After you set the encapsulation, you still have to set the interface mode to trunk. Honestly, it's pretty rare that you'd continue to use the ISL encapsulation method. Cisco is moving away from ISL—its new routers don't even support it.

Defining the Allowed VLANs on a Trunk

As I've mentioned, trunk ports send and receive information from all VLANs by default, and if a frame is untagged, it's sent to the management VLAN. This applies to the extended range VLANs as well.

However, you can remove VLANs from the allowed list to prevent traffic from certain VLANs from traversing a trunked link. Here's how you'd do that:

```
S1#config t
S1(config)#int F0/1
S1(config-if)#switchport trunk allowed vlan ?
  WORD    VLAN IDs of the allowed VLANs when this port is in
trunking mode
  add     add VLANs to the current list
  all     all VLANs
  except  all VLANs except the following
  none    no VLANs
  remove  remove VLANs from the current list
S1(config-if)#switchport trunk allowed vlan remove ?
  WORD    VLAN IDs of disallowed VLANS when this port is in trunking mode
S1(config-if)#switchport trunk allowed vlan remove 4
```

The preceding command configured the trunk link on S1 port F0/1, causing it to drop all traffic sent and received for VLAN 4. You could try to remove VLAN 1 on a trunk link, but it would still send and receive management like CDP, PAgP, LACP, DTP, and VTP, so there would really be no point.

To remove a range of VLANs, just use a hyphen:

```
S1(config-if)#switchport trunk allowed vlan remove 4-8
```

If by chance someone has removed some VLANs from a trunk link and you want to set the trunk back to default, just use this command:

```
S1(config-if)#switchport trunk allowed vlan all
```

Or this command to accomplish the same thing:

```
S1(config-if)#no switchport trunk allowed vlan
```

Next, I want to show you how to configure or change the native VLAN on a trunk.

Changing or Modifying the Trunk Native VLAN

You really don't want to change the trunk port native VLAN from VLAN 1, but you can, and some people do it for security reasons. To change the native VLAN, use the following command:

```
S1#config t
S1(config)#int F0/1
S1(config-if)#switchport trunk ?
  allowed  Set allowed VLAN characteristics when interface is
in trunking mode
  native   Set trunking native characteristics when interface
is in trunking mode
  pruning  Set pruning VLAN characteristics when interface is
in trunking mode
S1(config-if)#switchport trunk native ?
  vlan  Set native VLAN when interface is in trunking mode
S1(config-if)#switchport trunk native vlan ?
  <1-4094>  VLAN ID of the native VLAN when this port is in
 trunking mode
S1(config-if)#switchport trunk native vlan 40
S1(config-if)#^Z
```

So, you've changed the native VLAN on the trunk link to 40, and by using the show running-config command, you can see the configuration under the trunk link:

```
!
interface FastEthernet0/1
 switchport trunk native vlan 40
 switchport trunk allowed vlan 1-3,9-4094
 switchport trunk pruning vlan 3,4
!
```

Hold on! You didn't really think it would be this easy. Here's the rub: If none of the switches have the same native VLAN configured on the trunk links, then you'll start to receive this error:

```
19:23:29: %CDP-4-NATIVE_VLAN_MISMATCH: Native VLAN mismatch
discovered on FastEthernet0/1 (40), with Core FastEthernet0/7 (1).
19:24:29: %CDP-4-NATIVE_VLAN_MISMATCH: Native VLAN mismatch
discovered on FastEthernet0/1 (40), with Core FastEthernet0/7 (1).
```

Actually, this is a good, noncryptic error, so either you go to the other end of the trunk link(s) and change the native VLAN or you set the native VLAN back to the default. Here's how you'd do that:

```
S1(config-if)#no switchport trunk native vlan
```

Now the trunk link is using the default VLAN 1 as the native VLAN. Just remember that each connection between switches must use the same native VLAN or you'll have some serious problems.

Exam Essentials

Remember how to configure a trunk port on a 2960 switch.   The 2960 switch runs only the 802.1q trunking method, so the command to trunk a port is simple:

```
Switch(config-if)#switchport mode trunk
```

Remember how to configure a trunk port on a 3560 switch.   The 3560 switch can use both the ISL and 802.1q frame-tagging methods, so you must set the encapsulation first. Here is an example of trunking a port on a 3560 switch using the 802.1q method:

```
Switch(config-if)#switchport trunk encapsulation dotlq
Switch(config-if)#switchport mode trunk
```

Remember how to change the native VLAN on a trunk link.   The native VLAN on every switch, by default, is VLAN 1. This means that the traffic is untagged. If you wanted to change the native VLAN, typically for security reasons, here is how you'd do that:

```
S1(config-if)#switchport trunk native vlan vlan
```

Configure, Verify, and Troubleshoot InterVLAN Routing

By default, only hosts that are members of the same VLAN can communicate. To change this and allow inter-VLAN communication, you need a router or a layer 3 switch. I'm going to start with the router approach.

To support ISL or 802.1q routing on a Fast Ethernet interface, the router's interface is divided into logical interfaces—one for each VLAN. These are called *subinterfaces*. From a Fast Ethernet or Gigabit interface, you can set the interface to trunk with the encapsulation command:

```
ISR#config t
ISR(config)#int F0/0.1
ISR(config-subif)#encapsulation ?
```

```
 dot1Q  IEEE 802.1q Virtual LAN
ISR(config-subif)#encapsulation dot1Q ?
 <1-4094>  IEEE 802.1q VLAN ID
```

Notice that my 2811 router (named ISR) supports only 802.1q. I'd need an older-model router to run the ISL encapsulation, but why bother?

The subinterface number is only locally significant, so it doesn't matter which subinterface numbers are configured on the router. Most of the time, I'll configure a subinterface with the same number as the VLAN I want to route. It's easy to remember that way, because the subinterface number is used only for administrative purposes.

It's really important that you understand that each VLAN is a separate subnet. I know. They don't *have* to be, but it really is a good idea to configure your VLANs as separate subnets, so just do that.

Now, I need to make sure you're fully prepared to configure inter-VLAN routing, as well as determine the port IP addresses of hosts connected in a switched VLAN environment. As always, it's a good idea to be able to fix any problems that may arise. To set you up for success, let me give you a few examples.

First, start by looking at Figure 2.16, and read the router and switch configuration within it. By this point, you should be able to determine the IP address, masks, and default gateways of each of the hosts in the VLANs.

The next step after that is to figure out which subnets are being used. By looking at the router configuration in the figure, you can see that we're using 192.168.1.64/26 with VLAN 1 and 192.168.1.128/27 with VLAN 10. By looking at the switch configuration, you can see that ports 2 and 3 are in VLAN 1 and port 4 is in VLAN 10. This means that HostA and HostB are in VLAN 1, and HostC is in VLAN 10.

FIGURE 2.16   Configuring Inter-VLAN

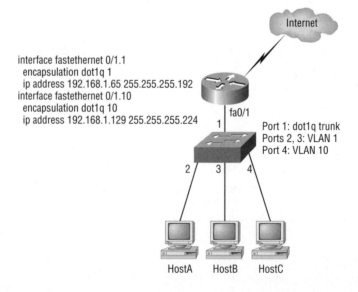

Here's what the hosts' IP addresses should be

HostA: 192.168.1.66, 255.255.255.192, default gateway 192.168.1.65

HostB: 192.168.1.67, 255.255.255.192, default gateway 192.168.1.65

HostC: 192.168.1.130, 255.255.255.224, default gateway 192.168.1.129

The hosts could be any address in the range—I just choose the first available IP address after the default gateway address. That wasn't so hard, was it?

Now, again using Figure 2.16, let's go through the commands necessary to configure switch port 1 to establish a link with the router and provide inter-VLAN communication using the IEEE version for encapsulation. Keep in mind that the commands can vary slightly depending on what type of switch you're dealing with.

For a 2960 switch, use the following:

```
2960#config t
2960(config)#interface fa0/1
2960(config-if)#switchport mode trunk
```

As you already know, the 2960 switch can run only the 802.1q encapsulation, so there's no need to specify it. You can't anyway! For a 3560, it's basically the same, but because it can run ISL and 802.1q, you have to specify the trunking protocol you're going to use.

 Remember that when you create a trunked link, all VLANs are allowed to pass data by default.

Let's look at Figure 2.17 and see what you can learn from it. This figure shows three VLANs, with two hosts in each of them.

The router in Figure 2.17 is connected to the fa0/1 switch port, and VLAN 2 is configured on port F0/6. Looking at the diagram, these are the things that Cisco expects you to know:

- The router is connected to the switch using subinterfaces.
- The switch port connecting to the router is a trunk port.
- The switch ports connecting to the clients and the hub are access ports, not trunk ports.

The configuration of the switch would look something like this:

```
2960#config t
2960(config)#int F0/1
2960(config-if)#switchport mode trunk
2960(config-if)#int F0/2
2960(config-if)#switchport access vlan 1
2960(config-if)#int F0/3
2960(config-if)#switchport access vlan 1
2960(config-if)#int F0/4
```

```
2960(config-if)#switchport access vlan 3
2960(config-if)#int F0/5
2960(config-if)#switchport access vlan 3
2960(config-if)#int F0/6
2960(config-if)#switchport access vlan 2
```

FIGURE 2.17   Inter-VLAN

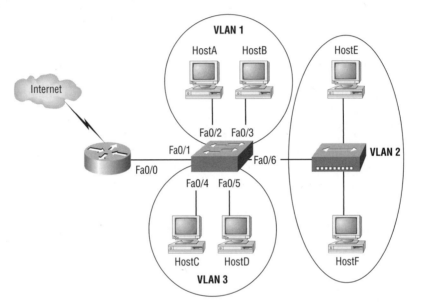

Before you configure the router, you need to design your logical network:

   VLAN 1: 192.168.10.16/28

   VLAN 2: 192.168.10.32/28

   VLAN 3: 192.168.10.48/28

The configuration of the router would then look like this:

```
ISR#config t
ISR(config)#int F0/0
ISR(config-if)#no ip address
ISR(config-if)#no shutdown
ISR(config-if)#int F0/0.1
ISR(config-subif)#encapsulation dot1q 1
ISR(config-subif)#ip address 192.168.10.17 255.255.255.240
ISR(config-subif)#int F0/0.2
ISR(config-subif)#encapsulation dot1q 2
```

```
ISR(config-subif)#ip address 192.168.10.33 255.255.255.240
ISR(config-subif)#int F0/0.3
ISR(config-subif)#encapsulation dot1q 3
ISR(config-subif)#ip address 192.168.10.49 255.255.255.240
```

The hosts in each VLAN would be assigned an address from their subnet range, and the default gateway would be the IP address assigned to the router's subinterface in that VLAN.

Exam Essentials

Remember that hosts in a VLAN can only communicate with hosts in the same VLAN.   If you have multiple VLANs and need inter-VLAN communication, you must configure a router or buy a more expensive layer 3 switch to provide the routing on the backplane of the switch.

Remember how to create a Cisco "router on a stick" to provide inter-VLAN communication. You can use a Cisco Fast Ethernet or Gigabit Ethernet interface to provide inter-VLAN routing. The switch port connected to the router must be a trunk port; then you must create virtual interfaces (subinterfaces) on the router port for each VLAN connecting. The hosts in each VLAN will use this subinterface address as their default gateway address.

Remember how to create a subinterface on a router port.   By creating a subinterface on a router, you can use one router port to allow inter-VLAN communication. You must create a subinterface for each VLAN. Here is an example of how to create a subinterface on a router port for VLAN 2:

```
Router#config t
Router(config)#int F0/0.1
Router(config-subif)#encapsulation dot1Q 2
```

Remember how to configure a trunk port on a 2960 switch.   The 2960 switch only runs the 802.1q trunking method, so the command to trunk a port is simple:

```
Switch(config-if)#switchport mode trunk
```

Configure, Verify, and Troubleshoot VTP

All Cisco switches are configured to be VTP servers by default. To configure VTP, first you have to configure the domain name you want to use. Of course, once you configure the VTP information on a switch, you need to verify it.

When you create the VTP domain, you have a bunch of options, including setting the domain name, password, operating mode, and pruning capabilities of the switch. Use the vtp global configuration mode command to set all this information. In the following example, I'll set the S1 switch to vtp server, the VTP domain to Lammle, and the VTP password to todd:

```
S1#config t
S1#(config)#vtp mode server
Device mode already VTP SERVER.
S1(config)#vtp domain Lammle
Changing VTP domain name from null to Lammle
S1(config)#vtp password todd
Setting device VLAN database password to todd
S1(config)#do show vtp password
VTP Password: todd
S1(config)#do show vtp status
VTP Version                    : 2
Configuration Revision         : 0
Maximum VLANs supported locally : 255
Number of existing VLANs       : 8
VTP Operating Mode             : Server
VTP Domain Name                : Lammle
VTP Pruning Mode               : Disabled
VTP V2 Mode                    : Disabled
VTP Traps Generation           : Disabled
MD5 digest                     : 0x15 0x54 0x88 0xF2 0x50 0xD9 0x03 0x07
Configuration last modified by 192.168.24.6 at 3-14-93 15:47:32
Local updater ID is 192.168.24.6 on interface Vl1 (lowest numbered VLAN
interface found)
```

Remember that all switches are set to VTP server mode by default, and if you want to change any VLAN information on a switch, you absolutely must be in VTP server mode. After you configure the VTP information, you can verify it with the show vtp status command as shown in the preceding output. The preceding switch output shows the VTP domain, the VTP password, and the switch's mode.

Take a minute to reflect on the fact that the show vtp status output shows that the maximum number of VLANs supported locally is only 255. Because you can create more than 1,000 VLANs on some switches, this seems as though it would definitely be a problem if you have more than 255 VLANs and you're using VTP.

Let's configure some switches and set them into the Lammle VTP domain. It is very important to remember that the VTP domain name is case sensitive.

```
Core#config t
Core(config)#vtp mode client
Setting device to VTP CLIENT mode.
Core(config)#vtp domain Lammle
```

```
Changing VTP domain name from null to Lammle
Core(config)#vtp password todd
Setting device VLAN database password to todd
Core(config)#do show vtp status
VTP Version                    : 2
Configuration Revision         : 0
Maximum VLANs supported locally : 1005
Number of existing VLANs       : 5
VTP Operating Mode             : Server
VTP Domain Name                : Lammle
VTP Pruning Mode               : Disabled
VTP V2 Mode                    : Disabled
VTP Traps Generation           : Disabled
MD5 digest                     : 0x2A 0x6B 0x22 0x17 0x04 0x4F 0xB8 0xC2
Configuration last modified by 192.168.10.19 at 3-1-93 03:13:16
Local updater ID is 192.168.24.7 on interface Vl1 (first interface found)
S2#config t
S2(config)#vtp mode client
Setting device to VTP CLIENT mode.
S2(config)#vtp domain Lammle
Changing VTP domain name from null to Lammle
S2(config)#vtp password todd
Setting device VLAN database password to todd
S2(config)#do show vtp status
VTP Version                    : 2
Configuration Revision         : 0
Maximum VLANs supported locally : 1005
Number of existing VLANs       : 5
VTP Operating Mode             : Client
VTP Domain Name                : Lammle
VTP Pruning Mode               : Disabled
VTP V2 Mode                    : Disabled
VTP Traps Generation           : Disabled
MD5 digest                     : 0x02 0x11 0x18 0x4B 0x36 0xC5 0xF4 0x1F
Configuration last modified by 0.0.0.0 at 0-0-00 00:00:00
```

Nice. Now that all the switches are set to the same VTP domain and password, the VLANs I created earlier on the S1 switch should be advertised to the Core and S2 VTP client switches. Let's take a look using the show vlan brief command on the Core and S2 switch:

```
Core#sh vlan brief
VLAN Name                Status    Ports
```

```
---- ------------------ --------- ----------------------
1    default             active    Fa0/1,Fa0/2,Fa0/3,Fa0/4
                                   Fa0/9,Fa0/10,Fa0/11,Fa0/12
                                   Fa0/13,Fa0/14,Fa0/15,
                                   Fa0/16,Fa0/17, Fa0/18, Fa0/19,
                                   Fa0/20,Fa0/21, Fa0/22, Fa0/23,
                                   Fa0/24, Gi0/1, Gi0/2
2    Sales               active
3    Marketing           active
4    Accounting          active
[output cut]

S2#sh vlan bri
VLAN Name                 Status    Ports
---- -------------------- --------- ----------------------
1    default             active    Fa0/3, Fa0/4, Fa0/5, Fa0/6
                                   Fa0/7, Fa0/8, Gi0/1
2    Sales               active
3    Marketing           active
4    Accounting          active
[output cut]
```

The VLAN database that I created on the S1 (2960) switch earlier in this chapter was uploaded to the Core and S2 switch via VTP advertisements. VTP is a great way to keep VLAN naming consistent across the switched network. You can now assign VLANs to the ports on the Core and S1 switches, and they'll communicate with the hosts in the same VLANs on the S1 switch across the trunked ports between switches.

 It's imperative that you can assign a VTP domain name, set the switch to VTP server mode, and create a VLAN!

Troubleshooting VTP

If VTP is not configured correctly, it will not work, so you absolutely must be capable of troubleshooting VTP. Let's take a look at a couple of configurations and solve the problems. Study the output from the two following switches:

```
SwitchA#sh vtp status
VTP Version                   : 2
Configuration Revision        : 0
Maximum VLANs supported locally : 64
```

```
Number of existing VLANs          : 7
VTP Operating Mode                : Server
VTP Domain Name                   : GlobalNet
VTP Pruning Mode                  : Disabled
VTP V2 Mode                       : Disabled
VTP Traps Generation              : Disabled


SwitchB#sh vtp status
VTP Version                       : 2
Configuration Revision            : 1
Maximum VLANs supported locally   : 64
Number of existing VLANs          : 7
VTP Operating Mode                : Server
VTP Domain Name                   : Lammle
VTP Pruning Mode                  : Disabled
VTP V2 Mode                       : Disabled
VTP Traps Generation              : Disabled
```

So, what's happening with these two switches? Why won't they share VLAN information? At first glance, it seems that both servers are in VTP server mode, but that's not the problem. Servers in VTP server mode will share VLAN information using VTP. The problem is that they're in two different VTP *domains*. SwitchA is in VTP domain GlobalNet and SwitchB is in VTP domain Lammle. They will never share VTP information because the VTP domain names are configured differently.

Now that you know how to look for common VTP domain configuration errors in your switches, let's take a look at another switch configuration:

```
SwitchC#sh vtp status
VTP Version                       : 2
Configuration Revision            : 1
Maximum VLANs supported locally   : 64
Number of existing VLANs          : 7
VTP Operating Mode                : Client
VTP Domain Name                   : Todd
VTP Pruning Mode                  : Disabled
VTP V2 Mode                       : Disabled
VTP Traps Generation              : Disabled
```

Why can't you create a VLAN on SwitchC? Well, the VTP domain name isn't the important thing in this example. What is critical here is the VTP *mode*. The VTP mode is client, and a VTP client cannot create, delete, add, or change VLANs. VTP clients keep only the VTP database in RAM, and that's not saved to NVRAM. So, in order to create a VLAN on this switch, you've got to make the switch a VTP server first.

Here's what will happen when you have the preceding VTP configuration:

```
SwitchC(config)#vlan 50
VTP VLAN configuration not allowed when device is in CLIENT mode.
```

So, to fix this problem, here's what you need to do:

```
SwitchC(config)#vtp mode server
Setting device to VTP SERVER mode
SwitchC(config)#vlan 50
SwitchC(config-vlan)#
```

Wait, you're not done. Now take a look at the output from these two switches and determine why SwitchB is not receiving VLAN information from SwitchA:

```
SwitchA#sh vtp status
VTP Version                    : 2
Configuration Revision         : 4
Maximum VLANs supported locally : 64
Number of existing VLANs       : 7
VTP Operating Mode             : Server
VTP Domain Name                : GlobalNet
VTP Pruning Mode               : Disabled
VTP V2 Mode                    : Disabled
VTP Traps Generation           : Disabled

SwitchB#sh vtp status
VTP Version                    : 2
Configuration Revision         : 14
Maximum VLANs supported locally : 64
Number of existing VLANs       : 7
VTP Operating Mode             : Server
VTP Domain Name                : GlobalNet
VTP Pruning Mode               : Disabled
VTP V2 Mode                    : Disabled
VTP Traps Generation           : Disabled
```

You may again be tempted to say it's because they're both VTP servers, but that is not the problem. All your switches can be servers and they can still share VLAN information. As a matter of fact, Cisco actually suggests that all switches stay VTP servers and that you just make sure the switch you want to advertise VTP VLAN information has the highest revision number. If all switches are VTP servers, then all of the switches will save the VLAN database. However, SwitchB isn't receiving VLAN information from SwitchA because SwitchB has a higher revision number than SwitchA. It's very important that you can recognize this problem.

Exam Essentials

Understand the purpose and configuration of VTP.   VTP provides propagation of the VLAN database throughout your switched network. All switches must be in the same VTP domain.

Remember the command to verify VTP.   Unfortunately, there are not a lot of ways to verify your VTP configuration. The best way is by using the command show vtp status. This shows you your domain name, password, and revision number.

Configure, Verify, and Troubleshoot RSTP Operation

Configuring RSTP actually is as easy as configuring any of our other 802.1d extensions. So, let's turn it on in the Core switch now and see what happens:

```
Core#config t
Core(config)#spanning-tree mode ?
  mst          Multiple spanning tree mode
  pvst         Per-Vlan spanning tree mode
  rapid-pvst   Per-Vlan rapid spanning tree mode
Core(config)#spanning-tree mode rapid-pvst
Core(config)#
1d02h: %LINEPROTO-5-UPDOWN: Line protocol on Interface Vlan1,
 changed state to down
1d02h: %LINEPROTO-5-UPDOWN: Line protocol on Interface Vlan1,
 changed state to up
```

Sweet! The Core switch is now running the 802.1w STP. Let's verify that:

```
Core(config)#do show spanning-tree
VLAN0001
  Spanning tree enabled protocol rstp
  Root ID    Priority    32769
             Address     000d.29bd.4b80
             This bridge is the root
             Hello Time   2 sec  Max Age 20 sec  Forward Delay 15 sec

  Bridge ID  Priority    32769  (priority 32768 sys-id-ext 1)
             Address     000d.29bd.4b80
```

```
Hello Time   2 sec  Max Age 20 sec  Forward Delay 15 sec
Aging Time 300
```

Interface	Role	Sts	Cost	Prio.Nbr	Type
Fa0/5	Desg	FWD	19	128.5	P2p Peer(STP)
Fa0/6	Desg	FWD	19	128.6	P2p Peer(STP)
Fa0/7	Desg	FWD	19	128.7	P2p Peer(STP)
Fa0/8	Desg	FWD	19	128.8	P2p Peer(STP)

This is interesting; it looks like nothing really happened. I can see on my two other switches that all ports have converged. Once everything was up, everything looked the same. The 802.1d and 802.1w switches seem to be cohabiting with no problem.

If you look under the hood more closely, you can see that the 802.1w switch has changed from 802.1w BPDUs to 802.1d BPDUs on the ports connecting to the other switches running 802.1d (which is all of them).

The S1 and S2 switches believe that the Core switch is actually running 802.1d because the Core reverted to 802.1d BPDUs just for them. Even though the S1 and S2 switches receive the 802.1w BPDUs, they don't understand them, so they simply drop them. However, the Core does receive the 802.1d BPDUs and accepts them from the S1 and S2 switches, not knowing which ports to run 802.1d on. In other words, turning 802.1w on for just one switch didn't really help our network at all!

One other important item to remember regarding RSTP is the port states. In order to converge quickly—the main reason to configure RSTP—the port states have gone from five to three. The RSTP port states are discarding, learning, and forwarding. The 802.1d port states are disabled, blocking, listening, learning, and forwarding.

Exam Essentials

Remember how to enable RSVP.   To enable RSVP, use the following command:

```
Router(config)#spanning-tree mode rapid-pvst
```

Remember to reboot the switch when changing to RSVP.   If you have a switch in your network that is not running 802.1w, then you need to reboot your switches when enabling RSTP to stop the 802.1d BPDU's from being sent out the switch port.

Understand the port states with RSTP.   STP doesn't seem that different unless you really start looking under the hood. However, RSTP transitions through different port states very quickly, especially compared with 802.1d. The new port states are discarding, learning, and forwarding, instead of the 8021d port states of disabled, blocking, listening, learning, and forwarding.

Interpret the Output of Various *SHOW* and *DEBUG* Commands to Verify the Operational Status of a Cisco Switched Network

For information on this objective, please review the objective "Verify network status and switch operation using basic utilities (including ping, traceroute, Telnet, SSH, arp, and ipconfig) and SHOW and DEBUG commands," which was covered earlier in this chapter.

Implement Basic Switch Security (Including Port Security, Trunk Access, Management VLAN Other Than VLAN 1, Etc.)

For information on the trunking part of this objective, please review the objective "Configure, verify, and troubleshoot trunking on Cisco switches," which was covered earlier in this chapter.

Just how do you stop someone from simply plugging a host into one of your switch ports—or worse, adding a hub, switch, or access point into the Ethernet jack in their office? By default, MAC addresses will just dynamically appear in your MAC forward/filter database. You can stop them in their tracks by using port security. Here are your options:

```
Switch#config t
Switch(config)#int F0/1
Switch(config-if)#switchport mode access
Switch(config-if)#switchport port-security ?
  aging          Port-security aging commands
  mac-address    Secure mac address
  maximum        Max secure addresses
  violation      Security violation mode
  <cr>
```

Because all of Cisco's latest switches ship with the ports in desirable mode (the port desires to trunk if it senses another switch just connected), you must first change the port from desirable mode to access mode or you won't be able to configure port security. Once that is done, you can continue with port-security commands.

You can see clearly in the preceding output that the `switchport port-security` command can be used with four options. Personally, I like the `port-security` command because it allows me to easily control users on my network. You can use the `switchport port-security mac-address` *mac-address* command to assign individual MAC addresses to each switch port, but if you choose to go there, you'd better have a lot of time on your hands.

If you want to set up a switch port to allow only one host per port, and to shut down the port if this rule is violated, use the following commands:

```
Switch(config-if)#switchport port-security maximum 1
Switch(config-if)#switchport port-security violation shutdown
```

These commands are probably the most popular because they prevent random users from connecting to a switch or access point that's in their office. The maximum setting of 1 (which is the port security default) means only one MAC address can be used on that port; if the user tries to add another host on that segment, the switch port will shut down. If that happens, you'd have to manually go into the switch and enable the port by cycling it with a shutdown and then a no shutdown command.

Probably one of my favorite commands is the sticky command. Not only does it perform a cool function, it has a cool name! You can find this command under the mac-address command:

```
Switch(config-if)#switchport port-security mac-address sticky
Switch(config-if)#switchport port-security maximum 2
Switch(config-if)#switchport port-security violation shutdown
```

Basically, what this does is provide static MAC address security without having to type in everyone's MAC address on the network. Now, let's verify the port security on one of the ports by using the `show port-security interface` command:

```
S1#sh port-security interface F0/3
Port Security              : Enabled
Port Status                : Secure-down
Violation Mode             : shutdown
Aging Time                 : 2 mins
Aging Type                 : Inactivity
SecureStatic Address Aging : Disabled
Maximum MAC Addresses      : 1
Total MAC Addresses        : 0
Configured MAC Addresses   : 0
Sticky MAC Addresses       : 0
Last Source Address:Vlan   : 0000.0000.0000:0
Security Violation Count   : 0
```

There are two other modes you can use instead of just shutting down the port. The protect mode means that another host can connect but its frames will just be dropped. Restrict mode is also pretty cool. It alerts you via SNMP that a violation has occurred on a port.

Exam Essentials

Remember how to set port security on a switch port.   If you want to set up a switch port to allow only one host per port, and to shut down the port if this rule is violated, use the following commands:

```
Switch#config t
Switch(config)#int F0/1
Switch(config-if)#switchport port-security maximum 1
Switch(config-if)#switchport port-security violation shutdown
```

Remember how to configure a trunk port on a 2960 switch.   The 2960 switch only runs the 802.1q trunking method, so the command to trunk a port is simple:

```
Switch(config-if)#switchport mode trunk
```

Review Questions

1. You need to configure a Catalyst switch so that it can be managed remotely. Which of the following would you use to accomplish this task?

   A. `Switch(configs)#int fa0/1`

      `Switch(configs-if)#ip address 192.168.10.252 255.255.255.0`

      `Switch(configs-if)#no shut`

   B. `Switch(configs)#int vlan 1`

      `Switch(configs-if)#ip address 192.168.10.252 255.255.255.0`

      `Switch(configs-if)#ip default-gateway 192.168.10.254 255.255.255.0`

   C. `Switch(configs)#ip default-gateway 192.168.10.254`

      `Switch(configs)#int vlan 1`

      `Switch(configs-if)#ip address 192.168.10.252 255.255.255.0`

      `Switch(configs-if)#no shut`

   D. `Switch(configs)#ip default-network 192.168.10.254`

      `Switch(configs)#int vlan 1`

      `Switch(configs-if)#ip address 192.168.10.252 255.255.255.0`

      `Switch(configs-if)#no shut`

2. What does a switch do when a frame is received on an interface and the destination hardware address is unknown or not in the filter table?

   A. Forwards the switch to the first available link

   B. Drops the frame

   C. Floods the network with the frame looking for the device

   D. Sends back a message to the originating station asking for a name resolution

3. If a switch receives a frame and the source MAC address is not in the MAC address table but the destination address is, what will the switch do with the frame?

   A. Discard it and send an error message back to the originating host

   B. Flood the network with the frame

   C. Add the source address and port to the MAC address table and forward the frame out the destination port

   D. Add the destination to the MAC address table and then forward the frame

4. You want to run the new 802.1w on your switches. Which of the following would enable this protocol?

   A. `Switch(config)#spanning-tree mode rapid-pvst`

   B. `Switch#spanning-tree mode rapid-pvst`

   C. `Switch(config)#spanning-tree mode 802.1w`

   D. `Switch#spanning-tree mode 802.1w`

5. In which circumstance are multiple copies of the same unicast frame likely to be transmitted in a switched LAN?

   A. During high-traffic periods

   B. After broken links are reestablished

   C. When upper-layer protocols require high reliability

   D. In an improperly implemented redundant topology

6. Which command was used to produce the following output:

   ```
   Vlan    Mac Address        Type         Ports
   ----    -----------        --------     -----
      1    0005.dccb.d74b     DYNAMIC      Fa0/1
      1    000a.f467.9e80     DYNAMIC      Fa0/3
      1    000a.f467.9e8b     DYNAMIC      Fa0/4
      1    000a.f467.9e8c     DYNAMIC      Fa0/3
      1    0010.7b7f.c2b0     DYNAMIC      Fa0/3
      1    0030.80dc.460b     DYNAMIC      Fa0/3
   ```

   A. `show vlan`

   B. `show ip route`

   C. `show mac address-table`

   D. `show mac address-filter`

7. If you want to disable STP on a port connected to a server, which command would you use?

   A. `disable spanning-tree`

   B. `spanning-tree off`

   C. `spanning-tree security`

   D. `spanning-tree portfast`

8. Refer to the graphic. Why does the switch have two MAC addresses assigned to the Fa0/1 port in the switch address table?

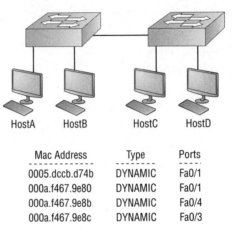

Mac Address	Type	Ports
0005.dccb.d74b	DYNAMIC	Fa0/1
000a.f467.9e80	DYNAMIC	Fa0/1
000a.f467.9e8b	DYNAMIC	Fa0/4
000a.f467.9e8c	DYNAMIC	Fa0/3

A. Data from HostC and HostD have been received by the switch port Fast Ethernet 0/1.

B. Data from two of the devices connected to the switch have been forwarded out to HostD.

C. HostC and HostD had their NIC replaced.

D. HostC and HostD are on different VLANs.

9. Layer 2 switching provides which of the following? (Choose four.)

A. Hardware-based bridging (ASIC)

B. Wire speed

C. Low latency

D. Low cost

E. Routing

F. WAN services

10. You type **show mac address-table** and receive the following output:

```
Switch#sh mac address-table
Vlan    Mac Address     Type        Ports
----    -----------     --------    -----
   1    0005.dccb.d74b  DYNAMIC     Fa0/1
   1    000a.f467.9e80  DYNAMIC     Fa0/3
   1    000a.f467.9e8b  DYNAMIC     Fa0/4
   1    000a.f467.9e8c  DYNAMIC     Fa0/3
   1    0010.7b7f.c2b0  DYNAMIC     Fa0/3
   1    0030.80dc.460b  DYNAMIC     Fa0/3
```

Suppose that the above switch received a frame with the following MAC addresses:

- Source MAC: 0005.dccb.d74b
- Destination MAC: 000a.f467.9e8c

What will it do?

A. It will discard the frame.

B. It will forward the frame out port Fa0/3 only.

C. It will forward it out Fa0/1 only.

D. It will send it out all ports except Fa0/1.

Answers to Review Questions

1. C. To manage a switch remotely, you must set an IP address under the management VLAN, which is, by default, `interface vlan 1`. Then, from global configuration mode, you set the default gateway with the `ip default-gateway` command.

2. C. Switches flood all frames that have an unknown destination address. If a device answers the frame, the switch will update the MAC address table to reflect the location of the device.

3. C. Because the source MAC address is not in the MAC address table, the switch will add the source address and the port it is connected to into the MAC address table and then forward the frame to the outgoing port.

4. A. 802.1w is also called Rapid Spanning-Tree Protocol. It is not enabled by default on Cisco switches, but it is a better STP to run because it has all the fixes that the Cisco extensions provide with 802.1d.

5. D. If the Spanning-Tree Protocol is not running on your switches and you connect them together with redundant links, you will have broadcast storms and multiple frame copies.

6. C. The command `show mac address-table` will display the forward/filter table, also called a CAM table on a switch.

7. D. If you have a server or other devices connected into your switch that you're totally sure won't create a switching loop if STP is disabled, you can use something called `portfast` on these ports. Using it means that the port won't spend the usual 50 seconds to come up while STP is converging.

8. A. A switch can have multiple MAC addresses associated with a port. In the graphic, a hub is connected to port Fa0/1, which has two hosts connected.

9. A, B, C, D. Switches, unlike bridges, are hardware based. Cisco says its switches are wire speed and provide low latency, and they are considered low cost compared to their prices in the 1990s.

10. B. Because the destination MAC address is in the MAC address table (forward/filter table), it will send it out port Fa0/3 only.

Chapter

3

Implement an IP Addressing Scheme and IP Services to Meet Network Requirements in a Medium-Sized Enterprise Branch Office Network

---

THE CISCO CCNA EXAM OBJECTIVES COVERED IN THIS CHAPTER INCLUDE THE FOLLOWING:

- ✓ Describe the operation and benefits of using private and public IP addressing.

- ✓ Explain the operation and benefits of using DHCP and DNS.

- ✓ Configure, verify, and troubleshoot DHCP and DNS operation on a router (including CLI/SDM).

- ✓ Implement static and dynamic addressing services for hosts in a LAN environment.

- ✓ Calculate and apply an addressing scheme, including VLSM IP addressing design, to a network.

- ✓ Determine the appropriate classless addressing scheme using VLSM and summarization to satisfy addressing requirements in a LAN/WAN environment.

✓ Describe the technological requirements for running IPv6 in conjunction with IPv4 (including protocols, dual stack, tunneling, etc.).

✓ Describe IPv6 addresses.

✓ Identify and correct common problems associated with IP addressing and host configurations.

This chapter will start with addressing an IP network. You're going to have to really apply yourself, because this takes time and practice in order to nail it, so be patient. Do whatever it takes to get this stuff dialed in, and you just must read Chapters 3 and 4 in my *CCNA Cisco Certified Network Associate Study Guide, 7th Edition* (Sybex, 2011).

After discussing IP subnetting, I'm going to review Variable Length Subnet Masks (VLSMs), as well as show you how to design and implement a network using VLSM networks, which is completely covered in Chapter 5 of my *CCNA Cisco Certified Network Associate Study Guide, 7th Edition.*

Once you have mastered VLSM design and implementation, I'll show you how to summarize classful boundaries.

I also hope you're ready to learn about the nuts and bolts of Internet Protocol version 6 (IPv6), because you're going to get the rub on it in this chapter.

Describe the Operation and Benefits of Using Private and Public IP Addressing

An IP address is a software address, not a hardware address—the latter is hard-coded on a network interface card (NIC) and used for finding hosts on a local network. IP addressing was designed to allow hosts on one network to communicate with a host on a different network regardless of the types of LANs in which the hosts are participating.

I am just going to review the more complicated aspects of IP addressing, but if you need to understand some of the basics, please run back to my study guide; remember that this is a review guide.

Class A Addresses

The designers of the IP address scheme said that the first bit of the first byte in a Class A network address must always be off, or 0. This means a Class A address must be between 0 and 127, inclusive.

Consider the following network address:

0xxxxxxx

If you turn off the other 7 bits and then turn them all on, you'll find the Class A range of network addresses:

00000000 = 0
01111111 = 127

So, a Class A network is defined in the first octet between 0 and 127, and it can't be less or more. (I'll talk about illegal addresses in a minute.)

In a Class A network address, the first byte is assigned to the network address, and the three remaining bytes are used for the node addresses. The Class A format is

network.node.node.node

Class B Addresses

In a Class B network, the RFCs state that the first bit of the first byte must always be turned on, but the second bit must always be turned off. If you turn the other 6 bits all off and then all on, you will find the range for a Class B network:

10000000 = 128
10111111 = 191

As you can see, this means that a Class B network is defined when the first byte is configured from 128 to 191.

In a Class B network address, the first 2 bytes are assigned to the network address, and the remaining 2 bytes are used for node addresses. The format is

network.network.node.node

For example, in the IP address 172.16.30.56, the network address is 172.16, and the node address is 30.56.

Class C Addresses

For Class C networks, the RFCs define that the first 2 bits of the first octet is always turned on, but the third bit can never be on. Following the same process as the previous classes, convert from binary to decimal to find the range. Here's the range for a Class C network:

11000000 = 192
11011111 = 223

So, if you see an IP address that starts at 192 and goes to 223, you'll know it is a Class C IP address.

The first 3 bytes of a Class C network address are dedicated to the network portion of the address, with only one measly byte remaining for the node address. The format is

network.network.network.node

Using the example IP address 192.168.100.102, the network address is 192.168.100, and the node address is 102.

Network Addresses: Special Purpose

Some IP addresses are reserved for special purposes, so network administrators cannot assign these addresses to nodes. Table 3.1 lists the members of this exclusive club and why they're included in it.

TABLE 3.1   Reserved IP Addresses

Address	Function
Network address of all 0s	Interpreted to mean "this network or segment"
Network address of all 1s	Interpreted to mean "all networks"
Network 127.0.0.0	Reserved for loopback tests. Designates the local node and allows that node to send a test packet to itself without generating network traffic.
Node address of all 0s	Interpreted to mean "network address" or any host on specified network
Node address of all 1s	Interpreted to mean "all nodes" on the specified network; for example, 128.2.255.255 means "all nodes" on network 128.2 (Class B address).
Entire IP address set to all 0s	Used by Cisco routers to designate the default route. Could also mean "any network."
Entire IP address set to all 1s (same as 255.255.255.255)	Broadcast to all nodes on the current network; sometimes called an "all 1s broadcast" or limited broadcast

Private IP Addresses

The creators of the IP addressing scheme also created what is called *private IP addresses*. These addresses can be used on a private network, but they're not routable through the Internet. This is designed for the purpose of creating a measure of much-needed security, but it also conveniently saves valuable IP address space.

The reserved private addresses are listed in Table 3.2.

TABLE 3.2   Reserved IP Address Space

Address Class	Reserved Address Space
Class A	10.0.0.0 through 10.255.255.255
Class B	172.16.0.0 through 172.31.255.255
Class C	192.168.0.0 through 192.168.255.255

Exam Essentials

Understand the three different classes of IP addresses and the associated network sizes. Know the ranges for class A, B, and C addresses and the rules for finding the associated network and node bits. Also, know the sizes of a class A, B, and C network.

Understand private IP addresses and NAT.   Private IP addresses are just like any other IP address, with the exception that they are not routable on the public Internet. Know the ranges for them and how they are used with NAT to connect to the Internet.

Explain the Operation and Benefits of Using DHCP and DNS

For information about this objective, see the section titled "Describe Common Networked Applications, Including Web Applications" in Chapter 1.

Configure, Verify, and Troubleshoot DHCP and DNS Operation on a Router (Including CLI/SDM)

Instead of using a server to provide IP addresses to clients, you can configure a router with a DHCP scope that will hand out IP addresses to hosts on a connected interface. Here is an example:

```
R2#config t
R2(config)#ip dhcp pool Admin
```

```
R2(dhcp-config)#network 10.1.8.0 255.255.255.0
R2(dhcp-config)#default-router 10.1.8.1
R2(dhcp-config)#ip name-server 10.1.8.2
R2(dhcp-config)#exit
R2(config)#ip dhcp excluded-address 10.1.8.1 10.1.8.2
R2(config)#
```

 NOTE   SDM is not covered in this Review Guide. However, it is covered in Appendix B on the CD of *CCNA Cisco Certified Network Associate Study Guide, 7th Edition* (Sybex, 2011).

Creating DHCP pools on a router is actually a pretty simple process. To do so, you just create the pool name, add the network/subnet and the default gateway, and exclude any addresses you don't want handed out (such as the default gateway address). You would usually add a DNS server as well. Note that the excluded addresses are set from global configuration mode.

Wait, you're not done. You created the pool, but which hosts can use this pool? This is where the interface configuration comes in. Notice the default-router address in the pool configuration. Any DHCP client connected off the interface Fa0/0 will grab a DHCP address from the pool. Here is the finished configuration:

```
R2(config)#interface fa0/0
R2(config-if)#ip address 10.1.8.1 255.255.255.0
```

Using DNS to Resolve Names

If you have a lot of devices and don't want to create a host table in each device, you can use a DNS server to resolve hostnames.

When a Cisco device receives a command it doesn't understand, it will try to resolve it through DNS by default. Watch what happens when I type the special command todd at a Cisco router prompt:

```
Corp#todd
Translating "todd"...domain server (255.255.255.255)
Translating "todd"...domain server (255.255.255.255)
Translating "todd"...domain server (255.255.255.255)
% Unknown command or computer name, or unable to find
  computer address
Corp#
```

It doesn't know my name or what command I am trying to type, so it tries to resolve this through DNS. This is really annoying because I need to hang out and wait for the name lookup to time out. You can get around this and prevent a time-consuming DNS lookup by using the no ip domain-lookup command on your router from global configuration mode.

If you have a DNS server on your network, you need to add a few commands to make DNS name resolution work:

- The first command is ip domain-lookup, which is turned on by default. It needs to be entered only if you previously turned it off (with the no ip domain-lookup command). The command can be used without the hyphen as well (ip domain lookup).

- The second command is ip name-server. This sets the IP address of the DNS server. You can enter the IP addresses of up to six servers.

- The last command is ip domain-name. Although this command is optional, it really should be set. It appends the domain name to the hostname you enter. Because DNS uses a FQDN system, you must have a full DNS name, in the form *domain*.com.

Here's an example that uses these three commands:

```
Corp#config t
Corp(config)#ip domain-lookup
Corp(config)#ip name-server ?
  A.B.C.D  Domain server IP address (maximum of 6)
Corp(config)#ip name-server 192.168.0.70
Corp(config)#ip domain-name lammle.com
Corp(config)#^Z
Corp#
```

After the DNS configurations are set, you can test the DNS server by using a hostname to ping or Telnet a device like this:

```
Corp#ping R1
Translating "R1"...domain server (192.168.0.70) [OK]
Type escape sequence to abort.
Sending 5, 100-byte ICMP Echos to 10.2.2.2, timeout is
  2 seconds:
!!!!!
Success rate is 100 percent (5/5), round-trip min/avg/max
  = 28/31/32 ms
```

Notice that the router uses the DNS server to resolve the name.

Exam Essentials

Remember how to configure a DHCP pool on a router. From global config mode, use the command ip dhcp pool_name network_address mask. From the DHCP pool prompt, you can use the network command to add the subnet address. This creates the pool of addresses that can be assigned to hosts. Adding the default gateway is just as important, and the command is `default-router 1.2.3.4`. You can also add a DNS server by using the command `ip name-server 1.2.3.4`.

Remember how to configure a router to perform DNS lookups.   The command `ip domain-lookup` is used to enable DNS lookups on the router. The command `ip name-server` allows you to specify the IP address of the DNS server, up to 6, and finally, the command `ip domain-name` is used to set the DNS hierarchical name.

Implement Static and Dynamic Addressing Services for Hosts in a LAN Environment

Interface configuration is one of the most important router configurations because without interfaces, a router is pretty much a completely useless object. Interface configurations must be precise to enable communication with other devices. Network layer addresses, media type, bandwidth, and other administrator commands are all used to configure an interface.

Different routers use different methods to choose the interfaces used on them. For instance, the following command shows a Cisco 2522 router with 10 serial interfaces, labeled 0 through 9:

```
Router(config)#int serial ?
 <0-9> Serial interface number
```

Now it's time to choose the interface you want to configure. Once you do that, you will be in interface configuration for that specific interface. The following command would be used to choose serial port 5, for example:

```
Router(config)#int serial 5
Router(config)-if)#
```

The 2522 router has one Ethernet 10BaseT port. To configure that interface, type **interface ethernet 0**, as shown here:

```
Router(config)#int ethernet ?
 <0-0> Ethernet interface number
Router(config)#int ethernet 0
Router(config-if)#
```

The above router is a fixed-configuration router. This means that when you buy that model, you're stuck with that physical configuration—a huge reason why I don't use them very much. I certainly never would use them in a production setting anymore.

To configure an interface, I always used the `interface` *type* *number* sequence, but with the 2600 and 2800 series routers (actually, any ISR router for that matter), there's a physical slot in the router, with a port number on the module plugged into that slot. So, on a modular router, the configuration would be `interface` *type* *slot/port*, as shown here:

```
Router(config)#int fastethernet ?
 <0-1> FastEthernet interface number
Router(config)#int fastethernet 0
% Incomplete command.
Router(config)#int fastethernet 0?
/
Router(config)#int fastethernet 0/?
 <0-1> FastEthernet interface number
```

Note that you can't just type **int fastethernet 0**. You must type the full command: *type* *slot/port*, or **int fastethernet 0/0** (or **int fa 0/0**).

For the ISR series, it's basically the same, only you have even more options. For example, the built-in Fast Ethernet interfaces work with the same configuration I used with the 2600 series:

```
Todd(config)#int fastEthernet 0/?
  <0-1>  FastEthernet interface number
Todd(config)#int fastEthernet 0/0
Todd(config-if)#
```

But the rest of the modules are different, they use three numbers instead of two. The first 0 is the router itself, and then you choose the slot and then the port. Here's an example of a serial interface on my 2811:

```
Todd(config)#interface serial ?
  <0-2>  Serial interface number
Todd(config)#interface serial 0/0/?
  <0-1>  Serial interface number
Todd(config)#interface serial 0/0/0
Todd(config-if)#
```

This can look a little dicey, but I promise it's really not that hard. It helps to remember that you should always view a `running-config` output first so that you know which interfaces you have to deal with. Here's my 2801 output:

```
Todd(config-if)#do show run
Building configuration...
[output cut]
!
interface FastEthernet0/0
```

```
 no ip address
 shutdown
 duplex auto
 speed auto
!
interface FastEthernet0/1
 no ip address
 shutdown
 duplex auto
 speed auto
!
interface Serial0/0/0
 no ip address
 shutdown
 no fair-queue
!
interface Serial0/0/1
 no ip address
 shutdown
!
interface Serial0/1/0
 no ip address
 shutdown
!
interface Serial0/2/0
 no ip address
 shutdown
 clock rate 2000000
!
 [output cut]
```

For the sake of brevity, I didn't include my complete running-config, but I've displayed all you need. You can see the two built-in Fast Ethernet interfaces, the two serial interfaces in slot 0 (0/0/0 and 0/0/1), the serial interface in slot 1 (0/1/0), and the serial interface in slot 2 (0/2/0). Once you see the interfaces like this, it makes it a lot easier for you to understand how the modules are inserted into the router.

Just understand that if you type **interface e0** on a 2500, **interface fastethernet 0/0** on a 2600, or **interface serial 0/1/0** on a 2800, all you're doing is choosing an interface to configure, and basically, they're all configured the same way after that.

I'm going to continue with my router interface discussion in the next sections, and I'll include how to bring up the interface and set an IP address on a router interface.

Bringing Up an Interface

You can disable an interface with the interface command shutdown and enable it with the no shutdown command.

If an interface is shut down, it'll display administratively down when you use the show interfaces command (sh int for short):

```
Todd#sh int f0/1
FastEthernet0/1 is administratively down, line protocol is down
[output cut]
```

Another way to check an interface's status is to use the show running-config command. All interfaces are shut down by default. You can bring up the interface with the no shutdown command (no shut for short):

```
Todd#config t
Todd(config)#int f0/1
Todd(config-if)#no shutdown
Todd(config-if)#
*Feb 28 22:45:08.455: %LINK-3-UPDOWN: Interface FastEthernet0/1,
    changed state to up
Todd(config-if)#do show int f0/1
FastEthernet0/1 is up, line protocol is up
[output cut]
```

Configuring an IP Address on an Interface

Even though you don't have to use IP on your routers, it's usually what people actually do use. To configure IP addresses on an interface, use the ip address command from interface configuration mode:

```
Todd(config)#int f0/1
Todd(config-if)#ip address 172.16.10.2 255.255.255.0
```

Don't forget to enable the interface with the no shutdown command. Remember to look at the command show interface *int* to see if the interface is administratively shut down or not. The show running-config command will also give you this information.

The ip address *address mask* command starts the IP processing on the interface.

If you want to add a second subnet address to an interface, you have to use the secondary parameter. If you type another IP address and press Enter, it will replace the existing IP address and mask. This is definitely a most excellent feature of the Cisco IOS.

So, let's try it. To add a secondary IP address, just use the secondary parameter:

```
Todd(config-if)#ip address 172.16.20.2 255.255.255.0 ?
  secondary  Make this IP address a secondary address
  <cr>
Todd(config-if)#ip address 172.16.20.2 255.255.255.0 secondary
Todd(config-if)#^Z
Todd(config-if)#do sh run
Building configuration...
[output cut]

interface FastEthernet0/1
 ip address 172.16.20.2 255.255.255.0 secondary
 ip address 172.16.10.2 255.255.255.0
 duplex auto
 speed auto
!
```

I really wouldn't recommend having multiple IP addresses on an interface because it's ugly and inefficient, but I showed you this method just in case you someday find yourself dealing with an MIS manager who's in love with really bad network design and makes you administer it.

If you want to create a pool of addresses on a router using the CLI, here is how you do that:

```
R2#config t
R2(config)#ip dhcp pool Todd
R2(dhcp-config)#network 10.1.8.0 255.255.255.0
R2(dhcp-config)#default-router 10.1.8.1
R2(dhcp-config)#ip name-server 192.168.0.70
R2(dhcp-config)#exit
R2(config)#ip dhcp excluded-address 10.1.8.1
R2(config)#
```

Creating DHCP pools on a router is actually a pretty simple process. To do so, you just create the pool name, add the network/subnet and the default gateway, and exclude any addresses you don't want handed out (like the default gateway address)—and you will usually add a DNS server as well.

Exam Essentials

Remember how to add an IP address to an interface.   To configure IP addresses on an interface, use the ip address command from interface configuration mode. Here is an example:

```
Todd(config)#int f0/1
Todd(config-if)#ip address 172.16.10.2 255.255.255.0
```

Remember how to configure a DHCP pool on a router.   I provided this information in the section titled "Configure, Verify, and Troubleshoot DHCP and DNS Operation on a Router (Including CLI/SDM)," but please review it.

Calculate and Apply an Addressing Scheme, Including VLSM IP Addressing Design, to a Network

I'm going to show you a simple way to take one network and create many networks using subnet masks of different lengths on different types of network designs. This is called VLSM networking, and it does bring up another subject: classful and classless networking.

Neither RIPv1 nor IGRP routing protocols have a field for subnet information, so the subnet information gets dropped. What this means is that if a router running RIP has a subnet mask of a certain value, it assumes that *all* interfaces within the classful address space have the same subnet mask. This is called classful routing, and RIP and IGRP are both considered classful routing protocols. If you mix and match subnet mask lengths in a network running RIP or IGRP, that network just won't work.

Classless routing protocols, however, do support the advertisement of subnet information. Therefore, you can use VLSM with routing protocols such as RIPv2, EIGRP, and OSPF. The benefit of this type of network is that you save a bunch of IP address space with it.

As the name suggests, with VLSMs you can have different subnet masks for different router interfaces. Look at Figure 3.1 to see an example of why classful network designs are inefficient.

FIGURE 3.1   Typical classful network

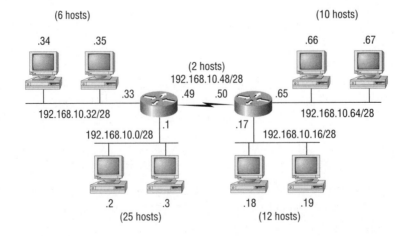

Looking at this figure, you'll notice that there are two routers, each with two LANs and connected together with a WAN serial link. In a typical classful network design (RIP or IGRP routing protocols), you could subnet a network like this:

192.168.10.0 = Network

255.255.255.240 (/28) = Mask

The subnets would be 0, 16, 32, 48, 64, 80, and so on. This allows you to assign 16 subnets to the internetwork. But how many hosts would be available on each network? Well, each subnet provides only 14 hosts. This means that each LAN has 14 valid hosts available—one LAN doesn't even have enough addresses needed for all the hosts. But the point-to-point WAN link also has 14 valid hosts. It's too bad you can't just nick some valid hosts from that WAN link and give them to the LANs.

All hosts and router interfaces have the same subnet mask—again, this is called classful routing. If you want this network to be more efficient, you definitely need to add different masks to each router interface.

But there's still another problem—the link between the two routers will never use more than two valid hosts. This wastes valuable IP address space, and it's the big reason that I'm going to talk to you about VLSM network design.

VLSM Design

Let's take Figure 3.1 and use a classless design, which will become the new network shown in Figure 3.2. In the previous example, one LAN didn't have enough addresses because every router interface and host used the same subnet mask, so address space was wasted—which is not so good. What would be good is to provide only the needed number of hosts on each router interface. To do this, you can use what are referred to as Variable Length Subnet Masks (VLSMs).

FIGURE 3.2   Classless network design

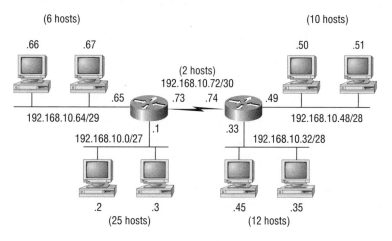

Now remember that you can use different sized masks on each router interface. If you use a /30 on the WAN links and a /27, /28, and /29 on the LANs, you'll get 2 hosts per WAN interface, and 30, 14, and 6 hosts per LAN interface. Nice. This makes a huge difference. Not only can you get just the right number of hosts on each LAN, but you still have room to add more WANs and LANs using this same network.

> Remember, in order to implement a VLSM design on your network, you need to have a routing protocol that sends subnet mask information with the route updates. This would be RIPv2, EIGRP, and OSPF. RIPv1 and IGRP will not work in classless networks and are considered classful routing protocols.

Exam Essentials

Understand the difference between classful and classless networks.   Classful networks are networks that have the same subnet mask on every node. Classless networks are networks that allow different sized masks on each subnet, called variable length subnet masks.

Remember which routing protocols are classful and which routing protocols are classless. Classful routing protocols are RIP and IGRP, and classless routing protocols are RIPv2, EIGRP, and OSPF.

Determine the Appropriate Classless Addressing Scheme Using VLSM and Summarization to Satisfy Addressing Requirements in a LAN/WAN Environment

To create VLSMs quickly and efficiently, you need to understand how block sizes and charts work together to create the VLSM masks. Table 3.3 shows you the block sizes used when creating VLSMs with Class C networks. For example, if you need 25 hosts, then you'll need a block size of 32. If you need 11 hosts, you'll use a block size of 16. If you need 40 hosts, then you'll need a block size of 64. You cannot just make up block sizes—they've got to be the block sizes shown in Table 3.3. So, memorize the block sizes in this table—it's easy. They're the same numbers you used with subnetting.

TABLE 3.3 Block Sizes

Prefix	Mask	Hosts	Block Size
/25	128	126	128
/26	192	62	64
/27	224	30	32
/28	240	14	16
/29	248	6	8
/30	252	2	4

The next step is to create a VLSM table. Figure 3.3 shows you the table used in creating a VLSM network. The reason that you use this table is so that you don't accidentally overlap networks.

You'll find the sheet shown in Figure 3.3 very valuable because it lists every block size you can use for a network address. Notice that the block sizes are listed starting from a block size of 4 all the way to a block size of 128.

If you have two networks with block sizes of 128, you'll quickly see that you can have only two networks. With a block size of 64, you can have only four networks, and so on, all the way to having 64 networks if you use only block sizes of 4. Remember that this takes into account that you are using the command `ip subnet-zero` in your network design.

Now, just fill in the chart in the lower-left corner, and then add the subnets to the worksheet and you're good to go.

So, let's take what you've learned so far about block sizes and VLSM tables and create a VLSM using the Class C network address 192.168.10.0 for the network in Figure 3.4. Then fill out the VLSM table, as shown in Figure 3.5.

In Figure 3.4, there are four WAN links and four LANs connected together. We need to create a VLSM network that will allow us to save address space. Looks like there are two block sizes of 32, a block size of 16, and a block size of 8; and the WANs each have a block size of 4. Take a look and see how I filled out the VLSM chart in Figure 3.5.

There is still plenty of room for growth with this VLSM network design. We never could accomplish that with one subnet mask using classful routing. Let's do another one. Figure 3.6 shows a network with 11 networks, two block sizes of 64, one of 32, five of 16, and three of 4.

First, create your VLSM table and use your block size chart to fill in the table with the subnets you need. Figure 3.7 shows a possible solution.

FIGURE 3.3   The VLSM table

Variable Length Subnet Masks Worksheet

Subnet	Mask	Subnets	Hosts	Block
/26	192	4	62	64
/27	224	8	30	32
/28	240	16	14	16
/29	248	32	6	8
/30	252	64	2	4

Class C Network   192.168.10.0

Network	Hosts	Block	Subnet	Mask
A				
B				
C				
D				
E				
F				
G				
H				
I				
J				
K				
L				
MNetwork	Hosts	Block	Subnet	Mask

Notice that this entire chart is filled and there is room for only one more block size of 4. Only with a VLSM network can you provide this type of address space savings.

Keep in mind that it doesn't matter where you start your block sizes as long as you always count from zero. For example, if you had a block size of 16, you must start at 0 and count from there—0, 16, 32, 48, etc. You can't start a block size of 16 from, say, 40 or anything other than increments of 16.

FIGURE 3.4 A VLSM network, example one

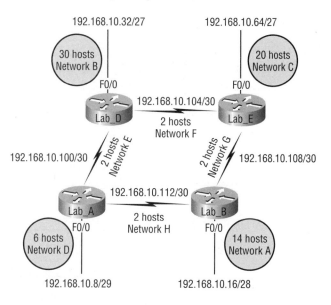

Here's another example: If you have block sizes of 32, you must start at zero like this: 0, 32, 64, 96, and so on. Just remember that you don't get to start wherever you want; you must always start counting from zero. In the example in Figure 3.7, I started at 64 and 128, with my two block sizes of 64. I didn't have much choice because my options are 0, 64, 128, and 192. However, I was able to add the block sizes of 32, 16, 8, and 4 wherever I wanted, just as long as they were in the correct increments of that block size.

You have three locations you need to address, and the IP network you have received is 192.168.55.0 to use as the addressing for the entire network. You'll use `ip subnet-zero` and RIPv2 as the routing protocol. (RIPv2 supports VLSM networks, RIPv1 does not.) Figure 3.8 shows the network diagram and the IP address of the RouterA S0/0 interface.

From the list of IP addresses on the right of the figure, which IP address will be placed in each router's Fa0/0 interface and serial 0/1 of RouterB?

To answer this question, first look for clues in Figure 3.8. The first clue is that interface S0/0 on RouterA has IP address 192.168.55.2/30 assigned, which makes for an easy answer. A /30, as you know, is 255.255.255.252, which gives you a block size of 4. Your subnets are 0, 4, 8, and so on. Because the known host has an IP address of 2, the only other valid host in the zero subnet is 1, so the third answer down is what you want for the S0/1 interface of RouterB.

The next clues are the listed number of hosts for each of the LANs. RouterA needs 7 hosts, a block size of 16 (/28); RouterB needs 90 hosts, a block size of 128 (/25); and RouterC needs 23 hosts, a block size of 32 (/27). Figure 3.9 provides the solution for the VLSM design.

FIGURE 3.5   A VLSM network, example two

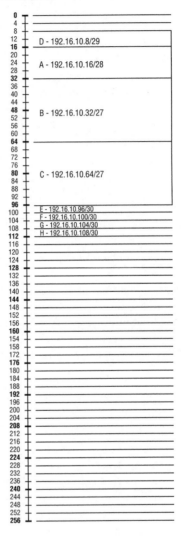

Variable Length Subnet Masks Worksheet

Subnet	Mask	Subnets	Hosts	Block
/26	192	4	62	64
/27	224	8	30	32
/28	240	16	14	16
/29	248	32	6	8
/30	252	64	2	4

Class C Network   192.16.10.0

Network	Hosts	Block	Subnet	Mask
A	12	16	/28	240
B	20	32	/27	224
C	25	32	/27	224
D	4	8	/29	248
E	2	4	/30	252
F	2	4	/30	252
G	2	4	/30	252
H	2	4	/30	252

Once you figured out the block size needed for each LAN, this was actually a pretty simple question. All you needed to do was look for the right clues and, of course, know your block sizes.

FIGURE 3.6   A VLSM table, example one

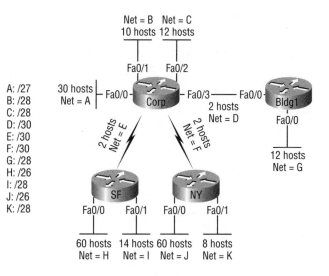

Summarization

Summarization, also called *route aggregation*, allows routing protocols to advertise many networks as one address. The purpose of this is to reduce the size of routing tables on routers to save memory, which also shortens the amount of time it takes for IP to parse the routing table and find the path to a remote network.

Figure 3.10 shows how a summary address would be used in an internetwork.

Summarization is actually somewhat simple because all you really need to have down are the block sizes that you just used when reviewing subnetting and VLSM design. For example, if you want to summarize the following networks into one network advertisement, you just have to find the block size first; then you can easily find your answer:

192.168.16.0 through network 192.168.31.0

What's the block size? There are exactly 16 Class C networks, so this neatly fits into a block size of 16.

Now that you know the block size, you can find the network address and mask used to summarize these networks into one advertisement. The network address used to advertise the summary address is always the first network address in the block—in this example, 192.168.16.0. To figure out a summary mask, in this same example, what mask is used to get a block size of 16? Yes, 240 is correct. This 240 would be placed in the third octet—the octet you are summarizing. So, the mask would be 255.255.240.0.

FIGURE 3.7 A VLSM table, example two

Variable Length Subnet Masks Worksheet

Subnet	Mask	Subnets	Hosts	Block
/26	192	4	62	64
/27	224	8	30	32
/28	240	16	14	16
/29	248	32	6	8
/30	252	64	2	4

Class C Network   192.168.10.0

Network	Hosts	Block	Subnet	Mask
A	30	32	32	224
B	10	16	0	240
C	12	16	16	240
D	2	4	244	252
E	2	4	248	252
F	2	4	252	252
G	12	16	208	240
H	60	64	64	192
I	14	16	192	240
J	60	64	128	192
K	8	16	224	240
L				30
M				10

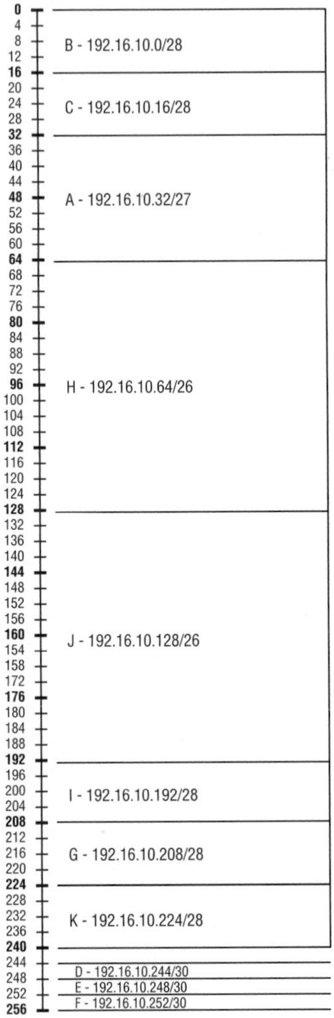

Worksheet scale (0–256):
B - 192.16.10.0/28
C - 192.16.10.16/28
A - 192.16.10.32/27
H - 192.16.10.64/26
J - 192.16.10.128/26
I - 192.16.10.192/28
G - 192.16.10.208/28
K - 192.16.10.224/28
D - 192.16.10.244/30
E - 192.16.10.248/30
F - 192.16.10.252/30

Here's another example:

Networks 172.16.32.0 through 172.16.50.0

This is not as clean as the previous example because there are two possible answers, and here's why: Because you're starting at network 32, your options for block sizes are 4, 8, 16, 32, 64, and so on, and block sizes of 16 and 32 could work as this summary address.

Answer #1: If you used a block size of 16, then the network address is 172.16.32.0 with a mask of 255.255.240.0 (240 provides a block of 16). However, this only summarizes from 32 to 47, which means that networks 48 through 50 would be advertised as single networks. This is probably the best answer, but that depends on your network design. Let's look at the next answer.

Answer #2: If you used a block size of 32, then your summary address would still be 172.16.32.0, but the mask would be 255.255.224.0 (224 provides a block of 32). The possible problem with this answer is that it will summarize networks 32 to 63, and you only have networks 32 to 50. This is no problem if you're planning on adding networks 51 to 63 later into the same network, but you could have serious problems in your internetwork if somehow networks 51 to 63 were to show up and be advertised from somewhere else in your network. This is the reason why answer number one is the safest answer.

FIGURE 3.8 A VLSM design

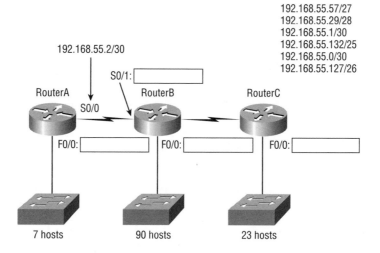

FIGURE 3.9 A solution to the VLSM design

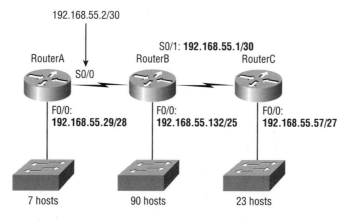

FIGURE 3.10   Summary address used in an internetwork

```
10.0.0.0/16 ⎤              10.0.0.0/8
10.1.0.0/16 ⎥         ───────────────▶
10.2.0.0/16... ⎥
10.255.0.0/16 ⎦
```

Exam Essentials

Remember your block sizes.   Block sizes are used to help you subnet, but they can also be helpful when creating summaries on contiguous boundaries. Block sizes are 1, 2, 4, 8, 16, 32, 64, 128, and so on. However, using a block size larger than 128 is not typical.

Remember how to create classless networks.   Classless networking, also called variable length subnet masking, uses blocks of addresses that can be assigned on each router interface. A different mask can be used on each interface to allow the granular addressing of hosts, which saves address space. In order to use classless networking, you must use a routing protocol like RIPv2, EIGRP, or OSPF.

Determine the summary address and mask from a given set of subnets.   To determine your summary address, you must be able to put the network/subnets into a block size. Once you find your block of networks, the network address is always the first address in the range, and the subnet mask tells you the block size in the interesting octet.

Describe the Technological Requirements for Running IPv6 in Conjunction with IPv4 (Including Protocols, Dual Stack, Tunneling, Etc.)

The IPv6 header and address structure has been completely overhauled, and many of the features that were basically just afterthoughts and addendums in IPv4 are now included as full-blown standards in IPv6. It's seriously well equipped, poised, and ready to manage the mind-blowing demands of the Internet to come.

The Benefits and Uses for IPv6

Today's networks, as well as the Internet, have a ton of unforeseen requirements that simply were not considerations when IPv4 was created. We've tried to compensate with a collection of add-ons that can actually make implementing them more difficult than they would be if they were applied according to a standard. By default, IPv6 has improved upon and included many of those features as standard and mandatory. One of these sweet new standards is *IPSec*. Another little beauty is known as *mobility*, and as its name suggests, it allows a device to roam from one network to another without dropping connections.

But the efficiency features are what are really going to rock the house! For starters, the header in an IPv6 packet has half the fields, and those fields are aligned to 64 bits, which gives us some seriously souped-up processing speed—compared to IPv4, lookups happen at light speed. Most of the information that used to be bound into the IPv4 header was taken out, and now you can choose to put it, or parts of it, back into the header in the form of an optional extension header that follows the basic header fields.

Of course, there's that whole new universe of addresses (3.4×10^{38}). But where did we get them? I mean, that huge proliferation of addresses had to come from somewhere! IPv6 gives us a substantially larger address space, meaning the address is a whole lot bigger—four times bigger, as a matter of fact! An IPv6 address is actually 128 bits in length. For now, let me just say that all that additional room permits more levels of hierarchy inside the address space and a more flexible address architecture. It also makes routing much more efficient and scalable because the addresses can be aggregated a lot more effectively—and IPv6 also allows multiple addresses for hosts and networks.

IPv4 uses broadcasts very prolifically, causing a bunch of problems, the worst of which is, of course, the dreaded *broadcast storm*—an uncontrolled deluge of forwarded broadcast traffic that can bring an entire network to its knees and devour every last bit of bandwidth. Another nasty thing about broadcast traffic is that it interrupts each and every device on the network. When a broadcast is sent out, every machine has to stop what it's doing and respond to the traffic, whether the broadcast is meant for it or not.

Fortunately, there is no such thing as a broadcast in IPv6 because it uses multicast traffic instead, and there are two other types of communication as well: unicast, which is the same as it is in IPv4, and a new type called *anycast*. Anycast communication allows the same address to be placed on more than one device so that when traffic is sent to one device addressed in this way, it is routed to the nearest host that shares the same address. This is just the beginning—we'll get more into the various types of communication in the section called "Address Types."

Dual Stacking (ISATAP)

ISATAP (Intra-Site Automatic Tunnel Addressing Protocol) is an IPv6 transition mechanism meant to transmit IPv6 packets between dual-stack nodes on top of an IPv4 network.

This is the most common type of migration strategy because, well, it's the easiest on us—it allows our devices to communicate using either IPv4 or IPv6. *Dual stacking* lets you upgrade your devices and applications on the network one at a time. As more and more hosts and devices on the network are upgraded, more of your communication will happen over IPv6, and after you've arrived—everything's running on IPv6, and you get to remove all the old IPv4 protocol stacks you no longer need.

Plus, configuring dual stacking on a Cisco router is amazingly easy—all you have to do is enable IPv6 forwarding and apply an address to the interfaces already configured with IPv4. It'll look something like this:

```
Corp(config)#ipv6 unicast-routing
Corp(config)#interface fastethernet 0/0
Corp(config-if)#ipv6 address 2001:db8:3c4d:1::/64 eui-64
Corp(config-if)#ip address 192.168.255.1 255.255.255.0
```

To be honest, it's a good idea to understand the various tunneling techniques because it'll probably be awhile before everyone starts running IPv6 as a solo routed protocol.

6to4 Tunneling

6to4 tunneling is really useful for carrying IPv6 data over a network that's still IPv4. It's quite possible that you'll have IPv6 subnets or other portions of your network that are all IPv6, and those networks will have to communicate with each other. This isn't too complicated, but when you consider that you might find this happening over a WAN or some other network that you don't control, well, that could be a bit ugly. Even if you can't control the whole tamale, you can create a tunnel that will carry the IPv6 traffic across the IPv4 network.

The whole idea of tunneling isn't a difficult concept, and creating tunnels really isn't as hard as you might think. All it really comes down to is snatching the IPv6 packet that's happily traveling across the network and sticking an IPv4 header onto the front of it. It's kind of like catch-and-release fishing, except that the fish doesn't get something plastered on its face before being thrown back into the stream.

To get a picture of this, take a look at Figure 3.11.

FIGURE 3.11   Creating a 6to4 tunnel

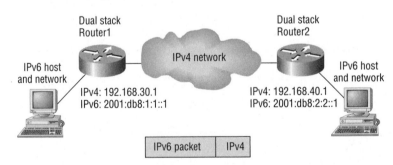

IPv6 packet encapsulated in an IPv4 packet

To make this happen, you're going to need a couple of dual-stacked routers, which I just demonstrated for you, so you should be good to go. Now you have to add a little configuration to place a tunnel between those routers. Tunnels are pretty simple. You just have to tell each router where the tunnel begins and where you want it to end up. Referring again to Figure 3.11, configure the tunnel on each router:

```
Router1(config)#int tunnel 0
Router1(config-if)#ipv6 address 2001:db8:1:1::1/64
Router1(config-if)#tunnel source 192.168.30.1
Router1(config-if)#tunnel destination 192.168.40.1
Router1(config-if)#tunnel mode ipv6ip

Router2(config)#int tunnel 0
Router2(config-if)#ipv6 address 2001:db8:2:2::1/64
Router2(config-if)#tunnel source 192.168.40.1
Router2(config-if)#tunnel destination 192.168.30.1
Router2(config-if)#tunnel mode ipv6ip
```

With this in place, the IPv6 networks can now communicate over the IPv4 network. Now, I've got to tell you that this is not meant to be a permanent configuration; your end goal should still be to run a total, complete IPv6 network end to end.

One important note here: If the IPv4 network that you're traversing in this situation has a NAT translation point, it would absolutely break the tunnel encapsulation you've just created! Over the years, NAT has been upgraded a lot so that it can handle specific protocols and dynamic connections, and without one of these upgrades, NAT likes to demolish most connections. Because this transition strategy isn't present in most NAT implementations, that means trouble.

There is a way around this little problem, and it's called *Teredo*; it allows all your tunnel traffic to be placed in UDP packets. NAT doesn't blast away at UDP packets, so they won't get broken as other protocols packets do. With Teredo in place and your packets disguised under their UDP cloak, the packets will easily slip by NAT alive and well.

Exam Essentials

Understand why IPv6 was needed.   Without IPv6, the world would be depleted of IP addresses.

Remember the IPv6 tunnel mechanisms.   The three default tunnel types included in the IPv6 stack are 6to4, ISATAP, and Teredo.

Describe IPv6 Addresses

Just as understanding how IP addresses are structured and used is critical with IPv4 addressing, it's also vital when it comes to IPv6. You've already read about the fact that at 128 bits, an IPv6 address is much larger than an IPv4 address. Because of this, as well as the new ways the addresses can be used, you've probably guessed that IPv6 will be more complicated to manage. As I explained earlier, I'll break down the basics and show you what the address looks like, how you can write it, and what many of its common uses are. It's going to be a little weird at first, but before you know it, you'll have it nailed.

Let's take a look at Figure 3.12, which has a sample IPv6 address broken down into sections.

FIGURE 3.12   An IPv6 address

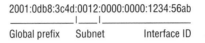

As you can see, the address is truly much larger. Note that it has eight groups of numbers instead of four and also that those groups are separated by colons instead of periods, and there are letters in that address. Yes, the address is expressed in hexadecimal just like a MAC address. You could say this address has eight 16-bit hexadecimal colon-delimited blocks. That's already quite a mouthful, and you probably haven't even tried to say the address out loud yet.

One other thing I want to point out will be useful when you set up your test network to play with IPv6, because I know you're going to want to do that. When you use a web browser to make an HTTP connection to an IPv6 device, you have to type the address into the browser with brackets around the literal address. If you don't enclose the address in brackets, the browser will have no way to identify the information because a colon is already being used by the browser to specify a port number.

Here's an example of how this looks:

```
http://[2001:0db8:3c4d:0012:0000:0000:1234:56ab]/default.html
```

Now obviously, if you can, you would rather use names to specify a destination (like www.lammle.com). Even though it's definitely going to be a pain, sometimes you'll just have to bite the bullet and type in an address number. So, it should be pretty clear that DNS is going to become extremely important when implementing IPv6.

Shortened Expression

The good news is there are a few tricks to help rescue you when you're writing those monster addresses. For one thing, you can actually leave out parts of an address to abbreviate it, but to get away with doing that you have to follow a couple of rules. First, you can drop any leading zeros in each of the individual blocks. The sample address from earlier would then look like this:

```
2001:db8:3c4d:12:0:0:1234:56ab
```

Okay, that's a definite improvement—at least you don't have to write all of those extra zeros. But what about whole blocks that don't have anything in them except zeros? Well, you can lose those, too—at least some of them. Again referring to the sample address, you can remove the two blocks of zeros by replacing them with double colons, like this:

`2001:db8:3c4d:12::1234:56ab`

Cool. You replaced the blocks of all zeros with double colons. The rule you have to follow to get away with this is that you can only replace one contiguous block of zeros in an address. So, if your address has four blocks of zeros and each of them is separated, you just don't get to replace them all. Check out this example:

`2001:0000:0000:0012:0000:0000:1234:56ab`

And just know that you *can't* do this:

`2001::12::1234:56ab`

Instead, this is the best that you can do:

`2001::12:0:0:1234:56ab`

The reason why the above example is your best shot is that if you remove two sets of zeros, the device looking at the address will have no way of knowing where the zeros go back in. Basically, the router would look at the incorrect address and say, "Well, do I place two blocks into the first set of double colons and two into the second set, or do I place three blocks into the first set and one block into the second set?" It would go on and on because the information the router needs just isn't there.

Address Types

Experienced networking professionals are all familiar with IPv4's unicast, broadcast, and multicast addresses that basically define to whom or at least to how many other devices we're talking. As I mentioned, IPv6 adds to that trio and introduces the anycast. Broadcasts, as traditionally known, have been eliminated in IPv6 because of their cumbersome inefficiency.

So, let's find out what each of these types of IPv6 addressing and communication methods do for us.

Unicast   Packets addressed to a unicast address are delivered to a single interface. For load balancing, multiple interfaces across several devices can use the same address, but I'll call that an "anycast" address. There are a few different types of unicast addresses, but I won't get into that here.

Global Unicast Addresses   These are typical publicly routable addresses, and they're the same as they are in IPv4. Global addresses start at 2000::/3.

Link-Local Addresses   These are like the private addresses in IPv4 in that they're not meant to be routed. Think of them as a handy tool that gives you the ability to throw a temporary LAN together for meetings or for creating a small LAN that's not going to be routed but still needs to share and access files and services locally.

Unique Local Addresses These addresses are also intended for non-routing purposes over the Internet, but they are nearly globally unique, so it's unlikely you'll ever have one of them overlap. Unique local addresses were designed to replace site-local addresses, so they basically do almost exactly what IPv4 private addresses do—allow communication throughout a site while being routable to multiple local networks. Site-local addresses were denounced as of September 2004.

Multicast Again, these are the same as in IPv4, packets addressed to a multicast address are delivered to all interfaces identified by the multicast address. Sometimes people call them *one-to-many addresses*. It's really easy to spot a multicast address in IPv6 because they always start with *FF*.

Anycast Like multicast addresses, an anycast address identifies multiple interfaces, but there's a big difference: The anycast packet is only delivered to one address—actually, to the first one it finds defined in terms of routing distance. Again, this address is special because you can apply a single address to more than one interface and device. You could call them one-to-one-of-many addresses, but just saying "anycast" is a lot easier.

You're probably wondering if there are any special, reserved addresses in IPv6 because they're there in IPv4. There are plenty of them! Let's go over them now.

Special Addresses

I'm going to list some of the addresses and address ranges that you should definitely make a point to remember because you'll eventually use them. They're all special or reserved for specific use; but unlike IPv4, IPv6 gives us a galaxy of addresses, so reserving a few here and there doesn't hurt a thing.

0:0:0:0:0:0:0:0 Equals ::. This is the equivalent of IPv4's 0.0.0.0, and it is typically the source address of a host when you're using stateful configuration.

0:0:0:0:0:0:0:1 Equals ::1. The equivalent of 127.0.0.1 in IPv4

0:0:0:0:0:0:192.168.100.1 This is how an IPv4 address would be written in a mixed IPv6/IPv4 network environment.

2000::/3 The global unicast address range

FC00::/7 The unique local unicast range

FE80::/10 The link-local unicast range

FF00::/8 The multicast range

3FFF:FFFF::/32 Reserved for examples and documentation.

2001:0DB8::/32 Also reserved for examples and documentation.

2002::/16 Used with 6to4, which is the transition system—the structure that allows IPv6 packets to be transmitted over an IPv4 network without the need to configure explicit tunnels.

Exam Essentials

Understand why IPv6 was needed.   Without IPv6, the world would be depleted of IP addresses.

Understand link-local.   Link-local is like an IPv4 private IP address, but it can't be routed at all, not even in your organization.

Understand unique local.   This, like link-local, is like private IP addresses in IPv4 and cannot be routed to the Internet. However, the difference between link-local and unique local is that unique local can be routed within your organization or company.

Remember IPv6 addressing.   IPv6 addressing is not like IPv4 addressing. IPv6 addressing has much more address space and is 128 bits long, represented in hexadecimal, unlike IPv4, which is only 32-bits long and represented in decimal.

Identify and Correct Common Problems Associated with IP Addressing and Host Configurations

Please see the following section in Chapter 2:

- Verify Network Status and Switch Operation Using Basic Utilities (Including ping, traceroute, Telnet, SSH, arp, and ipconfig) and SHOW and DEBUG Commands."

  Please see the following section in Chapter 1:

- "Identify and Correct Common Network Problems at Layers 1, 2, 3, and 7 Using a Layered Model Approach."

Review Questions

The following questions are designed to test your understanding of this chapter's material. For more information on how to get additional questions, please see this book's Introduction.

1. On a VLSM network, which mask should you use on point-to-point WAN links in order to reduce the waste of IP addresses?

   A. /27

   B. /28

   C. /29

   D. /30

   E. /31

2. Which of the following is true when describing a global unicast address?

   A. Packets addressed to a unicast address are delivered to a single interface.

   B. These are typical publicly routable addresses, just like a regular publicly routable address in IPv4.

   C. These are like private addresses in IPv4 in that they are not meant to be routed over the Internet.

   D. These addresses are meant for non-routing purposes, but they are almost globally unique, so it is unlikely they will have an address overlap.

3. Which of the following is true when describing a link-local address?

   A. Packets addressed to a broadcast address are delivered to a single interface.

   B. These are typical publicly routable addresses, just like a regular publicly routable address in IPv4.

   C. These are like private addresses in IPv4 in that they are not meant to be routed over the Internet.

   D. These addresses are meant for non-routing purposes, but they are almost globally unique, so it is unlikely they will have an address overlap.

4. Which of the following are IPv6 translation mechanisms? (Choose three.)

   A. 6to4 tunneling

   B. GRE tunneling

   C. ISATAP tunneling

   D. Teredo tunneling

5. Which of the following statements are true of IPv6 address representation? (Choose two.)

  A. The first 64 bits represent the dynamically created interface ID.

  B. A single interface may be assigned multiple IPv6 addresses of any type.

  C. Every IPv6 interface contains at least one loopback address.

  D. Leading zeroes in an IPv6 16-bit hexadecimal field are mandatory.

6. How many bits are in an IPv6 address field?

  A. 24

  B. 4

  C. 3

  D. 16

  E. 32

  F. 128

7. Which of the following is true when describing a unicast address?

  A. Packets addressed to a unicast address are delivered to a single interface.

  B. These are your typical publicly routable addresses, just like a regular publicly routable address in IPv4.

  C. These are like private addresses in IPv4 in that they are not meant to be routed.

  D. These addresses are meant for non-routing purposes, but they are almost globally unique, so it is unlikely they will have an address overlap.

8. Which of the following descriptions about IPv6 is correct?

  A. Addresses are not hierarchical and are assigned at random.

  B. Broadcasts have been eliminated and replaced with multicasts.

  C. There are 2.7 billion addresses.

  D. An interface can only be configured with one IPv6 address.

9. Which of the following is true when describing a unique local address?

  A. Packets addressed to a unicast address are delivered to a single interface.

  B. These are your typical publicly routable addresses, just like a regular publicly routable address in IPv4.

  C. These are like private addresses in IPv4 in that they are not meant to be routed.

  D. These addresses are meant for non-routing purposes, but they are almost globally unique, so it is unlikely they will have an address overlap.

10. Which of the following is true when describing a multicast address?

  A. Packets addressed to a unicast address are delivered to a single interface.

  B. Packets are delivered to all interfaces identified by the address. This is also called a one-to-many address.

  C. Identifies multiple interfaces and is only delivered to one address. This address can also be called one-to-one-of-many.

  D. These addresses are meant for non-routing purposes, but they are almost globally unique, so it is unlikely they will have an address overlap.

Answer to Review Questions

1.   D. A point-to-point link uses only two hosts. A /30, or 255.255.255.252, mask provides two hosts per subnet.

2.   B. Unlike unicast addresses, global unicast addresses are meant to be routed.

3.   C. Link-local addresses are meant for throwing together a temporary LAN for meetings or a small LAN that is not going to be routed but needs to share and access files and services locally.

4.   A, C, D. 6to4, ISATAP (Ddual Sstack), and Teredo are translation tunnel mechanisms.

5.   B, C. If you verify your IP configuration on your host, you'll see that you have multiple IPv6 addresses, including a loopback address. The last 64 bits represent the dynamically created interface ID, and leading zeros are not mandatory in a 16-bit IPv6 field.

6.   D. There are 16 bits (four hex characters) in an IPv6 field.

7.   A. Packets addressed to a unicast address are delivered to a single interface. For load balancing, multiple interfaces can use the same address.

8.   B. There are no broadcasts with IPv6. Unicast, multicast, anycast, global, and link-local unicast are used.

9.   D. These addresses are meant for non-routing purposes like link-local, but they are almost globally unique, so it is unlikely they will have an address overlap. Unique local addresses were designed as a replacement for site-local addresses.

10. B. Packets addressed to a multicast address are delivered to all interfaces identified by the multicast address, the same as in IPv4. It is also called a one-to-many address. You can always tell a multicast address in IPv6 because multicast addresses always start with FF.

Chapter

4

Configure, Verify, and Troubleshoot Basic Router Operation and Routing on Cisco Devices

---

THE CISCO CCNA EXAM OBJECTIVES COVERED IN THIS CHAPTER INCLUDE THE FOLLOWING:

- ✓ Describe basic routing concepts (including packet forwarding and the router lookup process).

- ✓ Describe the operation of Cisco routers (including the router bootup process, POST, and router components).

- ✓ Select the appropriate media, cables, ports, and connectors to connect routers to other network devices and hosts.

- ✓ Configure, verify, and troubleshoot RIPv2.

- ✓ Access and utilize the router to set basic parameters (including CLI/SDM).

- ✓ Connect, configure, and verify the operational status of a device interface.

- ✓ Verify device configuration and network connectivity using ping, traceroute, Telnet, SSH, or other utilities.

- ✓ Perform and verify routing configuration tasks for a static or default route given specific routing requirements.

- ✓ Manage IOS configuration files (including save, edit, upgrade, and restore).

- ✓ Manage Cisco IOS.

- ✓ Compare and contrast methods of routing and routing protocols.

- ✓ Configure, verify, and troubleshoot OSPF.

- ✓ Configure, verify, and troubleshoot EIGRP.

- ✓ Verify network connectivity (including using ping, traceroute, and Telnet or SSH).

- ✓ Troubleshoot routing issues.

- ✓ Verify router hardware and software operation using the SHOW and DEBUG commands.

- ✓ Implement basic router security.

In this chapter, I'm going to discuss the IP routing process. This is an important subject to understand because it pertains to all routers and configurations that use IP. *IP routing* is the process of moving packets from one network to another network using routers.

Describe Basic Routing Concepts (Including Packet Forwarding and the Router Lookup Process)

The term *routing* describes the process of taking a packet from one device and sending it through the network to another device on a different network. Routers don't really care about hosts—they only care about networks and the best path to each network. The logical network address of the destination host is used to get packets to a network through a routed network, and then the hardware address of the host is used to deliver the packet from a router to the correct destination host.

If your network has no routers, it should be apparent that you are not routing. Routers route traffic to all the networks in your internetwork. To be able to route packets, a router must know, at a minimum, the following:

- Destination address
- Neighboring routers from which it can learn about remote networks
- Possible routes to all remote networks
- The best route to each remote network
- How to maintain and verify routing information

The router learns about remote networks from neighboring routers or from an administrator. The router then builds a routing table (a map of the internetwork) that describes how to find the remote networks. If a network is directly connected, then the router already knows how to get to it.

If a network isn't directly connected to the router, the router must use one of two ways to learn how to get to the remote network: *static routing*, meaning that someone must hand-type all network locations into the routing table, or something called dynamic routing. In *dynamic routing*, a protocol on one router communicates with the same protocol running on neighboring routers. The routers then update each other about all the networks they know about and place this information into the routing table. If a change occurs in the network, the dynamic routing protocols automatically inform all routers about the event. If static routing is used, the administrator is responsible for updating all changes by hand into all routers. Typically, in a large network, a combination of both dynamic and static routing is used.

Let's take a look at a simple example that demonstrates how a router uses the routing table to route packets out of an interface. I'll go into a more detailed discussion of the process in the next section.

Figure 4.1 shows a simple two-router network. Lab_A has one serial interface and three LAN interfaces.

FIGURE 4.1   A simple routing example

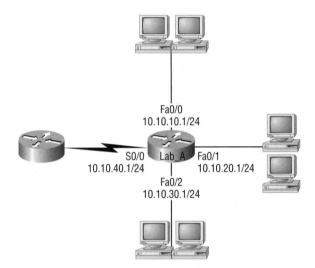

By looking at Figure 4.1, can you see which interface Lab_A will use to forward an IP datagram to a host with an IP address of 10.10.10.10?

By using the command show ip route, you can see the routing table (map of the internetwork) that Lab_A uses to make forwarding decisions:

```
Lab_A#sh ip route
[output cut]
Gateway of last resort is not set
C       10.10.10.0/24 is directly connected, FastEthernet0/0
C       10.10.20.0/24 is directly connected, FastEthernet0/1
C       10.10.30.0/24 is directly connected, FastEthernet0/2
C       10.10.40.0/24 is directly connected, Serial 0/0
```

The C in the routing table output means that the networks listed are "directly connected." Until a routing protocol—something like RIP, EIGRP, and so on—is added to the routers in the internetwork (or use static routes), only directly connected networks will be in the routing table.

So, let's get back to the original question: By looking at the figure and the output of the routing table, can you tell what IP will do with a received packet that has a destination IP address of 10.10.10.10? The router will packet-switch the packet to interface FastEthernet0/0, and this interface will frame the packet and then send it out on the network segment.

Let's try another example: Based on the output of the next routing table, from which interface will a packet with a destination address of 10.10.10.14 be forwarded?

```
Lab_A#sh ip route
[output cut]
Gateway of last resort is not set
C       10.10.10.16/28 is directly connected, FastEthernet0/0
C       10.10.10.8/29 is directly connected, FastEthernet0/1
C       10.10.10.4/30 is directly connected, FastEthernet0/2
C       10.10.10.0/30 is directly connected, Serial 0/0
```

First, you can see that the network is subnetted and each interface has a different mask. Because 10.10.10.14 would be a host in the 10.10.10.8/29 subnet connected to the FastEthernet0/1 interface, the packet will be forwarded out the FastEthernet0/1 interface.

For more information on IP routing, please see Chapter 8 of the *CCNA Cisco Certified Network Associate Study Guide, 7th Edition* (Sybex, 2011).

Exam Essentials

Understand the basic IP routing process.   You need to remember that the frame changes at each hop but that the packet is never changed or manipulated in any way until it reaches the destination device.

Understand the term *routing.*   Routing refers to the process of examining a packet from one device, determining its destination, locating the best path to that destination, and sending it through the network to the destination device. Routers don't really care about hosts—they care only about networks and the best path to each network.

List the information required by a router to route packets.   To be able to route packets, a router must know, at a minimum, the following:

- The destination address
- The neighboring routers from which it can learn about remote networks
- The possible routes to all remote networks
- The best route to each remote network
- How to maintain and verify routing information

Describe the Operation of Cisco Routers (Including the Router Bootup Process, POST, and Router Components)

To configure and troubleshoot a Cisco internetwork, you need to know the major components of Cisco routers and understand what each one does. Table 4.1 describes the major Cisco router components.

TABLE 4.1   Cisco Router Components

Component	Description
Bootstrap	Stored in the microcode of the ROM, the bootstrap is used to bring a router up during initialization. It will boot the router and then load the IOS.
POST (Power-On Self-Test)	Stored in the microcode of the ROM, the POST is used to check the basic functionality of the router hardware and determine which interfaces are present.
ROM Monitor	Stored in the microcode of the ROM, the ROM monitor is used for manufacturing, testing, and troubleshooting.
Mini-IOS	Called the RXBOOT or bootloader by Cisco, the mini-IOS is a small IOS in ROM that can be used to bring up an interface and load a Cisco IOS into flash memory. The mini-IOS can also perform a few other maintenance operations.
RAM (Random Access Memory)	Used to hold packet buffers, ARP cache, routing tables, and the software and data structures that allow the router to function. Running-config is stored in RAM, and most routers expand the IOS from flash into RAM upon boot.
ROM (Read-Only Memory)	Used to start and maintain the router. Holds the POST and the bootstrap program, as well as the mini-IOS.
Flash Memory	Stores the Cisco IOS by default. Flash memory is not erased when the router is reloaded. It is EEPROM (Electronically Erasable Programmable Read-Only Memory) created by Intel.

Component	Description
NVRAM (Nonvolatile RAM)	Used to hold the router and switch configuration. NVRAM is not erased when the router or switch is reloaded. Does not store an IOS. The configuration register is stored in NVRAM.
Configuration Register	Used to control how the router boots up. This value can be found as the last line of the show version command output and by default is set to 0x2102, which tells the router to load the IOS from flash memory as well as to load the configuration from NVRAM.

The Router Boot Sequence

When a router boots up, it performs a series of steps, called the *boot sequence*, to test the hardware and load the necessary software. The boot sequence consists of the following steps:

1. The router performs a POST. The POST tests the hardware to verify that all components of the device are present and operational. For example, the POST checks for the different interfaces on the router. The POST is stored in and runs from ROM *(Read-Only Memory)*.

2. The bootstrap then looks for and loads the Cisco IOS software. The *bootstrap* is a program in ROM that is used to execute programs. The bootstrap program is responsible for finding where each IOS program is located and then loading the file. By default, the IOS software is loaded from flash memory in all Cisco routers.

 The default order of an IOS loading from a router is flash, TFTP server, and then ROM.

3. The IOS software looks for a valid configuration file stored in NVRAM. This file is called startup-config and is present in NVRAM only if an administrator copies the running-config file into NVRAM. (Cisco's new Integrated Services Router (ISR) has a small startup-config file preloaded.)

4. If a startup-config file is in NVRAM, the router will copy this file and place it in RAM and then call the file running-config. The router will use this file to run the router. The router should then be operational. If a startup-config file is not present in NVRAM, the router will attempt to locate a TFTP server that may contain this file. It will do so by broadcasting out any interface that detects carrier detect (CD), and if that fails, it will start the setup mode configuration process.

Exam Essentials

Remember the default configuration register setting.   The default configuration register setting is 0x2102, which means "load the IOS from flash and the configuration from NVRAM."

Remember where the IOS is stored by default.   The IOS is stored and loaded from flash memory by default on all Cisco routers.

Define and identify the location of all router components.   Identify all components listed in Table 4.1 and their locations.

Select the Appropriate Media, Cables, Ports, and Connectors to Connect Routers to Other Network Devices and Hosts

See the section titled "Select the Appropriate Media, Cables, Ports, and Connectors to Connect Switches to Other Network Devices and Hosts" in Chapter 2, "Configure, Verify, and Troubleshoot a Switch with VLANs and Interswitch Communications," for coverage of LAN media, cables, and connections.

Router WAN Connections

As you can imagine, there are a few things you will need to know before you connect your WAN in order to make sure everything goes well. For starters, you have to understand the kind of WAN Physical layer implementation that Cisco provides and be familiar with the various types of WAN serial connectors.

The good news is that Cisco serial connections support almost any type of WAN service. The typical WAN connection is a dedicated leased line using HDLC, PPP, and Frame Relay with speeds that can kick it up to 45Mbps (T3).

HDLC, PPP, and Frame Relay can use the same Physical layer specifications. I'll go over the various types of connections and then tell you all about the WAN protocols specified in the CCNA objectives.

Serial Transmission

WAN serial connectors use *serial transmission*, which takes place 1 bit at a time over a single channel.

 Parallel transmission can pass at least 8 bits at a time, but all WANs use serial transmission.

Cisco routers use a proprietary 60-pin serial connector that you have to get from Cisco or a provider of Cisco equipment. Cisco also has a new, smaller proprietary serial connection that's about ⅒ the size of the 60-pin basic serial cable, called the *smart-serial*. You must make sure that you have the right type of interface in your router before using this cable connector.

The type of connector you have on the other end of the cable depends on your service provider and their particular end-device requirements. Among the types of connectors in use are

- EIA/TIA-232

- EIA/TIA-449

- V.35 (used to connect to a CSU/DSU)

- EIA-530

Make sure that you're clear on these things. Serial links are described in frequency or cycles per second (hertz). The amount of data that can be carried within these frequencies is called *bandwidth*. Bandwidth is the amount of data in bits per second that the serial channel can carry.

Data Terminal Equipment and Data Communication Equipment

By default, router interfaces are *data terminal equipment (DTE),* and they connect into *data communication equipment (DCE)* like a *channel service unit/data service unit (CSU/DSU)*. The CSU/DSU then plugs into a demarcation location (demarc) and is the service provider's last responsibility. Most of the time, the *demarc* is a jack that has an RJ-45 (8-pin modular) female connector located in a telecommunications closet.

Figure 4.2 shows a typical DTE-DCE-DTE connection and the devices used in the network.

FIGURE 4.2   A DTE-DCE-DTE WAN connection

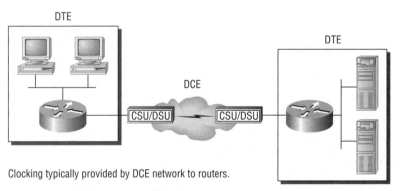

Clocking typically provided by DCE network to routers.

In non-production environments, a DCE network is not always present.

The idea behind a WAN is to be able to connect two DTE networks through a DCE network. The DCE network includes the CSU/DSU, through the provider's wiring and switches, all the way to the CSU/DSU at the other end. The network's DCE device (CSU/DSU) provides clocking to the DTE-connected interface (the router's serial interface).

As mentioned, the DCE network provides clocking to the router—this is the CSU/DSU. If you have a nonproduction network and you're using a WAN crossover type of cable and do not have a CSU/DSU, then you need to provide clocking on the DCE end of the cable by using the clock rate command.

Terms such as *EIA/TIA-232, V.35, X.21,* and *HSSI (High-Speed Serial Interface)* describe the Physical layer between the DTE (router) and DCE device (CSU/DSU).

Exam Essentials

Understand the difference between DTE and DCE connections.   Data terminal equipment (DTE) is considered your router connected to a WAN and is the customer's responsibility. DTE devices connect into data communication equipment (DCE), typically considered the CSU/DSU, which then connects into the providers network.

Configure, Verify, and Troubleshoot RIPv2

RIP version 2 is almost the same as RIP version 1, but there are some important differences that make RIPv2 more scalable than RIPv1. Both RIPv1 and RIPv2 are *distance-vector protocols*, which means that each router running RIP sends its complete routing tables out on all active interfaces at periodic time intervals. Also, the timers and loop-avoidance schemes are the same in both RIP versions (i.e., holddown timers and split horizon rule). Both RIPv1 and RIPv2 are configured as classful addressing protocols, and both have the same administrative distance (120). Table 4.2 lists the differences between RIPv1 and RIPv2.

TABLE 4.2   RIPv1 Compared to RIPv2

RIPv1	RIPv2
Distance vector	Distance vector
Maximum hop count of 15	Maximum hop count of 15
Classful	Classless
Broadcast based	Uses multicast 224.0.0.9

RIPv1	RIPv2
No support for VLSM	Supports VLSM networks
No authentication	Allows for MD5 authentication
No support for discontiguous networks	Supports discontiguous networks

RIPv2, unlike RIPv1, is a classless routing protocol (even though it is configured as classful, like RIPv1), which means that it sends subnet mask information along with the route updates. By sending the subnet mask information with the updates, RIPv2 can support variable length subnet masks (VLSMs) as well as the summarization of network boundaries. In addition, RIPv2 can support discontiguous networking.

Configuring RIPv2 is pretty straightforward. Here's an example:

```
Lab_C(config)#router rip
Lab_C(config-router)#network 192.168.40.0
Lab_C(config-router)#network 192.168.50.0
Lab_C(config-router)#version 2
```

Now all you have to do is add the command **version 2** under the (config-router)# prompt, and you are running RIPv2.

  RIPv2 is classless and works in VLSM and discontiguous networks.

Let's look at our routing table after enabling RIPv2.

```
      10.0.0.0/24 is subnetted, 12 subnets
C         10.1.11.0 is directly connected, FastEthernet0/1
C         10.1.10.0 is directly connected, FastEthernet0/0
R         10.1.9.0 [120/2] via 10.1.5.1, 00:00:23, Serial0/0/1
R         10.1.8.0 [120/2] via 10.1.5.1, 00:00:23, Serial0/0/1
R         10.1.12.0 [120/1] via 10.1.11.2, 00:00:18, FastEthernet0/1
R         10.1.3.0 [120/1] via 10.1.5.1, 00:00:23, Serial0/0/1
```

RIP has found four new routes in the routing table. I'm going to turn on debugging and see if that shows us anything new.

```
*Mar 17 19:34:00.123: RIP: sending v2 update to 224.0.0.9 via
    Serial0/0/1 (10.1.5.2)
*Mar 17 19:34:00.123: RIP: build update entries
*Mar 17 19:34:00.123:    10.1.10.0/24 via 0.0.0.0, metric 1, tag 0
*Mar 17 19:34:00.123:    10.1.11.0/24 via 0.0.0.0, metric 1, tag 0
```

```
*Mar 17 19:34:00.123:    10.1.12.0/24 via 0.0.0.0, metric 2, tag 0col
*Mar 17 19:34:03.795: RIP: received v2 update from 10.1.5.1 on
   Serial0/0/1
```
[output cut]

This shows that the networks are being advertised every 30 seconds, and they're sending the advertisements as v2 and as a multicast address of 224.0.0.9. Let's take a look at the show ip protocols output:

```
Router#sh ip protocols
Routing Protocol is "rip"
  Outgoing update filter list for all interfaces is not set
  Incoming update filter list for all interfaces is not set
  Sending updates every 30 seconds, next due in 27 seconds
  Invalid after 180 seconds, hold down 180, flushed after 240
  Redistributing: rip
  Default version control: send version 2, receive version 2
    Interface          Send  Recv  Triggered RIP  Key-chain
    FastEthernet0/1     2     2
    Serial0/0/1         2     2
  Automatic network summarization is not in effect
  Maximum path: 4
  Routing for Networks:
    10.0.0.0
  Passive Interface(s):
    FastEthernet0/0
    Serial0/0/0
  Routing Information Sources:
    Gateway         Distance      Last Update
    10.1.11.2           120       00:00:00
    10.1.5.1            120       00:00:02
  Distance: (default is 120)
```

The router is now sending and receiving RIPv2.

Exam Essentials

Remember the multicast address of RIPv2.   RIPv2 does not use broadcasts like RIPv1; instead, it uses a multicast address of 224.0.0.9 to communicate with other routers running RIPv2.

Understand how to configure RIPv2.   RIPv2 has a very simple configuration. You just add the command version 2 under the RIP configuration.

Compare and contrast RIPv1 and RIPv2.   Identify the important differences that make RIPv2 more scalable than RIPv1 as listed in Table 4.2.

Access and Utilize the Router to Set Basic Parameters (Including CLI/SDM)

If you boot a router, the interface status messages appear, and if you press Enter, the Router> prompt will appear. This is called *user exec mode* (user mode), and it's mostly used to view statistics, but it's also a stepping stone to logging in to privileged mode.

You can only view and change the configuration of a Cisco router in *privileged exec mode* (privileged mode), which you can enter with the enable command as follows:

```
Router>enable
Router#
```

You now end up with a Router# prompt, which indicates that you're in *privileged mode*, where you can view the router's configuration. Privileged mode is also used to access global configuration mode, where changes can be made to the configuration. You can go back from privileged mode into user mode by using the disable command as follows:

```
Router#disable
Router>
```

At this point, you can type **logout** from either mode to exit the console:

```
Router>logout

Router con0 is now available
Press RETURN to get started.
```

In the following sections, I am going to show you how to perform some basic administrative configurations.

Overview of Router Modes

To configure from a CLI, you can make global changes to the router by typing configure terminal (or config t for short), which puts you in global configuration mode and changes what's known as the running-config. A global command (a command run from global config) is set only once and affects the entire router.

You can type **config** from the privileged-mode prompt and then just press Enter to take the default of terminal, as shown here:

```
router#config
Configuring from terminal, memory, or network [terminal]? [press enter]
Enter configuration commands, one per line. End with CNTL/Z.
router(config)#
```

At this point, you make changes that affect the router as a whole (globally)—hence the term *global configuration mode*. To change the running-config—the current configuration running in dynamic RAM (DRAM)—you use the configure terminal command, as I just demonstrated.

To change the startup-config—the configuration stored in NVRAM—you use the configure memory command (or config mem for short), which merges the startup-config file into the running-config file in RAM. If you want to change a router configuration stored on a TFTP host, you use the configure network command (or config net for short), which also merges the file with the running-config file in RAM.

The configure terminal, configure memory, and configure network are all used to configure information into RAM on a router, although typically only the configure terminal command is used. However, it is possible that the commands config mem and config net can be useful if you want to to reapply your startup-config file and don't want to reboot your router.

Here are some of the other options under the configure command:

```
router(config)#exit or press cntl-z
router#config ?
  confirm              Confirm replacement of running-config with a new config file
  memory               Configure from NV memory
  network              Configure from a TFTP network host
  overwrite-network    Overwrite NV memory from TFTP network host
  replace              Replace the running-config with a new config file
  terminal             Configure from the terminal
  <cr>
```

As you can see, Cisco has added a few more commands in the 12.4 IOS.

Defining Router Terms

Table 4.3 defines some of the terms used so far.

TABLE 4.3 Router Terms

Mode	Definition
User EXEC mode	Limited to basic monitoring commands
Privileged EXEC mode	Provides access to all other router commands
Global configuration mode	Commands that affect the entire system
Specific configuration mode	Commands that affect interfaces/processes only
Setup mode	Interactive configuration dialog

Gathering Basic Routing Information

The show version command will provide basic configuration for the system hardware as well as the software version and the boot images. Here's an example:

```
router#show version
Cisco IOS Software, 2800 Software (C2800NM-ADVSECURITYK9-M), Version
   12.4(12), RELEASE SOFTWARE (fc1)
Technical Support: http://www.cisco.com/techsupport
Copyright (c) 1986-2006 by Cisco Systems, Inc.
Compiled Fri 17-Nov-06 12:02 by prod_rel_team
```

The preceding section of output describes the Cisco IOS running on the router. The following section describes the read-only memory (ROM) that's used to boot the router and holds the POST:

```
ROM: System Bootstrap, Version 12.4(13r)T, RELEASE SOFTWARE (fc1)
```

The next section shows how long the router has been running, how it was restarted, where the Cisco IOS was loaded from, and the IOS name (if you see a system restarted by bus error, that is a very bad thing). Flash is the default.

```
router uptime is 2 hours, 30 minutes
System returned to ROM by power-on
System restarted at 09:04:07 UTC Sat Aug 25 2007
System image file is "flash:c2800nm-advsecurityk9-mz.124-12.bin"
```

The next section displays the processor, the amount of DRAM and flash memory, and the interfaces the POST found on the router:

```
[some output cut]
Cisco 2811 (revision 53.50) with 249856K/12288K bytes of memory.
Processor board ID FTX1049A1AB
2 FastEthernet interfaces
4 Serial(sync/async) interfaces
1 Virtual Private Network (VPN) Module
DRAM configuration is 64 bits wide with parity enabled.
239K bytes of non-volatile configuration memory.
62720K bytes of ATA CompactFlash (Read/Write)
Configuration register is 0x2102
```

The configuration register value is listed last.

Router and Switch Administrative Configurations

In this section, I'm going to lead you through configuring commands that will help you administrate your network.

The administrative functions that you can configure on a router and switch are the following:

- Hostnames
- Banners
- Passwords
- Interface descriptions

None of these will make your routers or switches work better or faster. However, if you take the time to set these configurations on each of your network devices, troubleshooting and maintaining your network will be much easier.

Hostnames

You can set the identity of the router with the `hostname` command. This is only locally significant, which means that it has no bearing on how the router performs name lookups or how the router works on the internetwork. I'll cover an additional function of the `hostname` command when I discuss PPP in Chapter 8, "Implement and Verify WAN Links."

Here's an example:

```
router#config t
Enter configuration commands, one per line. End with
   CNTL/Z.
router(config)#hostname Todd
Todd(config)#
```

Even though it's pretty tempting to configure the hostname after your own name, it's definitely a better idea to name the router something pertinent to the location. This is because giving it a hostname that's somehow relevant to where the device actually lives will make finding it a whole lot easier.

Banners

You can use a banner to display a security notice to anyone who attempts to Telnet or dial into your internetwork. You can create a banner to give anyone who shows up on the router exactly the information you want them to have.

There are four available banner types: exec process creation banner, incoming terminal line banner, login banner, and message of the day (MOTD) banner. All four of these banner types are illustrated in the following code:

```
Todd(config)#banner ?
  LINE          c banner-text c, where 'c' is a delimiting character
  exec          Set EXEC process creation banner
  incoming      Set incoming terminal line banner
  login         Set login banner
```

```
motd            Set Message of the Day banner
prompt-timeout  Set Message for login authentication timeout
slip-ppp        Set Message for SLIP/PPP
```

MOTD is the most extensively used banner. It provides a message to every person dialing into or connecting to the router via Telnet or auxiliary port, or even through a console port. Its configuration is as follows:

```
Todd(config)#banner motd ?
LINE c banner-text c, where 'c' is a delimiting character
Todd(config)#banner motd #
Enter TEXT message. End with the character '#'.
$ Acme.com network, then you must disconnect immediately.
#
Todd(config)#^Z
Todd#
00:25:12: %SYS-5-CONFIG_I: Configured from console by
  console
Todd#exit

Router con0 is now available

Press RETURN to get started.

If you are not authorized to be in Acme.com network, then you must disconnect
immediately.
Todd#
```

The preceding MOTD banner essentially tells everyone connecting to the router that if they're not on the guest list, they need to leave! The delimiting character is used to tell the router when the message is done. You can use any character you want for it, but you can't use the delimiting character in the message itself. The best way to use a delimiting character is to write your message, press Enter, type the delimiting character, and then press Enter again. It will still work if you don't press the second Enter, but if you have more than one banner, they'll be combined as one message on a single line.

Setting Passwords

Five passwords are used to secure your Cisco routers: console, auxiliary, Telnet (VTY), enable, and enable secret. Enable secret and enable passwords are used to set the password that's used to secure privileged mode. This will prompt a user for a password when the `enable` command is used. The other three are used to configure a password when user mode is accessed through the console port, through the auxiliary port, or via Telnet.

Let's take a closer look at each of these now.

Enable Passwords

You set the enable passwords from global configuration mode like this:

```
Todd(config)#enable ?
 last-resort Define enable action if no TACACS servers
             respond
 password    Assign the privileged level password
 secret      Assign the privileged level secret
 use-tacacs  Use TACACS to check enable passwords
```

Here's an example of setting the enable passwords:

```
Todd(config)#enable secret todd
Todd(config)#enable password todd
The enable password you have chosen is the same as your
  enable secret. This is not recommended. Re-enter the
  enable password.
```

If you try to set the enable secret and enable password using the same word, the router will give you a nice, polite warning to change the second password. If you don't have older legacy routers, don't even bother to use the enable password.

User-mode passwords are assigned by using the line command as follows:

```
Todd(config)#line ?
  <0-337>  First Line number
  aux      Auxiliary line
  console  Primary terminal line
  tty      Terminal controller
  vty      Virtual terminal
  x/y      Slot/Port for Modems
  x/y/z    Slot/Subslot/Port for Modems
```

Here are the lines to be concerned with:

aux   Sets the user-mode password for the auxiliary port. It's usually used for attaching a modem to the router, but it can be used as a console as well.

console   Sets a console user-mode password.

vty   Sets a Telnet password on the router. If this password isn't set, then Telnet can't be used by default.

To configure the user-mode passwords, you configure the line you want and use either the login or no login command to tell the router to prompt for authentication. The next section provides a complete example of each line configuration.

Auxiliary Password

To configure the auxiliary password, go into global configuration mode and type **line aux ?**. You can see that the only choice is 0–0 (that's because there's only one port):

```
Todd#config t
Enter configuration commands, one per line. End with CNTL/Z.
Todd(config)#line aux ?
  <0-0>  First Line number
Todd(config)#line aux 0
Todd(config-line)#login
% Login disabled on line 1, until 'password' is set
Todd(config-line)#password aux
Todd(config-line)#login
```

It's important to remember to use the login command, or the auxiliary port won't prompt for authentication.

If you set the login command under a line and then don't set a password, the line won't be usable. It will prompt for a password that doesn't exist. This is why Cisco won't let you set the login command before a password is set on a line. So, this is a good feature, not a hassle!

 Although Cisco has this new "password feature" on its routers, starting with its newer IOS (12.2 and above), it's not in all its IOSs.

Console Password

To set the console password, use the line console 0 command at the (config) prompt. You could type **line console 0** at the (config-line) prompt instead, but the help screens won't function from that prompt—type **exit** to get back one level, and you'll find that your help screens will work.

Here's the example:

```
Todd(config-line)#line console ?
% Unrecognized command
Todd(config-line)#exit
Todd(config)#line console ?
  <0-0>  First Line number
Todd(config-line)#password console
Todd(config-line)#login
```

Because there's only one console port in this example, you can choose only line console 0. You can set all your line passwords to the same password, but for security reasons, I'd recommend that you make them different.

Telnet Password

To set the user-mode password for Telnet access into the router, use the `line vty` command. Routers that aren't running the Enterprise edition of the Cisco IOS default to five VTY lines, 0 through 4. If you're using the Enterprise edition, you'll have significantly more lines. The best way to find out how many lines you have is to use the question mark, as shown here:

```
Todd(config-line)#line vty 0 ?
% Unrecognized command
Todd(config-line)#exit
Todd(config)#line vty 0 ?
  <1-1180>  Last Line number
  <cr>
Todd(config)#line vty 0 1180
Todd(config-line)#password telnet
Todd(config-line)#login
```

Remember: You cannot get help from your (`config-line`)# prompt. You must go back to privilege mode in order to use the question mark (?).

> You may or may not have to set the password command before the login command on the VTY lines; It depends on the IOS version. The result is the same either way.

If you try to Telnet into a router that doesn't have a VTY password set, you'll receive an error stating that the connection is refused because the password isn't set. So, if you Telnet into a router and receive the message

```
Todd#telnet SFRouter
Trying SFRouter (10.0.0.1)…Open

Password required, but none set
[Connection to SFRouter closed by foreign host]
Todd#
```

then the remote router (SFRouter in this example) does not have the VTY (Telnet) password set.

After your routers are configured with an IP address, you can use the Telnet program to configure and check your routers instead of having to use a console cable. You can use the Telnet program by typing **telnet** from any command prompt.

Setting Up Secure Shell (SSH)

Instead of Telnet, you can use Secure Shell (SSH), which creates a more secure session than the Telnet application, which uses an unencrypted data stream. SSH uses encrypted keys to send data so that your username and password are not sent in the clear.

Here are the steps to setting up SSH:

1. Set your hostname:

   Router(config)#**hostname Todd**

2. Set the domain name (both the hostname and domain name are required for the encryption keys to be generated):

   Todd(config)#**ip domain-name Lammle.com**

3. Set the username to allow SSH client access:

   Todd(config)#**username Todd password Lammle**

4. Generate the encryption keys for securing the session:

   ```
   Todd(config)#crypto key generate rsa general-keys modulus ?
     <360-2048>  size of the key modulus [360-2048]
   Todd(config)#crypto key generate rsa general-keys modulus 1024
   The name for the keys will be: Todd.Lammle.com
   % The key modulus size is 1024 bits
   % Generating 1024 bit RSA keys, keys will be non-exportable...[OK]
   *June 24 19:25:30.035: %SSH-5-ENABLED: SSH 1.99 has been enabled
   ```

5. Enable SSH version 2 on the router (although this isn't mandatory, it is highly suggested):

   Todd(config)#**ssh version 2**

6. Connect to the VTY lines of the router:

   Todd(config)#**line vty 0 1180**

7. Configure SSH and then Telnet as access protocols:

   Todd(config-line)#**transport input ssh telnet**

   If you do not use the keyword telnet at the end of the command string, then only SSH will work on the router. I am not recommending one method over the other, but just understand that SSH is more secure than Telnet.

Descriptions

Setting descriptions on an interface is helpful to the administrator and, like the hostname, only locally significant. The description command is a helpful one because you can, for instance, use it to keep track of circuit numbers.

Here's an example:

```
Todd#config t
Todd(config)#int s0/0/0
Todd(config-if)#description Wan to SF circuit number 6fdda12345678
Todd(config-if)#int fa0/0
Todd(config-if)#description Sales VLAN
Todd(config-if)#^Z
Todd#
```

You can view the description of an interface with either the show running-config command or the show interface command:

```
Todd#sh run
[output cut]
!
interface FastEthernet0/0
 description Sales VLAN
 ip address 10.10.10.1 255.255.255.248
 duplex auto
 speed auto
!
interface Serial0/0/0
 description Wan to SF circuit number 6fdda 12345678
 no ip address
 shutdown
!
[output cut]
Todd#sh int f0/0
FastEthernet0/0 is up, line protocol is down
  Hardware is MV96340 Ethernet, address is 001a.2f55.c9e8 (bia 001a.2f55.c9e8)
  Description: Sales VLAN
 [output cut]


Todd#sh int s0/0/0
Serial0/0/0 is administratively down, line protocol is down
  Hardware is GT96K Serial
  Description: Wan to SF circuit number 6fdda12345678
```

 SDM objectives are covered solely on the CD of the *CCNA Cisco Certified Network Associate Study Guide, 7th Edition* (Sybex, 2011).

Exam Essentials

Remember how to configure your administrative functions. Administrative functions are your hostname, banners, passwords, and interface descriptions.

Remember what is required to configure SSH on your router. You must configure both your hostname and domain name on the router in order for SSH to be enabled.

Define the available router modes and identify them by their prompts. Understand the difference in functionality of user mode, privileged mode, and configuration mode. Identify each by its prompt.

Connect, Configure, and Verify the Operational Status of a Device Interface

Interface configuration is one of the most important router configurations. Without interfaces, a router is pretty much a completely useless object—plus, interface configurations must be totally precise to enable communication with other devices. Network layer addresses, media type, bandwidth, and other administrator commands are all used to configure an interface.

Based on the router model, you use different syntax to access interface configuration mode. To determine the proper syntax for identifying interfaces on your router, use the question mark to find your interface numbers as follows:

```
Router(config)#int serial ?
 <0-9> Serial interface number
```

Now it's time to choose the interface you want to configure. Once you do that, you will be in the interface configuration for that specific interface. For example, you would use the following command to choose serial port 5:

```
Router(config)#int serial 5
Router(config)-if)#
```

The router in this example has one Ethernet 10BaseT port, so you can type **interface ethernet 0** to configure that interface as follows:

```
Router(config)#int ethernet ?
 <0-0> Ethernet interface number
Router(config)#int ethernet 0
Router(config-if)#
```

As I showed you previously, the 2500 router is a fixed configuration router. This means that when you buy that model, you're stuck with that physical configuration (which is a huge reason why I don't use them much, and I certainly would never use them in a production setting anymore).

In the interface configuration examples so far, I have used the interface *type number* syntax, but the 2600 and 2800 series routers (actually, any ISR router for that matter) use a physical slot in the router, with a port number on the module plugged into that slot. So on a modular router, the configuration would be interface ***type slot/port***, as shown here:

```
Router(config)#int fastethernet ?
  <0-1> FastEthernet interface number
Router(config)#int fastethernet 0
% Incomplete command.
Router(config)#int fastethernet 0?
/
Router(config)#int fastethernet 0/?
  <0-1> FastEthernet interface number
```

Note that you can't just type **int fastethernet 0**. You must type the full command: ***type slot/port***, or **int fastethernet 0/0** (or **int fa 0/0**).

For the ISR series, it's basically the same, only you get even more options. For example, the built-in Fast Ethernet interfaces work with the same syntax I just used in the last example with the 2600 series:

```
Todd(config)#int fastEthernet 0/?
  <0-1>  FastEthernet interface number
Todd(config)#int fastEthernet 0/0
Todd(config-if)#
```

The rest of the modules are different. They use three numbers instead of two. The first 0 is the router itself, and then you choose the slot, and then the port. Here's an example of a serial interface on my 2811:

```
Todd(config)#interface serial ?
  <0-2>  Serial interface number
Todd(config)#interface serial 0/0/?
  <0-1>  Serial interface number
Todd(config)#interface serial 0/0/0
Todd(config-if)#
```

This can look a little dicey, but I promise it's really not that hard. It helps to remember that you should always view a running-config output first so that you know the interfaces with which you have to deal. Here's my 2801 output:

```
Todd(config-if)#do show run
Building configuration...
```

```
[output cut]
!
interface FastEthernet0/0
 no ip address
 shutdown
 duplex auto
 speed auto
!
interface FastEthernet0/1
 no ip address
 shutdown
 duplex auto
 speed auto
!
interface Serial0/0/0
 no ip address
 shutdown
 no fair-queue
!
interface Serial0/0/1
 no ip address
 shutdown
!
interface Serial0/1/0
 no ip address
 shutdown
!
interface Serial0/2/0
 no ip address
 shutdown
 clock rate 2000000
!
 [output cut]
```

For the sake of brevity, I didn't include my complete running-config, but I displayed all you need. You can see the two built-in Fast Ethernet interfaces, the two serial interfaces in slot 0 (0/0/0 and 0/0/1), the serial interface in slot 1 (0/1/0), and the serial interface in slot 2 (0/2/0). Once you see the interfaces like this, it's a lot easier to understand how the modules are inserted into the router.

Just understand that if you type **interface e0** on a 2500, **interface fastethernet 0/0** on a 2600, or **interface serial 0/1/0** on a 2800, all you're doing is choosing an interface to configure—and basically, they're all configured the same way after that.

I'm going to continue with the router interface discussion in the next sections. I'll include how to bring up the interface and set an IP address on a router interface.

Bringing Up an Interface

You can disable an interface with the interface command `shutdown` and enable it with the `no shutdown` command.

If an interface is shut down, it will display `administratively down` when you use the `show interfaces` command (`sh int` for short) as shown here:

```
Todd#sh int f0/1
FastEthernet0/1 is administratively down, line protocol is down
[output cut]
```

Another way to check an interface's status is via the `show running-config` command. All interfaces are shut down by default. You can bring up the interface with the `no shutdown` command (`no shut` for short) as shown here:

```
Todd#config t
Todd(config)#int f0/1
Todd(config-if)#no shutdown
Todd(config-if)#
*Feb 28 22:45:08.455: %LINK-3-UPDOWN: Interface FastEthernet0/1,
     changed state to up
Todd(config-if)#do show int f0/1
FastEthernet0/1 is up, line protocol is up
[output cut]
```

Configuring an IP Address on an Interface

Although it's not a requirement, IP is the most common LAN protocol used on a router and the most common type of interface addressing you will perform. To configure IP addresses on an interface, use the `ip address` command from interface configuration mode as follows:

```
Todd(config)#int f0/1
Todd(config-if)#ip address 172.16.10.2 255.255.255.0
```

Don't forget to enable the interface with the `no shutdown` command. Remember to look at the command `show interface` *int* to see if it's administratively shut down or not. The `show running-config` command will also give you this information.

 The `ip address` *address mask* command starts the IP processing on the interface.

Serial Interface Commands

Before you configure a serial interface, you'll need some key information. The interface will usually be attached to a CSU/DSU type of device that provides clocking for the line to the router, as shown in Figure 4.3.

FIGURE 4.3 A typical WAN connection

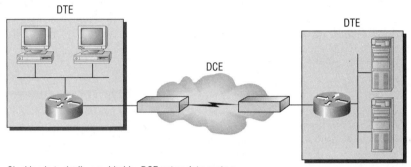

Clocking is typically provided by DCE network to routers.
In nonproduction environments, a DCE network is not always present.

Here you can see that the serial interface is used to connect to a DCE network via a CSU/DSU that provides the clocking to the router interface. If you have a back-to-back configuration (for example, one that's used in a lab environment as in Figure 4.4), one end—the data communication equipment (DCE) end of the cable—must provide clocking.

By default, Cisco routers are all data terminal equipment (DTE) devices, which means that you must configure an interface to provide clocking if you need it to act as a DCE device. Again, you would not provide clocking on a production T1 connection, for example, because you would have a CSU/DSU connected to your serial interface, as Figure 4.4 shows.

FIGURE 4.4 Providing clocking in a nonproduction network

Set clock rate if needed.

Todd#config t
Todd(config)#interface serial 0
Todd(config-if)#clock rate 64000

DCE

DTE

DCE side determined by cable.
Add clocking to DCE side only.

show controllers will show the cable connection type.

You configure a DCE serial interface with the clock rate command, like this:

```
Todd#config t
Enter configuration commands, one per line. End with CNTL/Z.
Todd(config)#int s0/0/0
Todd(config-if)#clock rate 1000000
```

The clock rate command is set in bits per second. Besides looking at the cable end to check for a label of DCE or DTE, you can see if a router's serial interface has a DCE cable connected with the show controllers int command as shown here:

```
Todd#sh controllers s0/0/0
Interface Serial0/0/0
Hardware is GT96K
DTE V.35idb at 0x4342FCB0, driver data structure at 0x434373D4
```

Here is an example of an output that shows a DCE connection:

```
Todd#sh controllers s0/2/0
Interface Serial0/2/0
Hardware is GT96K
DCE V.35, clock rate 1000000
```

The next command you need to get acquainted with is the bandwidth command. Every Cisco router ships with a default serial link bandwidth of T1 (1.544Mbps), but this has nothing to do with how data is transferred over a link. The bandwidth of a serial link is used by routing protocols such as EIGRP and OSPF to calculate the best cost (path) to a remote network. So, if you're using RIP routing, the bandwidth setting of a serial link is irrelevant because RIP uses only hop count to determine that.

Here's an example using the **bandwidth** command:

```
Todd#config t
Todd(config)#int s0/0/0
Todd(config-if)#bandwidth ?
  <1-10000000>  Bandwidth in kilobits
  inherit       Specify that bandwidth is inherited
  receive       Specify receive-side bandwidth
Todd(config-if)#bandwidth 1000
```

Note that, unlike the clock rate command, the bandwidth command is configured in kilobits.

 Even though the new ISR router automatically detects the DCE connection and sets the clock rate to 2000000, you should still understand how to use the clock rate command.

Viewing, Saving, and Erasing Configurations

You can manually save the file from DRAM to NVRAM by using the `copy running-config startup-config` command (or the shortcut `copy run start`), as shown here:

```
Todd#copy running-config startup-config
Destination filename [startup-config]? [press enter]
Building configuration...
[OK]
Todd#
Building configuration...
```

When you see a question with an answer in [], it means that if you just press Enter, you're choosing the default answer.

Also, when the command asked for the destination filename, the default answer was `startup-config`. It asks for one because you can copy the configuration pretty much anywhere you want to copy it. Take a look:

```
Todd#copy running-config ?
  archive:        Copy to archive: file system
  flash:          Copy to flash: file system
  ftp:            Copy to ftp: file system
  http:           Copy to http: file system
  https:          Copy to https: file system
  ips-sdf         Update (merge with) IPS signature configuration
  null:           Copy to null: file system
  nvram:          Copy to nvram: file system
  rcp:            Copy to rcp: file system
  running-config  Update (merge with) current system configuration
  scp:            Copy to scp: file system
  startup-config  Copy to startup configuration
  syslog:         Copy to syslog: file system
  system:         Copy to system: file system
  tftp:           Copy to tftp: file system
  xmodem:         Copy to xmodem: file system
  ymodem:         Copy to ymodem: file system
```

You can view the files by typing **show running-config** or **show startup-config** from privileged mode. The `sh run` command, which is a shortcut for `show running-config`, tells you that you are viewing the current configuration:

```
Todd#show running-config
Building configuration...
```

```
Current configuration : 3343 bytes
!
version 12.4
[output cut]
```

The sh start command—one of the shortcuts for the show startup-config command—indicates the configuration that will be used the next time the router is reloaded. It also indicates how much NVRAM is being used to store the startup-config file. Here's an example:

```
Todd#show startup-config
Using 1978 out of 245752 bytes
!
version 12.4
[output cut]
```

Verifying Your Configuration

Once you take a look at the running-config, if all appears well, you can verify your configuration with utilities such as ping and Telnet. Ping is Packet Internet Groper, a program that uses ICMP echo requests and replies. Ping sends a packet to a remote host. If that host responds, you know that the host is alive—but you don't know if it's alive and also *well*. Just because you can ping a Microsoft server does not mean you can log in. Even so, ping is an awesome starting point for troubleshooting an internetwork.

You can also ping with different protocols. You can test this by typing **ping ?** at either the router user-mode or privileged-mode prompt, as shown here:

```
Router#ping ?
  WORD       Ping destination address or hostname
  appletalk  Appletalk echo
  clns       CLNS echo
  decnet     DECnet echo
  ip         IP echo
  ipv6       IPv6 echo
  ipx        Novell/IPX echo
  srb        srb echo
  tag        Tag encapsulated IP echo
  <cr>
```

If you want to find a neighbor's Network layer address, you need to access the router or switch and type **show cdp entry * protocol** from that device to get the Network layer addresses you need for pinging.

Traceroute uses ICMP with IP time to live (TTL) time-outs to track the path a packet takes through an internetwork, in contrast to ping, which just finds the host and responds. Traceroute can also be used with multiple protocols.

```
Router#traceroute ?
  WORD       Trace route to destination address or hostname
  appletalk  AppleTalk Trace
  clns       ISO CLNS Trace
  ip         IP Trace
  ipv6       IPv6 Trace
  ipx        IPX Trace
  <cr>
```

Telnet, FTP, and HTTP use IP at the Network layer and TCP at the Transport layer to create a session with a remote host, and as such are really the best tools for verifying connectivity at the IP layer. If you can Telnet, ftp, or http into a device, your IP connectivity just has to be good.

```
Router#telnet ?
WORD IP address or hostname of a remote system
<cr>
```

From the router prompt, you just type a hostname or IP address, and it will assume you want to Telnet—you don't need to type the actual `telnet` command.

In the following sections, I am going to show you how to verify the interface statistics.

Verifying with the *show interface* Command

Another way to verify your configuration is by typing `show interface` commands, the first of which is `show interface ?`. That will reveal all the available interfaces to configure.

> The `show interfaces` command displays the configurable parameters and statistics of all interfaces on a router.

This command is very useful for verifying and troubleshooting router and network issues. The following output is from my freshly erased and rebooted 2811 router:

```
Router#sh int ?
  Async         Async interface
  BVI           Bridge-Group Virtual Interface
  CDMA-Ix       CDMA Ix interface
  CTunnel       CTunnel interface
  Dialer        Dialer interface
  FastEthernet  FastEthernet IEEE 802.3
```

```
Loopback           Loopback interface
MFR                Multilink Frame Relay bundle interface
Multilink          Multilink-group interface
Null               Null interface
Port-channel       Ethernet Channel of interfaces
Serial             Serial
Tunnel             Tunnel interface
Vif                PGM Multicast Host interface
Virtual-PPP        Virtual PPP interface
Virtual-Template   Virtual Template interface
Virtual-TokenRing  Virtual TokenRing
accounting         Show interface accounting
counters           Show interface counters
crb                Show interface routing/bridging info
dampening          Show interface dampening info
description        Show interface description
etherchannel       Show interface etherchannel information
irb                Show interface routing/bridging info
mac-accounting     Show interface MAC accounting info
mpls-exp           Show interface MPLS experimental accounting info
precedence         Show interface precedence accounting info
pruning            Show interface trunk VTP pruning information
rate-limit         Show interface rate-limit info
stats              Show interface packets & octets, in & out, by switching
                   path
status             Show interface line status
summary            Show interface summary
switching          Show interface switching
switchport         Show interface switchport information
trunk              Show interface trunk information
|                  Output modifiers
<cr>
```

The only "real" physical interfaces are Fast Ethernet, Serial, and Async; the rest are all logical interfaces or commands with which to verify.

The next command is show interface fastethernet 0/0. It reveals the hardware address, logical address, and encapsulation method, as well as statistics on collisions, as shown here:

```
Router#sh int f0/0
FastEthernet0/0 is up, line protocol is up
  Hardware is MV96340 Ethernet, address is 001a.2f55.c9e8 (bia 001a.2f55.c9e8)
  Internet address is 192.168.1.33/27
```

```
MTU 1500 bytes, BW 100000 Kbit, DLY 100 usec,
    reliability 255/255, txload 1/255, rxload 1/255
  Encapsulation ARPA, loopback not set
  Keepalive set (10 sec)
  Auto-duplex, Auto Speed, 100BaseTX/FX
  ARP type: ARPA, ARP Timeout 04:00:00
  Last input never, output 00:02:07, output hang never
  Last clearing of "show interface" counters never
  Input queue: 0/75/0/0 (size/max/drops/flushes); Total output drops: 0
  Queueing strategy: fifo
  Output queue: 0/40 (size/max)
  5 minute input rate 0 bits/sec, 0 packets/sec
  5 minute output rate 0 bits/sec, 0 packets/sec
      0 packets input, 0 bytes
      Received 0 broadcasts, 0 runts, 0 giants, 0 throttles
      0 input errors, 0 CRC, 0 frame, 0 overrun, 0 ignored
      0 watchdog
      0 input packets with dribble condition detected
      16 packets output, 960 bytes, 0 underruns
      0 output errors, 0 collisions, 0 interface resets
      0 babbles, 0 late collision, 0 deferred
      0 lost carrier, 0 no carrier
      0 output buffer failures, 0 output buffers swapped out
Router#
```

The preceding interface is working and looks to be in good shape. The show interfaces command will show you if you are receiving errors on the interface. It will also show you the maximum transmission units (MTUs), bandwidth (BW), reliability (255/255 means perfect), and load (1/255 means no load).

You can see the bandwidth is 100,000Kbit, which is 100,000,000 (Kbit means to add three zeros), which is 100Mbits per second, or FastEthernet. Gigabit would be 1,000,000Kbits per second.

The most important statistic of the show interface command is the output of the line and data-link protocol status. If the output reveals that FastEthernet 0/0 is up and the line protocol is up, then the interface is up and running:

```
Router#sh int fa0/0
FastEthernet0/0 is up, line protocol is up
```

The first parameter refers to the Physical layer, and it's up when it receives carrier detect. The second parameter refers to the Data Link layer, and it looks for keepalives from the connecting end. (*Keepalives* are used between devices to make sure that connectivity has not dropped.)

Here's an example of where the problem usually is found—on serial interfaces:

```
Router#sh int s0/0/0
Serial0/0 is up, line protocol is down
```

If you see that the line is up but the protocol is down, as shown in the preceding example, you're experiencing a clocking (keepalive) or framing problem—which is possibly an encapsulation mismatch. Check the keepalives on both ends to make sure that they match, that the clock rate is set, if needed, and that the encapsulation type is the same on both ends. Therefore, the output in the preceding example would be considered a Data Link layer problem.

If you discover that both the line interface and the protocol are down, it's a cable or interface problem. The following output would be considered a Physical layer problem:

```
Router#sh int s0/0/0
Serial0/0 is down, line protocol is down
```

If one end is administratively shut down (as shown in the following example), the remote end would present as down:

```
Router#sh int s0/0/0
Serial0/0 is administratively down, line protocol is down
```

To enable the interface, use the command no shutdown from interface configuration mode.

The next show interface serial 0/0/0 command demonstrates the serial line and the maximum transmission unit (MTU)—1,500 bytes by default. It also shows the default bandwidth (BW) on all Cisco serial links: 1.544Kbps. This is used to determine the bandwidth of the line for routing protocols such as EIGRP and OSPF. Another important configuration to notice is the keepalive, which is 10 seconds by default. Each router sends a keepalive message to its neighbor every 10 seconds, and if both routers aren't configured for the same keepalive time, it won't work.

```
Router#sh int s0/0/0
Serial0/0 is up, line protocol is up
 Hardware is HD64570
 MTU 1500 bytes, BW 1544 Kbit, DLY 20000 usec,
   reliability 255/255, txload 1/255, rxload 1/255
 Encapsulation HDLC, loopback not set, keepalive set
  (10 sec)
 Last input never, output never, output hang never
 Last clearing of "show interface" counters never
 Queueing strategy: fifo
 Output queue 0/40, 0 drops; input queue 0/75, 0 drops
 5 minute input rate 0 bits/sec, 0 packets/sec
```

```
5 minute output rate 0 bits/sec, 0 packets/sec
  0 packets input, 0 bytes, 0 no buffer
  Received 0 broadcasts, 0 runts, 0 giants, 0 throttles
  0 input errors, 0 CRC, 0 frame, 0 overrun, 0 ignored,
  0 abort
  0 packets output, 0 bytes, 0 underruns
  0 output errors, 0 collisions, 16 interface resets
  0 output buffer failures, 0 output buffers swapped out
  0 carrier transitions
  DCD=down DSR=down DTR=down RTS=down CTS=down
```

You can clear the counters on the interface by typing the command **clear counters**, as shown here:

```
Router#clear counters ?
  Async            Async interface
  BVI              Bridge-Group Virtual Interface
  CTunnel          CTunnel interface
  Dialer           Dialer interface
  FastEthernet     FastEthernet IEEE 802.3
  Group-Async      Async Group interface
  Line             Terminal line
  Loopback         Loopback interface
  MFR              Multilink Frame Relay bundle interface
  Multilink        Multilink-group interface
  Null             Null interface
  Serial           Serial
  Tunnel           Tunnel interface
  Vif              PGM Multicast Host interface
  Virtual-Template  Virtual Template interface
  Virtual-TokenRing  Virtual TokenRing
  <cr>

Router#clear counters s0/0/0
Clear "show interface" counters on this interface
  [confirm][Enter]
Router#
00:17:35: %CLEAR-5-COUNTERS: Clear counter on interface
  Serial0/0/0 by console
Router#
```

Verifying with the *show ip interface* Command

The show ip interface command will provide you with information regarding the layer 3 configurations of a router's interfaces, as in the following example:

```
Router#sh ip interface
FastEthernet0/0 is up, line protocol is up
  Internet address is 1.1.1.1/24
  Broadcast address is 255.255.255.255
  Address determined by setup command
  MTU is 1500 bytes
  Helper address is not set
  Directed broadcast forwarding is disabled
  Outgoing access list is not set
  Inbound  access list is not set
  Proxy ARP is enabled
  Security level is default
  Split horizon is enabled
[output cut]
```

This output includes the status of the interface, the IP address and mask, information on whether an access list is set on the interface, and basic IP information.

Using the *show ip interface brief* Command

The show ip interface brief command is probably one of the most helpful commands that you can ever use on a Cisco router. This command provides a quick overview of the router's interfaces, including the logical address and status:

```
Router#sh ip int brief
Interface        IP-Address      OK? Method Status    Protocol
FastEthernet0/0  unassigned      YES unset  up          up
FastEthernet0/1  unassigned      YES unset  up          up
Serial0/0/0      unassigned      YES unset  up          down
Serial0/0/1      unassigned      YES unset  administratively down down
Serial0/1/0      unassigned      YES unset  administratively down down
Serial0/2/0      unassigned      YES unset  administratively down down
```

Remember, administratively down means that you need to type no shutdown under the interface configuration. Notice that Serial0/0/0 is up/down, which means that the Physical layer is good and carrier detect is sensed, but no keepalives are being received from the remote end. In a nonproduction network, like the one I am working with, the clock rate isn't set.

Exam Essentials

Remember how to enable a router interface.   From within the interface configuration, use the no shutdown command to enable a router interface.

Identify and configure router interfaces.   Use the show interfaces command to identify your router interface and the interface command at the global configuration prompt to configure the interface.

Determine the DCE end of a back-to-back serial connection and configure clocking.   In a lab environment, one end of the cable should be marked DCE. If you're trying to determine this remotely, you can use the show versions command to identify the DCE end of the cable. The clock rate command is used to set the clock rate on the DCE end.

View, edit, save, and delete configurations.   Use the show running-config and the show startup-config commands to view the configuration in RAM and NVRAM, respectively. To save changes made to the running-config, use the copy start run command.

Understand the output from the show interface command.   An interface should show that Serial0/0 is up and line protocol is up, which means all is operational. If it shows Serial0/0 is up and line protocol is down, then you have a Data Link layer problem. If Serial0/0 is down and line protocol is down, then there is a Physical layer problem.

Verify Device Configuration and Network Connectivity Using ping, traceroute, Telnet, SSH, or Other Utilities

For coverage of this objective, please see the section titled "Verify Network Status and Switch Operation Using Basic Utilities (Including ping, traceroute, Telnet, SSH, arp, and ipconfig) and *SHOW* and *DEBUG* Commands)" in Chapter 2, as well as the section titled "Access and Utilize the Router to Set Basic Parameters (Including CLI/SDM)" in this chapter.

Perform and Verify Routing Configuration Tasks for a Static or Default Route Given Specific Routing Requirements

A fundamental knowledge of routing is required to pass the CCNA exam. This section will provide a solid review of static and default routing.

Static routing occurs when you manually add routes in each router's routing table. There are pros and cons to static routing, but that's true for all routing processes.

Static routing has the following benefits:

- There is no overhead on the router CPU, which means that you could possibly buy a cheaper router than you would need if you were using dynamic routing.

- There is no bandwidth usage between routers, which means that you could possibly save money on WAN links.

- It adds security, because the administrator can choose to allow routing access to certain networks only.

Static routing has the following disadvantages:

- The administrator must really understand the internetwork and how each router is connected in order to configure routes correctly.

- If a network is added to the internetwork, the administrator has to add a route to it on all routers—by hand.

- It's not feasible in large networks because maintaining it would be a full-time job in itself.

The command syntax you use to add a static route to a routing table is as follows:

```
ip route [destination_network] [mask] [next-hop_address or
  exitinterface] [administrative_distance] [permanent]
```

Here's a description of each command in the string:

ip route   The command used to create the static route.

destination_network   The network you're placing in the routing table.

mask   The subnet mask being used on the network.

next-hop_address   The address of the next-hop router that will receive the packet and forward it to the remote network. This is a router interface that's on a directly connected network. You must be able to ping the router interface before you add the route. If you type in the wrong next-hop address or the interface to that router is down, the static route will show up in the router's configuration but not in the routing table.

exitinterface   You can use this instead of the next-hop address if you want, and it will show up as a directly connected route.

administrative_distance   By default, static routes have an administrative distance of 1 (or even 0 if you use an exit interface instead of a next-hop address). You can change the default value by adding an administrative weight at the end of the command. I'll talk a lot more about this subject later in the chapter when we get to the section entitled "Compare and Contrast Methods of Routing and Routing Protocols."

permanent   If the interface is shut down or the router can't communicate with the next-hop router, the route will automatically be discarded from the routing table. Choosing the permanent option keeps the entry in the routing table no matter what happens.

Before we dive into configuring static routes, let's take a look at the following sample static route:

```
Router(config)#ip route 172.16.3.0 255.255.255.0 192.168.2.4
```

Here is how this command is interpreted:

- The ip route command tells you simply that it is a static route.
- 172.16.3.0 is the remote network to which you want to send packets.
- 255.255.255.0 is the mask of the remote network.
- 192.168.2.4 is the next hop, or router, to which you will send packets.

To configure a default route, you use wildcards in the network address and mask locations of a static route. In fact, you can just think of a default route as a static route that uses wildcards instead of network and mask information.

There's another command you can use to configure a gateway of last resort—the ip default-network command. Figure 4.5 shows a network that needs to have a gateway-of-last-resort statement configured.

FIGURE 4.5   Configuring a gateway of last resort

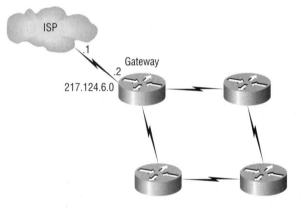

The interface leading to the ISP is Serial 0/0. Here are three commands (all providing the same solution) for adding a gateway of last resort on the gateway router to the ISP:

```
Gateway(config)#ip route 0.0.0.0 0.0.0.0 217.124.6.1
```

```
Gateway(config)#ip route 0.0.0.0 0.0.0.0 s0/0
```

```
Gateway(config)#ip default-network 217.124.6.0
```

As I said, all three of these commands would accomplish the goal of setting the gateway of last resort, but there are some small differences between them. First, the exit interface solution would be used over the other two solutions because it has an AD of 0. Also, the `ip default-network` command would advertise the default network when you configure an IGP (like RIP) on the router. This is so other routers in your internetwork will receive this route as a default route automatically.

Exam Essentials

Understand how to configure a static route.   A static route is configured from global configuration mode. Here is the command structure: `ip route` *remote_network remote_mask next_hop_address/exit_interface*.

Understand how to configure a default route, which is also called a gateway of last resort. A default route is configured from global configuration mode. Here is the command structure: `ip route 0.0.0.0 0.0.0.0` *next_hop_address/exit_interface*.

Compare and contrast static and dynamic routing.   Static routing creates less network traffic and fewer CPU cycles on the router but cannot choose the best router or react to outages. Dynamic routing creates more traffic and workload on the router but can choose the best route and react to outages.

Manage IOS Configuration Files (Including Save, Edit, Upgrade, and Restore)

Any changes that you make to the router configuration are stored in the `running-config` file. If you don't enter a `copy run start` command after you make a change to `running-config`, that change will not be saved if the router reboots or is powered down. So, you will probably want to make another backup of the configuration information just in case the router or switch completely dies on you. Even if your machine is healthy and happy, it's good to have a backup copy of the configuration for reference and documentation.

   In the following sections, I'll describe how to copy the configuration of a router to a TFTP server and how to restore that configuration.

Backing Up the Cisco Router Configuration

To copy the router's configuration from a router to a TFTP server, you can use either the `copy running-config tftp` or the `copy startup-config tftp` command. Either one will back up the router configuration that's currently running in DRAM or that's stored in NVRAM.

Verifying the Current Configuration

To verify the configuration in DRAM, use the show running-config command (sh run for short) like this:

```
Router#show running-config
Building configuration...

Current configuration : 776 bytes
!
version 12.4
```

The current configuration information indicates that the router is running version 12.4 of the IOS.

Verifying the Stored Configuration

Next, you should check the configuration stored in NVRAM. To see this, use the show startup-config command (sh start for short) like this:

```
Router#show startup-config
Using 776 out of 245752 bytes
!
version 12.4
```

The second line shows you how much room your backup configuration is using. Here, you can see that NVRAM is 239KB (again, memory is easier to see with the show version command when using an ISR router) and that only 776 bytes of it are used.

If you're not sure that the files are the same and the running-config file is what you want, you can use the copy running-config startup-config command to verify that both files are, in fact, the same. I'll go through this with you in the next section.

Copying the Current Configuration to NVRAM

To ensure that your running-config will always be reloaded if the router is rebooted, you should copy it to NVRAM where it will become the startup-config. In the new IOS version 12.0, you're prompted for the filename you want to use.

```
Router#copy running-config startup-config
Destination filename [startup-config]?[enter]
Building configuration...
[OK]
Router#
```

The filename prompt appears because the copy command has many options, as shown in the following output:

```
Router#copy running-config ?
  archive:         Copy to archive: file system
  flash:           Copy to flash: file system
  ftp:             Copy to ftp: file system
  http:            Copy to http: file system
  https:           Copy to https: file system
  ips-sdf          Update (merge with) IPS signature configuration
  null:            Copy to null: file system
  nvram:           Copy to nvram: file system
  rcp:             Copy to rcp: file system
  running-config   Update (merge with) current system configuration
  scp:             Copy to scp: file system
  startup-config   Copy to startup configuration
  syslog:          Copy to syslog: file system
  system:          Copy to system: file system
  tftp:            Copy to tftp: file system
  xmodem:          Copy to xmodem: file system
  ymodem:          Copy to ymodem: file system
```

We'll go over the copy command again in a minute.

Copying the Configuration to a TFTP Server

Once the file is copied to NVRAM, you can make a second backup to a TFTP server by using the copy running-config tftp command (copy run tftp for short), like this:

```
Router#copy running-config tftp
Address or name of remote host []?1.1.1.2
Destination filename [router-confg]?todd-confg
!!
776 bytes copied in 0.800 secs (970 bytes/sec)
Router#
```

In the preceding example, I entered the IP address of the TFTP server and named the file todd-confg because I had not set a hostname for the router. If you have a hostname already configured, the command will automatically use that hostname plus the extension -confg as the name of the file.

Restoring the Cisco Router Configuration

If you've changed your router's running-config file and want to restore the configuration to the version in the startup-config file, the easiest way to do this is to use the copy startup-config running-config command (copy start run for short). You can also use the older Cisco command config mem to restore a configuration. Of course, this will work only if you first copied running-config into NVRAM before making any changes.

If you did copy the router's configuration to a TFTP server as a second backup, you can restore the configuration using the copy tftp running-config command (copy tftp run for short) or the copy tftp startup-config command (copy tftp start for short), as shown here:

```
Router#copy tftp running-config
Address or name of remote host []?1.1.1.2
Source filename []?todd-confg
Destination filename[running-config]?[enter]
Accessing tftp://1.1.1.2/todd-confg...
Loading todd-confg from 1.1.1.2 (via FastEthernet0/0): !
[OK - 776 bytes]
776 bytes copied in 9.212 secs (84 bytes/sec)
Router#
*Mar  7 17:53:34.071: %SYS-5-CONFIG_I: Configured from
    tftp://1.1.1.2/todd-confg by console
Router#
```

The configuration file is an ASCII text file, meaning that before you copy the configuration stored on a TFTP server back to a router, you can make changes to the file with any text editor. Also, notice that the command was changed to a URL of tftp://1.1.1.2/todd-config.

 It is important to remember that when you copy or merge a configuration from a TFTP server to a router's RAM, the interfaces are shut down by default and you must manually enable each interface with the no shutdown command.

Erasing the Configuration

To delete the startup-config file on a Cisco router, use the command erase startup-config, like this:

```
Router#erase startup-config
Erasing the nvram filesystem will remove all configuration files!
    Continue? [confirm][enter]
[OK]
Erase of nvram: complete
*Mar  7 17:56:20.407: %SYS-7-NV_BLOCK_INIT: Initialized the geometry of nvram
```

```
Router#reload
System configuration has been modified. Save? [yes/no]:n
Proceed with reload? [confirm][enter]
 *Mar  7 17:56:31.059: %SYS-5-RELOAD: Reload requested by console.
   Reload Reason: Reload Command.
```

This command deletes the contents of NVRAM on the router. Typing **reload** at the privileged mode prompt and typing no to save changes will cause the router to reload and come up into setup mode.

Exam Essentials

Remember how to save the configuration of a router.   There are a couple of ways to do this, but the most common (and the most tested) method is copy running-config startup-config.

Remember how to erase the configuration of a router.   Type the privileged-mode command erase startup-config and reload the router.

Manage Cisco IOS

Before you upgrade or restore a Cisco IOS, you should copy the existing file to a TFTP host as a backup just in case the new image crashes and burns. You can use any TFTP host to accomplish this. By default, the flash memory in a router is used to store the Cisco IOS. In the following sections, I'll describe how to check the amount of flash memory, how to copy the Cisco IOS from flash memory to a TFTP host, and how to copy the IOS from a TFTP host to flash memory.

But before you back up an IOS image to a network server on your intranet, you've got to do these three things:

- Make sure that you can access the network server.
- Ensure that the network server has adequate space for the code image.
- Verify the file naming and path requirements.

If you have a laptop or a workstation's Ethernet port directly connected to a router's Ethernet interface (as shown in Figure 4.6), you need to verify the following before attempting to copy the image to or from the router:

- The TFTP server software must be running on the administrator's workstation.
- The Ethernet connection between the router and the workstation must be made with a crossover cable.
- The workstation must be on the same subnet as the router's Ethernet interface.

- The copy flash tftp command must be supplied the IP address of the workstation if you are copying from the router flash.
- If you're copying "into" flash, you need to verify that there's enough room in flash memory to accommodate the file to be copied.

FIGURE 4.6   Copying an IOS from a workstation to a router

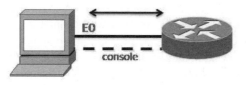

Verifying Flash Memory

Before you attempt to upgrade the Cisco IOS on your router with a new IOS file, it's a good idea to verify that your flash memory has enough room to hold the new image. You can verify the amount of flash memory and the file or files being stored in flash memory by using the show flash command (sh flash for short), like this:

```
Router#sh flash
-#- --length-- -----date/time------ path
1      21710744 Jan 2 2007 22:41:14 +00:00 c2800nm-advsecurityk9-mz.124-12.bin
[output cut]
32989184 bytes available (31027200 bytes used)
```

The ISR router in this example has 64MB of RAM, and roughly half of the memory is in use.

The show flash command will display the amount of memory consumed by the current IOS image, as well as the amount of memory available to hold current and new images. If there is not enough room for both the old and new images you want to load, the old image will be erased!

The amount of flash is actually easier to tally using the show version command on the ISR routers, as shown in the following example:

```
Router#show version
[output cut]
Cisco 2811 (revision 49.46) with 249856K/12288K bytes of memory.
Processor board ID FTX1049A1AB
2 FastEthernet interfaces
```

```
4 Serial(sync/async) interfaces
1 Virtual Private Network (VPN) Module
DRAM configuration is 64 bits wide with parity enabled.
239K bytes of non-volatile configuration memory.
62720K bytes of ATA CompactFlash (Read/Write)
```

You can see that the amount of flash shows up on the last line. By averaging up, you get 64MB of flash.

Notice that the filename in the show flash command example is c2800nm-advsecurityk9-mz.124-12.bin. The main difference in the output of the show flash and show version commands is that the show flash command displays the actual name of the file that the router is using to run the router, and the show version command shows all files in flash.

Backing Up the Cisco IOS

To back up the Cisco IOS to a TFTP server, you use the copy flash tftp command. It's a straightforward command that requires only the source filename and the IP address of the TFTP server.

The key to success in this backup routine is to make sure that you've got good, solid connectivity to the TFTP server. Check this by pinging the TFTP device from the router console prompt like this:

```
Router#ping 1.1.1.2
Type escape sequence to abort.
Sending 5, 100-byte ICMP Echos to 1.1.1.2, timeout
  is 2 seconds:
!!!!!
Success rate is 100 percent (5/5), round-trip min/avg/max
  = 4/4/8 ms
```

After you ping the TFTP server to make sure that IP is working, you can use the copy flash tftp command to copy the IOS to the TFTP server as shown here:

```
Router#copy flash tftp
Source filename []?c2800nm-advsecurityk9-mz.124-12.bin
Address or name of remote host []?1.1.1.2
Destination filename [c2800nm-advsecurityk9-mz.124-12.bin]?[enter]
!!!!!!!!!!!!!!!!!!!!!!!!!!!!!!!!!!!!!!!!!!!!!!!!!!!!!!!!!!!!!!!!!!!!!!!!!!!!!!!!!!!!
!!!!!!
21710744 bytes copied in 60.724 secs (357532 bytes/sec)
Router#
```

Just copy the IOS filename from either the show flash or show version command and then paste it when prompted for the source filename.

In the preceding example, the contents of flash memory were copied successfully to the TFTP server. The address of the remote host is the IP address of the TFTP host, and the source filename is the file in flash memory.

Restoring or Upgrading the Cisco Router IOS

If you need to restore the Cisco IOS to flash memory to replace an original file that has been damaged or if you want to upgrade the IOS, you can download the file from a TFTP server to flash memory by using the `copy tftp flash` command. This command requires the IP address of the TFTP host and the name of the file you want to download.

But before you begin, make sure that the file you want to place in flash memory is in the default TFTP directory on your host. When you issue the command, TFTP won't ask you where the file is, so if the file you want to use isn't in the default directory of the TFTP host, this just won't work.

```
Router#copy tftp flash
Address or name of remote host []?1.1.1.2
Source filename []?c2800nm-advsecurityk9-mz.124-12.bin
Destination filename [c2800nm-advsecurityk9-mz.124-12.bin]?[enter]
%Warning:There is a file already existing with this name
Do you want to over write? [confirm][enter]
Accessing tftp://1.1.1.2/c2800nm-advsecurityk9-mz.124-12.bin...
Loading c2800nm-advsecurityk9-mz.124-12.bin from 1.1.1.2 (via
    FastEthernet0/0): !!!!!!!!!!!!!!!!!!!!!!!!!!!!!!!!!!!!!!!!!!!!!!!!!!!!!!!!!!!
!!!!!!!!!!!!!!!!!!!!!!!!!!
[OK - 21710744 bytes]

21710744 bytes copied in 82.880 secs (261954 bytes/sec)
Router#
```

In this example, I copied the same file into flash memory, so it asked me if I wanted to overwrite it. Remember that I am "playing" with files in flash memory. If I just corrupted my file by overwriting the file, I wouldn't know this until I rebooted the router. When you're working with this command, be careful. If the file is corrupted, you'll need to do an IOS restore from ROMMON.

If you are loading a new file and you don't have enough room in flash memory to store both the new and existing copies, the router will ask to erase the contents of flash memory before writing the new file into flash memory.

Exam Essentials

Remember how to back up an IOS image.   By using the privileged-mode command copy flash tftp, you can back up a file from flash memory to a TFTP (network) server.

Remember how to restore or upgrade an IOS image.   By using the privileged-mode command copy tftp flash, you can restore or upgrade a file from a TFTP (network) server to flash memory.

Remember what you must complete before you back up an IOS image to a network server. Make sure that you can access the network server, ensure that the network server has adequate space for the code image, and verify the file naming and path requirements.

Compare and Contrast Methods of Routing and Routing Protocols

A *routing protocol* is used by routers to dynamically find all the networks in the internetwork and to ensure that all routers have the same routing table. Basically, a routing protocol determines the path of a packet through an internetwork. Examples of routing protocols are RIP, RIPv2, EIGRP, and OSPF.

Once all routers know about all networks, a *routed protocol* can be used to send user data (packets) through the established enterprise. Routed protocols are assigned to an interface and determine the method of packet delivery. Examples of routed protocols are IP and IPv6.

The *administrative distance (AD)* is used to rate the trustworthiness of routing information received on a router from a neighboring router. An administrative distance is an integer from 0 to 255, where 0 is the most trusted and 255 means no traffic will be passed via this route.

If a router receives two updates listing the same remote network, the first thing the router will check will be the AD. If one of the advertised routes has a lower AD than the other, then the route with the lowest AD will be placed in the routing table.

If both advertised routes to the same network have the same AD, then routing protocol metrics (such as *hop count* or bandwidth of the lines) will be used to find the best path to the remote network. The advertised route with the lowest metric will be placed in the routing table. If both advertised routes have the same AD as well as the same metrics, then the routing protocol will load-balance to the remote network (which means that it will send packets down each link).

Table 4.4 shows the default administrative distances that a Cisco router uses to decide which route to take to a remote network.

TABLE 4.4   Default Administrative Distances

Route Source	Default AD
Connected interface	0
Static route	1
EIGRP	90

Route Source	Default AD
IGRP	100
OSPF	110
RIP	120
External EIGRP	170
Unknown	255 (this route will never be used)

If a network is directly connected, the router will always use the interface connected to the network. If you configure a static route, the router will then believe that route over any other learned routes. You can change the administrative distance of static routes; by default, they have an AD of 1. For example, you might set the AD of a static route to 150 or 151. This would let you configure routing protocols without having to remove the static routes. They can be used as backup routes in case the routing protocol experiences a failure of some type.

For example, if you have a static route, a RIP-advertised route, and an IGRP-advertised route listing the same network, then, by default, the router will always use the static route unless you change the AD of the static route.

Routing Protocols

There are three classes of routing protocols:

Distance-Vector   The *distance-vector protocols* find the best path to a remote network by judging distance. Each time a packet goes through a router, that's called a *hop*. The route with the least number of hops to the network is determined to be the best route. The vector indicates the direction to the remote network. Both RIP and IGRP are distance-vector routing protocols. They send the entire routing table to directly connected neighbors.

Link-State   In *link-state protocols*, also called *shortest-path-first protocols*, the routers each create three separate tables. One of these tables keeps track of directly attached neighbors, one determines the topology of the entire internetwork, and one is used as the routing table. Link-state routers know more about the internetwork than any distance-vector routing protocol. OSPF is an IP routing protocol that is completely link-state. Link-state protocols send updates containing the state of their own links to all other routers on the network.

Hybrid   *Hybrid protocols* use aspects of both distance-vector and link-state—for example, EIGRP.

There's no set way of configuring routing protocols for use with every business. This is something you have to do on a case-by-case basis. If you understand how the different routing protocols work, you can make good, solid decisions that truly meet the individual needs of any business.

Exam Essentials

Be able to define a routing protocol. A *routing protocol* is used by routers to dynamically find all the networks in the internetwork and to ensure that all routers have the same routing table. Basically, a routing protocol determines the path of a packet through an internetwork. Examples of routing protocols are RIP, RIPv2, EIGRP, and OSPF.

Be able to define a routed protocol. Once all routers know about all networks, a *routed protocol* can be used to send user data (packets) through the established enterprise. Routed protocols are assigned to an interface and determine the method of packet delivery. Examples of routed protocols are IP and IPv6.

Define the three types of routing protocols. Routing protocols can be distance-vector, link-state, or hybrid. The distance-vector protocols find the best path to a remote network by judging distance. In link-state protocols, also called shortest-path-first protocols, the routers each create three separate tables. One of these tables keeps track of directly attached neighbors, one determines the topology, and one is used as the routing table. Hybrid protocols use aspects of both distance-vector and link-state—for example, EIGRP.

Configure, Verify, and Troubleshoot OSPF

Open Shortest Path First (OSPF) is an open standard routing protocol that's been implemented by a wide variety of network vendors, including Cisco. If you have multiple routers and not all of them are Cisco routers, then you can't use a Cisco proprietary protocol like EIGRP. So, your remaining CCNA objective options are basically RIP, RIPv2, and OSPF.

OSPF works by using the *Dijkstra algorithm*. First, a shortest path tree is constructed, and then the routing table is populated with the resulting best paths. OSPF converges quickly (although perhaps not as quickly as EIGRP), and it supports multiple, equal-cost routes to the same destination. Like EIGRP, it does support both IP and IPv6 routed protocols.

OSPF provides the following features:

- Consists of areas and autonomous systems
- Minimizes routing update traffic
- Allows scalability
- Supports VLSM/CIDR
- Has unlimited hop count
- Allows multi-vendor deployment (open standard)

OSPF is the first link-state routing protocol that most people are introduced to, so it's useful to see how it compares to more traditional distance-vector protocols such as RIPv2 and RIPv1. Table 4.5 gives you a comparison of these three protocols.

TABLE 4.5   OSPF and RIP Comparison

Characteristic	OSPF	RIPv2	RIPv1
Type of protocol	Link state	Distance vector	Distance vector
Classless support	Yes	Yes	No
VLSM support	Yes	Yes	No
Auto-summarization	No	Yes	Yes
Manual summarization	Yes	No	No
Discontiguous support	Yes	Yes	No
Route propagation	Multicast on change	Periodic multicast	Periodic broadcast
Path metric	Bandwidth	Hops	Hops
Hop count limit	None	15	15
Convergence	Fast	Slow	Slow
Peer authentication	Yes	Yes	No
Hierarchical network	Yes (using areas)	No (flat only)	No (flat only)
Updates	Event triggered	Route table updates	Route table updates
Route computation	Dijkstra	Bellman-Ford	Bellman-Ford

OSPF has many features beyond the few listed in Table 4.5, and all of them contribute to a fast, scalable, and robust protocol that can be actively deployed in thousands of production networks.

OSPF is designed to be implemented in a hierarchical fashion, which means separating the larger internetwork into smaller internetworks called *areas*. This is the best design for OSPF.

Here are some reasons for creating an OSPF hierarchically:

- To decrease routing overhead
- To speed up convergence
- To confine network instability to single areas of the network

These benefits make the additional configuration required by OSPF worth the effort.

Figure 4.7 shows a typical OSPF simple design. Notice how each router connects to the backbone—called *area 0*, or the *backbone area*. OSPF must have an area 0, and all other areas should connect to this area. (Areas that do not connect directly to area 0 by using virtual links are beyond the scope of this book.) Routers that connect other areas to the backbone area within an AS are called *Area Border Routers* (ABRs). Still, at least one interface of the ABR must be in area 0.

FIGURE 4.7   An OSPF design

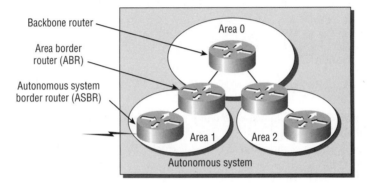

OSPF runs inside an autonomous system, but it can also connect multiple autonomous systems. The router that connects these ASs is called an *Autonomous System Boundary Router (ASBR)*.

Ideally, you would create other areas of networks to help keep route updates to a minimum and to keep problems from propagating throughout the network. However, that's beyond the scope of this chapter. Just make note of it.

Configuring OSPF Areas

After identifying the OSPF process, you need to identify the interfaces that you want to activate OSPF communications on as well as the area in which each resides. This will also configure the networks you're going to advertise to others. OSPF uses wildcards in the configuration—which are also used in access-list configurations.

Here's an OSPF basic configuration example:

```
Lab_A#config t
Lab_A(config)#router ospf 1
Lab_A(config-router)#network 10.0.0.0 0.255.255.255
 area ?
  <0-4294967295>  OSPF area ID as a decimal value
  A.B.C.D         OSPF area ID in IP address format
Lab_A(config-router)#network 10.0.0.0 0.255.255.255
 area 0
```

The areas can be any number from 0 to 4.2 billion. Don't get these numbers confused with the Process ID, which is from 1 to 65,535.

Remember, the OSPF Process ID number is irrelevant. It can be the same on every router on the network, or it can be different—it doesn't matter. It's locally significant and just enables the OSPF routing on the router.

There are several ways to verify proper OSPF configuration and operation. In the following sections, we'll review the OSPF show commands that you need to know in order to do this.

The *show ip route* Command

Let's start by taking a quick look at the routing table of a router named Corp by issuing a show ip route command with the following output:

```
    10.0.0.0/24 is subnetted, 12 subnets
O       10.1.11.0 [110/65] via 10.1.5.2, 00:01:31, Serial0/2/0
O       10.1.10.0 [110/65] via 10.1.5.2, 00:01:31, Serial0/2/0
O       10.1.9.0 [110/74] via 10.1.4.2, 00:01:31, Serial0/1/0
O       10.1.8.0 [110/65] via 10.1.4.2, 00:01:31, Serial0/1/0
O       10.1.12.0 [110/66] via 10.1.5.2, 00:01:31, Serial0/2/0
C       10.1.3.0 is directly connected, Serial0/0/1
C       10.1.2.0 is directly connected, Serial0/0/0
C       10.1.1.0 is directly connected, FastEthernet0/1
O       10.1.7.0 [110/74] via 10.1.3.2, 00:01:32, Serial0/0/1
                 [110/74] via 10.1.2.2, 00:01:32, Serial0/0/0
O       10.1.6.0 [110/74] via 10.1.3.2, 00:01:32, Serial0/0/1
                 [110/74] via 10.1.2.2, 00:01:32, Serial0/0/0
C       10.1.5.0 is directly connected, Serial0/2/0
C       10.1.4.0 is directly connected, Serial0/1/0
```

The Corp router shows the found routes for 12 networks, with the O representing OSPF internal routes (the Cs are obviously the directly connected networks). It also found dual routes to networks 10.1.6.0 and 10.1.7.0. No bandwidth or delay commands were executed under the interfaces, so the defaults are being used to determine the metric—but remember, OSPF uses only bandwidth to determine the best path to a network.

This is important: OSPF can load-balance only across links of equal costs. It can't load-balance across unequal-cost links as EIGRP can.

Next, I'll show you all the OSPF verification commands that you need to know.

The *show ip ospf* Command

The show ip ospf command is used to display OSPF information for one or all OSPF processes running on the router. Information contained therein includes the Router ID, area information, SPF statistics, and LSA timer information. Let's check the output from the Corp router:

```
Corp#sh ip ospf
 Routing Process "ospf 132" with ID 10.1.5.1
 Start time: 04:32:04.116, Time elapsed: 01:27:10.156
[output cut]
```

Notice the Router ID (RID) of 10.1.5.1, which is the highest IP address configured on the router.

The *show ip ospf database* Command

The show ip ospf database command will give you information about the number of routers in the internetwork (AS) plus the neighboring router's ID (this is the topology database I mentioned earlier). Unlike the show ip eigrp topology command, this command shows the "OSPF routers," not each and every link in the AS as EIGRP does.

The output is broken down by area. Here's a sample output, again from Corp:

```
Corp#sh ip ospf database

        OSPF Router with ID (10.1.5.1) (Process ID 132)

          Router Link States (Area 0)

Link ID        ADV Router      Age       Seq#       Checksum Link count
10.1.5.1       10.1.5.1        72        0x80000002 0x00F2CA 9
10.1.7.1       10.1.7.1        83        0x80000004 0x009197 6
10.1.9.1       10.1.9.1        73        0x80000001 0x00DA1C 4
10.1.11.1      10.1.11.1       67        0x80000005 0x00666A 4
10.1.12.1      10.1.12.1       67        0x80000004 0x007631 2

          Net Link States (Area 0)

Link ID        ADV Router      Age       Seq#       Checksum
10.1.11.2      10.1.12.1       68        0x80000001 0x00A337
```

You can see five routers and the RID of each router (the highest IP address on each router). The router output shows the link ID (remember that an interface is also a link) and the RID of the router on that link under the ADV router, or advertising router.

The *show ip ospf interface* Command

The show ip ospf interface command displays all interface-related OSPF information. Data is displayed about OSPF information for all interfaces or for specified interfaces. The following example shows the key information in boldface type:

```
Corp#sh ip ospf interface f0/1
FastEthernet0/1 is up, line protocol is up
  Internet Address 10.1.1.1/24, Area 0
  Process ID 132, Router ID 10.1.5.1, Network Type BROADCAST, Cost: 1
  Transmit Delay is 1 sec, State DR, Priority 1
  Designated Router (ID) 10.1.5.1, Interface address 10.1.1.1
  No backup designated router on this network
  Timer intervals configured, Hello 10, Dead 40, Wait 40, Retransmit 5
    oob-resync timeout 40
    Hello due in 00:00:01
  Supports Link-local Signaling (LLS)
  Index 1/1, flood queue length 0
  Next 0x0(0)/0x0(0)
  Last flood scan length is 0, maximum is 0
  Last flood scan time is 0 msec, maximum is 0 msec
  Neighbor Count is 0, Adjacent neighbor count is 0
  Suppress hello for 0 neighbor(s)
```

The following information is displayed by this command:

- Interface IP address
- Area assignment
- Process ID
- Router ID
- Network type
- Cost
- Priority
- DR/BDR election information (if applicable)
- Hello and Dead timer intervals
- Adjacent neighbor information

I used the show ip ospf interface f0/1 command because I knew that there would be a designated router elected on the FastEthernet broadcast multi-access network. We'll get into DR and DBR elections in detail in a minute.

The *show ip ospf neighbor* Command

The show ip ospf neighbor command is very useful because it summarizes the pertinent OSPF information regarding neighbors and the adjacency state. If a DR or BDR exists, that information will also be displayed. Here's a sample:

```
Corp#sh ip ospf neighbor
Neighbor ID   Pri   State     Dead Time     Address      Interface
10.1.11.1      0    FULL/  -  00:00:37      10.1.5.2     Serial0/2/0
10.1.9.1       0    FULL/  -  00:00:34      10.1.4.2     Serial0/1/0
10.1.7.1       0    FULL/  -  00:00:38      10.1.3.2     Serial0/0/1
10.1.7.1       0    FULL/  -  00:00:34      10.1.2.2     Serial0/0/0
```

It is important for you to understand this command, because it's extremely useful in production networks.

Let's take a look at the R3 and 871W routers' outputs:

```
R3#sh ip ospf neighbor
Neighbor ID   Pri   State     Dead Time     Address      Interface
10.1.5.1       0    FULL/  -  00:00:39      10.1.5.1     Serial0/0/1
10.1.11.2      1    FULL/BDR  00:00:31      10.1.11.2    FastEthernet0/1
871W#sh ip ospf nei
Neighbor ID   Pri   State     Dead Time     Address      Interface
10.1.11.1      1    FULL/DR   00:00:30      10.1.11.1    Vlan1
```

Because there's an Ethernet link (broadcast multi-access) on the Corp router, there's going to be an election to determine which will be the designated router and which will be the non-designated router. You can see that R3 became the designated router, and it won because it had the highest IP address on the network. You can change this, but that's the default.

The Serial 0/0/1 connection on Corp doesn't have a DR or BDR listed in the output because elections don't happen on point-to-point links by default. However, you can see that the Corp router is fully adjacent to two routers from its output.

Debugging OSPF

Debugging is a great tool for any protocol. Table 4.6 describes a few debugging commands for troubleshooting OSPF.

TABLE 4.6 Debugging Commands for Troubleshooting OSPF

Command	Description/Function
debug ip ospf packet	Shows Hello packets being sent and received on your router.

Command	Description/Function
debug ip ospf hello	Shows Hello packets being sent and received on your router. Shows more detail than the debug ip ospf packet output.
debug ip ospf adj	Shows DR and DBR elections on a broadcast and nonbroadcast multi-access network.

I'll start by showing you the output from the Corp router I received using the debug ip ospf packet command:

```
Corp#debug ip ospf packet
OSPF packet debugging is on
*Mar 23 01:20:42.199: OSPF: rcv. v:2 t:1 l:48 rid:172.16.10.3
     aid:0.0.0.0 chk:8075 aut:0 auk: from Serial0/1/0
Corp#
*Mar 23 01:20:45.507: OSPF: rcv. v:2 t:1 l:48 rid:172.16.10.2
     aid:0.0.0.0 chk:8076 aut:0 auk: from Serial0/0/0
*Mar 23 01:20:45.531: OSPF: rcv. v:2 t:1 l:48 rid:172.16.10.2
     aid:0.0.0.0 chk:8076 aut:0 auk: from Serial0/0/1
*Mar 23 01:20:45.531: OSPF: rcv. v:2 t:1 l:48 rid:172.16.10.4
     aid:0.0.0.0 chk:8074 aut:0 auk: from Serial0/2/0
*Mar 23 01:20:52.199: OSPF: rcv. v:2 t:1 l:48 rid:172.16.10.3
     aid:0.0.0.0 chk:8075 aut:0 auk: from Serial0/1/0
*Mar 23 01:20:55.507: OSPF: rcv. v:2 t:1 l:48 rid:172.16.10.2
     aid:0.0.0.0 chk:8076 aut:0 auk: from Serial0/0/0
*Mar 23 01:20:55.527: OSPF: rcv. v:2 t:1 l:48 rid:172.16.10.2
     aid:0.0.0.0 chk:8076 aut:0 auk: from Serial0/0/1
*Mar 23 01:20:55.531: OSPF: rcv. v:2 t:1 l:48 rid:172.16.10.4
     aid:0.0.0.0 chk:8074 aut:0 auk: from Serial0/2/0
```

In the preceding output, you can see that the router is both sending and receiving Hello packets every 10 seconds from neighbor (adjacent) routers. The next command will provide the same information, but with more detail. For example, you can see the multicast address used (224.0.0.5) and the area:

```
Corp#debug ip ospf hello
*Mar 23 01:18:41.103: OSPF: Send hello to 224.0.0.5 area 0 on
   Serial0/1/0 from 10.1.4.1
*Mar 23 01:18:41.607: OSPF: Send hello to 224.0.0.5 area 0 on
   FastEthernet0/1 from 10.1.1.1
```

```
*Mar 23 01:18:41.607: OSPF: Send hello to 224.0.0.5 area 0 on
   Serial0/0/0 from 10.1.2.1
*Mar 23 01:18:41.611: OSPF: Send hello to 224.0.0.5 area 0 on
   Serial0/2/0 from 10.1.5.1
*Mar 23 01:18:41.611: OSPF: Send hello to 224.0.0.5 area 0 on
   Serial0/0/1 from 10.1.3.1
*Mar 23 01:18:42.199: OSPF: Rcv hello from 172.16.10.3 area 0 from
   Serial0/1/0 10.1.4.2
*Mar 23 01:18:42.199: OSPF: End of hello processing
*Mar 23 01:18:45.519: OSPF: Rcv hello from 172.16.10.2 area 0 from
   Serial0/0/0 10.1.2.2
*Mar 23 01:18:45.519: OSPF: End of hello processing
*Mar 23 01:18:45.543: OSPF: Rcv hello from 172.16.10.2 area 0 from
   Serial0/0/1 10.1.3.2
*Mar 23 01:18:45.543: OSPF: End of hello processing
*Mar 23 01:18:45.543: OSPF: Rcv hello from 172.16.10.4 area 0 from
   Serial0/2/0 10.1.5.2
*Mar 23 01:18:45.543: OSPF: End of hello processing
```

The last debug command I'm going show you is the debug ip ospf adj command, which displays elections as they occur on broadcast and nonbroadcast multi-access networks:

```
Corp#debug ip ospf adj
OSPF adjacency events debugging is on
*Mar 23 01:24:34.823: OSPF: Interface FastEthernet0/1 going Down
*Mar 23 01:24:34.823: OSPF: 172.16.10.1 address 10.1.1.1 on
   FastEthernet0/1 is dead, state DOWN
*Mar 23 01:24:34.823: OSPF: Neighbor change Event on interface
   FastEthernet0/1
*Mar 23 01:24:34.823: OSPF: DR/BDR election on FastEthernet0/1
*Mar 23 01:24:34.823: OSPF: Elect BDR 0.0.0.0
*Mar 23 01:24:34.823: OSPF: Elect DR 0.0.0.0
*Mar 23 01:24:34.823: OSPF: Elect BDR 0.0.0.0
*Mar 23 01:24:34.823: OSPF: Elect DR 0.0.0.0
*Mar 23 01:24:34.823:          DR: none      BDR: none
*Mar 23 01:24:34.823: OSPF: Flush network LSA immediately
*Mar 23 01:24:34.823: OSPF: Remember old DR 172.16.10.1 (id)
*Mar 23 01:24:35.323: OSPF: We are not DR to build Net Lsa for
   interface FastEthernet0/1
*Mar 23 01:24:35.323: OSPF: Build router LSA for area 0, router ID
   172.16.10.1, seq 0x80000006
*Mar 23 01:24:35.347: OSPF: Rcv LS UPD from 172.16.10.2 on Serial0/0/1
   length 148 LSA count 1
```

```
*Mar 23 01:24:40.703: OSPF: Interface FastEthernet0/1 going Up
*Mar 23 01:24:41.203: OSPF: Build router LSA for area 0, router ID
    172.16.10.1, seq 0x80000007
*Mar 23 01:24:41.231: OSPF: Rcv LS UPD from 172.16.10.2 on Serial0/0/1
    length 160 LSA count 1
```

Exam Essentials

Be able to configure a single-area OSPF. A minimal single-area configuration involves only two commands: router ospf *process-id* and network *x.x.x.x y.y.y.y area Z*.

Be able to verify the operation of OSPF. There are many show commands that provide useful details on OSPF. You should be familiar with the output of each of the following:

> show ip ospf
>
> show ip ospf database
>
> show ip ospf interface
>
> show ip ospf neighbor
>
> show ip protocols

List the features of OSPF. OSPF provides the following features:

- Consists of areas and autonomous systems
- Minimizes routing update traffic
- Allows scalability
- Supports VLSM/CIDR
- Has unlimited hop count
- Allows multi-vendor deployment (open standard)

Contrast RIPv1, RIPv2, and OSPF. Understand the differences between these protocols as listed in Table 4.5: OSPF and RIP comparison.

List the benefits of a hierarchical OSPF design. The benefits of a hierarchical OSPF design are

- To speed up convergence
- To decrease routing overhead
- To confine network instability to single areas of the network

Configure, Verify, and Troubleshoot EIGRP

You can enter EIGRP commands using two modes: router configuration mode and interface configuration mode. *Router configuration mode* is used to enable the protocol, specify which networks will run EIGRP, and set global characteristics. *Interface configuration mode* is used to customize summaries, metrics, timers, and bandwidth.

To start an EIGRP session on a router, use the `router eigrp` command followed by the autonomous system number of your network. Then enter the network numbers connected to the router using the `network` command followed by the network number.

Let's look at an example of enabling EIGRP for autonomous system 20 on a router connected to two networks, with the network numbers being 10.3.1.0/24 and 172.16.10.0/24:

```
Router#config t
Router(config)#router eigrp 20
Router(config-router)#network 172.16.0.0
Router(config-router)#network 10.0.0.0
```

As with RIP, you use the classful network address (all subnet and host bits turned off) for EIGRP.

The AS number is irrelevant—as long as all routers use the same number. You can use any number from 1 to 65,535.

Verifying EIGRP

There are several commands that you can use on a router to troubleshoot and verify the EIGRP. Table 4.7 lists all of the most important commands that are used in conjunction with verifying EIGRP operation. It also offers a brief description of what each command does.

TABLE 4.7   EIGRP Troubleshooting Commands

Command	Description/Function
show ip route	Shows the entire routing table
show ip route eigrp	Shows only EIGRP entries in the routing table
show ip eigrp neighbors	Shows all EIGRP neighbors
show ip eigrp topology	Shows entries in the EIGRP topology table
debug eigrp packet	Shows Hello packets sent/received between adjacent routers
debug ip eigrp notification	Shows EIGRP changes and updates as they occur on your network

I'll demonstrate how you would use the commands in Table 4.7 on a router named Corp that is configured with EIGRP.

The following router output is from the Corp router in the example:

```
Corp#sh ip route
      10.0.0.0/24 is subnetted, 12 subnets
D        10.1.11.0 [90/2172416] via 10.1.5.2, 00:01:05, Serial0/2/0
D        10.1.10.0 [90/2195456] via 10.1.5.2, 00:01:05, Serial0/2/0
D        10.1.9.0 [90/2195456] via 10.1.4.2, 00:01:05, Serial0/1/0
D        10.1.8.0 [90/2195456] via 10.1.4.2, 00:01:05, Serial0/1/0
D        10.1.12.0 [90/2172416] via 10.1.5.2, 00:01:05, Serial0/2/0
C        10.1.3.0 is directly connected, Serial0/0/1
C        10.1.2.0 is directly connected, Serial0/0/0
C        10.1.1.0 is directly connected, FastEthernet0/1
D        10.1.7.0 [90/2195456] via 10.1.2.2, 00:01:06, Serial0/0/0
D        10.1.6.0 [90/2195456] via 10.1.2.2, 00:01:06, Serial0/0/0
C        10.1.5.0 is directly connected, Serial0/2/0
C        10.1.4.0 is directly connected, Serial0/1/0
```

Notice that EIGRP routes are indicated with simply a D designation (DUAL) and that the default AD of these routes is 90. This represents internal EIGRP routes.

Let's see what's in Corp's neighbor table:

```
Corp#sh ip eigrp neighbors
IP-EIGRP neighbors for process 10
```

H	Address	Interface	Hold Uptime	SRTT	RTO	Q	Seq
			(sec)	(ms)		Cnt	Num
1	10.1.3.2	Se0/0/1	14 00:35:10	1	200	0	81
3	10.1.5.2	Se0/2/0	10 02:51:22	1	200	0	31
2	10.1.4.2	Se0/1/0	13 03:17:20	1	200	0	20
0	10.1.2.2	Se0/0/0	10 03:19:37	1	200	0	80

Here is what this table tells us:

- The H field indicates the order in which the neighbor was discovered.

- The hold time is how long this router will wait for a Hello packet to arrive from a specific neighbor.

- The uptime indicates how long the neighborship has been established.

- The SRTT field is the smooth round-trip timer—an indication of the time it takes for a round trip from this router to its neighbor and back. This value is used to determine how long to wait after a multicast for a reply from this neighbor. If a reply isn't received in time, the router will switch to using unicasts in an attempt to complete the communication.

Now let's see what's in the Corp topology table by using the show ip eigrp topology command:

```
Corp#sh ip eigrp topology
IP-EIGRP Topology Table for AS(10)/ID(10.1.5.1)
Codes: P - Passive, A - Active, U - Update, Q - Query, R - Reply,
       r - reply Status, s - sia Status
P 10.1.11.0/24, 1 successors, FD is 2172416
        via 10.1.5.2 (2172416/28160), Serial0/2/0
P 10.1.10.0/24, 1 successors, FD is 2172416
        via 10.1.5.2 (2195456/281600), Serial0/2/0
P 10.1.9.0/24, 1 successors, FD is 2195456
        via 10.1.4.2 (2195456/281600), Serial0/1/0
P 10.1.8.0/24, 1 successors, FD is 2195456
        via 10.1.4.2 (2195456/72960), Serial0/1/0
P 10.1.12.0/24, 1 successors, FD is 2172416
        via 10.1.5.2 (2172416/28160), Serial0/2/0
P 10.1.3.0/24, 1 successors, FD is 76839936
        via Connected, Serial0/0/1
        via 10.1.2.2 (9849856/7719936), Serial0/0/0
P 10.1.2.0/24, 1 successors, FD is 2169856
        via Connected, Serial0/0/0
        via 10.1.2.2 (2681856/551936), Serial0/0/0
P 10.1.1.0/24, 1 successors, FD is 28160
        via Connected, FastEthernet0/1
P 10.1.7.0/24, 1 successors, FD is 793600
        via 10.1.2.2 (2195456/281600), Serial0/0/0
        via 10.1.3.2 (77081600/281600), Serial0/0/1
P 10.1.6.0/24, 1 successors, FD is 793600
        via 10.1.2.2 (2195456/281600), Serial0/0/0
        via 10.1.3.2 (77081600/281600), Serial0/0/1
P 10.1.5.0/24, 1 successors, FD is 2169856
        via Connected, Serial0/2/0
P 10.1.4.0/24, 1 successors, FD is 2169856
        via Connected, Serial0/1/0
```

Notice that every route is preceded by a P. This means that the route is in the *passive state*, which is a good thing because routes in the *active state* (A) indicate that the router has lost its path to this network and is searching for a replacement. Each entry also indicates the *feasible distance*, or FD, to each remote network plus the next-hop neighbor through which packets will travel to their destination. Plus, each entry also has two numbers in parentheses. The first indicates the feasible distance, and the second the advertised distance to a remote network.

Now here's where things get interesting—notice that under the 10.1.7.0 and 10.1.6.0 outputs there are two links to each network and that the feasible distance and advertised distance are different. What this means is that there is one successor to the networks and one feasible successor—a backup route! You need to remember that even though both routes to network 10.1.6.0 and 10.1.7.0 are in the topology table, only the successor route (the one with the lowest metrics) will be copied and placed into the routing table.

 In order for the route to be a feasible successor, its advertised distance must be less than the feasible distance of the successor route.

EIGRP will load-balance across both links automatically when they are of equal variance (equal cost), but EIGRP can load-balance across unequal-cost links as well if you use the variance command. The variance metric is set to 1 by default, meaning that only equal-cost links will load-balance. You can increase the metric value to a maximum of 128. Changing a variance value enables EIGRP to install multiple, loop-free routes with unequal cost in a local routing table.

So basically, if the variance is set to 1, only routes with the same metric as the successor will be installed in the local routing table. For example, if the variance is set to 2, any EIGRP-learned route with a metric less than two times the successor metric will be installed in the local routing table (if it is already a feasible successor).

Now's a great time for us to check out some debugging outputs. First, let's use the debug eigrp packet command that will show the Hello packets being sent between neighbor routers:

```
Corp#debug eigrp packet
EIGRP Packets debugging is on
    (UPDATE, REQUEST, QUERY, REPLY, HELLO, IPXSAP, PROBE, ACK, STUB,
    SIAQUERY, SIAREPLY)
Corp#
*Mar 21 23:17:35.050: EIGRP: Sending HELLO on FastEthernet0/1
*Mar 21 23:17:35.050:    AS 10, Flags 0x0, Seq 0/0 idbQ 0/0 iidbQ un/rely 0/0
*Mar 21 23:17:35.270: EIGRP: Received HELLO on Serial0/1/0 nbr 10.1.4.2
*Mar 21 23:17:35.270:    AS 10, Flags 0x0, Seq 0/0 idbQ 0/0 iidbQ
    un/rely 0/0 peerQ un/rely 0/0
*Mar 21 23:17:35.294: EIGRP: Received HELLO on Serial0/0/0 nbr 10.1.2.2
*Mar 21 23:17:35.294:    AS 10, Flags 0x0, Seq 0/0 idbQ 0/0 iidbQ
    un/rely 0/0 peerQ un/rely 0/0
*Mar 21 23:17:38.014: EIGRP: Received HELLO on Serial0/2/0 nbr 10.1.5.2
*Mar 21 23:17:38.014:    AS 10, Flags 0x0, Seq 0/0 idbQ 0/0 iidbQ
    un/rely 0/0 peerQ un/rely 0/0
```

Exam Essentials

Know the EIGRP features. EIGRP is a classless, advanced distance-vector protocol that supports IP, IPX, AppleTalk, and now IPv6. EIGRP uses a unique algorithm, called DUAL, to maintain route information and uses RTP to communicate with other EIGRP routers reliably.

Know how to configure EIGRP. Be able to configure basic EIGRP. This is configured the same as IGRP with classful addresses.

Know how to verify EIGRP operation. Know all of the EIGRP show commands and be familiar with their output and the interpretation of the main components of their output.

Verify Network Connectivity (Including Using ping, traceroute, and Telnet or SSH)

For information on these objectives, please see the section titled "Verify Device Configuration and Network Connectivity Using ping, traceroute, Telnet, SSH, or other Utilities" earlier in this chapter.

Troubleshoot Routing Issues

The best troubleshooting tools are show and debug commands, specifically show ip protocols and various routing protocol debugging commands. Let's take a look.

First, the show ip protocols command will show you the routing protocols configured on your router. Hopefully, you have only one. Here is an example:

```
Router#sh ip protocols
Routing Protocol is "rip"
  Outgoing update filter list for all interfaces is not set
  Incoming update filter list for all interfaces is not set
  Sending updates every 30 seconds, next due in 27 seconds
  Invalid after 180 seconds, hold down 180, flushed after 240
  Redistributing: rip
  Default version control: send version 2, receive version 2
    Interface        Send  Recv  Triggered RIP  Key-chain
    FastEthernet0/1   2     2
    Serial0/0/1       2     2
  Automatic network summarization is not in effect
  Maximum path: 4
```

```
Routing for Networks:
  10.0.0.0
Passive Interface(s):
  FastEthernet0/0
  Serial0/0/0
Routing Information Sources:
  Gateway         Distance      Last Update
  10.1.11.2         120         00:00:00
  10.1.5.1          120         00:00:02
Distance: (default is 120)
```

This router output shows that the router is running RIPv2, the interfaces participating in the routing process, the next-hop gateways (neighbors), and the administrative distance. Also, you can see that the maximum path is 4, which means that RIP will load-balance across four equal-cost links by default.

There are dozens of debugging commands you can use, and for RIP, the debug ip rip command is the best tool for debugging RIP routing.

```
*Mar 17 19:34:00.123: RIP: sending v2 update to 224.0.0.9 via
   Serial0/0/1 (10.1.5.2)
*Mar 17 19:34:00.123: RIP: build update entries
*Mar 17 19:34:00.123:   10.1.10.0/24 via 0.0.0.0, metric 1, tag 0
*Mar 17 19:34:00.123:   10.1.11.0/24 via 0.0.0.0, metric 1, tag 0
*Mar 17 19:34:00.123:   10.1.12.0/24 via 0.0.0.0, metric 2, tag 0col
*Mar 17 19:34:03.795: RIP: received v2 update from 10.1.5.1 on
   Serial0/0/1
```

This debugging output shows that RIPv2 is running with multicast address 224.0.0.9.

For EIGRP, I am going to show you two commands—the debug eigrp packet command and the debug ip eigrp notification command:

```
Router#debug eigrp packet
EIGRP Packets debugging is on
    (UPDATE, REQUEST, QUERY, REPLY, HELLO, IPXSAP, PROBE, ACK, STUB,
    SIAQUERY, SIAREPLY)
*Mar 21 23:17:35.050: EIGRP: Sending HELLO on FastEthernet0/1
*Mar 21 23:17:35.050:   AS 10, Flags 0x0, Seq 0/0 idbQ 0/0 iidbQ un/rely 0/0
*Mar 21 23:17:35.270: EIGRP: Received HELLO on Serial0/1/0 nbr 10.1.4.2
*Mar 21 23:17:35.270:   AS 10, Flags 0x0, Seq 0/0 idbQ 0/0 iidbQ
   un/rely 0/0 peerQ un/rely 0/0
*Mar 21 23:17:35.294: EIGRP: Received HELLO on Serial0/0/0 nbr 10.1.2.2
*Mar 21 23:17:35.294:   AS 10, Flags 0x0, Seq 0/0 idbQ 0/0 iidbQ
   un/rely 0/0 peerQ un/rely 0/0
```

```
*Mar 21 23:17:38.014: EIGRP: Received HELLO on Serial0/2/0 nbr 10.1.5.2
*Mar 21 23:17:38.014:    AS 10, Flags 0x0, Seq 0/0 idbQ 0/0 iidbQ
   un/rely 0/0 peerQ un/rely 0/0
```

The EIGRP 224.0.0.10 multicast is sent out every 5 seconds, and the Hello packets are sent out of every active interface, as well as all the interfaces to which neighbors are connected. Did you notice the AS number provided in the update? It is provided because the Hello update will just be discarded if a neighbor doesn't have the same AS number.

The debug ip eigrp notification command (called debug ip eigrp events on pre-12.4 routers) shouldn't show you anything at all. The only time you'll see output from this command is if there's a problem on your network—or if you've added or deleted a network from a router in your internetwork. Because I have a problem-free network, I'm going to shut down an interface on my router in order to see some output:

```
Router(config)#int f0/1
Router(config-if)#shut
*Mar 21 23:25:43.506: IP-EIGRP(Default-IP-Routing-Table:10): Callback:
   route_adjust FastEthernet0/1
*Mar 21 23:25:43.506: IP-EIGRP: Callback: ignored connected AS 0 10.1.1.0/24
*Mar 21 23:25:43.506:              into: eigrp AS 10
*Mar 21 23:25:43.506: IP-EIGRP(Default-IP-Routing-Table:10): Callback:
   callbackup_routes 10.1.1.0/24
Corp(config-if)#n
*Mar 21 23:25:45.506: %LINK-5-CHANGED: Interface FastEthernet0/1,
   changed state to administratively down
*Mar 21 23:25:46.506: %LINEPROTO-5-UPDOWN: Line protocol on Interface
   FastEthernet0/1, changed state to down
Router(config-if)#no shut
Router(config-if)#^Z
*Mar 21 23:25:49.570: %LINK-3-UPDOWN: Interface FastEthernet0/1,
   changed state to up
*Mar 21 23:25:49.570: IP-EIGRP(Default-IP-Routing-Table:10): Callback:
   lostroute 10.1.1.0/24
*Mar 21 23:25:49.570: IP-EIGRP(Default-IP-Routing-Table:0): Callback:
   redist connected (config change) FastEthernet0/1
*Mar 21 23:25:49.570: IP-EIGRP(Default-IP-Routing-Table:0): Callback:
   redist connected (config change) Serial0/0/0
*Mar 21 23:25:49.570: IP-EIGRP(Default-IP-Routing-Table:0): Callback:
   redist connected (config change) Serial0/0/1
*Mar 21 23:25:49.570: IP-EIGRP(Default-IP-Routing-Table:0): Callback:
   redist connected (config change) Serial0/1/0
*Mar 21 23:25:49.570: IP-EIGRP(Default-IP-Routing-Table:0): Callback:
   redist connected (config change) Serial0/2/0
```

```
*Mar 21 23:25:49.570: IP-EIGRP(Default-IP-Routing-Table:10): Callback:
    route_adjust FastEthernet0/1
```

As previously mentioned, debugging is a great tool for any protocol. Table 4.8 describes a few debugging commands for OSPF.

TABLE 4.8 Debugging Commands for Troubleshooting OSPF

Command	Description/Function
debug ip ospf packet	Shows Hello packets being sent and received on your router
debug ip ospf hello	Shows Hello packets being sent and received on your router. Shows more detail than the debug ip ospf packet output
debug ip ospf adj	Shows DR and DBR elections on a broadcast and nonbroadcast multi-access network

I'll start by showing you the output from the router I have, using the debug ip ospf packet command:

```
Router#debug ip ospf packet
OSPF packet debugging is on
*Mar 23 01:20:42.199: OSPF: rcv. v:2 t:1 l:48 rid:172.16.10.3
     aid:0.0.0.0 chk:8075 aut:0 auk: from Serial0/1/0
*Mar 23 01:20:45.507: OSPF: rcv. v:2 t:1 l:48 rid:172.16.10.2
     aid:0.0.0.0 chk:8076 aut:0 auk: from Serial0/0/0
*Mar 23 01:20:45.531: OSPF: rcv. v:2 t:1 l:48 rid:172.16.10.2
     aid:0.0.0.0 chk:8076 aut:0 auk: from Serial0/0/1
*Mar 23 01:20:45.531: OSPF: rcv. v:2 t:1 l:48 rid:172.16.10.4
     aid:0.0.0.0 chk:8074 aut:0 auk: from Serial0/2/0
*Mar 23 01:20:52.199: OSPF: rcv. v:2 t:1 l:48 rid:172.16.10.3
     aid:0.0.0.0 chk:8075 aut:0 auk: from Serial0/1/0
*Mar 23 01:20:55.507: OSPF: rcv. v:2 t:1 l:48 rid:172.16.10.2
     aid:0.0.0.0 chk:8076 aut:0 auk: from Serial0/0/0
```

In this output, you can see that the router is both sending and receiving Hello packets every 10 seconds from neighbor (adjacent) routers. The next command will provide the same information, but with more detail. For example, you can see the multicast address used (224.0.0.5) and the area in the following output:

```
Router#debug ip ospf hello
*Mar 23 01:18:41.103: OSPF: Send hello to 224.0.0.5 area 0 on
```

```
   Serial0/1/0 from 10.1.4.1
*Mar 23 01:18:41.607: OSPF: Send hello to 224.0.0.5 area 0 on
   FastEthernet0/1 from 10.1.1.1
*Mar 23 01:18:41.607: OSPF: Send hello to 224.0.0.5 area 0 on
   Serial0/0/0 from 10.1.2.1
*Mar 23 01:18:41.611: OSPF: Send hello to 224.0.0.5 area 0 on
   Serial0/2/0 from 10.1.5.1
*Mar 23 01:18:41.611: OSPF: Send hello to 224.0.0.5 area 0 on
   Serial0/0/1 from 10.1.3.1
*Mar 23 01:18:42.199: OSPF: Rcv hello from 172.16.10.3 area 0 from
   Serial0/1/0 10.1.4.2
*Mar 23 01:18:42.199: OSPF: End of hello processing
*Mar 23 01:18:45.519: OSPF: Rcv hello from 172.16.10.2 area 0 from
   Serial0/0/0 10.1.2.2
*Mar 23 01:18:45.519: OSPF: End of hello processing
```

The last debug command I'm going show you is the debug ip ospf adj command, which displays elections as they occur on broadcast and nonbroadcast multi-access networks:

```
Router#debug ip ospf adj
OSPF adjacency events debugging is on
*Mar 23 01:24:34.823: OSPF: Interface FastEthernet0/1 going Down
*Mar 23 01:24:34.823: OSPF: 172.16.10.1 address 10.1.1.1 on
   FastEthernet0/1 is dead, state DOWN
*Mar 23 01:24:34.823: OSPF: Neighbor change Event on interface
   FastEthernet0/1
*Mar 23 01:24:34.823: OSPF: DR/BDR election on FastEthernet0/1
*Mar 23 01:24:34.823: OSPF: Elect BDR 0.0.0.0
*Mar 23 01:24:34.823: OSPF: Elect DR 0.0.0.0
*Mar 23 01:24:34.823: OSPF: Elect BDR 0.0.0.0
*Mar 23 01:24:34.823: OSPF: Elect DR 0.0.0.0
*Mar 23 01:24:34.823:          DR: none    BDR: none
*Mar 23 01:24:34.823: OSPF: Flush network LSA immediately
*Mar 23 01:24:34.823: OSPF: Remember old DR 172.16.10.1 (id)
*Mar 23 01:24:35.323: OSPF: We are not DR to build Net Lsa for
   interface FastEthernet0/1
*Mar 23 01:24:35.323: OSPF: Build router LSA for area 0, router ID
   172.16.10.1, seq 0x80000006
*Mar 23 01:24:35.347: OSPF: Rcv LS UPD from 172.16.10.2 on Serial0/0/1
   length 148 LSA count 1
*Mar 23 01:24:40.703: OSPF: Interface FastEthernet0/1 going Up
```

```
*Mar 23 01:24:41.203: OSPF: Build router LSA for area 0, router ID
   172.16.10.1, seq 0x80000007
*Mar 23 01:24:41.231: OSPF: Rcv LS UPD from 172.16.10.2 on Serial0/0/1
   length 160 LSA count 1
```

Exam Essentials

Verify EIGRP with show and debug commands.   Use the debug eigrp packet, sh ip eigrp topology, sh ip eigrp neighbors, and sh ip route commands to verify EIGRP.

Remember what the command debug ip ospf packet provides to you.   Shows Hello packets being sent and received on your router.

Remember what the command debug ip ospf hello provides to you.   Shows Hello packets being sent and received on your router. Shows more detail than the debug ip ospf packet output.

Remember what the command debug ip ospf adj provides to you.   Shows DR and DBR elections on a broadcast and nonbroadcast multi-access network.

Verify Router Hardware and Software Operation Using the *show* and *debug* Commands

You can use the ping and traceroute commands to test connectivity to remote devices, and both of them can be used with many protocols, not just IP. Don't forget that the show ip route command is a good troubleshooting command for verifying your routing table, and the show interfaces command will show you the status of each interface.

I am going to go over both the debug command and the show processes command you need to troubleshoot a router.

Using the *ping* Command

So far, you've seen many examples of pinging devices to test IP connectivity and name resolution using the DNS server. To see all the different protocols that you can use with the *ping* program, type **ping ?**:

```
Corp#ping ?
  WORD  Ping destination address or hostname
  clns  CLNS echo
```

```
ip     IP echo
srb    srb echo
tag    Tag encapsulated IP echo
<cr>
```

The ping output displays the minimum, average, and maximum times it takes for a ping packet to find a specified system and return. Here's an example:

```
Corp#ping R1
Translating "R1"...domain server (192.168.0.70)[OK]
Type escape sequence to abort.
Sending 5, 100-byte ICMP Echos to 10.2.2.2, timeout
  is 2 seconds:
!!!!!
Success rate is 100 percent (5/5), round-trip min/avg/max
  = 1/2/4 ms
Corp#
```

You can see that the DNS server was used to resolve the name, and the device was pinged in 1ms (millisecond), an average of 2ms, and up to 4ms.

The ping command can be used in user mode and privileged mode but not in configuration mode.

Using the *traceroute* Command

Traceroute (the traceroute command, or trace for short) shows the path a packet takes to get to a remote device. It uses time to live (TTL) time-outs and ICMP error messages to outline the path a packet takes through an internetwork to arrive at a remote host.

Trace (the trace command) can be used from either user mode or privileged mode. Trace allows you to determine which router in the path to an unreachable network host should be examined more closely for the cause of the network's failure.

To see the protocols that you can use with the traceroute command, type **traceroute ?**:

```
Corp#traceroute ?
  WORD       Trace route to destination address or hostname
  appletalk  AppleTalk Trace
  clns       ISO CLNS Trace
  ip         IP Trace
  ipv6       IPv6 Trace
  ipx        IPX Trace
  <cr>
```

The trace command shows the hop or hops that a packet traverses on its way to a remote device. Here's an example:

```
Corp#traceroute r1

Type escape sequence to abort.
Tracing the route to R1 (10.2.2.2)

  1 R1 (10.2.2.2) 4 msec *  0 msec
Corp#
```

You can see that the packet went through only one hop to find the destination.

 Do not get confused! You can't use the tracert command—it's a Windows command. For a router, use the traceroute command.

Here's an example of using tracert from a Windows DOS prompt (notice the command tracert):

```
C:\>tracert www.whitehouse.gov


Tracing route to a1289.g.akamai.net [69.8.201.107]
over a maximum of 30 hops:

  1      *          *          *       Request timed out.
  2    53 ms     61 ms     53 ms  hlrn-dsl-gw15-207.hlrn.qwest.net
          [207.225.112.207]
  3    53 ms     55 ms     54 ms  hlrn-agw1.inet.qwest.net [71.217.188.113]
  4    54 ms     53 ms     54 ms  hlr-core-01.inet.qwest.net [205.171.253.97]
  5    54 ms     53 ms     54 ms  apa-cntr-01.inet.qwest.net [205.171.253.26]
  6    54 ms     53 ms     53 ms  63.150.160.34
  7    54 ms     54 ms     53 ms  www.whitehouse.gov [69.8.201.107]

Trace complete.
```

Let's move on and talk about how to troubleshoot your network using the debug command.

Debugging

The debug command is a troubleshooting command that's available from the privileged exec mode of Cisco IOS. It's used to display information about various router operations and the related traffic generated or received by the router, plus any error messages.

It's a useful and informative tool, but you really need to understand some important facts about its use. Debugging is regarded as a very high-priority task, because it can consume a huge amount of resources and the router is forced to process-switch the packets being debugged. So, you don't just use debug as a monitoring tool—it's meant to be used for a short period of time and only as a troubleshooting tool. By using it, you can discover some significant facts about both working and faulty software and/or hardware components.

Because debugging output takes priority over other network traffic, and because the **debug all** command generates more output than any other debug command, it can severely diminish the router's performance—even render it unusable. So, in virtually all cases, it's best to use more-specific debug commands.

As you can see from the following output, you can't enable debugging from user mode, only privileged mode:

```
Corp>debug ?
% Unrecognized command
Corp>en
Corp#debug ?
  aaa                       AAA Authentication, Authorization and Accounting
  access-expression         Boolean access expression
  adjacency                 adjacency
  all                       Enable all debugging
[output cut]
```

If you've got the freedom to pretty much take out a router and you really want to have some fun with debugging, you can use the debug all command as shown in the following example:

```
Corp#debug all

This may severely impact network performance. Continue? (yes/[no]):yes

All possible debugging has been turned on

2d20h: SNMP: HC Timer 824AE5CC fired
2d20h: SNMP: HC Timer 824AE5CC rearmed, delay = 20000
2d20h: Serial0/0: HDLC myseq 4, mineseen 0, yourseen 0, line down
2d20h:
2d20h: Rudpv1 Sent: Pkts 0,  Data Bytes 0,  Data Pkts 0
2d20h: Rudpv1 Rcvd: Pkts 0,  Data Bytes 0,  Data Pkts 0
2d20h: Rudpv1 Discarded: 0,  Retransmitted 0
2d20h:
2d20h: RIP-TIMER: periodic timer expired
2d20h: Serial0/0: HDLC myseq 5, mineseen 0, yourseen 0, line down
2d20h: Serial0/0: attempting to restart
```

```
2d20h: PowerQUICC(0/0): DCD is up.
2d20h: is_up: 0 state: 4 sub state: 1 line: 0
2d20h:
2d20h: Rudpv1 Sent: Pkts 0,   Data Bytes 0,   Data Pkts 0
2d20h: Rudpv1 Rcvd: Pkts 0,   Data Bytes 0,   Data Pkts 0
2d20h: Rudpv1 Discarded: 0,   Retransmitted 0
2d20h: un all
All possible debugging has been turned off
Corp#
```

To disable debugging on a router, you can use the command no in front of the debug command, like this:

```
Corp#no debug all
```

I typically just use the undebug all command, because it is so easy when using the shortcut as shown here:

```
Corp#un all
```

Remember that instead of using the debug all command, it's almost always better to use specific commands—and only for short periods of time. Here's an example of deploying debug ip rip that will show you RIP updates being sent and received on a router:

```
Corp#debug ip rip
RIP protocol debugging is on
Corp#
1w4d: RIP: sending v2 update to 224.0.0.9 via Serial0/0 (192.168.12.1)
1w4d: RIP: build update entries
1w4d:    10.10.10.0/24 via 0.0.0.0, metric 2, tag 0
1w4d:    171.16.125.0/24 via 0.0.0.0, metric 3, tag 0
1w4d:    172.16.12.0/24 via 0.0.0.0, metric 1, tag 0
1w4d:    172.16.125.0/24 via 0.0.0.0, metric 3, tag 0
1w4d: RIP: sending v2 update to 224.0.0.9 via Serial0/2 (172.16.12.1)
1w4d: RIP: build update entries
1w4d:    192.168.12.0/24 via 0.0.0.0, metric 1, tag 0
1w4d:    192.168.22.0/24 via 0.0.0.0, metric 2, tag 0
1w4d: RIP: received v2 update from 192.168.12.2 on Serial0/0
1w4d:     192.168.22.0/24 via 0.0.0.0 in 1 hops
Corp#un all
```

I'm sure you can see that the debug command is a very powerful command. Because of this, I'm also sure you realize that before you use any of the debugging commands, you should make sure you check the utilization of your router. This is important because in most cases, you don't want to negatively impact the device's ability to process the packets throughput on your internetwork. You can determine a specific router's utilization information by using the show processes command.

> Remember, when you Telnet into a remote device, you will not see console messages by default. For example, you will not see debugging output. To allow console messages to be sent to your Telnet session, use the terminal monitor command.

Using the *show processes* Command

As mentioned in the previous section, you've really got to be careful when using the debug command on your devices. If your router's CPU utilization is consistently at 50 percent or more, it's probably not a good idea to type in the debug all command unless you want to see what a router looks like when it crashes.

A feasible alternative is the show processes (or show processes cpu) command, which gives you the following information:

- CPU utilization
- Active processes and the corresponding details:
  - Process ID
  - Priority
  - Scheduler test (status)
  - CPU time used
  - Number of times invoked

In the following example, the first line shows the CPU utilization output for the last 5 seconds, 1 minute, and 5 minutes. The output provides 2%/0% in front of the CPU utilization for the last 5 seconds. The first number equals the total utilization, and the second one delimits the utilization due to interrupt routines.

```
Corp#sh processes
CPU utilization for five seconds: 2%/0%; one minute: 0%; five minutes: 0%
  PID QTy       PC Runtime (ms)   Invoked   uSecs    Stacks TTY Process
    1 Cwe 8034470C           0         1        0 5804/6000   0 Chunk Manager
    2 Csp 80369A88           4      1856        2 2616/3000   0 Load Meter
    3 M*         0         112        14 800010656/12000   0 Exec
    5 Lst 8034FD9C      268246     52101     5148 5768/6000   0 Check heaps
    6 Cwe 80355E5C          20         3     6666 5704/6000   0 Pool Manager
    7 Mst 802AC3C4           0         2        0 5580/6000   0 Timers
[output cut]
```

Basically, the output from the `show processes` command shows that the router is able to process debugging commands without being overloaded.

Exam Essentials

Remember the difference between the `traceroute` and `tracert` commands.   The command `trace` (or `traceroute`) is used with Cisco routers, switches, and Unix devices. However, the command `tracert` is used on Windows devices from the DOS prompt.

Remember which command to use before debugging a router.   Before using any `debug` command on a router, you should use the `show processes` command to verify the CPU utilization.

Implement Basic Router Security

An *access list* is essentially a list of conditions that categorize packets. This can be really helpful when you need to exercise control over network traffic.

One of the most common and easiest-to-understand uses of access lists is filtering unwanted packets when implementing security policies. For example, you can set up access lists to make very specific decisions about regulating traffic patterns so they'll allow only certain hosts to access web resources on the Internet while restricting others. With the right combination of access lists, network managers arm themselves with the power to enforce nearly any security policy they can invent.

Access lists can even be used in situations that don't necessarily involve blocking packets. For example, you can use them to control which networks will or won't be advertised by dynamic routing protocols. How you configure the access list is the same. The difference here is simply how you apply it—to a routing protocol instead of an interface. When you apply an access list in this way, it's called a *distribute list*, and it doesn't stop routing advertisements—it just controls their content. You can also use access lists to categorize packets for queuing or QoS-type services and for controlling which types of traffic can activate an ISDN link.

Creating access lists is a lot like programming a series of `if-then` statements—if a given condition is met, then a given action is taken. If the specific condition isn't met, nothing happens and the next statement is evaluated. Access-list statements are basically packet filters that packets are compared against, categorized by, and acted upon accordingly. Once the lists are built, they can be applied to either inbound or outbound traffic on any interface. Applying an access list causes the router to analyze every packet crossing that interface in the specified direction and then take the appropriate action. Here are a few important rules that a packet follows when it's being compared with an access list:

- It's always compared with each line of the access list in sequential order—that is, it will always start with the first line of the access list, then go to line 2, then line 3, and so on.

- It's compared with lines of the access list only until a match is made. Once the packet matches the condition on a line of the access list, the packet is acted upon and no further comparisons take place.

- There is an *implicit deny* at the end of each access list, which means that if a packet doesn't match the condition on any of the lines in the access list, the packet will be discarded.

Each of these rules has some powerful implications when filtering IP packets with access lists, so keep in mind that creating effective access lists takes some practice.

There are two main types of access lists:

Standard Access Lists   These use only the source IP address in an IP packet as the condition test. All decisions are made based on the source IP address. This means that standard access lists basically permit or deny an entire suite of protocols. They don't distinguish among any of the many types of IP traffic such as web, Telnet, UDP, and so on.

Extended Access Lists   Extended access lists can evaluate many of the other fields in the layer 3 and layer 4 headers of an IP packet. They can evaluate source and destination IP addresses, the protocol field in the Network layer header, and the port number at the Transport layer header. This gives extended access lists the ability to make much more granular decisions when controlling traffic.

Named Access Lists   I said there were two types of access lists but I listed three! Well, technically there really are only two because *named access lists* are either standard or extended and are not actually a new type. I'm just distinguishing them because they're created and referred to differently than standard and extended access lists, but they're functionally the same.

Once you create an access list, it's not really going to do anything until you apply it. To use an access list as a packet filter, you need to apply it to an interface on the router where you want the traffic filtered—and you need to specify to which direction of traffic you want the access list applied. There's a good reason for this—you may want different controls in place for traffic leaving your enterprise destined for the Internet than you'd want for traffic coming into your enterprise from the Internet. So, by specifying the direction of traffic, you can—and frequently you'll need to—use different access lists for inbound and outbound traffic on a single interface.

Inbound Access Lists   When an access list is applied to inbound packets on an interface, those packets are processed through the access list before being routed to the outbound interface. Any packets that are denied won't be routed, because they're discarded before the routing process is invoked.

Outbound Access Lists   When an access list is applied to outbound packets on an interface, those packets are routed to the outbound interface and then processed through the access list before being queued.

Here are some general guidelines that you should follow when you're creating and implementing access lists on a router:

- You can assign only one access list per interface per protocol per direction. This means that when creating IP access lists, you can have only one inbound access list and one outbound access list per interface.

NOTE When you consider the implications of the implicit deny at the end of any access list, it makes sense that you can't have multiple access lists applied on the same interface in the same direction for the same protocol. That's because any packets that don't match some condition in the first access list would be denied, and there wouldn't be any packets left over to compare against a second access list.

- Organize your access lists so that the more-specific tests are at the top of the access list.

- Anytime a new entry is added to the access list, it will be placed at the bottom of the list. Using a text editor for access lists is highly suggested.

- You cannot remove one line from an access list. If you try to do this, you will remove the entire list. It is best to copy the access list to a text editor before trying to edit the list. The only exception is when you're using named access lists.

- Unless your access list ends with a `permit any` command, all packets will be discarded if they do not meet any of the list's tests. Every list should have at least one `permit` statement or it will deny all traffic.

- Create access lists and then apply them to an interface. Any access list *not* applied to an interface will not filter traffic.

- Access lists are designed to filter traffic going through the router. They will not filter traffic that has originated from the router.

- Place IP standard access lists as close to the destination as possible. Standard ACLs can only filter based on source address. If placed too close to the source, the source device will be blocked from everything beyond the point where the ACL is applied.

- Place IP extended access lists as close to the source as possible. Because extended access lists can filter on very specific addresses and protocols, you don't want your traffic to traverse the entire network and then be denied. By placing this list as close to the source address as possible, you can filter traffic before it uses up your precious bandwidth.

Exam Essentials

Understand the term *implicit deny*.   At the end of every access list is an implicit deny. What this means is that if a packet does not match any of the lines in the access list, it will be discarded. Also, if you have nothing but deny statements in your list, then the list will not permit any packets.

Understand the standard IP access-list configuration command.   To configure a standard IP access list, use the access-list numbers 1–99 or 1300–1999 in global configuration mode. Choose `permit` or deny, and then choose the source IP address you want to filter on using one of the three techniques covered earlier.

Understand the extended IP access-list configuration command. To configure an extended IP access list, use the access-list numbers 100–199 or 2000–2699 in global configuration mode. Choose permit or deny, the Network layer protocol field, the source IP address you want to filter on, the destination address you want to filter on, and the Transport layer port number (if selected).

Understand the logic of ACL processing. All lines are processed in order until a match is found. Once the packet matches the condition on a line of the access list, the packet is acted upon and no further comparisons take place. There is an *implicit deny* at the end of each access list.

Contrast standard and extended ACLs. Standard ACLs can only filter based on source IP address, while extended ACLs can filter based on source and destination IP addresses and port numbers.

Describe the logic of inbound and outbound ACLs. Inbound ACLs are applied before a packet is routed and outgoing ACLs filter after routing has taken place.

Review Questions

1. Network 206.143.5.0 was assigned to the Acme Company to connect to its ISP. The Acme administrator would like to configure one router with the commands to access the Internet. Which commands could be configured on the Gateway router to allow Internet access to the entire network? (Choose two.)

   A. `Gateway(config)#ip route 0.0.0.0 0.0.0.0 206.143.5.2`

   B. `Gateway(config)#router rip`

   C. `Gateway(config-router)#network 206.143.5.0`

   D. `Gateway(config)#router rip`

   E. `Gateway(config-router)#network 206.143.5.0 default`

   F. `Gateway(config)#ip route 206.143.5.0 255.255.255.0 default`

   G. `Gateway(config)#ip default-network 206.143.5.0`

2. Which statements are true regarding classless routing protocols? (Choose two.)

   A. The use of discontiguous networks is not allowed.

   B. The use of variable length subnet masks is permitted.

   C. RIPv1 is a classless routing protocol.

   D. IGRP supports classless routing within the same autonomous system.

   E. RIPv2 supports classless routing.

3. Which two of the following are true regarding the distance-vector and link-state routing protocols?

   A. Link-state protocols send their complete routing tables out all active interfaces on periodic time intervals.

   B. Distance-vector protocols send their complete routing tables out all active interfaces on periodic time intervals.

   C. Link-state protocols send updates containing the state of their own links to all routers in the internetwork.

   D. Distance-vector protocols send updates containing the state of their own links to all routers in the internetwork.

4. Which command displays RIP routing updates?

   A. `show ip route`

   B. `debug ip rip`

   C. `show protocols`

   D. `debug ip route`

5. Which of the following is true regarding RIPv2?

   A. It has a lower administrative distance than RIPv1.

   B. It converges faster than RIPv1.

   C. It has the same timers as RIPv1.

   D. It is harder to configure than RIPv1.

6. Which command will copy the IOS to a backup host on your network?
   A. `transfer IOS to 172.16.10.1`
   B. `copy run start`
   C. `copy tftp flash`
   D. `copy start tftp`
   E. `copy flash tftp`

7. You are troubleshooting a connectivity problem in your corporate network and want to isolate the problem. You suspect that a router on the route to an unreachable network is at fault. What IOS user exec command should you issue?
   A. `Router>ping`
   B. `Router>trace`
   C. `Router>show ip route`
   D. `Router>show interface`
   E. `Router>show cdp neighbors`

8. You copy a configuration from a network host to a router's RAM. The configuration looks correct, yet it is not working at all. What could the problem be?
   A. You copied the wrong configuration into RAM.
   B. You copied the configuration into flash memory instead.
   C. The copy did not override the `shutdown` command in `running-config`.
   D. The IOS became corrupted after the `copy` command was initiated.

9. A network administrator wants to upgrade the IOS of a router without removing the image currently installed. What command will display the amount of memory consumed by the current IOS image and indicate whether enough room is available to hold both the current and new images?
   A. `show version`
   B. `show flash`
   C. `show memory`
   D. `show buffers`
   E. `show running-config`

10. Which command loads a new version of the Cisco IOS into a router?
    A. `copy flash ftp`
    B. `copy ftp flash`
    C. `copy flash tftp`
    D. `copy tftp flash`

Answers to Review Questions

1. A, E. There are actually three different ways to configure the same default route, but only two are shown in the answer. First, you can set a default route with the 0.0.0.0 0.0.0.0 mask and then specify the next hop, as in answer A. Or, you can use 0.0.0.0 0.0.0.0 and use the exit interface instead of the next hop. Finally, you can use answer E with the `ip default-network` command.

2. B, E. Classful routing means that all hosts in the internetwork use the same mask. Classless routing means that you can use Variable Length Subnet Masks (VLSMs) and can also support discontiguous networking.

3. B, C. The distance-vector routing protocol sends its complete routing table out all active interfaces on periodic time intervals. Link-state routing protocols send updates containing the state of their own links to all routers in the internetwork.

4. B. `Debug ip rip` is used to show the Internet Protocol (IP) Routing Information Protocol (RIP) updates being sent and received on the router.

5. C. RIPv2 is pretty much just like RIPv1. It has the same administrative distance and timers and is configured just like RIPv1.

6. E. To copy the IOS to a backup host, which is stored in flash memory by default, use the `copy flash tftp` command.

7. B. The command `traceroute` (`trace` for short), which can be issued from user mode or privileged mode, is used to find the path a packet takes through an internetwork and will also show you where the packet stops because of an error on a router.

8. C. Because the configuration looks correct, you probably didn't screw up the copy job. However, when you perform a copy from a network host to a router, the interfaces are automatically shut down and need to be manually enabled with the `no shutdown` command.

9. B. The `show flash` command will provide the current IOS name and size and the size of flash memory.

10. D. The command `copy tftp flash` will allow you to copy a new IOS into flash memory on your router.

Chapter

5

Explain and Select the Appropriate Administrative Tasks Required for a WLAN

THE CISCO CCNA EXAM OBJECTIVES COVERED IN THIS CHAPTER INCLUDE THE FOLLOWING:

- ✓ Describe standards associated with wireless media (including IEEE, Wi-Fi Alliance, and ITU/FCC).

- ✓ Identify and describe the purpose of the components in a small wireless network (including SSID, BSS, and ESS).

- ✓ Identify the basic parameters to configure on a wireless network to ensure that devices connect to the correct access point.

- ✓ Compare and contrast wireless security features and capabilities of WPA security (including open, WEP, and WPA-1/2).

- ✓ Identify common issues with implementing wireless networks (including interfaces and misconfigurations).

If you want to understand the basic wireless LANs, or WLANs, that are the most commonly used today, just think 10BaseT Ethernet with hubs. What this means is that WLANs typically run half-duplex communication—everyone is sharing the same bandwidth and only one user is communicating at a time. This isn't necessarily bad—it's just not good enough. Because most people rely on wireless networks today, it's critical that those networks evolve to keep up with everyone's rapidly escalating needs.

Cisco has reacted by coming up with the *Cisco Unified Wireless Solution*, which works, with all types of wireless connections—and it works securely, too!

Describe Standards Associated with Wireless Media (Including IEEE, Wi-Fi Alliance, and ITU/FCC)

Various agencies have been around for a very long time to help govern the use of wireless devices, frequencies, standards, and how the frequency spectrums are used. Table 5.1 shows the current agencies that help create, maintain, and enforce wireless standards worldwide.

TABLE 5.1 Wireless Agencies and Standards

Agency	Purpose	Website
Institute of Electrical and Electronics Engineers (IEEE)	Creates and maintains operational standards	www.ieee.org
Federal Communications Commission (FCC)	Regulates the use of wireless devices in the U.S.	www.fcc.gov
European Telecommunications Standards Institute (ETSI)	Chartered to produce common standards in Europe	www.etsi.org
Wi-Fi Alliance	Promotes and tests for WLAN interoperability	www.wi-fi.com
WLAN Association (WLANA)	Educates and raises consumer awareness regarding WLANs	www.wlana.org

Because WLANs transmit over radio frequencies, they're regulated by the same types of laws used to govern things like AM/FM radios. The Federal Communications Commission (FCC) regulates the use of wireless LAN devices, and the Institute of Electrical and Electronics Engineers (IEEE) creates standards based on the frequencies that the FCC releases for public use.

The FCC has released three unlicensed bands for public use: 900MHz, 2.4GHz, and 5.7GHz. The 900MHz and 2.4GHz bands are referred to as the *Industrial, Scientific, and Medical (ISM)* bands, and the 5GHz band is known as the *Unlicensed National Information Infrastructure (UNII)* band. Figure 5.1 shows where the unlicensed bands sit within the RF spectrum.

FIGURE 5.1   Unlicensed frequencies

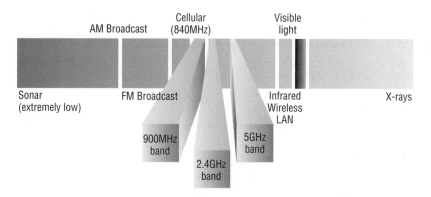

If you opt to deploy wireless in a range outside of the three public bands shown in Figure 5.1, you'll need to get a specific license from the FCC to do so. When the FCC opened the three frequency ranges for public use, many manufacturers were able to start offering myriad products that flooded the market, with 802.11b/g being the most widely used wireless network today.

The Wi-Fi Alliance grants certification for interoperability among 802.11 products offered by various vendors. This certification provides a sort of comfort zone for the users purchasing the many types of products, although in my personal experience, it's a whole lot easier to buy all of your access points from the same manufacturer.

In the current U.S. wireless LAN market, the IEEE has created and maintained several accepted operational standards and drafts. Let's take a look at these standards and then talk about how the most commonly used standards work.

The 802.11 Standards

As you learned in Chapter 2, "Configure, Verify, and Troubleshoot a Switch with VLANs and Interswitch Communications," the Ethernet standards group committee is 802.3. Likewise, wireless networking has its own 802 standards group, starting with 802.11 and including various other evolving standards groups such as 802.16 and 802.20. There is no doubt that cellular networks will become huge players in the wireless future—but for now, let's concentrate on the 802.11 standards committee and subcommittees.

IEEE 802.11 was the original standardized WLAN at 1 and 2Mbps. It runs in the 2.4GHz radio frequency and was ratified in 1997, even though not very many products popped up until around 1999 when 802.11b was introduced. All the committees listed in Table 5.2 are amendments to the original 802.11 standard—except for 802.11F and 802.11T, which are both stand-alone documents.

TABLE 5.2   802.11 Committees and Subcommittees

Committee	Purpose
IEEE 802.11a	54Mbps, 5GHz standard
IEEE 802.11b	Enhancements to 802.11 to support 5.5 and 11Mbps
IEEE 802.11c	Bridge operation procedures; included in the IEEE 802.1D standard
IEEE 802.11d	International roaming extensions
IEEE 802.11e	Quality of service
IEEE 802.11F	Inter-Access Point Protocol
IEEE 802.11g	54Mbps, 2.4GHz standard (backward compatible with 802.11b)
IEEE 802.11h	Dynamic Frequency Selection (DFS) and Transmit Power Control (TPC) at 5Ghz
IEEE 802.11i	Enhanced security
IEEE 802.11j	Extensions for Japan and U.S. public safety
IEEE 802.11k	Radio resource measurement enhancements
IEEE 802.11m	Maintenance of the standard; odds and ends
IEEE 802.11n	Higher throughput improvements using MIMO (multiple input, multiple output) antennas
IEEE 802.11p	Wireless Access for the Vehicular Environment (WAVE)
IEEE 802.11r	Fast roaming
IEEE 802.11s	ESS Extended Service Set Mesh Networking
IEEE 802.11T	Wireless Performance Prediction (WPP)

Committee	Purpose
IEEE 802.11u	Internetworking with non-802 networks (cellular, for example)
IEEE 802.11v	Wireless network management
IEEE 802.11w	Protected management frames
IEEE 802.11y	3650–3700 operation in the U.S.

2.4GHz (802.11b)

The first widely deployed wireless standard was 802.11b. It operates in the 2.4GHz unlicensed radio band and delivers a maximum data rate of 11Mbps. The 802.11b standard has been widely adopted by both vendors and customers who found that its 11Mbps data rate worked pretty well for most applications. However, 802.11b has been mostly replaced by 802.11g, which operates in the same frequency and can go up to 54 Mbps.

An interesting thing about all Cisco 802.11 WLAN products is that they have the ability to data-rate-shift while moving. This allows the person operating at 11Mbps to shift to 5.5Mbps and then to 2Mbps as the distance between the access point (AP) and the station increases. Furthermore, this rate shifting happens without losing connection and with no interaction from the user. Rate shifting also occurs on a transmission-by-transmission basis. This is important because it means that the access point can support multiple clients at varying speeds, depending on the location of each client.

The problem with 802.11b lies in the way in which the Data Link layer is dealt. In order to solve problems in the RF spectrum, a type of Ethernet collision detection was created called *CSMA/CA*, or *Carrier Sense Multiple Access with Collision Avoidance*. Check this out in Figure 5.2.

FIGURE 5.2   802.11b CSMA/CA

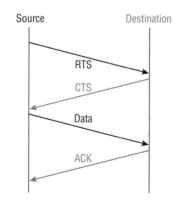

CSMA/CA is more involved than CSMA/CD, which is the contention method used on wired Ethernet. Since, unlike with wired Ethernet, stations cannot detect a collision, each and every wireless frame transfer must be acknowledged. Because of this rather cumbersome process, the method has tremendous overhead. When you also consider that every frame goes through the AP when it traverses from Station A to Station B, the overhead in a single frame transfer is compounded.

NOTE   Cordless phones and microwave ovens can cause interference in the 2.4GHz range.

In the United States, there are currently 11 channels that can be configured within the 2.4GHz range. However, only three of these channels are considered non-overlapping: 1, 6, and 11.

Figure 5.3 shows the 14 different channels (each 22MHz wide) that the FCC released within the 2.4GHz range:

FIGURE 5.3   ISM 2.4GHz channels

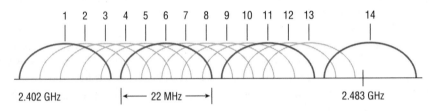

Because there are three channels (1, 6, and 11) that don't overlap, you can have three access points in the same general area without experiencing interference. One of the first things you should do when configuring an AP is set the AP channel.

2.4GHz (802.11g)

The 802.11g standard was ratified in June 2003 and is backward compatible with 802.11b. The 802.11g standard delivers the same 54Mbps maximum data rate as 802.11a, but it runs in the 2.4GHz range—the same as 802.11b.

Because 802.11b/g operate in the same 2.4GHz unlicensed band, migrating to 802.11g is an affordable choice for organizations with existing 802.11b wireless infrastructures. Just keep in mind that 802.11b products cannot be "software upgraded" to 802.11g, because 802.11g radios use a different chipset in order to deliver the higher data rate.

But still, much like Ethernet and FastEthernet, 802.11g products can be commingled with 802.11b products in the same network. Yet, for example, completely unlike Ethernet, if you have four users running 802.11g cards and one user starts using an 802.11b card, everyone connected to the same access point is then forced to run the 802.11b CSMA/CA method, which negatively affects the throughput. So to optimize performance, it's recommended that you disable the 802.11b-only mode on all your access points.

To explain this further, 802.11b uses a modulation technique called *Direct Sequence Spread Spectrum* (DSSS), which is not as robust as the Orthogonal Frequency Division Multiplexing (OFDM) modulation used by both 802.11g and 802.11a. The 802.11g clients using OFDM enjoy much better performance at the same ranges than the 802.11b clients do, but—and remember this—when 802.11g clients are operating at the 802.11b rates (11, 5.5, 2, and 1Mbps), they're actually using the same modulation that 802.11b uses.

5GHz (802.11a)

The IEEE ratified the 802.11a standard in 1999, but the first 802.11a products didn't begin appearing on the market until late 2001. The 802.11a standard delivers a maximum data rate of 54Mbps with 12 non-overlapping frequency channels.

Operating in the 5GHz radio band, 802.11a is also immune to interference from devices that operate in the 2.4GHz band, such as microwave ovens, cordless phones, and Bluetooth devices. The 802.11a standard isn't backward compatible with 802.11b because they have different frequencies, so you can't just "upgrade" part of your network and expect everything to work together in perfect harmony, but there are plenty of dual-radio devices that will work in both types of networks. A definite plus for 802.11a is that it can work in the same physical environment without interference from 802.11b users.

All 802.11a products also have the ability to data-rate-shift while moving. The 802.11a products allow the person operating at 54Mbps to shift to 48Mbps, 36Mbps, 24Mbps, 18Mbps, 12Mbps, 9Mbps, and finally 6Mbps at the farthest distance at which it can still communicate with the AP.

2.4GHz/5GHz (802.11n)

The 802.11n standard builds on previous 802.11 standards by adding *Multiple-Input Multiple-Output (MIMO)*, which uses multiple transmitters and receiver antennas to increase data throughput and range. The 802.11n standard can allow up to eight antennas, but most of today's APs use only four to six. This setup permits considerably higher data rates than 802.11a/b/g do.

The following three vital items are combined in 802.11n to enhance performance:

- At the Physical layer, the way a signal is sent is changed, enabling reflections and interferences to become an advantage instead of a source of degradation.

- Two 20MHz-wide channels are combined to increase throughput.

- At the MAC layer, a different way of managing packet transmission is used.

It's important to note that 802.11n isn't truly compatible with 802.11b, 802.11g, or even 802.11a, but it is designed to be backward compatible with them. The 802.11n standard achieves backward compatibility by changing the way frames are sent so they can be understood by 802.11a/b/g.

Here's a list of some of the primary components of 802.11n that together sum up why people claim 802.11n is more reliable and predictable:

40MHz Channels   Both 802.11g and 802.11a use 20MHz channels and employ tones on the sides of each unused channel in order to protect the main carrier. This means that 11Mbps go unused and are basically wasted. The 802.11n standard aggregates two carriers to double the speed from 54Mbps to more than 108. Add in those wasted 11Mbps rescued from the side tones and you get a grand total of 119Mbps.

MAC Efficiency   The 802.11 protocols require acknowledgment of each and every frame. The 802.11n can pass many packets before an acknowledgment is required, which saves you a huge amount of overhead. This is called *block acknowledgment.*

Multiple-Input Multiple-Output (MIMO)   Several frames are sent by several antennae over several paths and are then recombined by another set of antennae to optimize through-put and multipath resistance. This is called *spatial multiplexing.*

Comparing 802.11

Figure 5.4 lists every IEEE standard in use today, along with the year it was ratified, its frequency, the number of non-overlapping channels, the Physical layer transmission techniques, and the data rates.

FIGURE 5.4   Standards for Spectrums and Speeds

	802.11	802.11b	802.11a	802.11g		802.11n
Ratified	1997	1999	1999	2003		2010
Frequency Band	2.4GHz	2.4GHz	5GHz	2.4GHz		2.4GHz, 5GHz
No. of Channels	3	3	Up to 23	3		Varies
Transmission	IR, FHSS, DSSS	DSSS	OFDM	DSSS	OFDM	DSSS, CCK, OFDM
Data Rates (Mbps)	1, 2	1, 2, 5.5, 11	6, 9, 12, 18, 24, 36, 48, 54	1, 2, 5.5, 11	6, 9, 12, 18, 24, 36, 48, 54	100+

Exam Essentials

Remember the three overlapping channels used with the 2.4GHz range.   In the United States, only 11 channels are configurable, with channels 1, 6, and 11 being non-overlapping.

Remember how many channels are non-overlapping in the 5GHz range. The 802.11a standard delivers a maximum data rate of 54Mbps with 12 non-overlapping frequency channels.

Understand the IEEE 802.11a specification. The 802.11a standard runs in the 5GHz spectrum, and if you use the 802.11h extensions, you have 23 non-overlapping channels. The 802.11a standard can run up to 54Mbps, but only if you are less than 50 feet from an access point.

Understand the IEEE 802.11b specification. IEEE 802.11b runs in the 2.4GHz range and has three non-overlapping channels. It can handle long distances, but with a maximum data rate of up to 11Mpbs.

Understand the IEEE 802.11g specification. IEEE 802.11g is 802.11b's big brother and runs in the same 2.4GHz range, but it has a higher data rate of 54Mbps if you are less than 100 feet from an access point.

Understand the IEEE 802.11n specification. The 802.11n standard adds efficiency and improvements to existing standards. IEEE 802.11n uses the same frequencies as 802.11b/g and 802.11a, but it uses Multiple-In-Multiple-Out (MIMO) to significantly increase the amount of data that can be transmitted.

Identify the major agencies that create, maintain, and enforce wireless standards. The FCC, Wi-Fi Alliance, the IEEE, the ETSI, and the WLAN associations are important governing bodies as described in Table 5.1.

Identify and Describe the Purpose of the Components in a Small Wireless Network (Including SSID, BSS, and ESS)

Transmitting a signal using the typical 802.11 specifications works a lot like it does with a basic Ethernet hub: They're both two-way forms of communication, and they both use the same frequency to transmit and receive, often referred to as *half-duplex*, as mentioned earlier in the chapter. Wireless LANs (WLANs) use RFs that are radiated into the air from an antenna that creates radio waves. These waves can be absorbed, refracted, or reflected by walls, water, and metal surfaces, resulting in low signal strength. Because of this innate vulnerability to surrounding environmental factors, wireless will never offer the same robustness as a wired network, but wireless networks will continue to gain popularity despite this shortcoming.

Transmitting power can be increased to gain a greater transmitting distance, but doing so can create some nasty distortion, so it has to be done carefully. Using higher frequencies can attain higher data rates, but this is, unfortunately, at the cost of decreased transmitting distances. If lower frequencies are used, you get to transmit across greater distances but at lower data rates. This should make it pretty clear to you that understanding all the various types of WLANs you can implement is imperative in creating the LAN solution that best meets the specific requirements of the unique situation with which you're dealing.

Also important to note is the fact that the 802.11 specifications were developed so that no licensing would be required in most countries to ensure users the freedom to install and operate without any licensing or operating fees. This means that any manufacturer can create products and sell them at a local computer store or wherever. It also means that all our computers should be able to communicate wirelessly without configuring much, if anything at all.

Service Sets

Now that I've discussed the very basics of the wireless devices used in today's simple networks, I'll describe the different types of networks you'll run across or design and implement as your wireless networks grow. These include the following:

- Independent Basic Service Set (IBSS)
- Basic Service Set (BSS)
- Extended Service Set (ESS)

All types of networks define what is called a Service Set ID (SSID) that's used to advertise your wireless network so hosts can connect to the access point (AP). You can have multiple SSIDs configured on an access point for security reasons. For example, you can designate that one SSID is open access for a public hot spot, while another SSID can use WEP or WPA2 for the employees that work at this public hot spot. The SSID name is broadcasted out the AP by default so the clients can find the AP and connect to the wireless network, and of course you can turn this feature off for security reasons.

IBSS

Using an ad IBSS (ad hoc) network is the easiest way to install wireless 802.11 devices. In this mode, the wireless NICs (or other devices) can communicate directly without the need for an AP. A good example of this is two laptops with wireless NICs installed. If both cards are set up to operate in ad hoc mode, they can connect and transfer files as long as the other network settings, like the IP protocols, are set up to enable this as well.

To create an Independent Basic Service Set (IBSS), ad hoc network, you only need two or more wireless-capable devices. Once you've placed them within a range of 20 to 40 meters of each other, they'll "see" each other and be able to connect, assuming they share some basic configuration parameters. One computer may be able to share its Internet connection with the rest of the wireless stations in the IBSS.

BSS

A BSS involves only a single access point. You create a BSS, bring up an AP, and create a name for the service set ID (SSID). Users can then connect to and use this SSID to access the wireless network, which may also provide connectivity to wired resources. When the

AP connects to a wired network, it then becomes known as an Infrastructure Basic Service Set, or IBSS. Keep in mind that if you have a BSS/IBSS, users won't be able to maintain network connectivity when roaming from AP to AP because each AP is configured with a different SSID name.

BSS wireless networks are also really helpful if you happen to have a couple of hosts that need to establish wireless communication directly between only themselves. You can also make this happen through something called ad hoc networking, but if you have an AP between the hosts it's just called a BSS.

Figure 5.5 shows a basic service set using one SSID:

FIGURE 5.5   Basic Service Set (BSS)

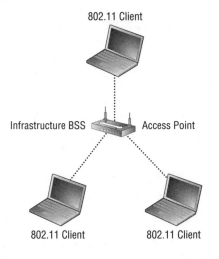

ESS

Mobile wireless clients can roam around within the same network if you set all your access points to the same SSID. Doing this creates an Extended Service Set (ESS). Figure 5.6 shows four APs configured with the same SSID in an office, thereby creating the ESS network.

For users to be able to roam throughout the wireless network—from AP to AP without losing their connection to the network—all APs must overlap by at least 10 percent and be set to different channels. As you'll recall, an 8.02.11b/g network has only three non-overlapping channels (1, 6, and 11), so design is super important here!

Exam Essentials

Differentiate the three types of service sets.   An IBSS is a service set with no AP and direct communication between the stations. A BSS is a service set consisting one AP and its associated stations. The ESS is two or more BSSs using the same SSID, which allows for seamless roaming between the APs.

FIGURE 5.6   Extended Service Set (ESS)

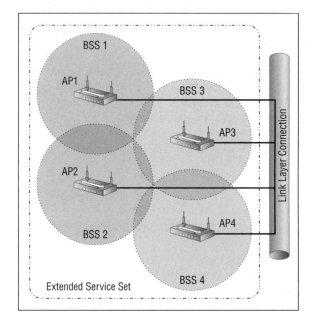

Identify the Basic Parameters to Configure on a Wireless Network to Ensure That Devices Connect to the Correct Access Point

It's true that a wireless interface can really be just another interface on a router—and it looks just like that in a routing table or a separate device called an access point. In order to bring up a wireless interface, more configurations are needed than for a simple Fast Ethernet interface.

Check out the following output, and then I'll tell you about the special configuration needs for this wireless interface.

```
R2(config-if)#int dot11radio0/3/0
R2(config-if)#ip address 10.1.8.1 255.255.255.0
R2(config-if)#description Connection to Corp ISR Router
R2(config-if)#no shut
```

```
R2(config-if)#ssid ADMIN
R2(config-if-ssid)#guest-mode
R2(config-if-ssid)#authentication open
R2(config-if-ssid)#infrastructure-ssid
R2(config-if-ssid)#no shut
```

What you see here is pretty commonplace until you get to the SSID configuration. This is the Service Set Identifier that creates a wireless network to which hosts can connect.

Unlike access points, the interface on the router is actually a routed interface, which is the reason the IP address is placed under the physical interface—typically, the IP address would be placed under the management VLAN or Bridge-Group Virtual Interface (BVI).

That guest-mode line means that the interface will broadcast the SSID so that wireless hosts will understand that they can connect to this interface.

Authentication open means just that: no authentication. (Even so, you still have to at least type that command to make the wireless interface work.)

Last, the infrastructure-ssid indicates that this interface can be used to communicate with other access points, or other devices on the infrastructure—meaning to the actual wired network itself and the resources on the wired network, such as servers.

You're not done yet. The DHCP pool for the wireless clients still needs to be configured:

```
R2#config t
R2(config)#ip dhcp pool Admin
R2(dhcp-config)#network 10.1.8.0 255.255.255.0
R2(dhcp-config)#default-router 10.1.8.1
R2(dhcp-config)#exit
R2(config)#ip dhcp excluded-address 10.1.8.1
R2(config)#
```

Creating DHCP pools on a router is actually a pretty simple process. To do so, you just create the pool name, add the network/subnet and the default gateway, and exclude any addresses you don't want handed out (like the default gateway address)—and you'd usually add a DNS server as well.

Understand that the pool is basically attached to an interface that has an address from the same subnet created by the DHCP pool. In the preceding example, this is interface dot11radio 0/3/0. You can easily create another pool and have it connected with a LAN interface as in FastEthernet 0/0 by assigning an address on FastEthernet 0/0 that is from the subnet pool.

Exam Essentials

Remember how to set a Service Set Identifier (SSID) on a wireless routed interface. From the interface mode of the wireless routed interface, use the ssid *ssid-name* command. This is the Service Set Identifier that creates a wireless network to which hosts can connect.

Remember how to configure a wireless interface on a router to allow hosts to communicate to a wired infrastructure.   Under the Router(config-if-ssid)# command prompt, use the command infrastructure-ssid to indicate that this interface can be used to communicate to other access points, or to the wired network.

Compare and Contrast Wireless Security Features and Capabilities of WPA Security (Including Open, WEP, and WPA-1/2)

The original 802.11 committee didn't add security standards that are robust enough to work in a corporate environment. However, an enterprise wireless network demands this security. First let's look at the basic security that was added into the original 802.11 standards and understand the shortcomings inherent in those methods.

Open Access

All Wi-Fi Certified wireless LAN products are shipped in "open-access" mode, with their security features turned off. While open access or no security may be appropriate and acceptable for public hot spots such as coffee shops, college campuses, and maybe airports, it's definitely not an option for an enterprise organization, and likely not even adequate for your private home network.

Security needs to be enabled on wireless devices during their installation in enterprise environments. It may come as quite a shock, but some companies actually don't enable any WLAN security features. Obviously, the companies that don't are exposing their networks to tremendous risk.

Products are shipped with open access so that even someone who knows absolutely nothing about computers can buy an access point, plug it into a cable or DSL modem, and voilà—be up and running. It's marketing, plain and simple, and simplicity sells.

SSIDs, WEP, and MAC Address Authentication

What the original designers of 802.11 did to create basic security was include the use of Service Set Identifiers (SSIDs), open or shared-key authentication, static Wired Equivalent Protocol (WEP), and optional Media Access Control (MAC) authentication. That sounds like a lot, but none of these really offers a serious security solution.

SSID is a common network name for the devices in a WLAN system that create the wireless LAN. An SSID prevents access by any client device that doesn't have the SSID. However, by default, an access point broadcasts its SSID in its beacon many times a second, so even if

SSID broadcasting is turned off, a wireless hacker can discover the SSID by monitoring the network and just waiting for a client response to the access point. That response information, as specified in the original 802.11 specifications, must be sent in the clear.

Two types of authentication were specified by the IEEE 802.11 committee: *open* and *shared-key authentication*. Open authentication involves little more than supplying the correct SSID—but it's the most common method in use today. With shared-key authentication, the access point sends the client device a challenge-text packet that the client must then encrypt with the correct WEP key and return to the access point. Without the correct key, authentication will fail and the client won't be allowed to associate with the access point. Shared-key authentication is still not considered secure because all an intruder has to do to get around this is detect both the cleartext challenge and the same challenge encrypted with a WEP key and then decipher the WEP key. For this reason, shared key isn't used in today's WLANs.

With open authentication, even if a client can complete authentication and associate with an access point, the use of WEP prevents the client from sending and receiving data from the access point unless the client has the correct WEP key. A WEP key is composed of either 40 or 128 bits and, in its basic form, is usually statically defined by the network administrator on the access point and all clients that communicate with that access point. When static WEP keys are used, a network administrator must perform the time-consuming task of entering the same keys on every device in the WLAN. Although there are easier methods to accomplish this today, this remains a cumbersome process.

Finally, allowed client MAC addresses can be statically typed into each access point in the form of a MAC address filter and the AP will deny access to any station whose MAC address is not on the list. Of course, because all MAC layer information must be sent in the clear, anyone equipped with a free wireless sniffer can just read the client packets sent to the access point and spoof their MAC address.

Encryption Methods

There are two basic encryption methods used in most wireless networks today: TKIP and AES. I'll cover TKIP first.

Temporal Key Integrity Protocol (TKIP)

The IEEE 802.11i task group and the Wi-Fi Alliance, joining forces, came up with a remediation to the WEP weaknesses called *Temporal Key Integrity Protocol (TKIP)*, which is based on the RC4 encryption algorithm.

TKIP affords protections to the authentication process, and it is also used after the authentication process to encrypt the data traffic thereafter. The Wi-Fi Alliance unveiled TKIP back in late 2002 and introduced it as Wi-Fi Protected Access (WPA). TKIP doesn't require an upgrade to legacy hardware equipment in order to use it. In the summer of 2004, the IEEE put its seal of approval on its final version and added 802.1X and AES-CCMP (AES-Counter Mode CBC-MAC Protocol). Upon publishing IEEE 802.11i-2004, the Wi-Fi Alliance responded positively by embracing the now-complete specification and dubbing it WPA2 for marketing purposes.

A big reason new hardware wasn't required to run TKIP is that it really just kind of wraps around the preexisting WEP RC4 encryption cipher, which was way too short, and upgrades it to a much more impenetrable 128-bit encryption. Another reason for TKIP's innate compatibility is that both its encryption mechanism and the RC4 algorithm used to power and define WEP remained the same.

AES

Both WPA/2 and the 802.11i standard call for the use of 128-bit Advanced Encryption Standard (AES) for data encryption. It's widely considered the best encryption available today and has been approved by the National Institute of Standards and Technology (NIST). It's also referred to as AES-CCMP, or AES Counter Mode with CBC-MAC authentication.

The only shortcoming of AES is that due to the computational requirements, you need a cryptographic processor to run it. Still, it's much more efficient and secure than RC4.

WPA or WPA 2 Pre-Shared Key

Although this is another form of basic security that's really just an add-on to the specifications, *WPA* or *WPA2 Pre-Shared Key (PSK)* is a better form of wireless security than any other *basic* wireless security method mentioned so far.

The PSK verifies users via a password or identifying code (also called a *passphrase*) on both the client machine and the access point. A client only gains access to the network if its password matches the access point's password. The PSK also provides keying material that TKIP or AES uses to generate an encryption key for each packet of transmitted data. While more secure than static WEP, PSK still has a lot in common with static WEP in that the PSK is stored on the client station and can be compromised if the client station is lost or stolen—even though finding this key isn't all that easy to do. To prevent PSK guessing, use a strong PSK passphrase that includes a mixture of letters, numbers, and non-alphanumeric characters.

Wi-Fi Protected Access (WPA) is a standard developed in 2003 by the Wi-Fi Alliance, formerly known as WECA. WPA provides a standard for authentication and encryption of WLANs that's intended to solve known security problems existing up to and including the year 2003. This takes into account the well-publicized AirSnort and man-in-the-middle WLAN attacks.

WPA is a step toward the IEEE 802.11i standard and uses many of the same components, with the exception of encryption—802.11i (WPA2) uses AES-CCMP encryption. The IEEE 802.11i standard replaced Wired Equivalent Privacy (WEP) with a specific mode of the Advanced Encryption Standard (AES) known as the Counter Mode Cipher Block Chaining-Message Authentication Code (CBC-MAC) protocol (CCMP). This allows AES-CCMP to provide both data confidentiality (encryption) and data integrity.

WPA's mechanisms are designed to be implementable by current hardware vendors, meaning that users should be able to implement WPA on their systems with only a firmware/software modification.

The IEEE 802.11i standard has been sanctioned by WPA and is termed WPA version 2.

Exam Essentials

Remember the two types of original 802.11 authentication.   Two types of authentication were specified by the IEEE 802.11 committee: open and shared-key authentication.

Remember the standard developed by the Wi-Fi Alliance.   Wi-Fi Protected Access (WPA) is a standard developed by the Wi-Fi Alliance that addresses the weaknesses inherent in the original 802.11 security model.

Identify Common Issues with Implementing Wireless Networks (Including Interfaces and Misconfigurations)

For information about this objective, see the section titled "Identify the Basic Parameters to Configure on a Wireless Network to Ensure That Devices Connect to the Correct Access Point" earlier in this chapter.

Review Questions

1. What is the frequency range of the IEEE 802.11b standard?
   A. 2.4Gbps
   B. 5Gbps
   C. 2.4GHz
   D. 5GHz

2. What is the frequency range of the IEEE 802.11a standard?
   A. 2.4Gbps
   B. 5Gbps
   C. 2.4GHz
   D. 5GHz

3. What is the frequency range of the IEEE 802.11g standard?
   A. 2.4Gbps
   B. 5Gbps
   C. 2.4GHz
   D. 5GHz

4. What is the encryption used in WPA2?
   A. AES-CCMP
   B. WEP
   C. PSK
   D. TKIP

5. How many non-overlapping channels are available with 802.11g?
   A. 3
   B. 12
   C. 23
   D. 40

6. How many non-overlapping channels are available with 802.11b?
   A. 3
   B. 12
   C. 23
   D. 40

7. After the 802.11h standard, how many non-overlapping channels are available with 802.11a?

A. 3

B. 12

C. 23

D. 40

8. What is the maximum data rate for the 802.11a standard?

A. 6Mbps

B. 11Mbps

C. 22Mbps

D. 54Mbps

9. What is the maximum data rate for the 802.11g standard?

A. 6Mbps

B. 11Mbps

C. 22Mbps

D. 54Mbps

10. What is the maximum data rate for the 802.11b standard?

A. 6Mbps

B. 11Mbps

C. 22Mbps

D. 54Mbps

Answers to Review Questions

1.   C. The IEEE 802.11b and IEEE 802.11g both run in the 2.4GHz RF range.

2.   D. The IEEE 802.11a standard runs in the 5GHz RF range.

3.   C. The IEEE 802.11b and IEEE 802.11g both run in the 2.4GHz RF range.

4.   A. WPA2 uses the Advanced Encryption Standard (AES) known as the Counter Mode Cipher Block Chaining-Message Authentication Code (CBC-MAC) protocol (CCMP).

5.   A. The IEEE 802.11g standard provides three non-overlapping channels.

6.   A. The IEEE 802.11b standard provides three non-overlapping channels.

7.   C. With the 802.11h standard, the IEEE 802.11a standard provides up to 23 non-overlapping channels.

8.   D. The IEEE 802.11a standard provides a maximum data rate of up to 54Mbps.

9.   D. The IEEE 802.11g standard provides a maximum data rate of up to 54Mbps.

10. B. The IEEE 802.11b standard provides a maximum data rate of up to 11Mbps.

Chapter

6

Identify Security Threats to a Network and Describe General Methods to Mitigate Those Threats

THE CISCO CCNA EXAM OBJECTIVES COVERED IN THIS CHAPTER INCLUDE THE FOLLOWING:

✓ Describe today's increasing network security threats and explain the need to implement a comprehensive security policy to mitigate the threats.

✓ Explain general methods to mitigate common security threats to network devices, hosts, and applications.

✓ Describe the functions of common security appliances and applications.

✓ Describe security recommended practices, including initial steps to secure network devices.

If you're a sysadmin, it's my guess that shielding sensitive, critical data, as well as your network's resources, from every possible evil exploit is a top priority. Cisco has some really effective security solutions that will arm you with the tools you need to make this happen.

In this chapter, you'll learn a lot about deterring the most common threats to your network's security with Cisco routers and IOS Firewalls that, together, offer quite a powerful, integrated detection package against many types of invasions. I'm going to give you the lowdown on how the Cisco IOS Firewall provides actual security and policy enforcement for both your internal and external networking needs. I'll also show you how to create secure connections to remote routers and switches.

Describe Today's Increasing Network Security Threats and Explain the Need to Implement a Comprehensive Security Policy to Mitigate the Threats

In medium-sized to large enterprise networks, the various strategies for security are based on a recipe of internal and perimeter routers plus firewall devices. Internal routers provide additional security to the network by screening traffic to various parts of the protected corporate network, and they do this by using access lists. Figure 6.1 shows where these devices are located in a typical secured network.

I'll use the terms *trusted network* and *untrusted network* throughout this chapter, so it's important that you can see where they are found in a typical secured network. The demilitarized zone (DMZ) can be global (real) Internet addresses or private addresses, depending on how you configure your firewall, but this is typically where you'll find the HTTP, DNS, email, and other Internet-type corporate servers.

As discussed previously, instead of having routers, you can use virtual local area networks (VLANs) with switches on the inside trusted network. Multilayer switches containing their own security features can sometimes replace internal (LAN) routers to provide higher performance in VLAN architectures.

First, let's discuss the security threats a typical secured internetwork faces; then I'll explain some methods of protecting the internetwork using the Cisco IOS Firewall feature set and access lists.

FIGURE 6.1   A typical secured network

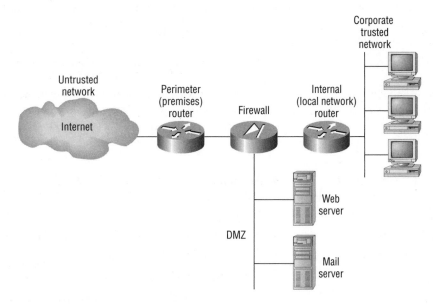

Recognizing Security Threats

Security attacks vary considerably in their complexity and threat level, and some even happen because of user error.

It all comes down to planning, or rather, lack thereof. Basically, the vital tool that the Internet has become today was absolutely unforeseen by those who brought it into being. This is a big reason why security is now such an issue—most IP implementations are innately insecure. Fortunately, Cisco has a few tricks up its sleeve to help us with this, but first, let's examine some common attack profiles:

Application Layer Attacks   These attacks commonly zero in on well-known holes in the software that is typically found running on servers. Favorite targets include FTP, sendmail, and HTTP. Because the permissions level granted to these accounts is most often "privileged," intruders simply access and exploit the machine that's running one of the applications I just mentioned.

Autorooters   You can think of these as a kind of hacker automaton. Hackers use something called a *rootkit* to probe, scan, and then capture data on a strategically positioned computer that's poised to give them "eyes" into entire systems—automatically!

Backdoors   These are simply paths leading into a computer or network. Through simple invasions, or via more elaborate "Trojan horse" code, intruders can use their implanted inroads into a specific host or even a network whenever they want to—until you detect and stop them, that is!

Denial of Service (DoS) and Distributed Denial of Service (DDoS) Attacks   Basically, a service is made unavailable by overwhelming the system that normally provides it. A Denial of Service attack is characterized by a flood of packets that are requesting a TCP connection to a server, and there are several different flavors:

TCP SYN Flood   This type of attack begins when a client initiates a seemingly run-of-the-mill TCP connection and sends a SYN message to a server. The server predictably responds by sending a SYN-ACK message back to the client machine, which then establishes the connection by returning an ACK message. This sounds fine, but it's actually during this process—when the connection is only halfway open—that the victim machine is literally flooded with a deluge of half-open connections and pretty much becomes paralyzed.

"Ping of Death" Attacks   TCP/IP's maximum packet size is 65,536 octets, and this attack is executed by simply pinging with oversized packets, causing a device to keep rebooting incessantly, freeze up, or just totally crash.

Tribe Flood Network (TFN) and Tribe Flood Network 2000 (TFN2K)   TFN and TFN2K initiate synchronized DoS attacks from multiple sources and can target multiple devices. This is achieved, in part, by something known as "IP spoofing," which I'll be describing soon.

Stacheldraht   This attack is actually a mélange of methods, and it translates from the German term for barbed wire. It basically incorporates TFN and adds a dash of encryption. It all begins with a huge invasion at the root level, leading up to a DoS attack.

IP Spoofing   This is pretty much what it sounds like it is—an intruder from within or outside your network masquerades as a trusted host machine by doing one of two things: presenting with an IP address that's inside your network's scope of trusted addresses, or using an approved, trusted external IP address. Because the hacker's true identity is veiled behind the spoofed address, this is often just the beginning of your problems.

Man-in-the-Middle Attacks   These attacks involve stealing packets when they are en route. A common guilty party could be someone working for your own ISP using a tool known as a *sniffer* (discussed later) and augmenting it with routing and transport protocols.

Network Reconnaissance   Before breaking into a network, hackers often gather all the information they can about it, because the more they know about the network, the better they can compromise it. They accomplish their objectives through methods such as port scans, DNS queries, and ping sweeps.

Packet Sniffers   This is the tool I mentioned earlier, but I didn't tell you what it is, and it may come as a surprise that it's actually software. Here's how it works: A network adapter card is set to promiscuous mode so that it will send all packets snagged from the network's Physical layer through to a special application to be viewed and sorted. A packet sniffer can nick some highly valuable, sensitive data including, but not limited to, passwords and usernames, making them prized among identity thieves.

Password Attacks   These come in many varieties, and even though they can be achieved via more sophisticated types of attacks like IP spoofing, packet sniffing, and Trojan horses, their sole purpose is to discover user passwords so that the thief can pretend to be a valid user and then access that user's privileges and resources.

Brute Force Attack   This is another software-oriented attack. It employs a program running on a targeted network that tries to log in to some type of shared network resource such as a server. For the hacker, it's ideal if the accessed accounts have a lot of privileges, because then they can form backdoors to gain access later and bypass the need for passwords entirely.

Port Redirection Attacks   This approach requires a host machine that the hacker has broken into and uses to get malicious traffic (that normally wouldn't be allowed passage) through a firewall.

Trojan Horse Attacks and Viruses   These two are actually pretty similar. Both Trojan horses and viruses infect user machines with malicious code and mess them up with varying degrees of paralysis, destruction, and even death! They do have their differences, though. Viruses are really just nasty programs attached to command.com, which just happens to be the main interpreter for all Windows systems. Viruses then run amok, deleting files and infecting any flavor of command.com they find on the diseased machine. The difference between a virus and a Trojan horse is that Trojans are actually complete applications encased inside code that makes them appear to be completely different entities—say, a simple, innocent game—instead of the ugly implements of destruction they truly are.

Trust Exploitation Attacks   These happen when someone exploits a trust relationship inside your network. For example, a company's perimeter network connection usually shelters important things like SMTP, DNS, and HTTP servers, making the servers really vulnerable because they're all on the same segment.

I'm not going to go into detail on how to mitigate each and every one of the security threats I just talked about, not only because that would be outside the scope of this book, but also because the methods I am going to teach you will truly protect you from being attacked in general. You will learn enough tricks to make all but the most determined hackers give up on you and search for easier prey. So basically, think of this as a chapter on how to practice "safe networking."

Exam Essentials

Remember the basic strategy for security.   In medium-sized to large enterprise networks, the various strategies for security are based on some recipe of internal and perimeter routers plus firewall devices.

Remember the four typical Denial of Service (DoS) attacks.   There are four typical DoS attacks used on today's networks: TCP SYN flood, Ping of Death, Tribe Flood Network (TFN), and Stacheldraht.

Explain General Methods to Mitigate Common Security Threats to Network Devices, Hosts, and Applications

Cisco IOS software runs on upward of 80 percent of the Internet backbone routers out there, and it's probably the most critical part of the network infrastructure. Therefore, the discussion for this section will assume that Cisco IOS's software-based security, known as the *Cisco IOS Firewall* feature set, is being used for the end-to-end Internet, intranet, and remote-access network security solutions. Let's take a look.

Cisco's IOS Firewall

Here's where you're going to find out how to mitigate some of the more common security threats on the list I gave you earlier in this chapter by using these Cisco IOS Firewall features:

Stateful IOS Firewall Inspection Engine   This is your perimeter protection feature because it gives your internal users secure access control on a per-application basis. People often call it *Context-Based Access Control (CBAC)*.

Intrusion Detection   A deep packet inspection tool that lets you monitor, intercept, and respond to abuse in real time by referencing 102 of the most common attack and intrusion detection signatures.

Firewall Voice Traversal   An application-level feature based on the protocol's understanding of call flow, as well as the relevant open channels. It supports both the H.323v2 and Session Initiation Protocol (SIP) voice protocols.

ICMP Inspection   Basically permits responses to ICMP packets, such as ping and traceroute, that come from inside your firewall while denying other ICMP traffic.

Authentication Proxy   A feature that makes users authenticate any time they want to access the network's resources through HTTP, HTTPS, FTP, and Telnet. It keeps personal network access profiles for users and automatically retrieves them from a RADIUS or TACACS+ server and applies them.

Destination URL Policy Management   A suite of features that's commonly referred to as *URL filtering*.

Per-User Firewalls   Personalized, user-specific, downloadable firewalls obtained through service providers. You can also get personalized ACLs and other settings via AAA server profile storage.

Cisco IOS Router and Firewall Provisioning   Allows for automatic router provisioning based on the role of the device, version updates, and security policies.

Denial of Service (DoS) Detection and Prevention   A feature that checks packet headers and drops any packets it finds suspicious.

Dynamic Port Mapping   A sort of adapter that permits applications supported by firewalls on nonstandard ports.

Java Applet Blocking   Protects you from any strange, unrecognized Java applets.

Basic and Advanced Traffic Filtering

You can use standard, extended, and even dynamic ACLs like Lock-and-Key traffic filtering with Cisco's IOS Firewall. You also get to apply access controls to any network segment you want. Plus, you can specify the exact kind of traffic you want to allow to pass through any segment.

Here are some of the variations of access control and security enhancing options available:

Policy-Based, Multi-Interface Support   Allows you to control user access by IP address and interface depending on your security policy.

Network Address Translation (NAT)   Conceals the internal network from the outside, increasing security.

Time-Based Access Lists   Determines security policies based on the exact time of day and the particular day of the week.

Peer Router Authentication   Guarantees that routers are getting dependable routing information from actual, trusted sources. (For this to work, you need a routing protocol that supports authentication, such as RIPv2, EIGRP, or OSPF.)

Now that you've been briefed on security threats, relevant features of the Cisco IOS Firewall, and how to use that software to your advantage, let's dive deep into the world of access lists and learn how to use ACLs to mitigate security threats.

Exam Essentials

Remember the basic services that the Cisco IOS Firewall provides.   The Cisco IOS Firewall provides, at a minimum, a stateful IOS firewall inspection engine, intrusion detection, firewall voice traversal, ICMP inspection, and authentication proxy, among many other services.

Describe the Functions of Common Security Appliances and Applications

In this section, I'll discuss the most commonly used advanced access control lists and applications used by Cisco routers. First, however, I am going to mention two security appliances typically found on a network.

Security Appliances

The two most noteworthy technologies that you can use to provide network security are intrusion prevention systems (IPS) and intrusion detection systems (IDS).

An IPS is an appliance that monitors network activities for malicious or unwanted behavior and can react in real time to block or prevent those activities. For example, an IPS will operate in-line to monitor all network traffic for malicious code or attacks. When an attack is detected, it can drop the offending packets while still allowing all other traffic to pass.

An IDS generally detects unwanted manipulations to computer systems, mainly through the Internet. The manipulations may take the form of attacks by crackers. An IDS is used to detect many types of malicious network traffic and computer usage that can't be detected by a conventional firewall. This includes network attacks against vulnerable services, data-driven attacks on applications, host-based attacks such as privilege escalation, unauthorized logins and access to sensitive files, and malware (viruses, Trojan horses, and worms).

Lock and Key (Dynamic ACLs)

This type of ACL depends on either remote or local Telnet authentication in combination with extended ACLs.

Before you can configure a dynamic ACL, you need to apply an extended ACL on your router to stop the flow of traffic through it. The only way anyone can get through the blockade is if they telnet the router and gain authentication. It works like this: The Telnet connection the user initiated gets dropped and is replaced with a single-entry dynamic ACL that's appended to the extended ACL already in place. This allows traffic to get through for a specific amount of time—and as you may have guessed, time-outs can and do happen.

Reflexive ACLs

These ACLs filter IP packets depending on upper-layer session information, and they often permit outbound traffic to pass but place limitations on inbound traffic. You can't define reflexive ACLs with numbered or standard IP ACLs, or any other protocol ACLs for that matter. They can be used along with other standard or static extended ACLs, but they're only defined with extended named IP ACLs.

Context-Based Access Control (Cisco IOS Firewall)

Context-Based Access Control (CBAC) is available only if you have the Cisco IOS Firewall set in the IOS. It's used to allow or deny connections based on the context in which the connections are requested.

CBAC's job is to scrutinize any and all traffic that's attempting to come through the firewall, so it can find out about and control the state information for TCP and UDP sessions. It uses the information it's gathered to determine whether to create a temporary pathway into the firewall's access lists.

To make this happen, just configure `ip inspect` lists in the same direction that the traffic is flowing. If you don't do this, any return traffic will be unable to get back through, which will negatively impact any session connections originating from inside the internal network.

Take a look at Figure 6.2, which illustrates in a very simple way how a Cisco IOS Firewall (CBAC) works.

FIGURE 6.2 A Cisco IOS Firewall (CBAC)

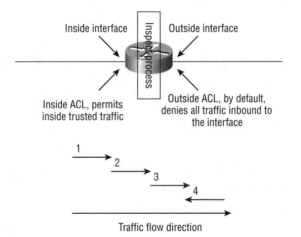

A router that's configured with the Cisco IOS Firewall will process traffic in the following manner:

1. If the inside ACL approves, the router will get all of the inside packets sent to it.

2. The approved traffic is subjected to the firewall's `ip inspect` process, which adds the approved connection's state information into the state table.

3. The traffic passes through the IP inspect process, which then creates a dynamic ACL entry and puts it into the outside ACL so that the return traffic will be allowed to pass back through the router.

Authentication Proxy

I have Authentication Proxy set on all of my routers. In order for me to do that, I also had to have the Cisco IOS Firewall feature set up. I have the configuration set up this way because the authentication proxy is a good thing to have on my side.

This is true because it authenticates inbound users, outbound users, or both. Those who would normally be blocked by an ACL can just bring up a browser to get through the firewall and then authenticate on a TACACS+ or RADIUS server.

Exam Essentials

Remember the two types of security appliances typically found on a network.   The two types of security appliances that you'll typically find on a network are intrusion prevention systems (IPS) and intrusion detection systems (IDS).

Understand what CBAC is.   Context-Based Access Control scrutinizes any and all traffic that's attempting to come through the firewall, so it can find out about and control the state information for TCP and UDP sessions.

Describe Security Recommended Practices, Including Initial Steps to Secure Network Devices

Here's a list of the many security threats you can mitigate with ACLs:

- IP address spoofing, inbound
- IP address spoofing, outbound
- Denial of service (DoS) TCP SYN attacks, blocking external attacks
- DoS TCP SYN attacks, using TCP Intercept
- DoS smurf attacks
- Filtering ICMP messages, inbound
- Filtering ICMP messages, outbound
- Filtering traceroute

You should never configure a private network to allow IP packets that contain the source address of any internal hosts or networks. Moreover, when configuring ACLs from the Internet to your production network, you should follow these rules in order to mitigate security problems:

- Deny any addresses from your internal networks.
- Deny any local host addresses (127.0.0.0/8).
- Deny any reserved private addresses.
- Deny any addresses in the IP multicast address range (224.0.0.0/4).

None of these addresses should be allowed to enter your internetwork!

Exam Essentials

Remember the security rules that you should follow when configuring ACLs from the Internet to your production network. Deny any addresses from your internal networks, deny any local host addresses (127.0.0.0/8), deny any reserved private addresses, and deny any addresses in the IP multicast address range (224.0.0.0/4).

Review Questions

1. Which Cisco IOS Firewall feature set allows you to use a browser to get through the firewall and then authenticate on a TACACS+ or RADIUS server?

    A. Reflexive ACLs

    B. Authentication proxy

    C. CBAC

    D. Dynamic ACLs

2. What does the Cisco IOS use to scrutinize any and all traffic that's attempting to come through the firewall so that it can find out about and control the state information for TCP and UDP sessions?

    A. Reflexive ACLs

    B. Authentication proxy

    C. CBAC

    D. Dynamic ACLs

3. Which type of ACLs filter IP packets depending on upper-layer session information and can permit outbound traffic to pass but place limitations on inbound traffic?

    A. Reflexive ACLs

    B. Authentication proxy

    C. CBAC

    D. Dynamic ACLs

4. Which type of ACL depends on either remote or local Telnet authentication in combination with extended ACLs?

    A. Reflexive ACLs

    B. Authentication proxy

    C. CBAC

    D. Dynamic ACLs

5. Which two of the following are considered to be Denial of Service attacks (DoS)?

    A. TCP SYN flood

    B. Application layer attacks

    C. Ping of Death attacks

    D. Autorooters

6. Which of the following commonly zero in on well-known holes in the software that is typically found running on servers?

   A. Application layer attacks

   B. Autorooters

   C. Backdoors

   D. Denial of Service (DoS) attacks

7. Which of the following refers to paths leading into a computer or network that can be used for Trojan horse code?

   A. Application layer attacks

   B. Autorooters

   C. Backdoors

   D. Denial of Service (DoS)

8. Which of the following probe, scan, and then capture data on a strategically positioned computer?

   A. Application layer attacks

   B. Autorooters

   C. Backdoors

   D. Denial of Service (DoS) attacks

9. Which of the following makes a service unavailable by overwhelming the system that normally provides it?

   A. Application layer attacks

   B. Autorooters

   C. Backdoors

   D. Denial of Service (DoS) attacks

10. Which two of the following are security appliances that can be installed in a network?

    A. IDS

    B. IPS

    C. AAA

    D. SDM

Answers to Review Questions

1. B. Users who would normally be blocked by an ACL can just bring up a browser to get through the firewall and then authenticate on a TACACS+ or RADIUS server.

2. C. The Context-based Access Control's (CBAC's) job is to scrutinize any and all traffic that's attempting to come through the firewall so it can find out about and control the state information for TCP and UDP sessions. It also uses the information it's gathered to determine whether to create a temporary pathway into the firewall's access lists.

3. A. Reflexive ACLs filter IP packets depending on upper-layer session information, and they often permit outbound traffic to pass but place limitations on inbound traffic. You can't define reflexive ACLs with numbered or standard IP ACLs, or any other protocol ACLs for that matter.

4. D. Dynamic ACLs first drop the Telnet connection that the user initiated and replace it with a single-entry dynamic ACL that's appended to the extended ACL already in place. This causes traffic to be allowed through for a specific amount of time.

5. A, C. The four typical types of Denial of Service attacks are TCP SYN flood, Ping of Death, Tribe Flood Network (TFN), and Stacheldraht.

6. A. Application layer attacks commonly zero in on well-known holes in the software that's typically found running on servers. Favorite targets include FTP, sendmail and HTTP.

7. C. Backdoors are simply paths leading into a computer or network. However, through simple invasions, or via more elaborate Trojan horse code, hackers can use them as inroads into a specific host or even a network.

8. B. Intruders use something called a rootkit to probe, scan, and then capture data on a strategically positioned computer that's poised to give them "eyes" into entire systems.

9. D. DoS attacks make a service unavailable by overwhelming the system that normally provides it, and there are several different versions.

10. A, B. The two technologies that you can use to provide network security are intrusion prevention systems (IPS), which (hopefully) prevent intrusions, and intrusion detection systems (IDS), which only detect intrusions and tell you about them.

Chapter

7

Implement, Verify, and Troubleshoot NAT and ACLs in a Medium-Sized Enterprise Branch Office Network

THE CISCO CCNA EXAM OBJECTIVES COVERED IN THIS CHAPTER INCLUDE THE FOLLOWING:

- ✓ Describe the purpose and types of ACLs.

- ✓ Configure and apply ACLs based on network filtering requirements (including CLI/SDM).

- ✓ Configure and apply ACLs to limit Telnet and SSH access to the router using (including SDM/CLI).

- ✓ Verify and monitor ACLs in a network environment.

- ✓ Troubleshoot ACL issues.

- ✓ Explain the basic operation of NAT.

- ✓ Configure NAT for given network requirements using (including CLI/SDM).

- ✓ Troubleshoot NAT issues.

The proper use and configuration of access lists is a vital part of router configuration because access lists are such versatile networking accessories. Contributing mightily to the efficiency and operation of your network, access lists give network managers a huge amount of control over traffic flow throughout the enterprise. With access lists, managers can gather basic statistics on packet flow and security policies can be implemented. Sensitive devices can also be protected from unauthorized access.

In this chapter, we'll look more closely at ACLs, Network Address Translation (NAT), Dynamic NAT, and Port Address Translation (PAT), also known as *NAT Overload*.

Describe the Purpose and Types of ACLs

For information on this objective, please see the section titled "Implement Basic Router Security" in Chapter 4, "Configure, Verify, and Troubleshoot Basic Router Operation and Routing on Cisco Devices."

Configure and Apply ACLs Based on Network Filtering Requirements (Including CLI/SDM)

In this section, configuring standard and extended access lists will be covered. This will include a look at a technique for specifying ranges of addressing called *wildcard masking* that can be used with all three types of access lists. First, let's look at how standard ALs are configured and applied.

Configuring Standard IP Access Lists

As you learned in Chapter 4, standard IP access lists filter network traffic by examining the source IP address in a packet. You create a *standard IP access list* by using the access-list numbers 1–99 or 1300–1999 (expanded range). Access-list types are generally differentiated using a number. Based on the number used when the access list is created, the router knows which type of syntax to expect as the list is entered. By using numbers 1–99 or 1300–1999, you're telling the router that you want to create a standard IP access list, so the router will expect syntax specifying only the source IP address in the test lines.

The following is an example of the many access-list number ranges that you can use to filter traffic on your network (the protocols for which you can specify access lists depend on your IOS version):

```
Corp(config)#access-list ?
  <1-99>            IP standard access list
  <100-199>         IP extended access list
  <1100-1199>       Extended 48-bit MAC address access list
  <1300-1999>       IP standard access list (expanded range)
  <200-299>         Protocol type-code access list
  <2000-2699>       IP extended access list (expanded range)
  <700-799>         48-bit MAC address access list
  compiled          Enable IP access-list compilation
  dynamic-extended  Extend the dynamic ACL absolute timer
  rate-limit        Simple rate-limit specific access list
```

Let's take a look at the syntax used when creating a standard access list:

```
Corp(config)#access-list 10 ?
  deny    Specify packets to reject
  permit  Specify packets to forward
  remark  Access list entry comment
```

As I said, by using the access-list numbers 1–99 or 1300–1999, you're telling the router that you want to create a standard IP access list.

After you choose the access-list number, you need to decide whether you're creating a permit or deny statement. For this example, you will create a deny statement:

```
Corp(config)#access-list 10 deny ?
  Hostname or A.B.C.D  Address to match
  any                  Any source host
  host                 A single host address
```

The next step requires a more detailed explanation. Three options are available. You can use the any parameter to permit or deny any host or network, you can use an IP address to specify either a single host or a range of them, or you can use the host command to specify a specific host only. The any command is pretty obvious—any source address matches the statement, so every packet compared against this line will match. The host command is relatively simple, as you can see in the following example:

```
Corp(config)#access-list 10 deny host ?
  Hostname or A.B.C.D  Host address
Corp(config)#access-list 10 deny host 172.16.30.2
```

This tells the list to deny any packets from host 172.16.30.2. The default parameter is host. In other words, if you type **access-list 10 deny 172.16.30.2**, the router assumes that you mean host 172.16.30.2.

But there's another way to specify either a particular host or a range of hosts—you can use wildcard masking. In fact, to specify any range of hosts, you have to use wildcard masking in the access list.

Wildcard Masking

Wildcards are used with access lists to specify an individual host, a network, or a certain range of a network or networks. To understand a *wildcard*, you need to understand what a *block size* is. A block size is used to specify a range of addresses. Some of the different block sizes available are 64, 32, 16, 8, and 4.

When you need to specify a range of addresses, you choose the next-largest block size for your needs. For example, if you need to specify 34 networks, you need a block size of 64. If you want to specify 18 hosts, you need a block size of 32. If you specify only two networks, then a block size of 4 would work.

Wildcards are used with the host or network address to tell the router a range of available addresses to filter. To specify a host, the address would look like this:

172.16.30.5 0.0.0.0

The four zeros represent each octet of the address. Whenever a zero is present, it means that octet in the address must match exactly. To specify that an octet can be any value, the value of 255 is used. As an example, here's how a /24 subnet is specified with a wildcard:

172.16.30.0 0.0.0.255

This tells the router to match up the first three octets exactly, but the fourth octet can be any value.

That was the easy part. What if you want to specify only a small range of subnets? This is where the block sizes come into play. You have to specify the range of values in a block size. In other words, you can't choose to specify 20 networks. You can only specify the exact amount as the block size value. For example, the range would have to be either 16 or 32, but not 20.

Let's say you want to block access to part of the network that is in the range from 172.16.8.0 through 172.16.15.0. That is a block size of 8. Your network number would be 172.16.8.0, and the wildcard would be 0.0.7.255. The 7.255 is what the router uses to determine the block size. The network and wildcard tell the router to start at 172.16.8.0 and go up a block size of eight addresses to network 172.16.15.0.

All you have to do is remember that the wildcard is always one number less than the block size. So, in this example, the wildcard would be 7 because the block size is 8. If you used a block size of 16, the wildcard would be 15.

The following example tells the router to match the first three octets exactly but that the fourth octet can be anything:

Corp(config)#**access-list 10 deny 172.16.10.0 0.0.0.255**

The next example tells the router to match the first two octets and that the last two octets can be any value:

```
Corp(config)#access-list 10 deny 172.16.0.0
  0.0.255.255
```

Try to figure out the next line:

```
Corp(config)#access-list 10 deny 172.16.16.0 0.0.3.255
```

This configuration tells the router to start at network 172.16.16.0 and use a block size of 4. The range would be 172.16.16.0 through 172.16.19.255.

The following example shows an access list starting at 172.16.16.0 and going up a block size of 8 to 172.16.23.255:

```
Corp(config)#access-list 10 deny 172.16.16.0 0.0.7.255
```

The next example starts at network 172.16.32.0 and goes up a block size of 16 to 172.16.47.255:

```
Corp(config)#access-list 10 deny 172.16.32.0 0.0.15.255
```

The next example starts at network 172.16.64.0 and goes up a block size of 64 to 172.16.127.255:

```
Corp(config)#access-list 10 deny 172.16.64.0 0.0.63.255
```

The last example starts at network 192.168.160.0 and goes up a block size of 32 to 192.168.191.255:

```
Corp(config)#access-list 10 deny 192.168.160.0 0.0.31.255
```

Here are two more things to keep in mind when working with block sizes and wildcards:

- Each block size must start at 0 or a multiple of the block size. For example, you can't say that you want a block size of 8 and then start at 12. You must use 0–7, 8–15, 16–23, and so on. For a block size of 32, the ranges are 0–31, 32–63, 64–95, and so on.

- Using the command any does the same thing as writing out the wildcard 0.0.0.0 255.255.255.255.

 Wildcard masking is a crucial skill to master when you are creating IP access lists. It's used identically when you are creating standard and extended IP access lists.

Using a Standard Access List

In this section, you'll learn how to use a standard access list to stop specific users from gaining access to the Finance Department LAN.

In Figure 7.1, a router has three LAN connections and one WAN connection to the Internet. Users on the Sales LAN should not have access to the Finance LAN, but they should be able to access the Internet and the Marketing Department. The Marketing LAN needs to access the Finance LAN for application services.

FIGURE 7.1   Three LANs and a WAN connection

On the router in the figure, the following standard IP access list is configured:

```
Lab_A#config t
Lab_A(config)#access-list 10 deny 172.16.40.0 0.0.0.255
Lab_A(config)#access-list 10 permit any
```

It's very important to know that using the any command is the same thing as saying the following using wildcard masking:

```
Lab_A(config)#access-list 10 permit 0.0.0.0 255.255.255.255
```

Because the wildcard mask says that none of the octets is to be evaluated, every address matches the test condition. So, this is functionally the same as using the any keyword.

At this point, the access list is configured to deny source addresses from the Sales LAN access to the Finance LAN and allow everyone else. Don't forget that no action will be taken until the access list is applied on an interface in a specific direction. Where should this access list be placed? If you place it as an incoming access list on E0, you might as well shut down the Ethernet interface because all of the Sales LAN devices will be denied access to all networks attached to the router. The best place to apply this access list is on the E1 interface as an outbound list:

```
Lab_A(config)#int e1
Lab_A(config-if)#ip access-group 10 out
```

This completely stops traffic from 172.16.40.0 from getting out Ethernet 1. It has no effect on the hosts from the Sales LAN accessing the Marketing LAN and the Internet because traffic to those destinations doesn't go through interface E1. Any packet trying to exit out E1 will have to go through the access list first. If an inbound list were to be placed on E0, then any packet trying to enter interface E0 would have to go through the access list before being routed to an exit interface.

Let's take a look at another example of a standard access list. Figure 7.2 shows an internetwork of two routers with three LANs and one serial WAN connection.

FIGURE 7.2   Two routers with three LANs and one serial WAN connection

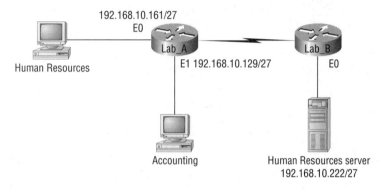

You need to stop the Accounting users from accessing the Human Resources server attached to the Lab_B router but allow all other users access to that LAN. What standard access list would you create and where would you place it?

Standard access lists, by rule of thumb, are placed closest to the destination—in this example, Ethernet 0 outbound on the Lab_B router. Here is the access list that should be placed on the Lab_B router:

```
Lab_B#config t
Lab_B(config)#access-list 10 deny 192.168.10.128 0.0.0.31
Lab_B(config)#access-list 10 permit any
Lab_B(config)#interface Ethernet 0
Lab_B(config-if)#ip access-group 10 out
```

Before we move on to restricting Telnet access on a router, let's take a look at one more standard access list example, but it will require some thought. This example begins with a router that has four LAN connections and one WAN connection to the Internet, as shown in Figure 7.3.

You need to write an access list that will stop access from each of the four LANs shown in the diagram to the Internet. Each of the LANs shows a single host's IP address, and from that you need to determine the subnet and use wildcards to configure the access list.

FIGURE 7.3 A router with four LAN connections and one WAN connection to the Internet

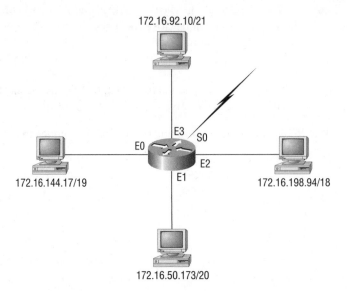

172.16.92.10/21

E3   S0
E0
E2
172.16.144.17/19   E1   172.16.198.94/18

172.16.50.173/20

Here is an example of what your answer should look like (starting with the network on E0 and working through to E3):

```
Router(config)#access-list 1 deny 172.16.128.0 0.0.31.255
Router(config)#access-list 1 deny 172.16.48.0 0.0.15.255
Router(config)#access-list 1 deny 172.16.192.0 0.0.63.255
Router(config)#access-list 1 deny 172.16.88.0 0.0.7.255
Router(config)#access-list 1 permit any
Router(config)#interface serial 0
Router(config-if)#ip access-group 1 out
```

Controlling VTY (Telnet) Access

For information on this subobjective, see the section titled "Configure and Apply ACLs to Limit Telnet and SSH Access to the Router Using (Including SDM/CLI)" later in this chapter.

Extended Access Lists

In the previous standard IP access list example, you had to block all access from the Sales LAN to the Finance Department. What if you needed Sales to gain access to a certain server on the Finance LAN but not to other network services for security reasons? With a standard IP access list, you can't allow users to get to one network service and not another. Said another way, when you need to make decisions based on both source and destination addresses, a standard access list won't allow you to do that because it only makes decisions based on the source address.

However, an *extended access list* will hook you up because extended access lists allow you to specify the source and destination addresses as well as the protocol and port number that identify the upper-layer protocol or application. By using extended access lists, you can effectively allow users access to a physical LAN and stop them from accessing specific hosts—or even specific services on those hosts.

Here's an example of an extended IP access list:

```
Corp(config)#access-list ?
  <1-99>            IP standard access list
  <100-199>         IP extended access list
  <1100-1199>       Extended 48-bit MAC address access list
  <1300-1999>       IP standard access list (expanded range)
  <200-299>         Protocol type-code access list
  <2000-2699>       IP extended access list (expanded range)
  <700-799>         48-bit MAC address access list
  compiled          Enable IP access-list compilation
  dynamic-extended  Extend the dynamic ACL absolute timer
  rate-limit        Simple rate-limit specific access list
```

The first command shows the access-list numbers available. You'll use the extended access-list range from 100 to 199. Be sure to notice that the range 2000–2699 is also available for extended IP access lists.

At this point, you need to decide what type of list entry you are making. For this example, you'll choose a deny list entry.

```
Corp(config)#access-list 110 ?
  deny     Specify packets to reject
  dynamic  Specify a DYNAMIC list of PERMITs or DENYs
  permit   Specify packets to forward
  remark   Access list entry comment
```

Once you choose the access-list type, you'll need to select a protocol field entry.

```
Corp(config)#access-list 110 deny ?
  <0-255>  An IP protocol number
  ahp      Authentication Header Protocol
  eigrp    Cisco's EIGRP routing protocol
  esp      Encapsulation Security Payload
  gre      Cisco's GRE tunneling
  icmp     Internet Control Message Protocol
  igmp     Internet Gateway Message Protocol
  ip       Any Internet Protocol
  ipinip   IP in IP tunneling
  nos      KA9Q NOS compatible IP over IP tunneling
```

```
ospf      OSPF routing protocol
pcp       Payload Compression Protocol
pim       Protocol Independent Multicast
tcp       Transmission Control Protocol
udp       User Datagram Protocol
```

 If you want to filter by Application layer protocol, you have to choose the appropriate layer 4 transport protocol after the permit or deny statement. For example, to filter Telnet or FTP, you should specify TCP because both Telnet and FTP use TCP at the Transport layer. If you were to choose IP, you wouldn't be allowed to specify a specific application protocol later.

Here, you'll choose to filter an Application layer protocol that uses TCP by selecting TCP as the protocol. You'll specify the specific TCP port later. Next, you will be prompted for the source IP address of the host or network (you can choose the any command to deny any source address):

```
Corp(config)#access-list 110 deny tcp ?
  A.B.C.D  Source address
  any      Any source host
  host     A single source host
```

After the source address is selected, the destination address will be chosen:

```
Corp(config)#access-list 110 deny tcp any ?
  A.B.C.D  Destination address
  any      Any destination host
  eq       Match only packets on a given port number
  gt       Match only packets with a greater port number
  host     A single destination host
  lt       Match only packets with a lower port number
  neq      Match only packets not on a given port number
  range    Match only packets in the range of port numbers
```

In the following example, any source IP address that has a destination IP address of 172.16.30.2 has been denied.

```
Corp(config)#access-list 110 deny tcp any host 172.16.30.2 ?
  ack          Match on the ACK bit
  dscp         Match packets with given dscp value
  eq           Match only packets on a given port number
  established  Match established connections
  fin          Match on the FIN bit
  fragments    Check non-initial fragments
```

```
gt            Match only packets with a greater port number
log           Log matches against this entry
log-input     Log matches against this entry, including input interface
lt            Match only packets with a lower port number
neq           Match only packets not on a given port number
precedence    Match packets with given precedence value
psh           Match on the PSH bit
range         Match only packets in the range of port numbers
rst           Match on the RST bit
syn           Match on the SYN bit
time-range    Specify a time-range
tos           Match packets with given TOS value
urg           Match on the URG bit
<cr>
```

You can press Enter here and leave the access list as is—but if you do that, all TCP traffic to host 172.16.30.2 will be denied, regardless of the destination port. You can be even more specific: Once you have the host addresses in place, you can just specify the type of service you are denying. The help screen shown in the following example displays the available options. You can choose a port number or use the application or protocol name:

```
Corp(config)#access-list 110 deny tcp any host 172.16.30.2 eq ?
  <0-65535>    Port number
  bgp          Border Gateway Protocol (179)
  chargen      Character generator (19)
  cmd          Remote commands (rcmd, 514)
  daytime      Daytime (13)
  discard      Discard (9)
  domain       Domain Name Service (53)
  drip         Dynamic Routing Information Protocol (3949)
  echo         Echo (7)
  exec         Exec (rsh, 512)
  finger       Finger (79)
  ftp          File Transfer Protocol (21)
  ftp-data     FTP data connections (20)
  gopher       Gopher (70)
  hostname     NIC hostname server (101)
  ident        Ident Protocol (113)
  irc          Internet Relay Chat (194)
  klogin       Kerberos login (543)
  kshell       Kerberos shell (544)
  login        Login (rlogin, 513)
  lpd          Printer service (515)
```

```
nntp          Network News Transport Protocol (119)
pim-auto-rp   PIM Auto-RP (496)
pop2          Post Office Protocol v2 (109)
pop3          Post Office Protocol v3 (110)
smtp          Simple Mail Transport Protocol (25)
sunrpc        Sun Remote Procedure Call (111)
syslog        Syslog (514)
tacacs        TAC Access Control System (49)
talk          Talk (517)
telnet        Telnet (23)
time          Time (37)
uucp          Unix-to-Unix Copy Program (540)
whois         Nicname (43)
www           World Wide Web (HTTP, 80)
```

At this point, let's block Telnet (port 23) to host 172.16.30.2 only. The log parameter that I added is used to log messages every time the access list is hit and can be used to monitor inappropriate access attempts as follows:

Corp(config)#**access-list 110 deny tcp any host 172.16.30.2 eq 23 log**

You need to keep in mind that the next line is an implicit deny any by default. If you apply this access list to an interface, you might as well shut the interface down, because by default there is an implicit deny all at the end of every access list. You've got to close the access list with the following command:

Corp(config)#**access-list 110 permit ip any any**

Remember, the 0.0.0.0 255.255.255.255 is the same command as any, so the command could look like this:

Corp(config)#**access-list 110 permit ip 0.0.0.0 255.255.255.255**
0.0.0.0 255.255.255.255

Once the access list is created, you need to apply it to an interface (it's the same command as the IP standard list):

Corp(config-if)#**ip access-group 110 in**

Or this:

Corp(config-if)#**ip access-group 110 out**

In the following section, we'll look at an example of how to use an extended access list.

Extended Access List Example 1

Using Figure 7.1 from the IP standard access list example, let's use the same network and deny access to a host at 172.16.30.5 on the Finance Department LAN for both Telnet and FTP services. All other services on this and all other hosts are acceptable for the Sales and Marketing departments to access.

The following access list should be created:

```
Lab_A#config t
Lab_A(config)#access-list 110 deny tcp any host
  172.16.30.5 eq 21
Lab_A(config)#access-list 110 deny tcp any host
  172.16.30.5 eq 23
Lab_A(config)#access-list 110 permit ip any any
```

The access-list 110 tells the router you are creating an extended IP access list. The tcp is the protocol field in the Network layer header. If the list doesn't say tcp here, you cannot filter by port numbers 21 and 23 as shown in the example. (These are FTP and Telnet, and they both use TCP for connection-oriented services.) The any command is the source, which means any IP address, and the host is the destination IP address.

 Instead of using the host 172.16.30.5 command when you created the extended access list, you could have entered **172.16.30.5 0.0.0.0** and there would be no difference in the result—other than the router would change the command to host 172.16.30.5 in the running-config.

After the list is created, it needs to be applied to the Ethernet 1 interface outbound. This applies the policy you created to all hosts and effectively blocks all FTP and Telnet access to 172.16.30.5 from outside the local LAN. If this list were created to only block access from the Sales LAN, then you'd have put this list closer to the source, or on Ethernet interface 0. So, in this situation, you'd apply the list to inbound traffic.

Go ahead and apply the list to interface E1 and block all outside FTP and Telnet access to the host:

```
Lab_A(config-if)#ip access-group 110 out
```

Extended Access List Example 2

In this example, we'll again use Figure 7.3, which has four LANs and a serial connection. We need to stop Telnet access to the networks attached to the Ethernet 1 and Ethernet 2 interfaces. If we used only one access list, it would not be a very effective one because of the latency that would be caused on the Ethernet 1 and 2 interfaces (because every packet going out those interfaces must be looked at), but if we used two lists, the latency could be less on each interface if configured correctly. However, because you're studying the CCNA objectives and not working in a real-world environment, we're going to look at this with only one access list.

The configuration on the router would look something like this, although the answer can vary:

```
Router(config)#access-list 110 deny tcp any 172.16.48.0 0.0.15.255
eq 23
Router(config)#access-list 110 deny tcp any 172.16.192.0 0.0.63.255
eq 23
Router(config)#access-list 110 permit ip any any
Router(config)#interface Ethernet 1
Router(config-if)#ip access-group 110 out
Router(config-if)#interface Ethernet 2
Router(config-if)#ip access-group 110 out
```

The important information you need to understand from this list is as follows: First, you need to verify that the number range is correct for the type of access list you are creating—in this example, it's extended, so the range must be 100–199. Second, you need to verify that the protocol field matches the upper-layer process or application—in this example, port 23 (Telnet).

The protocol parameter must be TCP because Telnet uses TCP. If the question stated to use TFTP, for example, then the protocol parameter would have to be UDP because TFTP uses UDP. Third, verify that the destination port number matches the application you are filtering for—in this case, port 23 matches Telnet, which is correct. Finally, the test statement `permit ip any any` is important to have at the end of the list to enable all packets other than Telnet packets destined for the LANs connected to Ethernet 1 and Ethernet 2.

> The SDM objectives are covered on the CD of the *CCNA Cisco Certified Network Associate Study Guide, 7th Edition* (Sybex, 2011).

Exam Essentials

Understand the standard IP access list configuration command.   To configure a standard IP access list, use the access-list numbers 1–99 or 1300-1999 in global configuration mode. Choose `permit` or deny, and then choose the source IP address you want to filter on using one of the three techniques covered earlier.

Understand the extended IP access list configuration command.   To configure an extended IP access list, use the access-list numbers 100–199 or 2000-2699 in global configuration mode. Choose `permit` or deny, the Network layer protocol, the source IP address you want to filter on, the destination address you want to filter on, and finally the Transport layer protocol (if selected).

Use wildcard masks effectively to filter the IP addresses to which an ACL applies. Wildcards are used with the host or network address to tell the router a range of available addresses to filter.

Contrast standard and extended ACLs.   Standard access lists can only filter based on the source IP address. Extended access lists allow you to specify the source and destination address as well as the protocol and port number that identify the upper-layer protocol or application.

Configure and Apply ACLs to Limit Telnet and SSH Access to the Router Using (Including SDM/CLI)

You'll probably have a difficult time trying to stop users from telnetting to a large router, because any active interface on a router is fair game for VTY access. You could try to create an extended IP access list that limits Telnet access to every IP address on the router. But if you did that, you'd have to apply it inbound on every interface, and that really wouldn't scale well to a large router with dozens, or even hundreds, of interfaces. Here's a much better solution: Use a standard IP access list to control access to the VTY lines themselves.

When you apply an access list to the VTY lines, you don't need to specify the Telnet protocol because access to the VTY implies terminal access. You also don't need to specify a destination address, because it really doesn't matter which interface address the user used as a target for the Telnet session. You really only need to control where the user is coming from—their source IP address.

To create and apply an ACL to the VTY line(s), follow these steps:

1.   Create a standard IP access list that permits only the host or hosts you want to be able to telnet into the routers.

2.   Apply the access list to the VTY line with the access-class command.

Here is an example of allowing only host 172.16.10.3 to telnet into a router:

```
Lab_A(config)#access-list 50 permit 172.16.10.3
Lab_A(config)#line vty 0 4
Lab_A(config-line)#access-class 50 in
```

Because of the implied deny any at the end of the list, the access list stops any host from telnetting into the router except the host 172.16.10.3, regardless of which individual IP address on the router is used as a target.

Cisco recommends that you use Secure Shell (SSH) instead of Telnet on the VTY lines of a router.

Secure Shell (SSH)

Instead of Telnet, you can use *Secure Shell* (SSH), which creates a more secure session than the Telnet application, which uses an unencrypted data stream. SSH uses encrypted keys to send data so that your username and password are not sent in the clear.

Here are the steps to setting up SSH:

1. Set your hostname:

   ```
   Router(config)#hostname Todd
   ```

2. Set the domain name (both the hostname and domain name are required for the encryption keys to be generated):

   ```
   Todd(config)#ip domain-name Lammle.com
   ```

3. Generate the encryption keys for securing the session:

   ```
   Todd(config)#crypto key generate rsa general-keys modulus ?
     <360-2048>  size of the key modulus [360-2048]
   Todd(config)#crypto key generate rsa general-keys modulus 1024
   The name for the keys will be: Todd.Lammle.com
   % The key modulus size is 1024 bits
   % Generating 1024 bit RSA keys, keys will be non-exportable...[OK]
   *June 24 19:25:30.035: %SSH-5-ENABLED: SSH 1.99 has been enabled
   ```

4. Set the maximum idle timer for a SSH session:

   ```
   Todd(config)#ip ssh time-out ?
     <1-120>  SSH time-out interval (secs)
   Todd(config)#ip ssh time-out 60
   ```

5. Set the maximum failed attempts for an SSH connection:

   ```
   Todd(config)#ip ssh authentication-retries ?
     <0-5>  Number of authentication retries
   Todd(config)#ip ssh authentication-retries 2
   ```

6. Connect to the VTY lines of the router:

   ```
   Todd(config)#line vty 0 1180
   ```

7. Configure SSH and then Telnet as access protocols:

   ```
   Todd(config-line)#transport input ssh telnet
   ```

If you do not use the keyword `telnet` at the end of the command string, only SSH will work on the router. I am not suggesting you use either way. Just understand that SSH is more secure than Telnet.

Exam Essentials

Remember the command on a VTY line that enables you to use SSH on a Cisco router.   The command to set SSH on a VTY line is `transport input ssh telnet`, although the command `telnet` at the end of the line is optional.

Control telnet access to a router by applying ACLs to the VTY lines.   To create and apply an ACL to the VTY line(s), follow these steps:

1. Create a standard IP access list that permits only the host or hosts you want to be able to telnet into the routers.
2. Apply the access list to the VTY line with the `access-class` command.

Configure SSH on a VTY line.   To configure SSH on a VTY line, follow these steps:

1. Set your hostname.
2. Set the domain name (both the hostname and domain name are required for the encryption keys to be generated).
3. Generate the encryption keys for securing the session.
4. Set the maximum idle timer for a SSH session.
5. Set the maximum failed attempts for an SSH connection.
6. Connect to the VTY lines of the router.
7. Configure SSH and then Telnet as access protocols.

Verify and Monitor ACLs in a Network Environment

Again, it's always good to be able to verify a router's configuration. Table 7.1 lists the commands that can be used to verify the configuration.

TABLE 7.1   Commands Used to Verify Access List Configuration

Command	Effect
`show access-list`	Displays all access lists and their parameters configured on the router. This command does not show you the list on which the interface is set.

TABLE 7.1   Commands Used to Verify Access List Configuration *(continued)*

Command	Effect
show access-list 110	Shows only the parameters for the access list 110. This command does not show you the list on which the interface is set.
show ip access-list	Shows only the IP access lists configured on the router.
show ip interface	Shows which interfaces have access lists set.
show running-config	Shows the access lists and which interfaces have access lists set.
show mac access-group	Displays MAC access lists applied to all layer 2 interfaces or the specified layer 2 interface (used on layer 2 switches only).

You're already somewhat familiar with the show running-config command, so let's take a look at the output from some of the other commands.

The show access-list command will list all access lists on the router, whether they're applied to an interface or not:

```
Lab_A#show access-list
Standard IP access list 10
    deny    172.16.40.0, wildcard bits 0.0.0.255
    permit any
Standard IP access list BlockSales
    deny    172.16.40.0, wildcard bits 0.0.0.255
    permit any
Extended IP access list 110
    deny tcp any host 172.16.30.5 eq ftp
    deny tcp any host 172.16.30.5 eq telnet
    permit ip any any
Lab_A#
```

First, notice that access lists 10 and 110, as well as a named access list (BlockSales), appear on this list. Second, when I created access list 110 that is shown in the output, I entered actual numbers for TCP ports (23), but for readability the show command generates the protocol names rather than TCP ports.

Here's the output of the show ip interface command:

```
Lab_A#show ip interface e1
Ethernet1 is up, line protocol is up
  Internet address is 172.16.30.1/24
```

```
    Broadcast address is 255.255.255.255
    Address determined by non-volatile memory
    MTU is 1500 bytes
    Helper address is not set
    Directed broadcast forwarding is disabled
    Outgoing access list is BlockSales
    Inbound access list is not set
    Proxy ARP is enabled
    Security level is default
    Split horizon is enabled
    ICMP redirects are always sent
    ICMP unreachables are always sent
    ICMP mask replies are never sent
    IP fast switching is disabled
    IP fast switching on the same interface is disabled
    IP Null turbo vector
    IP multicast fast switching is disabled
    IP multicast distributed fast switching is disabled
    Router Discovery is disabled
    IP output packet accounting is disabled
    IP access violation accounting is disabled
    TCP/IP header compression is disabled
    RTP/IP header compression is disabled
    Probe proxy name replies are disabled
    Policy routing is disabled
    Network address translation is disabled
    Web Cache Redirect is disabled
    BGP Policy Mapping is disabled
Lab_A#
```

Be sure to notice the bold line indicating that the outgoing list on this interface is BlockSales but the inbound access list isn't set. Let's discuss one more verification command and then we'll move on.

As I've already mentioned, you can use the show running-config command to see any and all access lists. However, on a layer 2 switch, you can verify your interface configurations with the show mac access-group command:

```
S1#sh mac access-group
Interface FastEthernet0/1:
    Inbound access-list is not set
    Outbound access-list is not set
Interface FastEthernet0/2:
```

```
    Inbound access-list is not set
    Outbound access-list is not set
S1#
```

Depending on how many interfaces you set your MAC access lists on, you can use the `interface` command to view individual interfaces:

```
S1#sh mac access-group interface f0/6
Interface FastEthernet0/6:
    Inbound access-list is Todd_MAC_List
    Outbound access-list is not set
```

Exam Essentials

Remember the command to verify an access list on an interface.   To see whether an access list is set on an interface and in which direction it is filtering, use the `show ip interface` command. This command will not show you the contents of the access list, merely which access lists are applied on the interface.

Remember the command to verify the access lists configuration.   To see the configured access lists on your router, use the `show access-list` command. This command will not show you which interfaces have access lists set.

Troubleshoot ACL Issues

When you're troubleshooting ACL problems, the first thing you should do is make sure an access list is not blocking traffic. It is crucial that you be able to quickly view the contents of access lists as well as where they are.

 For more information concerning this objective, please see the previous section, "Verify and Monitor ACLs in a Network Environment."

Explain the Basic Operation of NAT

NAT was originally designed to slow the depletion of available IP address space by allowing many private IP addresses to be represented by some smaller number of public IP addresses. In this regard, its original intent was similar to Classless Inter-Domain Routing (CIDR).

Since then, NAT has also become a useful tool for network migrations and mergers, server load sharing, and creating "virtual servers." So, in this section, I'm going to describe the basics of NAT functionality and the terminology common to NAT.

Here's a list of situations when it's best to have NAT on your side:

- You need to connect to the Internet and your hosts don't have globally unique IP addresses
- You change to a new ISP that requires you to renumber your network
- You need to merge two intranets with duplicate addresses

You typically use NAT on a border router, such as the corporate router in Figure 7.4.

FIGURE 7.4 Where to configure NAT

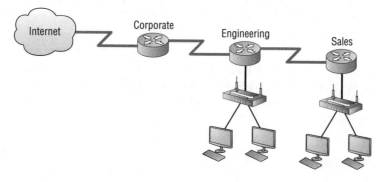

For all of its benefits, NAT has some drawbacks as well. For the pros and cons linked to using NAT, check out Table 7.2.

TABLE 7.2 Advantages and Disadvantages of Implementing NAT

Advantages	Disadvantages
Conserves legally registered addresses	Translation introduces switching path delays
Reduces address overlap occurrences	Loss of end-to-end IP traceability
Increases flexibility when connecting to the Internet	Certain applications will not function with NAT enabled
Eliminates address renumbering as the network changes	

The most obvious advantage associated with NAT is that it allows you to conserve your legally registered address scheme. This is why we haven't run out of IPv4 addresses.

Types of Network Address Translation

In this section, I'm going to go over the three types of NAT:

Static NAT   This type of NAT is designed to allow one-to-one mapping between local and global addresses. Keep in mind that the static version requires you to have one real Internet IP address for every host on your network.

Dynamic NAT   This version gives you the ability to map an unregistered IP address to a registered IP address from out of a pool of registered IP addresses. You don't have to statically configure your router to map an inside to an outside address as you do when using static NAT, but you do have to have enough real, bona fide IP addresses for everyone who's going to be sending packets to and receiving them from the Internet.

Overloading   This is the most popular type of NAT configuration. Overloading really is a form of dynamic NAT that maps multiple unregistered IP addresses to a single registered IP address—many-to-one—by using different ports. Because of that, it's also known as *Port Address Translation (PAT)*. By using PAT (NAT Overload), you get to have thousands of users connect to the Internet using only one real global IP address.

Exam Essentials

Remember the best advantage to using Network Address Translation.   The largest advantage to using NAT on your network is that it conserves legally registered addresses.

Remember the three types of NAT.   The three types of NAT are static, dynamic, and NAT overload.

Configure NAT for Given Network Requirements Using (Including CLI/SDM)

In this section, I'll show you how to configure static, dynamic, and NAT overload on a Cisco router using the command line interface (CLI).

Static NAT Configuration

Let's take a look at a simple basic static NAT configuration:

```
ip nat inside source static 10.1.1.1 170.46.2.2
!
interface Ethernet0
```

```
ip address 10.1.1.10 255.255.255.0
ip nat inside
!
interface Serial0
ip address 170.46.2.1 255.255.255.0
ip nat outside
```

In this example, the first command specifies `static nat` and the public IP address (10.1.1.1) to be mapped to the private IP address (172.46.2.2).

The second and third commands indicate which router interface is considered to be the private network (`ip nat inside`) and which will be the public network (`ip nat outside`).

Dynamic NAT Configuration

Dynamic NAT maps a pool of public addresses to the private IP addresses on the inside. Port numbers are not used, so there must be a public IP address for every user trying to get outside the local network.

Here is a sample output of a dynamic NAT configuration:

```
ip nat pool todd 170.168.2.2 170.168.2.254
    netmask 255.255.255.0
ip nat inside source list 1 pool todd
!
interface Ethernet0
ip address 10.1.1.10 255.255.255.0
ip nat inside
!
interface Serial0
ip address 170.168.2.1 255.255.255.0
ip nat outside
!
access-list 1 permit 10.1.1.0 0.0.0.255
```

In this example, the first command specifies a `nat pool` named `todd` that ranges from 17.168.2.2 to 17.168.2.254.

The second command specifies that the pool named `todd` will be used for translation on the inside interface and that access list number 1 will be used to determine the private ip addresses allowed to use the single public IP address.

The third and fourth commands indicate which router interface is considered to be the private network (`ip nat inside`) and which will be the public network (`ip nat outside`).

The final command creates an access list that determines which IP addresses on the private network are allowed to be mapped to the single public IP address.

PAT (Overloading) Configuration

This last example shows how to configure inside global address overloading. This is the typical NAT in use today. It is rare that you would use static or dynamic NAT unless you were statically mapping a server, for example.

Here is a sample output of a PAT configuration:

```
ip nat pool globalnet 170.168.2.1 170.168.2.1
   netmask 255.255.255.0
ip nat inside source list 1 pool globalnet overload
!
interface Ethernet0/0
 ip address 10.1.1.10 255.255.255.0
 ip nat inside
!
interface Serial0/0
 ip address 170.168.2.1 255.255.255.0
 ip nat outside
!
access-list 1 permit 10.1.1.0 0.0.0.255
```

In this example, the first command specifies a nat pool named globalnet that ranges from 17.168.2.1 to 17.168.2.1.

The second command specifies that the pool named globalnet will be used for translation on the inside interface, with the overload parameter indicating that the address will be used multiple times.

The third and fourth commands indicate which router interface is considered to be the private network (ip nat inside) and which will be the public network (ip nat outside).

The final command creates an access list that determines which IP addresses on the private network are allowed to be mapped to the single public IP address.

Exam Essentials

Remember the command to enable NAT on your inside network.   On your inside interface(s), use the command ip nat inside.

Remember the command to enable NAT on your outside network.   On your outside interface(s), use the command ip nat outside.

Configure static NAT, dynamic NAT, and PAT.   Specify a nat pool (dynamic and NAT and PAT) or specify a public IP address (statics).

For dynamic and NAT and PAT, specify the name of the pool to be used for translation on the inside interface, using the overload parameter if the address will be used multiple times.

Indicate which router interface is considered to be the private network (ip nat inside) and which will be the public network (ip nat outside).

For dynamic and NAT and PAT, create an access list that determines which IP addresses on the private network are allowed to be mapped to the single public IP address.

Troubleshoot NAT Issues

Let's go through a couple of NAT examples and see if you can figure out the configuration that needs to be used. To start, look at Figure 7.5 and ask yourself two things: Where would you implement NAT in this design, and what type of NAT would you configure to use the fewest public IP addresses?

FIGURE 7.5   Where to implement NAT

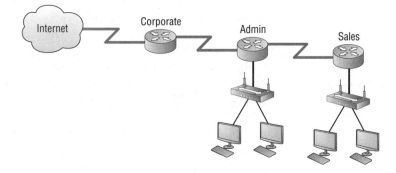

In Figure 7.5, the NAT configuration would be placed on the corporate router and the configuration will be dynamic NAT with overload (PAT). In the following NAT example, what type of NAT is being used?

```
ip nat pool todd-nat 170.168.10.10 170.168.10.20 netmask 255.255.255.0
```

This command uses dynamic NAT. The `pool` in the command gives the answer away, plus there is more than one address in the pool, which means PAT is probably not being used. In the next NAT example, you'll use Figure 7.6 to see if you can figure out the configuration needed.

The example in Figure 7.6 shows a border router that needs to be configured with NAT and that will allow the use of six public IP addresses, 192.1.2.109 through 114. However, on the inside network, you have 63 hosts that use the private addresses of 192.168.10.65 through 126. What would your NAT configuration be on the border router?

Two different answers would work here, but the following would be my first choice:

```
ip nat pool Todd 192.1.2.109 192.1.2.109 netmask 255.255.255.248
access-list 1 permit 192.168.10.64 0.0.0.63
ip nat inside source list 1 pool Todd overload
```

FIGURE 7.6 Configuring PAT

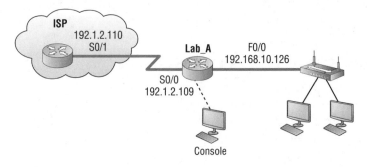

The command ip nat pool Todd 192.1.2.109 192.1.2.109 netmask 255.255.255.248 sets the pool name as Todd and creates a dynamic pool of addresses for the NAT to use address 192.1.2.109. Instead of the netmask command, you can use the prefix-length 29 statement. The second answer would end up with the same result of having only 192.1.2.109 as your inside global, but you can type this in and have it work too: **ip nat pool Todd 102.1.2.109 192.1.2.114 netmask 255.255.255.248**. This is a waste because the second through sixth addresses would only be used if there were a conflict with a TCP port number.

The ip nat inside source list 1 pool Todd overload command sets the dynamic pool to use PAT by using the overload command.

Be sure to add the ip nat inside and ip nat outside statements on the appropriate interfaces.

Exam Essentials

Remember to always check your interface configurations when troubleshooting NAT. Be sure to add the ip nat inside and ip nat outside statements on the appropriate interfaces.

Remember to check for the overload command when using Port Address Translation (PAT). The command ip nat inside source list *list-number* pool *pool-name* overload command sets the dynamic pool to use PAT by using the overload command.

Review Questions

1. Which of the following commands connect access list 110 inbound to interface ethernet0?

   A. Router(config)#**ip access-group 110 in**

   B. Router(config)#**ip access-list 110 in**

   C. Router(config-if)#**ip access-group 110 in**

   D. Router(config-if)#**ip access-list 110 in**

2. What command will permit SMTP mail only to host 1.1.1.1.?

   A. access-list 10 permit smtp host 1.1.1.1

   B. access-list 110 permit ip smtp host 1.1.1.1

   C. access-list 10 permit tcp any host 1.1.1.1 eq smtp

   D. access-list 110 permit tcp any host 1.1.1.1 eq smtp

3. You configure the following access list:

   ```
   access-list 110 deny tcp 10.1.1.128 0.0.0.63 any eq smtp
   access-list 110 deny tcp any eq 23
   int ethernet 0
   ip access-group 110 out
   ```

   What will the result of this access list be?

   A. Email and Telnet will be allowed out E0.

   B. Email and Telnet will be allowed in E0.

   C. Everything but email and Telnet will be allowed out E0.

   D. No IP traffic will be allowed out E0.

4. Which of the following series of commands will restrict Telnet access to the router?

   A. Lab_A(config)#**access-list 10 permit 172.16.1.1**

   Lab_A(config)#**line con0**

   Lab_A(config-line)#**ip access-group 10 in**

   B. Lab_A(config)#**access-list 10 permit 172.16.1.1**

   Lab_A(config)#**line vty 0 4**

   Lab_A(config-line)#**access-class 10 out**

   C. Lab_A(config)#**access-list 10 permit 172.16.1.1**

   Lab_A(config)#**line vty 0 4**

   Lab_A(config-line)#**access-class 10 in**

   D. Lab_A(config)#**access-list 10 permit 172.16.1.1**

   Lab_A(config)#**line vty 0 4**

   Lab_A(config-line)#**ip access-group 10 in**

5. Which of the following is true regarding access lists applied to an interface?

   A. You can place as many access lists as you want on any interface until you run out of memory.

   B. You can apply only one access list on any interface.

   C. One access list may be configured, per direction, for each layer 3 protocol configured on an interface.

   D. You can apply two access lists to any interface.

6. You are working on a router that has established privilege levels that restrict access to certain functions. How can you view and confirm the access lists that have been applied to the Ethernet 0 interface on your router?

   A. `show access-lists`

   B. `show interface Ethernet 0`

   C. `show ip access-lists`

   D. `show ip interface Ethernet 0`

7. Which command would you place on an interface connected to a private network?

   A. `ip nat inside`

   B. `ip nat outside`

   C. `ip outside global`

   D. `ip inside local`

8. Which command would you place on interface connected to the Internet?

   A. `ip nat inside`

   B. `ip nat outside`

   C. `ip outside global`

   D. `ip inside local`

9. Which of the following is another term for Port Address Translation (PAT)?

   A. NAT Fast

   B. NAT Static

   C. NAT Overload

   D. Overloading Static

10. Which of the following are disadvantages of using NAT? (Choose three.)

   A. Translation introduces switching path delays.

   B. Conserves legally registered addresses

   C. Causes loss of end-to-end IP traceability

   D. Increases flexibility when connecting to the Internet

   E. Certain applications will not function with NAT enabled.

   F. Reduces address overlap occurrence

Answers to Review Questions

1. C. To place an access list on an interface, use the `ip access-group` command in interface configuration mode.

2. D. When trying to find the best answer to an access-list question, always check the access-list number and then the protocol. When filtering to an upper-layer protocol, you must use an extended list, numbers 100–199 and 2000–2699. Also, when you filter to an upper-layer protocol, you must use either `tcp` or `udp` in the protocol field. If it says `ip` in the protocol field, you cannot filter to an upper-layer protocol. SMTP uses TCP.

3. D. If you add an access list to an interface and you do not have at least one `permit` statement, then you will effectively shut down the interface because of the implicit `deny any` at the end of every list.

4. C. Telnet access to the router is restricted by using either a standard or extended IP access list inbound on the VTY lines of the router. The command `access-class` is used to apply the access list to the VTY lines.

5. C. A Cisco router has rules regarding the placement of access lists on a router interface. You can place one access list per direction for each layer 3 protocol configured on an interface.

6. D. The only command that shows which access lists have been applied to an interface is `show ip interface Ethernet 0`. The command `show access-lists` displays all configured access lists, and `show ip access-lists` displays all configured IP access lists, but neither command indicates whether the displayed access lists have been applied to an interface.

7. A. As with access lists, you must configure your interfaces before NAT will provide any translations. On the inside networks, you would use the command `ip nat inside`. On the outside interface, you will use the command `ip nat outside`.

8. B. As with access lists, you must configure your interfaces before NAT will provide any translations. On the inside networks, you would use the command `ip nat inside`. On the outside interface, you will use the command `ip nat outside`.

9. C. Another term for Port Address Translation is NAT Overload because that is the command used to enable Port Address Translation.

10. A, C, E. NAT is not perfect and can cause some issues in some networks, but most networks work just fine. NAT can cause delays and troubleshooting problems, and some applications just won't work.

Chapter

8

Implement and Verify WAN Links

THE CISCO CCNA EXAM OBJECTIVES COVERED IN THIS CHAPTER INCLUDE THE FOLLOWING:

✓ Describe different methods for connecting to a WAN.

✓ Configure and verify a basic WAN serial connection.

✓ Configure and verify Frame Relay on Cisco routers.

✓ Troubleshoot WAN implementation issues.

✓ Describe VPN technology (including importance, benefits, role, impact, and components).

✓ Configure and verify a PPP connection between Cisco routers.

The Cisco IOS supports many Wide Area Network (WAN) protocols that can extend your local LANs to LANs at remote sites. It would not be cost-effective or efficient to install your own cable and connect all of your company's remote locations. A better and less expensive way to connect remote LANs is to lease the existing installations that service providers already have in place.

In this chapter, I'm going to discuss the various types of connections, technologies, and devices used in conjunction with WAN connections. I'll show you how to implement and configure High-Level Data Link Control (HDLC), Point-to-Point Protocol (PPP), and Frame Relay. I'll also introduce you to WAN security concepts, tunneling, and virtual private network basics.

Describe Different Methods for Connecting to a WAN

For complete coverage of WAN connection types, see the section titled "WAN Support" in Chapter 1, "Describe How a Network Works."

Building on the Chapter 1 discussion of WAN technologies, this section covers terms and concepts related to the bandwidth of a WAN connection.

WAN Connection Bandwidth

Here are some basic bandwidth terms that are used for WAN connections:

Digital Signal 0 (DS0) This is the basic digital signaling rate of 64Kbps, equivalent to one channel. Europe uses the E0 and Japan uses the J0 to reference the same channel speed. Typically used in a T-carrier transmission, this generic term is used by several multiplexed digital carrier systems. This is the smallest capacity digital circuit. 1 DS0 = 1 voice/data line.

T1 Also referred to as a DS1, this contains 24 DS0 circuits bundled together with a total bandwidth of 1.544Mbps.

E1 This is the European equivalent of the T1. It contains 30 DS0 circuits bundled together with a bandwidth of 2.048Mbps.

T3 Referred to as a DS3, this has 28 DS1s bundled together, or 672 DS0s, with a bandwidth of 44.736Mbps.

OC-3 Optical Carrier (OC) 3 uses fiber, is made up of three DS3s bundled together, and contains 2,016 DS0s with a total bandwidth of 155.52Mbps.

OC-12 Optical Carrier (OC) 12 is make up of four OC-3s bundled together and contains 8,064 DS0s with a total bandwidth of 622.08Mbps.

OC-48 Optical Carrier (OC) 48 is made up of four OC12s bundled together and contains 32,256 DS0s with a total bandwidth of 2488.32Mbps.

Exam Essentials

Identify terms used to describe the bandwidth of WAN connections. These terms include Digital Signal 0 (DS0), T1, E1, T3, OC-3, OC-12, and OC-48.

Configure and Verify a Basic WAN Serial Connection

In this section, the protocols used in WAN transmission are discussed.

 For coverage of serial transmission and DTE/DCE equipment, see the section titled "Router WAN Connections" in Chapter 4, "Configure, Verify, and Troubleshoot Basic Router Operation and Routing on Cisco Devices."

High-Level Data Link Control (HDLC) Protocol

The High-Level Data Link Control (HDLC) protocol is a popular ISO-standard, bit-oriented, Data Link layer protocol. It specifies an encapsulation method for data on synchronous serial data links using frame characters and checksums. HDLC is a point-to-point protocol used on leased lines. No authentication can be used with HDLC.

In byte-oriented protocols, control information is encoded using entire bytes. On the other hand, bit-oriented protocols use single bits to represent the control information. Some common bit-oriented protocols include SDLC, LLC, HDLC, TCP, and IP.

HDLC is the default encapsulation used by Cisco routers over synchronous serial links. Cisco's HDLC is proprietary. It won't communicate with any other vendor's HDLC implementation—but then again, all HDLC implementations are proprietary. Figure 8.1 shows the Cisco HDLC format.

As shown in the figure, every vendor has a proprietary HDLC encapsulation method because each vendor has a different way for the HDLC protocol to encapsulate multiple Network layer protocols. If the vendors didn't have a way for HDLC to communicate the different layer 3 protocols, then HDLC would only be able to carry one protocol. This proprietary header is placed in the data field of the HDLC encapsulation.

FIGURE 8.1 Cisco HDLC frame format

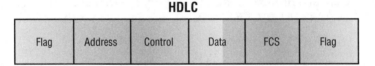

• Each vendor's HDLC has a proprietary data field to support multiprotocol environments.

• Supports only single-protocol environments.

Configuring HDLC on Cisco Routers

Configuring HDLC encapsulation on an interface is really pretty straightforward. To configure it from the CLI, follow these simple router commands:

```
Router#config t
Enter configuration commands, one per line. End with CNTL/Z.
Router(config)#int s0
Router(config-if)#encapsulation hdlc
Router(config-if)#^Z
Router#
```

So, let's say you have only one Cisco router, and you need to connect to a non-Cisco router because your other Cisco router is on order. What would you do? You couldn't use the default HDLC serial encapsulation because it wouldn't work. Instead, you would use something like PPP, an ISO-standard way of identifying the upper-layer protocols. You can check out RFC 1661 for more information on the origins and standards of PPP. Let's discuss PPP in more detail and how to connect to routers using the PPP encapsulation.

Point-to-Point Protocol (PPP)

Let's spend a little time on Point-to-Point Protocol (PPP). Remember that it's a Data Link layer protocol that can be used over either asynchronous serial (dial-up) or synchronous serial (ISDN) media. It uses Link Control Protocol (LCP) to build and maintain data-link connections. Network Control Protocol (NCP) is used to allow multiple Network layer protocols (routed protocols) to be used on a point-to-point connection.

Figure 8.2 shows the protocol stack compared to the OSI reference model.

FIGURE 8.2   Point-to-Point Protocol stack

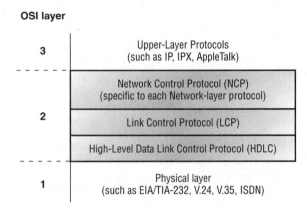

PPP contains the following four main components:

EIA/TIA-232-C, V.24, V.35, and ISDN   A Physical layer international standard for serial communication.

HDLC   A method for encapsulating datagrams over serial links.

LCP   A method of establishing, configuring, maintaining, and terminating the point-to-point connection.

NCP   A method of establishing and configuring different Network layer protocols. NCP is designed to allow the simultaneous use of multiple Network layer protocols. Some examples of protocols here are IPCP (Internet Protocol Control Protocol) and IPXCP (Internetwork Packet Exchange Control Protocol).

It is very important to note that the PPP Protocol stack is specified at the Physical and Data Link layers only. NCP is used to allow communication of multiple Network layer protocols by encapsulating the protocols across a PPP data link.

> Remember that if you have a Cisco router and a non-Cisco router connected with a serial connection, you must configure PPP or another encapsulation method, such as Frame Relay, because the HDLC default just won't work.

Configuring PPP on Cisco Routers

Configuring PPP encapsulation on an interface is the same as HDLC. To configure it from the CLI, follow these simple router commands:

```
Router#config t
Enter configuration commands, one per line. End with CNTL/Z.
Router(config)#int s0
```

```
Router(config-if)#encapsulation ppp
Router(config-if)#^Z
Router#
```

Exam Essentials

Remember the default serial encapsulation on Cisco routers.   Cisco routers use a proprietary High-Level Data Link Control (HDLC) encapsulation on all their serial links by default.

Remember the PPP Data Link layer protocols.   The three Data Link layer protocols are Network Control Protocol (NCP), which defines the Network layer protocols; Link Control Protocol (LCP), a method of establishing, configuring, maintaining, and terminating the point-to-point connection; and High-Level Data Link Control (HDLC), the MAC layer protocol that encapsulates the packets.

Configure and Verify Frame Relay on Cisco Routers

Frame Relay is still one of the most popular WAN services deployed over the past decade, and there's a good reason for this—cost! It's a rare network design or designer that has the privilege to ignore that all-important cost factor.

   By default, Frame Relay is classified as a non-broadcast multi-access (NBMA) network, meaning it doesn't send any broadcasts like RIP updates across the network.

Frame Relay Implementation and Monitoring

As I've said, there are a ton of Frame Relay commands and configuration options, but I'm going to zero in on the ones you really need to know when studying for the CCNA exam objectives. I'm going to start with one of the simplest configuration options: two routers with a single PVC between them. Next, I'll show you a more complex configuration using subinterfaces, and I'll demonstrate some of the monitoring commands available to verify the configuration.

Single Interface

Let's get started by looking at a simple example. Say that I just want to connect two routers with a single PVC. Here's how that configuration would look:

```
RouterA#config t
Enter configuration commands, one per line.  End with CNTL/Z.
RouterA(config)#int s0/0
```

```
RouterA(config-if)#encapsulation frame-relay
RouterA(config-if)#ip address 172.16.20.1 255.255.255.0
RouterA(config-if)#frame-relay lmi-type ansi
RouterA(config-if)#frame-relay interface-dlci 101
RouterA(config-if)#^Z
RouterA#
```

The first step is to specify the encapsulation as Frame Relay. There are two encapsulation types available: either Cisco or IETF. Notice that since I didn't specify a particular encapsulation type the proprietary Cisco default type was used. If the other router were non-Cisco, I would've specified IETF. Next, I assigned an IP address to the interface, and then I specified a Link Management Interface (LMI) type. The LMI type is used between the local router and the Frame Relay switch. It can be set one of two ways, and your provider will indicate to you which to use. In this case, I set it to ANSI (the default being Cisco). Finally, I added the Data Link Connection Identifier (DLCI) of 101, which indicates the PVC I want to use (again, given to me by my ISP) and assumes that there's only one PVC on this physical interface.

That's all there is to it. If both sides are configured correctly, the circuit will come up.

Subinterfaces

As you learned earlier, you can have multiple virtual circuits on a single serial interface and yet treat each as a separate interface. You can make this happen by creating *subinterfaces*. Think of a subinterface as a logical interface defined by the IOS software. Several subinterfaces will share a single hardware interface, yet for configuration purposes, they operate as if they were separate physical interfaces, something known as multiplexing.

To configure a router in a Frame Relay network so that it will avoid split horizon issues by not permitting routing updates, just configure a separate subinterface for each PVC, with a unique DLCI and subnet assigned to the subinterface.

You define subinterfaces using a command like int s0.*subinterface number*. First, you have to set the encapsulation on the physical serial interface, and then you can define the subinterfaces—generally one subinterface per PVC. Here's an example:

```
RouterA(config)#int s0
RouterA(config-if)#encapsulation frame-relay
RouterA(config-if)#int s0.?
  <0-4294967295>  Serial interface number
RouterA(config-if)#int s0.16 ?
  multipoint      Treat as a multipoint link
  point-to-point  Treat as a point-to-point link
RouterA(config-if)#int s0.16 point-to-point
```

Make sure you don't have an IP address under the physical interface if you have configured subinterfaces.

You can define a serious amount of subinterfaces on any given physical interface, but keep in mind that there are only about 1,000 available DLCIs. In the preceding example, I chose to use subinterface 16 because that represents the DLCI number assigned to that PVC by the carrier. There are two types of subinterfaces:

Point-to-Point   Used when a single virtual circuit connects one router to another. Each point-to-point subinterface requires its own subnet.

A point-to-point subinterface maps a single IP subnet per DLCI and addresses and resolves NBMA split horizon issues.

Multipoint   This is when the router is the center of a star of virtual circuits that are using a single subnet for all routers' serial interfaces connected to the frame switch. You'll usually find this implemented with the hub router in this mode and the spoke routers in physical interface (always point-to-point) or point-to-point subinterface mode.

Monitoring Frame Relay

Several commands are used frequently to check the status of your interfaces and PVCs once you have Frame Relay encapsulation set up and running. To list them, use the `show frame ?` command like this:

```
RouterA>sho frame ?
end-to-end      Frame-relay end-to-end VC information
fragment        show frame relay fragmentation information
ip              show frame relay IP statistics
lapf            show frame relay lapf status/statistics
lmi             show frame relay lmi statistics
map             Frame-Relay map table
pvc             show frame relay pvc statistics
qos-autosense   show frame relay qos-autosense information
route           show frame relay route
svc             show frame relay SVC stuff
traffic         Frame-Relay protocol statistics
vofr            Show frame-relay VoFR statistics
```

The most common parameters that you view with the `show frame-relay` command are lmi, pvc, and map.

Now, let's take a look at the most frequently used commands and the information they provide.

The *show frame-relay lmi* Command

The `show frame-relay lmi` command will give you the LMI traffic statistics exchanged between the local router and the Frame Relay switch. Here's an example:

```
Router#sh frame lmi
```

```
LMI Statistics for interface Serial0 (Frame Relay DTE)
LMI TYPE = CISCO
   Invalid Unnumbered info 0          Invalid Prot Disc 0
   Invalid dummy Call Ref 0           Invalid Msg Type 0
   Invalid Status Message 0           Invalid Lock Shift 0
   Invalid Information ID 0           Invalid Report IE Len 0
   Invalid Report Request 0           Invalid Keep IE Len 0
   Num Status Enq. Sent 0             Num Status msgs Rcvd 0
   Num Update Status Rcvd 0           Num Status Timeouts 0
Router#
```

The router output from the show frame-relay lmi command displays any LMI errors, plus the LMI type.

The *show frame pvc* Command

The show frame pvc command will present you with a list of all configured PVCs and DLCI numbers. It provides the status of each PVC connection and traffic statistics too. It will also give you the number of BECN and FECN packets received on the router per PVC. (BECN and FECN are discussed in detail in the *CCNA Cisco Certified Network Associate Study Guide, 7th Edition*.)

Here is an example:

```
RouterA#sho frame pvc

PVC Statistics for interface Serial0 (Frame Relay DTE)

DLCI = 16,DLCI USAGE = LOCAL,PVC STATUS =ACTIVE,
INTERFACE = Serial0.1
 input pkts 50977876     output pkts 41822892
  in bytes 3137403144
 out bytes 3408047602    dropped pkts 5
  in FECN pkts 0
 in BECN pkts 0        out FECN pkts 0       out BECN pkts 0
 in DE pkts 9393       out DE pkts 0
 pvc create time 7w3d, last time pvc status changed 7w3d

DLCI = 18,DLCI USAGE =LOCAL,PVC STATUS =ACTIVE,
INTERFACE = Serial0.3
 input pkts 30572401     output pkts 31139837
  in bytes 1797291100
 out bytes 3227181474    dropped pkts 5
  in FECN pkts 0
 in BECN pkts 0        out FECN pkts 0       out BECN pkts 0
```

```
 in DE pkts 28      out DE pkts 0
 pvc create time 7w3d, last time pvc status changed 7w3d
```

If you only want to see information about PVC 16, you can type the command **show frame-relay pvc 16**.

The *show interface* Command

You can use the show interface command to check for LMI traffic. The show interface command displays information about the encapsulation, as well as layer 2 and layer 3 information. It also displays line, protocol, DLCI, and LMI information. Check it out:

```
RouterA#sho int s0
Serial0 is up, line protocol is up
 Hardware is HD64570
 MTU 1500 bytes, BW 1544 Kbit, DLY 20000 usec, rely
  255/255, load 2/255
 Encapsulation FRAME-RELAY, loopback not set, keepalive
  set (10 sec)
 LMI enq sent 451751,LMI stat recvd 451750,LMI upd recvd
  164,DTE LMI up
 LMI enq recvd 0, LMI stat sent 0, LMI upd sent 0
 LMI DLCI 1023 LMI type is CISCO frame relay DTE
 Broadcast queue 0/64, broadcasts sent/dropped 0/0,
  interface broadcasts 839294
```

The LMI DLCI in this code is used to define the type of LMI being used. If it happens to be 1023, it's the default LMI type of Cisco. If LMI DLCI is zero, then it's the ANSI LMI type (Q.933A uses 0 as well). If LMI DLCI is anything other than 0 or 1023, call your provider; they've got issues!

The *show frame map* Command

The show frame map command displays the Network layer–to–DLCI mappings. Here's how that looks:

```
RouterB#show frame map
Serial0 (up): ipx 20.0007.7842.3575 dlci 16(0x10,0x400),
              dynamic, broadcast,, status defined, active
Serial0 (up): ip 172.16.20.1 dlci 16(0x10,0x400),
              dynamic, broadcast,, status defined, active
Serial1 (up): ipx 40.0007.7842.153a dlci 17(0x11,0x410),
              dynamic, broadcast,, status defined, active
Serial1 (up): ip 172.16.40.2 dlci 17(0x11,0x410),
              dynamic, broadcast,, status defined, active
```

Notice that the serial interfaces have two mappings—one for IP and one for IPX. Also important is that the Network layer addresses were resolved with the dynamic protocol Inverse ARP (IARP). After the DLCI number is listed, you can see some numbers in parentheses. The first one is 0x10, which is the hex equivalent for the DLCI number 16, used on serial 0. The 0x11 is the hex for DLCI 17 used on serial 1. The second numbers, 0x400 and 0x410, are the DLCI numbers configured in the Frame Relay frame. They're different because of the way the bits are spread out in the frame.

The *debug frame lmi* Command

The debug frame lmi command will show output on the router consoles by default (as with any debug command). The information this command gives you will enable you to verify and troubleshoot the Frame Relay connection by helping you determine whether the router and switch are exchanging the correct LMI information. Here's an example:

```
Router#debug frame-relay lmi
Serial3/1(in): Status, myseq 214
RT IE 1, length 1, type 0
KA IE 3, length 2, yourseq 214, myseq 214
PVC IE 0x7 , length 0x6 , dlci 130, status 0x2 , bw 0
Serial3/1(out): StEnq, myseq 215, yourseen 214, DTE up
datagramstart = 0x1959DF4, datagramsize = 13
FR encap = 0xFCF10309
00 75 01 01 01 03 02 D7 D6

Serial3/1(in): Status, myseq 215
RT IE 1, length 1, type 1
KA IE 3, length 2, yourseq 215, myseq 215
Serial3/1(out): StEnq, myseq 216, yourseen 215, DTE up
datagramstart = 0x1959DF4, datagramsize = 13
FR encap = 0xFCF10309
00 75 01 01 01 03 02 D8 D7
```

Exam Essentials

Understand what the LMI is in Frame Relay.   The LMI is a signaling standard between a CPE device (router) and a frame switch. The LMI is responsible for managing and maintaining the status between these devices. This also provides transmission keepalives to ensure that the PVC does not shut down because of inactivity.

Understand the different Frame Relay encapsulations.   Cisco uses two different Frame Relay encapsulation methods on their routers. Cisco is the default, and means that the router is connected to a Cisco Frame Relay switch; Internet Engineering Task Force (IETF) means that your router is connecting to anything except a Cisco Frame Relay switch.

Remember what the CIR is in Frame Relay. The CIR is the rate, in bits per second, at which the Frame Relay switch agrees to transfer data.

Configure a Frame Relay connection. The first step is to specify the encapsulation as Frame Relay. Next, assign an IP address to the interface. Next, specify an LMI type. Finally, add the Data Link Connection Identifier (DLCI).

Identify commands used to verify a Frame Relay connection. Use the `show frame-relay lmi`, `show frame pvc`, `show interface`, `show frame map`, and the `debug frame lmi` commands to verify the Frame Relay functionality.

Troubleshoot WAN Implementation Issues

If you have a point-to-point link, but the encapsulations aren't the same, the link will never come up. Figure 8.3 shows one link with PPP and one with HDLC.

FIGURE 8.3 Mismatched WAN encapsulations

```
hostname Pod1R1                          hostname Pod1R2
username Pod1R2 password Cisco           username Pod1R1 password cisco
  interface serial 0                       interface serial 0
  ip address 10.0.1.1 255.255.255.0        ip address 10.0.1.2 255.255.255.0
  encapsulation ppp                        encapsulation HDLC
```

Look at router Pod1R1 in this output:

```
Pod1R1#sh int s0/0
Serial0/0 is up, line protocol is down
  Hardware is PowerQUICC Serial
  Internet address is 10.0.1.1/24
  MTU 1500 bytes, BW 1544 Kbit, DLY 20000 usec,
    reliability 254/255, txload 1/255, rxload 1/255
  Encapsulation PPP, loopback not set
  Keepalive set (10 sec)
  LCP REQsent
Closed: IPCP, CDPCP
```

The serial interface is down, and LCP is sending requests but will never receive any responses because router Pod1R2 is using the HDLC encapsulation. To fix this problem, you would have to go to router Pod1R2 and configure the PPP encapsulation on the serial interface. There's one more thing though—even though the usernames are configured and they're wrong, it doesn't matter because the command `ppp authentication chap` isn't used under the serial interface configuration and the username command isn't relevant in this example.

Always remember that you just can't have PPP on one side and HDLC on the other. The two are incompatible.

Mismatched IP Addresses

A tricky problem to spot is if you have HDLC or PPP configured on your serial interface, but your IP addresses are wrong. Things seem to be just fine because the interfaces will show that they are up. For example, take a look at Figure 8.4, which shows two routers connected with different subnets: router Pod1R1 with 10.0.1.1/24 and router Pod1R2 with 10.2.1.2/24.

FIGURE 8.4 Mismatched IP addresses

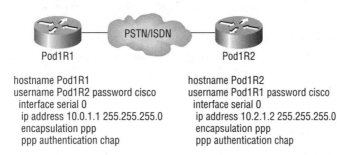

It should be obvious that this will never work, but take a look at the output:

```
Pod1R1#sh int s0/0
Serial0/0 is up, line protocol is up
  Hardware is PowerQUICC Serial
  Internet address is 10.0.1.1/24
  MTU 1500 bytes, BW 1544 Kbit, DLY 20000 usec,
     reliability 255/255, txload 1/255, rxload 1/255
  Encapsulation PPP, loopback not set
  Keepalive set (10 sec)
  LCP Open
  Open: IPCP, CDPCP
```

The IP addresses between the routers are wrong, but the link looks like it is working fine. This is because PPP, like HDLC and Frame Relay, is a layer 2 WAN encapsulation and doesn't care about IP addresses at all. So, yes, the link is up, but you can't use IP across this link because it is misconfigured.

To find and fix this problem, you can use the show running-config or the show interfaces command on each router, or you can use the show cdp neighbors detail command as follows:

```
Pod1R1#sh cdp neighbors detail
-------------------------
Device ID: Pod1R2
Entry address(es):
  IP address: 10.2.1.2
```

You can view and verify the directly connected neighbor's IP address and then solve your problem.

Troubleshooting Frame Relay Networks

Troubleshooting Frame Relay networks isn't any harder than troubleshooting any other type of network as long as you know what to look for. In this section, I'll go over some basic problems that commonly occur in Frame Relay configuration and how to solve them.

First, I'll discuss encapsulation. As you learned recently, there are two Frame Relay encapsulations: Cisco and IETF. Cisco is the default, and it means that you have a Cisco router on each end of the Frame Relay network. If you don't have a Cisco router on the remote end of your Frame Relay network, then you need to run the IETF encapsulation as shown here:

```
RouterA(config)#int s0
RouterA(config-if)#encapsulation frame-relay ?
  ietf  Use RFC1490 encapsulation
  <cr>
RouterA(config-if)#encapsulation frame-relay ietf
```

Once you verify that you're using the correct encapsulation, you then need to check out your Frame Relay mappings. For example, take a look at Figure 8.5.

FIGURE 8.5   Frame Relay mappings

```
RouterA#show running-config
interface s0/0
ip address 172.16.100.2 255.255.0.0
encapsulation frame-relay
frame-relay map ip 172.16.100.1 200 broadcast
```

So, why can't RouterA talk to RouterB across the Frame Relay network? If you take a close look at the `frame-relay map` statement, you will see that the DLCI mappings are incorrect. You cannot use a remote DLCI to communicate to the Frame Relay switch; you must use *your* DLCI number. The mapping should have included DLCI 100 instead of DLCI 200.

Now that you know how to ensure that you have the correct Frame Relay encapsulation, and that DLCIs are only locally significant, let's look into some routing protocol problems typically associated with Frame Relay. See if you can find a problem with the two configurations in Figure 8.6.

FIGURE 8.6   Frame Relay routing problems

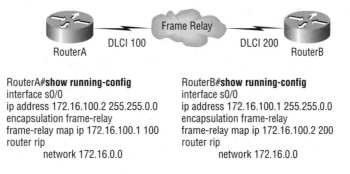

The configuration appears to be correct, but remember that Frame Relay is a NBMA network by default, meaning that it doesn't send any broadcasts across the PVC. So, because the mapping statements do not have the `broadcast` argument at the end of the line, broadcasts, like RIP updates, won't be sent across the PVC.

Exam Essentials

Remember the two Frame Relay encapsulation methods.   There are two Frame Relay encapsulations: Cisco and IETF. Cisco is the default, and it means that you have a Cisco router on each end of the Frame Relay network. If you don't have a Cisco router on the remote end of your Frame Relay network, then you need to run the IETF encapsulation.

Remember that DLCI numbers are considered locally significant.   You cannot use a remote DLCI to communicate to the Frame Relay switch—you must use *your* DLCI number.

Identify commands used to troubleshoot Frame Relay problems, including IP address mismatch, encapsulation mismatch, and LMI mismatch.   Use the `show interface`, `show cdp neighbors detail`, and the `show frame relay map` commands to troubleshoot IP address mismatches, encapsulation mismatches, and LMI mismatches.

Describe VPN Technology (Including Importance, Benefits, Role, Impact, and Components)

A *virtual private network (VPN)* allows the creation of private networks across the Internet, enabling privacy and tunneling of non-TCP/IP protocols. VPNs are used daily to give remote users and disjointed networks connectivity over a public medium like the Internet instead of using more expensive permanent means.

Types of VPNs are named based on the role they play in a business. There are three different categories of VPNs:

Remote Access VPNs   *Remote access VPNs* allow remote users like telecommuters to securely access the corporate network wherever and whenever needed.

Site-to-Site VPNs   *Site-to-site VPNs*, or intranet VPNs, allow a company to connect its remote sites to the corporate backbone securely over a public medium like the Internet instead of requiring more expensive WAN connections like Frame Relay.

Extranet VPNs   *Extranet VPNs* allow an organization's suppliers, partners, and customers to be connected to the corporate network in a limited way for business-to-business (B2B) communications.

There are two ways to create a VPN. The first approach uses IPSec to create authentication and encryption services between endpoints on an IP network. The second approach is via tunneling protocols, allowing you to establish a tunnel between endpoints on a network. Understand that the tunnel itself is a means for data or protocols to be encapsulated inside another protocol.

Here are some brief descriptions of the most common tunneling protocols:

Layer 2 Forwarding (L2F)   *Layer 2 Forwarding (L2F)* is a Cisco-proprietary tunneling protocol, and it was their first tunneling protocol created for virtual private dial-up networks (VPDNs). VPDN allows a device to use a dial-up connection to create a secure connection to a corporate network. L2F was later replaced by L2TP, which is backward compatible with L2F.

Point-to-Point Tunneling Protocol (PPTP)   *Point-to-Point Tunneling Protocol (PPTP)* was created by Microsoft to allow the secure transfer of data from remote networks to the corporate network.

Layer 2 Tunneling Protocol (L2TP)   *Layer 2 Tunneling Protocol (L2TP)* was created by Cisco and Microsoft to replace L2F and PPTP. L2TP merged the capabilities of both L2F and PPTP into one tunneling protocol.

Generic Routing Encapsulation (GRE)   *Generic Routing Encapsulation (GRE)* is another Cisco-proprietary tunneling protocol. It forms virtual point-to-point links, allowing a variety of protocols to be encapsulated in IP tunnels.

Exam Essentials

Understand the term virtual private network (VPN).   A *virtual private network (VPN)* allows the creation of private networks across the Internet, enabling privacy and tunneling of non-TCP/IP protocols. VPNs are used daily to give remote users and disjointed networks connectivity over a public medium, such as the Internet, instead of using more expensive permanent means.

Remember the three categories of VPNs.   Types of VPNs are named based on the roles they play in business. There are three different categories of VPNs: remote access VPNs, site-to-site VPNs, and extranet VPNs.

Identify tunneling protocols.   The tunneling protocols available for VPNs are Layer 2 Forwarding (L2F), Point-to-Point Tunneling Protocol (PPTP), Layer 2 Tunneling Protocol (L2TP), and Generic Routing Encapsulation (GRE).

Configure and Verify a PPP Connection between Cisco Routers

After you configure your serial interface to support PPP encapsulation, you can configure authentication using PPP between routers. First, you need to set the hostname of the router, if it's not already set. Then you need to set the username and password for the remote router that will be connecting to your router.

Here's an example:

```
Router#config t
Enter configuration commands, one per line. End with CNTL/Z.
Router(config)#hostname RouterA
RouterA(config)#username RouterB password cisco
```

When using the hostname command, remember that the username is the hostname of the remote router that's connecting to your router. Don't forget that it's case sensitive. Also, the password on both routers must be the same. It's a plaintext password that you can see with a show run command; you can encrypt the password by using the command service password-encryption. You must have a username and password configured for each remote system to which you plan to connect. The remote routers must also be configured with usernames and passwords.

After you set the hostname, usernames, and passwords, set the username and password for the remote router that will be connecting to your router; choose the authentication type, either CHAP or PAP (discussed in detail in the *CCNA Cisco Certified Network Associate Study Guide, 7th Edition*):

```
RouterA#config t
Enter configuration commands, one per line. End with CNTL/Z.
```

```
RouterA(config)#int s0
RouterA(config-if)#ppp authentication chap pap
RouterA(config-if)#^Z
RouterA#
```

If both methods are configured on the same line, as shown here, only the first method will be used during link negotiation. The second method acts as a backup just in case the first method fails.

Verifying PPP Encapsulation

Now that PPP encapsulation is enabled, I'll show you how to verify that it's up and running. First, let's take a look at a figure of a sample network. Figure 8.7 shows two routers connected with either a point-to-point serial or ISDN connection.

FIGURE 8.7 PPP authentication

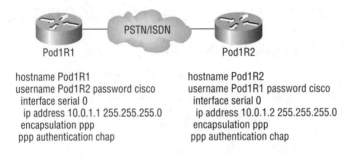

```
hostname Pod1R1                    hostname Pod1R2
username Pod1R2 password cisco     username Pod1R1 password cisco
 interface serial 0                 interface serial 0
  ip address 10.0.1.1 255.255.255.0  ip address 10.0.1.2 255.255.255.0
  encapsulation ppp                  encapsulation ppp
  ppp authentication chap            ppp authentication chap
```

You can start verifying the configuration with the show interface command as follows:

```
Pod1R1#sh int s0/0
Serial0/0 is up, line protocol is up
  Hardware is PowerQUICC Serial
  Internet address is 10.0.1.1/24
  MTU 1500 bytes, BW 1544 Kbit, DLY 20000 usec,
     reliability 239/255, txload 1/255, rxload 1/255
  Encapsulation PPP
  loopback not set
  Keepalive set (10 sec)
  LCP Open
  Open: IPCP, CDPCP
[output cut]
```

Notice that the sixth line lists encapsulation as PPP, and the ninth line shows that the LCP is open. This means that it has negotiated the session establishment and all is well. The 10th line indicates that NCP is listening for the protocols IP and CDP.

Let's look at an example of an incorrect configuration and determine the problem. Look at the configuration shown in Figure 8.8.

FIGURE 8.8   Failed PPP authentication

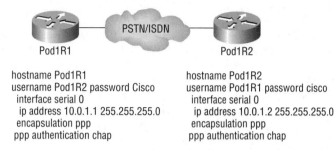

hostname Pod1R1
username Pod1R2 password Cisco
  interface serial 0
  ip address 10.0.1.1 255.255.255.0
  encapsulation ppp
  ppp authentication chap

hostname Pod1R2
username Pod1R1 password cisco
  interface serial 0
  ip address 10.0.1.2 255.255.255.0
  encapsulation ppp
  ppp authentication chap

The C is capitalized on the Pod1R2 username command found in the configuration of router Pod1R1. This is wrong because the usernames and passwords are case sensitive. Let's take a look at the show interface command and see what happens:

```
Pod1R1#sh int s0/0
Serial0/0 is up, line protocol is down
  Hardware is PowerQUICC Serial
  Internet address is 10.0.1.1/24
  MTU 1500 bytes, BW 1544 Kbit, DLY 20000 usec,
     reliability 243/255, txload 1/255, rxload 1/255
  Encapsulation PPP, loopback not set
  Keepalive set (10 sec)
  LCP Closed
  Closed: IPCP, CDPCP
```

First, notice in the first line of output that Serial0/0 is up, line protocol is down. This is because there are no keepalives coming from the remote router. Next, notice that the LCP is closed because the authentication failed.

Debugging PPP Authentication

To display the CHAP authentication process as it occurs between two routers in the network, just use the command debug ppp authentication.

If your PPP encapsulation and authentication are set up correctly on both routers, and your usernames and passwords are all good, the debug ppp authentication command will display output that looks like this:

```
d16h: Se0/0 PPP: Using default call direction
1d16h: Se0/0 PPP: Treating connection as a dedicated line
1d16h: Se0/0 CHAP: O CHALLENGE id 219 len 27 from "Pod1R1"
```

```
1d16h: Se0/0 CHAP: I CHALLENGE id 208 len 27 from "Pod1R2"
1d16h: Se0/0 CHAP: O RESPONSE id 208 len 27 from "Pod1R1"
1d16h: Se0/0 CHAP: I RESPONSE id 219 len 27 from "Pod1R2"
1d16h: Se0/0 CHAP: O SUCCESS id 219 len 4
1d16h: Se0/0 CHAP: I SUCCESS id 208 len 4
```

If you have the username wrong, as in the PPP authentication failure example in Figure 8.8, the output would look something like this:

```
1d16h: Se0/0 PPP: Using default call direction
1d16h: Se0/0 PPP: Treating connection as a dedicated line
1d16h: %SYS-5-CONFIG_I: Configured from console by console
1d16h: Se0/0 CHAP: O CHALLENGE id 220 len 27 from "Pod1R1"
1d16h: Se0/0 CHAP: I CHALLENGE id 209 len 27 from "Pod1R2"
1d16h: Se0/0 CHAP: O RESPONSE id 209 len 27 from "Pod1R1"
1d16h: Se0/0 CHAP: I RESPONSE id 220 len 27 from "Pod1R2"
1d16h: Se0/0 CHAP: O FAILURE id 220 len 25 msg is "MD/DES compare failed"
```

PPP with CHAP authentication is a three-way authentication, and if the usernames and passwords are not configured exactly the way they should be, the authentication will fail and the link will be down.

Exam Essentials

Configure and verify a PPP connection.   To configure a PPP connection, set the hostname of the router, set the username and password for the remote router that will be connecting to your router, and choose the authentication type, either CHAP or PAP. To verify, use the show interfaces and the debug ppp authentication commands.

Review Questions

1. Which command will display the CHAP authentication process as it occurs between two routers in the network?

    A. `show chap authentication`

    B. `show interface serial 0`

    C. `debug ppp authentication`

    D. `debug chap authentication`

2. Suppose that you have a customer who has a central headquarters (HQ) and six branch offices. They anticipate adding six more branches in the near future. They want to implement a WAN technology that will allow the branches to economically connect to HQ, and you have no free ports on the HQ router. Which of the following would you recommend?

    A. PPP

    B. HDLC

    C. Frame Relay

    D. ISDN

3. How should a router that is being used in a Frame Relay network be configured to keep split horizon issues from preventing routing updates?

    A. Configure a separate subinterface for each PVC with a unique DLCI and subnet assigned to the subinterface.

    B. Configure each Frame Relay circuit as a point-to-point line to support multicast and broadcast traffic.

    C. Configure many subinterfaces in the same subnet.

    D. Configure a single subinterface to establish multiple PVC connections to multiple remote router interfaces.

4. Which encapsulations can be configured on a serial interface? (Choose three.)

    A. Ethernet

    B. Token Ring

    C. HDLC

    D. Frame Relay

    E. PPP

5. The Acme Corporation is implementing dial-up services to enable remote-office employees to connect to the local network. The company uses multiple routed protocols, needs authentication of users connecting to the network, and because some calls will be long distance, needs callback support. Which of the following protocols is the best choice for these remote services?

   A. 802.1

   B. Frame Relay

   C. HDLC

   D. PPP

   E. PAP

6. Which WAN encapsulations can be configured on an asynchronous serial connection? (Choose two.)

   A. PPP

   B. ATM

   C. HDLC

   D. SDLC

   E. Frame Relay

7. Using the following output of the show interfaces command as a reference, why won't the serial link between the Corp router and the Remote router come up?

```
Corp#sh int s0/0
Serial0/0 is up, line protocol is down
  Hardware is PowerQUICC Serial
  Internet address is 10.0.1.1/24
  MTU 1500 bytes, BW 1544 Kbit, DLY 20000 usec,
     reliability 254/255, txload 1/255, rxload 1/255
  Encapsulation PPP, loopback not set


Remote#sh int s0/0
Serial0/0 is up, line protocol is down
  Hardware is PowerQUICC Serial
  Internet address is 10.0.1.2/24
  MTU 1500 bytes, BW 1544 Kbit, DLY 20000 usec,
     reliability 254/255, txload 1/255, rxload 1/255
  Encapsulation HDLC, loopback not set
```

   A. The serial cable is faulty.

   B. The IP addresses are not in the same subnet.

   C. The subnet masks are not correct.

   D. The keepalive settings are not correct.

   E. The layer 2 frame types are not compatible.

8. A remote site has just been connected to the central office. However, remote users cannot access applications at the central office. The remote router can be pinged from the central office router. After reviewing the command output shown below, which do you think is the most likely reason for the problem?

```
Central#show running-config
!
interface Serial0
 ip address 10.0.8.1 255.255.248.0
 encapsulation frame-relay
 frame-relay map ip 10.0.15.2 200
!
Router rip
Network 10.0.0.0
```

```
Remote#show running-config
!
interface Serial0
 ip address 10.0.15.2 255.255.248.0
 encapsulation frame-relay
 frame-relay map ip 10.0.8.1 100
!
Router rip
Network 10.0.0.0
```

A. The Frame Relay PVC is down.

B. The IP addressing on the Central/Remote router link is incorrect.

C. RIP routing information is not being forwarded.

D. Frame Relay Inverse ARP is not properly configured.

9. Which of the following describes an industry-wide standard suite of protocols and algorithms that allows for secure data transmission over an IP-based network that functions at the layer 3 Network layer of the OSI model?

A. HDLC

B. Cable

C. VPN

D. IPSec

E. xDSL

10. Which of the following describes the creation of private networks across the Internet, enabling privacy and tunneling of non-TCP/IP protocols?

   A. HDLC

   B. Cable

   C. VPN

   D. IPSec

   E. xDSL

Answers to Review Questions

1. C. The command `debug ppp authentication` will show you the authentication process that PPP uses between point-to-point connections.

2. C. The key is "there are no free ports" on your router. Only Frame Relay can provide a connection to multiple locations with one interface in an economical manner.

3. A. If you have a serial port configured with multiple DLCIs connected to multiple remote sites, split horizon rules stop route updates received on an interface from being sent out the same interface. By creating subinterfaces for each PVC, you can avoid the split horizon issues when using Frame Relay.

4. C, D, E. Ethernet and Token Ring are LAN technologies and cannot be configured on a serial interface. PPP, HDLC, and Frame Relay are layer 2 WAN technologies that are typically configured on a serial interface.

5. D. PPP is your only option, as HDLC and Frame Relay do not support these types of business requirements. PPP provides dynamic addressing, authentication using PAP or CHAP, and callback services.

6. A, B. Although it is a correct answer, we have not discussed ATM because it is not covered in depth on the CCNA exam. PPP is used mostly for dial-up (async) services, but ATM could be used as well, although it typically is not used anymore because PPP is so efficient.

7. E. This is an easy question because the Remote router is using the default HDLC serial encapsulation and the Corp router is using the PPP serial encapsulation. You should go to the Remote router and set that encapsulation to PPP or change the Corp router back to the default of HDLC.

8. C. Even though the IP addresses don't look correct, they are in the same subnet, so answer B is not correct. The question states that you can ping the other side, so the PVC must be up; therefore, answer A can't be correct. You cannot configure IARP, so only answer C can be correct. Because a Frame Relay network is a non-broadcast multi-access network by default, broadcasts such as RIP updates cannot be sent across the PVC unless you use the broadcast statement at the end of the `frame-relay map` command.

9. D. IPSec is an industry-wide standard suite of protocols and algorithms that allows for secure data transmission over an IP-based network that functions at the layer 3 Network layer of the OSI model.

10. C. A *virtual private network (VPN)* allows the creation of private networks across the Internet, enabling privacy and tunneling of non-TCP/IP protocols. A VPN can be set up across any type of link.

Appendix

About the Companion CD

IN THIS APPENDIX:

✓ What you'll find on the CD

✓ System requirements

✓ Using the CD

✓ Troubleshooting

What You'll Find on the CD

The following sections are arranged by category and summarize the software and other goodies you'll find on the CD. If you need help installing the items provided on the CD, refer to the installation instructions in the "Using the CD" section of this appendix.

Sybex Test Engine

The CD contains the Sybex test engine, which includes two bonus exams located only on the CD.

Electronic Flashcards

These handy electronic flashcards are just what they sound like. One side contains a question or fill-in-the-blank question, and the other side shows the answer.

PDF of Glossary of Terms

We have included an electronic version of the Glossary in `.pdf` format. You can view the electronic version of the Glossary with Adobe Reader.

Adobe Reader

We've also included a copy of Adobe Reader so you can view PDF files that accompany the book's content. For more information on Adobe Reader or to check for a newer version, visit Adobe's website at `www.adobe.com/products/reader/`.

System Requirements

Make sure your computer meets the minimum system requirements shown in the following list. If your computer doesn't match up to most of these requirements, you may have problems using the software and files on the companion CD. For the latest and greatest information, please refer to the `ReadMe` file located at the root of the CD-ROM.

- A PC running Microsoft Windows 98, Windows 2000, Windows NT4 (with SP4 or later), Windows Me, Windows XP, Windows Vista, or Windows 7
- An Internet connection
- A CD-ROM drive

Using the CD

To install the items from the CD to your hard drive, follow these steps:

1. Insert the CD into your computer's CD-ROM drive. The license agreement appears.

> *Windows users*: The interface won't launch if you have autorun disabled. In that case, click Start ➤ Run (for Windows Vista or Windows 7, Start ➤ All Programs ➤ Accessories ➤ Run). In the dialog box that appears, type **D:\ Start.exe**. (Replace *D* with the proper letter if your CD drive uses a different letter. If you don't know the letter, see how your CD drive is listed under My Computer.) Click OK.

2. Read the license agreement, and then click the Accept button if you want to use the CD.

The CD interface appears. The interface allows you to access the content with just one or two clicks.

Troubleshooting

Wiley has attempted to provide programs that work on most computers with the minimum system requirements. Alas, your computer may differ, and some programs may not work properly for some reason.

The two likeliest problems are that you don't have enough memory (RAM) for the programs you want to use or you have other programs running that are affecting installation or running of a program. If you get an error message such as "Not enough memory" or "Setup cannot continue," try one or more of the following suggestions and then try using the software again:

Turn off any antivirus software running on your computer. Installation programs sometimes mimic virus activity and may make your computer incorrectly believe that it's being infected by a virus.

Close all running programs. The more programs you have running, the less memory is available to other programs. Installation programs typically update files and programs; so if you keep other programs running, installation may not work properly.

Have your local computer store add more RAM to your computer. This is, admittedly, a drastic and somewhat expensive step. However, adding more memory can really help the speed of your computer and allow more programs to run at the same time.

Customer Care

If you have trouble with the book's companion CD-ROM, please call the Wiley Product Technical Support phone number at (800) 762-2974. Outside the United States, call +1(317) 572-3994. You can also contact Wiley Product Technical Support at http://sybex.custhelp .com. John Wiley & Sons will provide technical support only for installation and other general quality-control items. For technical support on the applications themselves, consult the program's vendor or author.

To place additional orders or to request information about other Wiley products, please call (877) 762-2974.

Index

Note to the reader: Throughout this index **boldfaced** page numbers indicate primary discussions of a topic. *Italicized* page numbers indicate illustrations.

Symbols and numbers

: (colon), IPv6, 146
- (hyphen), VLANs, 97
[] (square brackets), IPv6, 146
2.4 GHz, *240*
    IEEE 802.11b, **239–240**
    IEEE 802.11g, 238, **240–241**
    IEEE 802.11n, **241–242**
5.5 Mbps, 238, 239
5GHz
    IEEE 802.11a, 238, **241**
    IEEE 802.11n, **241–242**
10Base2, 65
10Base5, 65
10BaseT
    half-duplex Ethernet, 46
    IEEE 802.3, 65
10GBase-Extended Range (ER), 66
10GBase-Extra Long Wavelength (EW), 66
10GBase-Long Range (LR), 66
10GBase-Long Wavelength (LW), 66
10GBase-Short Range (SR), 66
10GBase-Short Wavelength (SW), 66
10GBase-T, 66
11 Mbps, 238, 239
40Mhz, 242
54Mbps, 238
100Base-CX, 65
100Base-FX, 65
100Base-TX, 65
1000Base-LX, 65
1000Base-SX, 65
1000Base-T, 65
1000Base-ZX, 65
3650-3700 operation, 239

A

A. *See* active state
ABRs. *See* Area Border Routers
access, 94
access lists, **227–230**, 285, 286
    extended, 228, **276–282**
    standard, 228, 270–271, 273–276
access points (AP), 245, **246–248**
access-class, 283
ACLs, **262**, **269–294**
    CLI/SDM, **270–283**
    filters, **270–283**
    Telnet, **283–285**
    troubleshooting, **288–290**
    verification, **285–288**
active state (A), 214
AD. *See* administrative distance
address learning, **71–73**
Address Resolution Protocol (ARP), 15, 38, 158, 309
addressing, 36–38
administrative distance (AD), 200–201, 213
administrative_distance, 190
administratively down, 130, 188
Advanced Encryption Standard (AES), **250**
AES. *See* Advanced Encryption Standard
AES-CCMP. *See* AES-Counter Mode CBC-MAC Protocol
AES-Counter Mode CBC-MAC Protocol (AES-CCMP), 249
anycast, 143, 148
AP. *See* access points
applications, **10–15**
Application layer, 18, 257, 278
application servers, 17
application-specific integrated circuit (ASIC), 42
areas, 202–205
area 0, 204
Area Border Routers (ABRs), 204
ARP. *See* Address Resolution Protocol
ASBR. *See* Autonomous System Boundary Router
ASCII, 195
ASIC. *See* application-specific integrated circuit
Asynchronous Transfer Mode (ATM), 52
ATM. *See* Asynchronous Transfer Mode

authentication, 170
    CBC-MAC, 250
    MAC, **248–249**
    Peer Router Authentication, 261
    PPP, *316*, 316–317, *317*
    ppp authentication chap, 310
    proxy, 260, **263**
Authentication, 247
auto-detect mechanisms, 47
Autonomous System Boundary Router (ASBR), 204
autorooters, 257
aux, 170
auxiliary passwords, 170

B

B2B. *See* business-to-business
back ups
    IOS, **198–199**
    routers, **192–194**
backbone area, 204
BackboneFast, 86
backdoors, 257
backoff algorithms, 63
bandwidth, 180
bandwidth (BW), 67, 180, 185
    static routing, 190
    WAN, **300–301**
    routers, 161
banners, 168–169
base MAC addresses, 80–81
Basic Service Set (BSS), **243–244**, *245*
binding, 16
block sizes, *135*, 135–138, 139, 272–273
boot sequence, **159**
bootstrap, 158, *159*
Bootstrap Protocol (BootP), **13–15**
BPDUs, 110
bridges, 2, 4, 43, **68–69**, 70
    multiport, 4, *5*
Bridge-Group Virtual Interface (BVI), 247

broadcast domains, 2, 4,
    44–45, 68
    flat networks, 88
    hosts, 67
    VLANs, 89
broadcast storm, 67, 143
brute force attack, 259
BSS. *See* Basic Service Set
business-to-business (B2B), 314
BVI. *See* Bridge-Group
    Virtual Interface
BW. *See* bandwidth

C

C, 156
cable TV (CATV), 51
CAM. *See* content
    addressable memory
Capability, 25
carrier detect (CD), 159
Carrier Sense Multiple Access
    with Collision Avoidance
    (CSMA/CA), 239, *239*, 240
Carrier Sense Multiple Access
    with Collision Detection
    (CSMA/CD), *45*, **45–47**,
    62–63, *63*, 240
CATV. *See* cable TV
CBAC. *See* Context-Based
    Access Control
CBC-MAC. *See* Counter
    Mode Cipher Block
    Chaining-Message
    Authentication Code
CD. *See* carrier detect
CDP. *See* Cisco Discovery
    Protocol
cdp holdtime, 24
cdp timers, 24
central office (CO), 48
channel service unit/data service
    unit (CSU/DSU), **161–162**,
    179, *179*
CIDR. *See* Classless
    Inter-Domain Routing
circuit switching, 49
Cisco Discovery Protocol (CDP),
    23–30, *30*, *31*
Class A IP addresses, 121–122
Class B IP addresses, 122
Class C IP addresses, 122–123
classful routing, *132*
Classless Inter-Domain Routing
    (CIDR), 288

classless routing, 132, *133*,
    134–142, 163
CLI. *See* command-line interface
client mode, VTP, *85*, 86,
    107–108
CLI/SDM, **270–283**, 290–293
clock rate, 180, 189
clocking, 179, *179*
CO. *See* central office
collision domains, 4, 6, 7, **44**, 45,
    47, 68, 89
command.com, 259
command-line interface (CLI), 74
    PPP, 303–304
    router IP addresses, 131
config vlan, 92
config-line, 171
config-router, 163
configuration register, 159
configure memory, 166
configure network, 166
configure terminal, 165
connectionless protocol, 21
connection-oriented
    communication, 20
console, 170
console passwords, 171
content addressable memory
    (CAM), 80
Context-Based Access Control
    (CBAC), 260, **262–263**, *263*
copy flash tftp, 197, 198
copy run start, 192
copy running-config startup-
    config, 181
copy running-config tftp, 192
copy startup-config tftp, 192
copy tftp flash, 199
copy tftp running-config, 195
copy tftp startup-config, 195
copy-startup-config running-
    config, 194–195
Counter Mode Cipher Block
    Chaining-Message
    Authentication Code
    (CBC-MAC), 250
CPE. *See* customer
    premises equipment
CRC, 38
crossover cable, *60*, **60**, 75
CSMA/CA. *See* Carrier Sense
    Multiple Access with
    Collision Avoidance
CSMA/CD. *See* Carrier Sense
    Multiple Access with
    Collision Detection
CSU/DSU. *See* channel service
    unit/data service unit

Current configuration, 193
customer premises equipment
    (CPE), 48

D

data communication equipment
    (DCE), **161**, **161–162**,
    179, 180
Data Link Connection Identifier
    (DLCI), 305–313
Data Link layer, 18, 36, 38, 45
    Ethernet, **47–48**, 62
    Frame Relay, 50
    HDLC, 301
    ISDN, 302
data terminal equipment (DTE),
    161, **161–162**, 179
datagrams, 36
DCE. *See* data
    communication equipment
DDoS. *See* Distributed Denial
    of Service
DEBUG, **111–113**
debug, 221–227, *223*
debug all, 224–225
debug eigrp packet, 212, 215,
    217–218
debug frame lmi, 309
debug ip eigrp events, 218
debug ip eigrp notification,
    212, 218
debug ip ospf adj, 209–211,
    219, 220
debug ip ospf hello, 209–210,
    219–220
debug ip ospf packet, 208, 219
debug ip rip, 225
debug ppp authentication, 317
debugging
    OSPF, 208–211, 219
    PPP, 317–318
de-encapsulation, 36
default gateway, 76, 100
default routing, **189–192**
default-network, 192
default-router 1.2.3.4., 127
delimiting characters, 169
demarcation point, 48, 161
Denial of Service (DoS), 258, 260
deny, 282
deny any, 280
Department of Defense (DoD),
    8–10, *9*
description, 173
desirable mode, 111–112

destination URL policy
    management, 260
Device ID, 25
DFS. *See* Dynamic Frequency
    Selection
DHCP. *See* Dynamic Host
    Configuration Protocol
Digital, Intel, and Xerox
    (DIX), 64
Digital Signal 0 (DS0), 300
Digital Subscriber Line (DSL), **52**
Digital Subscriber Line access
    Multiplexer (DSLAM), 52
Dijkstra algorithm, 202
Direct Sequence Spread Spectrum
    (DSSS), 241
disable, 165
distance-vector protocols,
    162, 201
distribute list, 227
Distributed Denial of Service
    (DDoS), 258
DIX. *See* Digital, Intel, and Xerox
DLCI. *See* Data Link
    Connection Identifier
DNS. *See* Domain Name Service
DoD. *See* Department of Defense
domains, 107. *See also* broadcast
    domains; collision domains;
    fully qualified domain name
Domain Name Service (DNS),
    12–13, 77, 127, 146
    hostnames, **125–126**
    IP addresses, 39, 126
    troubleshooting, **124–127**
DoS. *See* Denial of Service
DRAM. *See* dynamic RAM
DS0. *See* Digital Signal 0
DSL. *See* Digital Subscriber Line
DSLAM. *See* Digital Subscriber
    Line access Multiplexer
DSSS. *See* Direct Sequence
    Spread Spectrum
DTE. *See* data
    terminal equipment
DTP. *See* Dynamic
    Trunking Protocol
dual stacking, **143–144**
duplex, 83
dynamic, *95*
dynamic ACLs, **262**
Dynamic Frequency Selection
    (DFS), 238
Dynamic Host Configuration
    Protocol (DHCP), **13–15**, *14*
    conflicts, 14–15
    global configuration
        mode, 125

pools
    interfaces, 247
    routers, 125, 131
    wireless networks, 247
    troubleshooting, **124–127**
dynamic NAT, 290, **291**
dynamic RAM (DRAM), 166,
    181, 193
dynamic routing, 32,
    155–156, 192
Dynamic Trunking Protocol
    (DTP), 96

E

E1, 300
EEPROM. *See* Electronically
    Erasable Programmable
    Read-Only Memory
EIA/TIA-232-C, 303
EIGRP, 33
    AD, 213
    load-balance, 215
    serial interfaces, 180
    troubleshooting, 211–216
    verification, 212–215
Electronically Erasable
    Programmable Read-Only
    Memory (EEPROM), 158
enable password, 170
enable secret, 170
encapsulation, 35, *35*, 36
    DTP, 96
    Frame Relay, 305, 313
    GRE, 314
    HDLC, 310
    IEEE 802.1q, 95, 97
    PPP, 303, 311, **316–317**
    WAN, *310*
encapsulation, 99–100
encryption, 249–250, 315
encryption keys, **172–173**, 284
ER. *See* 10GBase-Extended Range
erase startup-config, 195
ESS. *See* Extended Service Set
ESS Extended Service Set Mesh
    Networking, 238
Ethernet, **44**, 47, *47*, **59–67**, *60*,
    61, 83. *See also specific*
    Ethernet types
    CSMA/CA, 240
    CSMA/CD, 62–63, *63*
    Data Link layer, **47–48**, 62
    distance constraints, 89
    Physical layer, 62, *64*, **64–66**
    UTP, 83

ETSI. *See* European
    Telecommunications
    Standards Institute
European Telecommunications
    Standards Institute
    (ETSI), 236
EW. *See* 10GBase-Extra Long
    Wavelength
exitinterface, 190
extended access lists, 228,
    276–282
Extended Service Set (ESS), **245**
extranet VPN, 314

F

Fast Ethernet, 62, 64, 83, 128
    ISR, 176
    running-config, 129
fast roaming, 238
FastEthernet 0/0, 185
FCC. *See* Federal Communications
    Commission
FCS, 38
FD. *See* feasible distance
FDDI, 48, 84
feasible distance (FD), 214
Federal Communications
    Commission (FCC), 236
File Transfer Protocol (FTP), **11**,
    183, 257
filters
    ACLs, **270–283**
    Application layer, 278
    forward/filter table, *71*, *73*,
        73–74, 111
    frames, 73
    URL, 260
fixed-configuration routers, 127
flash memory, 158, 199
    IOS, 159, 196
    verification, **197–198**
flat networks, 88, *88*
forward/filter table, *71*, *73*,
    73–74, 111
FQDN. *See* fully qualified
    domain name
frames, 36, 43, 73, 239
Frame Relay, 50
    encapsulation, 305, 313
    IETF, 305
    mappings, 312, *312*
    routers, **304–310**, 313, *313*
    single interface, 304–305
    subinterfaces, 305–306
    troubleshooting, **312–313**
    WAN, 160

FTP. *See* File Transfer Protocol
full-duplex Ethernet, **46–47**
fully qualified domain name
    (FQDN), 13

G

Gateway(config)#, 191
gateways, 17, 76, 100
gateway of last resort, 191, *191*
Generic Routing Encapsulation
    (GRE), 314
Gigabit Ethernet, 62, 64, 83
global configuration mode,
    125, 166
global unicast addresses, 147
globalnet, 292
graphical user interface (GUI), 12
gratuitous ARP, 15
GRE. *See* Generic
    Routing Encapsulation
guest-mode, 247
GUI. *See* graphical user interface

H

half-duplex Ethernet, 46–47, 243
HDLC. *See* High-Level
    Data-Link Control
HFC. *See* hybrid fibre-coaxial
High-Level Data-Link Control
    (HDLC), **51**, **301–302**, *302*
    encapsulation, 310
    WAN, 160
High-Speed Serial Data
    Connector (HSSDC), 65
Holdtime, 24–25
hop count, 200, 202
hosts, 17
    broadcast domain, 67
    switches, 72, 83
hostname, 168, 315
hostnames
    DNS, **125–126**
    ping, 126
    SSH, 284
    Telnet, 126, 183
Host-to-Host layer, 9, 19,
    20, **22–23**
HSSDC. *See* High-Speed Serial
    Data Connector
HTTP, 34
    Application layer attacks, 257
    IPv6, 146
    Network layer, 183

hubs, 5
    collision domains, 7
    routers, 6
    switches, 44
hybrid fibre-coaxial (HFC), 51
hybrid protocols, 201

I

IARP. *See* Inverse ARP
IBSS. *See* Independent Basic
    Service Set
ICMP. *See* Internet Control
    Message Protocol
IEEE. *See* Institute of Electrical
    and Electronics Engineers
IETF. *See* Internet Engineering
    Task Force
if-then, 227
I/G. *See* Individual/Group
IGP, 192
IGRP, 132
implicit deny, 228, 229
inbound access lists, 228
Independent Basic Service Set
    (IBSS), **243**, 245
Individual/Group (I/G), 48
Industrial, Scientific and Medical
    (ISM), 237
infrastructure-ssid, 247
Institute of Electrical and
    Electronics Engineers
    (IEEE), 236, 237
    IEEE 801.3ae, 66
    IEEE 801.q, 75
    IEEE 802.1d, 109–110
    IEEE 802.1q, **87**, 95, 97
    IEEE 802.1w, **86–87**
    IEEE 802.3, 65
        Ethernet Physical layer, 64
        half-duplex Ethernet, 46
    IEEE 802.3ab, 64, 65
    IEEE 802.3u, 64, 65
    IEEE 802.3z, 65
    IEEE 802.11, **237–239**
        WLAN security, **248–249**
    IEEE 802.11a, 238, **241**
    IEEE 802.11b, 238, *239*,
        239–240
    IEEE 802.11d, 238
    IEEE 802.11e, 238
    IEEE 802.11f, 238
    IEEE 802.11g, 238, **240–241**
    IEEE 802.11h, 238
    IEEE 802.11i, 238, 250
    IEEE 802.11j, 238
    IEEE 802.11k, 238

IEEE 802.11n, **241–242**
    MIMO, 238, 241, 242
    Physical layer, 241
IEEE 802.11r, 238
IEEE 802.11s, 238
IEEE 802.11t, 238
IEEE 802.11v, 239
IEEE 802.11w, 239
IEEE 802.11y, 239
Integrated Services Digital
    Network (ISDN), **50–51**,
    302, 303, 316
Integrated Services Router (ISR),
    159, 176, 180, 193
Inter-Access Point Protocol, 238
interfaces. *See also* network
    interface card; serial interface
    configuration, **175–188**, 211
        verification, **182–188**
    descriptions, 173–174
    DHCP pools, 247
    extended access lists, 280
    Fast Ethernet, 128
    GUI, 12
    IP addresses, **130–131**, 178
        masks, 130
        no shut down, 178
    routers, **127–131**
        masks, 134
    running-config, 128, 176–177
    show running-config, 178
    shutdown, 130
    VTY, 283
interface e0, 129, 177
interface fastethernet 0/0, 129,
    176, 177
interface range, 94
interface serial 0/1/0, 129, 177
interface *type number*, 128, 176
interface *type slot/port*, 128, 176
International Organization for
    Standardization (ISO), 15
international roaming, 238
Internet Control Message
    Protocol (ICMP), 183, 260
Internet Engineering Task Force
    (IETF), 305, 309
Internet layer, 9
Internet Protocol Control
    Protocol (IPCP), 303
Internetwork Packet
    Exchange Control Protocol
    (IPXCP), 303
Inter-Switch Link (ISL), 75
    routers, 97
inter-VLAN, *100*
    IP addresses, 101
    routers, *102*
        troubleshooting, **99–103**

Intra-Site Automatic Tunnel
    Addressing Protocol
    (ISATAP), **143–144**
intrusion detection, 260
Inverse ARP (IARP), 309
IOS, **192–200**
    access lists, 271
    back up, **198–199**
    bootstrap, 159
    copy flash tftp, 198
    flash memory, 159, 196
    NVRAM, 159
    privileged mode, 223
    restore, **199**
    ROM, 159
    routers, *197*
    show flash, 198
    show version, 198
    TFTP, 159, 196
IOS Firewall, **260–261**
IOS Router and Firewall
    Provisioning, 260
ip address *address mask*, 130, 178
IP addresses, **121–124**. *See also*
    access lists; IPv4; IPv6;
    TCP/IP
    Class A, 121–122
    Class B, 122
    Class C, 122–123
    copy flash tftp, 197, 198
    DHCP, 13, 14–15
    DNS, 12, 39, 126
    interfaces, **130–131**, 178
    inter-VLAN, 101
    IPv6, **145–148**, *146*
    many-to-one, 290
    mismatched, *311*, 311–312
    Network layer, 38
    NIC, 34, 39, 40, 121
    OSPF, 202
    packets, 157
    ping, 77
    private, 123–124
    routers, 4, 33–34, *34*, 130,
        156–158
        CLI, 131
    show cpd neighbor, 27
    special purposes, 122
    subinterfaces, 305
    summarization, **139–142**
    switches, **75–76**, 79
    Telnet, 172, 183
    troubleshooting, **39–42**, *40*
    VLAN switches, 100
    VLSM, **132–134**
    WAN, *311*, 311–312
ip default-gateway, 76
ip default-network, 191

ip dhcp pool_name network_
    address mask, 126
ip domain-lookup, 126
ip name-server, 126, 127
ip name-server 1.2.3.4., 127
ip nat inside, 291, 292
ip nat outside, 291, 292
ip route, 190
IP spoofing, 258
IP stack, 8
    failure, 40
ip subnet-zero, 137
ipconfig /all, 42
IPCP. *See* Internet Protocol
    Control Protocol
IPSec, 143
IPv4, **142–149**
    ISATAP, **143–144**
    NAT, 145, 289
    6to4 tunneling, **144–145**
IPv6, **142–149**
    IP addresses, **145–148**, *146*
    ISATAP, **143–144**
    OSPF, 202
    routers, 4
    6to4 tunneling, **144–145**
IPXCP. *See* Internetwork Packet
    Exchange Control Protocol
ISATAP. *See* Intra-Site Automatic
    Tunnel Addressing Protocol
ISDN. *See* Integrated Services
    Digital Network
ISL. *See* Inter-Switch Link
ISM. *See* Industrial, Scientific
    and Medical
ISO. *See* International
    Organization for
    Standardization
ISR. *See* Integrated
    Services Router

K

keepalives, 185

L

L2F. *See* Layer 2 Forwarding
L2TP. *See* Layer 2
    Tunneling Protocol
LAPB. *See* Link Access
    Procedure, Balanced
LAPD. *See* Link Access
    Procedure, D-Channel
latency, 43

latency, 69
layers. *See also specific layers*
    addressing, 36–38, *37*
    architecture, 16, *17*, *18*, 35
    Layer 2 Forwarding (L2F), 314
    layer 2 switches, 69–70
        address learning, **71–73**
        forward/filter table, *71*, *73*,
            73–74
    Layer 2 Tunneling Protocol
        (L2TP), 314
LCP. *See* Link Control Protocol
leased lines, *49*, 160
line, 170
Line Printer (LPR), 12
Line Printer Daemon (LPD), **12**
Link Access Procedure, Balanced
    (LAPB), **51**
Link Access Procedure,
    D-Channel (LAPD), **51**
Link Control Protocol (LCP),
    302, 303
link-local addresses, 147
Link-local Signaling (LLS), 207
link-state protocols, 201, 202
LLS. *See* Link-local Signaling
LMI, 306–307, 308
lmi, 306
LMI DLCI, 308
load-balance, 215
Local Interface, 25
local loop, 48, 51
Lock and Key ACLs, **262**
log, 280
logical interfaces, 184
login, 170
loop avoidance, 71
loopback, 40
LPD. *See* Line Printer Daemon
LPR. *See* Line Printer
LR. *See* 10GBase-Long Range
LW. *See* 10GBase-Long
    Wavelength

M

MAC. *See* Media Access Control
man-in-the-middle attacks, 258
many-to-one, IP addresses, 290
map, 306
mask, 190
masks. *See also* subnet masks;
    wildcard masks
    interfaces, 130
    router interfaces, 134
    VLANs, 100

maximum transmission units
(MTUs), 185, 186
Media Access Control (MAC)
authentication, **248–249**
base MAC addresses, 80–81
Ethernet, 47, *47*
forward/filter table, 111
IEEE 802.11n, 242
security, 112
show mac address-group, 286
show mac address-table,
80–81
switches, 71–73
ports, 112
memory. *See specific*
memory types
message of the day (MOTD),
168–169
MIMO. *See* multiple input,
multiple output
Mini-IOS, 158
mobility, 143
mode, 94
MOTD. *See* message of the day
MPLS. *See* MultiProtocol
Label Switching
MTUs. *See* maximum
transmission units
multicast, 67, 148, 164
multiple input, multiple output
(MIMO), 238, 241, 242
multipoint, 306
multiport bridges, 4, 5
MultiProtocol Label Switching
(MPLS), 50, **52**

N

named access lists, 228
NAT. *See* Network
Address Translation
nat pool, 291, 292
National Institute of
Standards and Technology
(NIST), 250
NCP. *See* Network
Control Protocol
network, 126
Network Access layer, 9
Network Address Translation
(NAT), 261, **269–294**,
289, 293
CIDR, 288
CLI/SDM, 290–293
dynamic, 290, **291**
IPv4, 145, 289

overloading, 290, **292**
static, **290–291**
troubleshooting, **293–294**
virtual servers, 288
Network Control Protocol
(NCP), 302, 303
Network File System
(NFS), **11–12**
UDP, 21
network interface card (NIC),
34, 39, 40, 47, 121
Network layer, 18
addressing, 36
FTP, 183
HTTP, 183
IP addresses, 38
PDUs, 36
show cdp entry *
protocol, 182
Telnet, 183
network management stations
(NMSs), 17
network reconnaissance, 258
next-hop_address, 190
NFS. *See* Network File System
NIC. *See* network interface card
NIST. *See* National Institute of
Standards and Technology
NMSs. *See* network
management stations
no cdp run, 24
no debug all, 225
no ip domain-lookup, 126
no login, 170
no shutdown, 130, 178
nonnegotiate, 94
nonvolatile RAM
(NVRAM), 159
back up, 192
running-config, 159, 193–194
startup-config, 166
TFTP, 194
verification, 193

O

OC-3. *See* Optical Carrier 3
OC-12. *See* Optical Carrier 12
OC-48. *See* Optical Carrier 48
OFDM. *See* Orthogonal
Frequency Division
Multiplexing
one-to-many addresses.
See multicast
open access, 248

Open Shortest Path First (OSPF),
202–211
areas, 202–205
debugging, 208–211, 219
serial interfaces, 180
show, 211
Open Systems Interconnection
(OSI), 16–18
model, **8–10**, *9*, **15–19**
open-key authentication, 249
Optical Carrier 3 (OC-3), 301
Optical Carrier 12 (OC-12), 301
Optical Carrier 48 (OC-48), 301
organizationally unique identifier
(OUI), 47
Orthogonal Frequency Division
Multiplexing (OFDM), 241
OSI. *See* Open Systems
Interconnection
OSPF. *See* Open Shortest
Path First
OUI. *See* organizationally
unique identifier
outbound access lists, 228
overhead, 190
overloading, 290, **292**

P

P. *See* passive state
packets, 78–79, 157
Data Link layer, 38
routers, 155
sniffers, 258
switching, 4, **49–50**
Transport layer, 36
Packet InterNet Groper (ping),
42, **77–78**, **221–222**
DNS, 77
hostnames, 126
IP addresses, 77
NIC, 39
privileged mode, 77, 222
remote server, 41
router, 41
running-config, 182
user mode, 222
parallel transmission, 160
passive state (P), 214
passphrase, 250
passwords, **169–173**, 284
attacks, 259
PPP, 315
VTP, 103–106
PAT. *See* Port Address
Translation

PDUs. *See* Protocol Data Units
Peer Router Authentication, 261
permanent, 190
permit, 282
per-user firewalls, 260
Per-VLAN Spanning-Tree
    (PVST), **87**
physical interfaces, 184
Physical layer, 18, 185, 241
    DSL, 51
    Ethernet, 62, *64*, **64–66**
    Frame Relay, 50
    WAN, 160
ping. *See* Packet InterNet Groper
"Ping of Death" attacks, 258
Platform, 25
point of presence (POP), 48
point-to-point connection, 46, 316
Point-to-Point Protocol (PPP), 51,
    302–304, *303*
    authentication, *316*,
        316–317, *317*
    debugging, 317–318
    encapsulation, 303, 311,
        316–317
    ISDN, 316
    passwords, 315
    routers, 303–304
    show interface, 316
    verification, **315–318**
    WAN, 160
Point-to-Point Protocol over
    Ethernet (PPPoE), **51**
Point-to-Point Tunneling
    Protocol (PPTP), 314
Policy-Based, Multi-Interface
    Support, 261
pool, 293
POP. *See* point of presence
ports. *See also* switch ports
    base MAC addresses, 80–81
    latency, 43
    numbers, Transport layer,
        37, 37–38
    redirection attacks, 259
    RJ-45, 83
    RSTP, 110
    security, 112
    trunks, 101
    VLANs, 89, 91
Port Address Translation (PAT),
    290, *292*, *294*
Port ID, 25
PortFast, 86
power-on self-test (POST), 84,
    158, 159, 167
PPP. *See* Point-to-Point Protocol
ppp authentication chap, 310

PPPoE. *See* Point-to-Point
    Protocol over Ethernet
PPTP. *See* Point-to-Point
    Tunneling Protocol
Presentation layer, 18
Pre-Shared Key (PSK), 250
private IP addresses, 123–124
privileged mode, 77, 165, 166,
    222, 223
Process/Application layer, 8, 21
protected management
    frames, 239
Protocol Data Units (PDUs),
    35–38
    layer addressing, 36–38, *37*
    layered architecture, 35
    Network layer, 36
    segments, 35–36
    Transport layer, 35, 36
PSK. *See* Pre-Shared Key
public safety, 238
PVC, 305
pvc, 306
PVST. *See* Per-VLAN
    Spanning-Tree

Q

quality of service, 238

R

radio frequency (RF), 243
radio measurements, 238
random access memory
    (RAM), 158, 166, 195.
    See also dynamic RAM;
    nonvolatile RAM
Rapid Spanning-Tree
    Protocol (RSTP)
    IEEE 802.1w, **86–87**
    troubleshooting, **109–110**
read-only memory (ROM), 158,
    159, 167
reference models, *16*, *17*, *18*
reflexive ACLs, **262**
reload, 196
remote access
    switches, **74–76**
    VPN, 314
remote server, 41
restore, 194–195, **199**
RF. *See* radio frequency
RID, 206

RIP, 33
RIPv1, 132, 202–203
RIPv2, **162–164**
    OSPF, 202–203
    VLSM, 137, 163
RJ-45, 61, *61*, *62*
    demarcation point, 161
    ports, 83
roaming, 238
rolled cable, **60–61**, *61*
ROM. *See* read-only memory
rootkit, 257
route aggregation.
    See summarization
Router#, 165
Router(config)#, 191
router eigrp, 212
router ospf *process-id*, 211
routers/routing, 2, *3*, **31–34**, *32*,
    90, *156*. *See also specific*
    router/routing types
    administrative configuration,
        167–175
    back ups, **192–194**
    boot sequence, **159**
    broadcast domain, 4, 68
    classful, *132*
    classless, 132, *133*,
        134–142, 163
    configuration mode, 211
    debug, 221–227
    default, **189–192**
    DHCP pools, 125, 131
    DNS, 127
    dynamic, 32, 155–156, 192
    flash memory, 199
    Frame Relay, **304–310**,
        313, *313*
    global configuration
        mode, 166
    HDLC, 302
    hostname, 168
    hubs, 6
    interfaces, **127–131**
        masks, 134
    inter-VLAN, **99–103**, *102*
    IOS, *197*
    IP addresses, 4, 33–34, *34*,
        130, **156–158**
        CLI, 131
    IPv6, 4
    ISL, 97
    network segmentation, **68**
    packets, 155
    passwords, **169–173**
    ping, 41
    POST, 159
    PPP, **303–304**

privileged mode, 165, 166
protocols, 200–202
restore, 194–195
running-config, 192
security, **227–230**
serial interface, 3
setup mode, 166
show, 221–227
specific configuration
    mode, 166
static, 156, **189–192**
subinterfaces, 101
subnet masks, 134
switches, 4
traceroute, 79
troubleshooting, 216–221
user mode, 165, 166
VLANs, **88–91**, 91
WAN, 160
    serial transmission,
      160–161
wildcard masking, 272
RSTP. *See* Rapid
    Spanning-Tree Protocol
running-config, 165
    DRAM, 193
    Fast Ethernet, 129
    interfaces, 128, 176–177
    NVRAM, 159, 193–194
    ping, 182
    RAM, 166
    routers, 192
    Telnet, 182
running-config tftp, 194
RXBOOT, 158

S

SDLC. *See* Synchronous Data
    Link Control
secondary, 130–131
Secure Shell (SSH), **284–285**
    encryption keys, **172–173**, 284
    VTY, 283, 285
security
    appliances, **262**
    banners, 168–169
    IEEE 802.11i, 238
    MAC, 112
    ports, 112
    private IP addresses, 123
    routers, **227–230**
    SSID, **248–249**
    static routing, 190
    switches, 89, 256
    threats, 255–265
    VLANs, 89

wireless networks, **248–251**
    WLAN, **248–249**
segments, 2, **67–69**
    PDUs, 35–36
    switches, 43
    TCP, 20, *21*
    UDP, 22, *22*
sendmail, 257
serial interface, 3, *179*, **179–180**
serial transmission, 160–161
Serial0/0, 189
server mode, *85*, 86, 108
service password-encryption, 315
Service Set ID (SSID), **243–244**
    security, **248–249**
Session Initiation Protocol
    (SIP), 260
Session layer, 18
setup mode, 166
shared-key authentication, 249
shortest-path-first protocols.
    See link-state protocols
SHOW, **111–113**
show, 205, 211, 221–227
show access-list, 285
show access-list 110, 286
show cdp, 24
show cdp entry * protocol, 182
show cdp neighbor, 24–28
show controllers *int*, 180
show cpd entry *, 27–28
show cpd neighbor, 25
show cpd neighbors detail, 26
show flash, 197–198
show frame ?, 306
show frame map, 308–309
show frame pvc, 307–308
show frame-relay, 306–307
show interface, 79, 189
    LMI, 308
    PPP, 316
    verification, **183–187**
show interface fastethernet
    0/0, 184
show interface *int*, 178
show interface serial 0/0/0, 186
show interface trunk, 93
show interfaces, 130, 185, 312
show ip access-list, 286
show ip arp, 42
show ip eigrp neighbors, 212, 213
show ip eigrp topology, 212, 214
show ip interface, **187**, 286
show ip interface brief, **187**
show ip ospf, **206**
show ip ospf database, **206**
show ip ospf interface, **207**
show ip ospf neighbor, **208**
show ip protocols, 164, 216–217

show ip route, 33, 156, **205**,
    212, 213
show ip route eigrp, 212
show mac address-group, 286,
    287–288
show mac address-table, **80–81**
show port-security interface, 112
show processes, 226–227
show running-config, 28–30, 79,
    286–287
    interfaces, 178
    mismatched IP addresses, 312
show spanning-tree, 82–83, 87
show startup-config, 181–182
show version, 167, 193, 197–198
show vlan, 93
show vtp status, 104
shutdown, 130
Simple Mail Transfer Protocol
    (SMTP), **12**
Simple Network Management
    Protocol (SNMP), **12**, 21
SIP. *See* Session Initiation Protocol
site-to-site VPN, 314
6to4 tunneling, *144*, **144–145**
smart-serial, 161
SMTP. *See* Simple Mail
    Transfer Protocol
sniffers, 258
SNMP. *See* Simple Network
    Management Protocol
Spanning Tree Protocol (STP), 71
specific configuration mode, 166
speed, 83
SR. *See* 10GBase-Short Range
SSH. *See* Secure Shell
SSID. *See* Service Set ID
standard access lists, 228,
    270–271, **273–276**
startup-config, 159, 181, 189
    NVRAM, 166
    restore, 194–195
static NAT, **290–291**
static routing, 156, **189–192**
STP. *See* Spanning Tree Protocol
straight-through cable,
    59–60, *60*
subinterfaces, 99–100,
    101, 305–306
subnets, 132–133
subnet masks. *See also* Variable
    Length Subnet Masks
    routers, 134
    static routing, 190
    VLSM, 132
summarization, **139–142**
SW. *See* 10GBase-Short
    Wavelength

switches, 2, *3*, 7, **69–74**, *89.*
    See also layer 2 switches
administrative configuration,
    167–175
bridges, 70
collision domains, 4, 68, 89
configuration, **74–76**
crossover cable, 75
DEBUG, **111–113**
frames, 43
hosts, 72, 83
hubs, 44
IEEE 802.1q, 95
IP addresses, **75–76**, 79
layer 2, 69–70
MAC, 71–73
multiport bridges, 5
network segmentation, **68**
POST, 84
remote access management,
    74–76, *76*
routers, 4
security, 89, 256
segments, 43
SHOW, **111–113**
troubleshooting, **95–99**
verification, **79–83**
VLANs, 7, 82, *91*, 256
    IP addresses, 100
VTP, **84–85**, **103–108**
switch ports, 83–84
    access mode, 112
    access ports, 101
    desirable mode, 111–112
    MAC, 112
    trunk ports, 101
    VLANs, 93, **94–95**
switchport, 94
switchport access, 95
switchport mode access, 95
switchport mode dynamic
    auto, 96
switchport mode dynamic
    desirable, 96
switchport mode trunk, 96
switchport nonnegotiate, 96
switchport port-security mac-
    address, 112
Synchronous Data Link Control
    (SDLC), 51
sys-id-ext, 82
system restarted by bus error, 167

T

T1, 300
T3, 300

tables, VLSM, 135, *136*, *139*, *140*
TCP. *See* Transmission
    Control Protocol
TCP SYN Flood, 258
TCP/IP, **8–10**, *10*, **15–19**, 40
Telnet, 11
    ACLs, **283–285**
    hostnames, 126, 183
    IP addresses, 172, 183
    Network layer, 183
    passwords, 170, 172
    running-config, 182
telnet, 285
Temporal Key Integrity Protocol
    (TKIP), **249–250**
Teredo, 145
TFN. *See* Tribe Flood Network
TFN2K. *See* Tribe Flood
    Network 2000
TFTP. *See* Trivial File
    Transfer Protocol
thin protocol, 20
time to live (TTL), 183, 222
timers, 24
TKIP. *See* Temporal Key
    Integrity Protocol
Token Ring, 48
toll network, 48
TPC. *See* Transmit Power Control
trace, 222–223
traceroute, 42, **78–79**, 222–223
    ICMP, 183
    TTL, 222
Transmission Control Protocol
    (TCP), **20**. *See also* TCP/IP
    Application layer, 278
    Host-to-Host layer, *22*, 22–23
    segments, 20, *21*
    Transport layer, 183
Transmit Power Control
    (TPC), 238
transparent bridging, 43
transparent mode, 85, *85*, 86
Transport layer, 18, 35, 36
    port numbers, *37*, 37–38
    TCP, 183
Tribe Flood Network (TFN), 258
Tribe Flood Network 2000
    (TFN2K), 258
Trivial File Transfer Protocol
    (TFTP), **11**, 195
    back up, 192
    IOS, 159, 196
    NVRAM, 194
Trojan horse, 257, 259
troubleshooting
    ACLs, **288–290**
    DHCP, **124–127**
    DNS, **124–127**

EIGRP, 211–216
Frame Relay, **312–313**
inter-VLAN routers, **99–103**
IP addresses, **39–42**, *40*
NAT, **293–294**
OSPF, **202–211**
RIPv2, **162–164**
routers, 216–221
RSTP, **109–110**
switches, **95–99**
VLANs, **92–95**
VTP, **103–108**
WAN, **310–313**
trunk, 94, 95
trunk [*parameter*], 95
trunks. *See also* Virtual
    Trunk Protocol
    DTP, 96
    ports, 101
    VLANs, **97–99**
trust exploitation attacks, 259
trusted networks, 256
TTL. *See* time to live

U

UDP. *See* User Datagram
    Protocol
unicast, 147
unique local addresses, 148
Unlicensed National Information
    Infrastructure (UNII),
    237, *237*
unshielded twisted pairs (UTP),
    61, *61*, 62, 83
untrusted networks, 256
UplinkFast, 86
URL filters, 260
User Datagram Protocol (UDP),
    13, **20–23**
    Host-to-Host layer, *22*, 22–23
    6to4 tunneling, 145
user mode, 165, 166, 170, 222
username, 284, 315
UTP. *See* unshielded twisted pairs

V

V.24, 303
V.35, 303
Variable Length Subnet Masks
    (VLSM), *137*, *138*, *141*
    block sizes, *135*, 135–138
    classful routing, *132*

classless routing, 132, *133*, **134–142**, 163
IP addresses, **132–134**
OSPF, 202
RIPv2, 137, 163
subnets, 132–133
summarization, **139–142**
tables, 135, *136*, *139*, *140*
verification
  ACLs, **285–288**
  default routing, **189–192**
  EIGRP, 212–215
  flash memory, **197–198**
  interface configuration, **182–188**
  NVRAM, 193
  PPP, **315–318**
  show interface, **183–187**
  show ip interface, 187
  static routing, **189–192**
  switches, **79–83**
  WAN, **299–318**
version 2, 164
virtual circuit, 20
virtual LANs (VLANs)
  broadcast domains, 89
  default gateway, 100
  masks, 100
  ports, 89, 91
  routers, **88–91**
  security, 89
  switches, 256
    IP addresses, 100
  switch ports, 93, **94–95**
  switches, 7, 82, *91*
  troubleshooting, **92–95**
  trunks, **97–99**
  VTP, **84–85**

virtual private network (VPN), **314–315**
  remote access, 314
virtual servers, NAT, 288
Virtual Trunk Protocol (VTP), 75
  client mode, *85*, 86, **107–108**
  domains, 107
  passwords, **103–106**
  server mode, *85*, 86, 108
    switches, 104
  switches, 84–85, **103–108**
  transparent mode, 85, *85*, 86
  troubleshooting, **103–108**
  VLANs, **84–85**
viruses, 259
VLANs. *See* virtual LANs
VLSM. *See* Variable Length Subnet Masks
voice, 94
VPN. *See* virtual private network
VTP. *See* Virtual Trunk Protocol
vtp, 103–104
vtp server, 104
VTY, 172, 283, 285
vty, 170

W

WAN
  BW, **300–301**
  connection types, 48–52, *49*, **300–301**
  encapsulation, *310*
  IP addresses, *311*, 311–312
  routers, 160
    serial transmission, 160–161

support, *50–52*
terms, 48
troubleshooting, **310–313**
verification, **299–318**
web servers, 17
WEP. *See* Wired Equivalent Protocol
Wi-Fi Alliance, 236, 237
Wi-Fi Protected Access (WPA), 249, **250**
wildcard masks, 270, **272–274**
Wired Equivalent Protocol (WEP), **248–249**, 250
wireless networks
  AP, **246–248**
  DHCP pools, 247
  IEEE 802.11v, 239
  open access, 248
  security, **248–251**
  SSID, 247
Wireless Performance Prediction (WPP), 238
WLAN Association (WLANA), 236
WLANs
  administration, **235–254**
  encryption, **249–250**
  security, **248–249**
WPA. *See* Wi-Fi Protected Access
WPA 2, **250**
WPP. *See* Wireless Performance Prediction

X

X Window, **12**
X.25, 50

The Best CCNA Quick Reference Book/CD Package on the Market!

Brush up on key CCNA topics with hundreds of challenging review questions!

- Two bonus CCNA exams available only on the CD. Each question includes a detailed explanation.
- Over 200 electronic flashcards.

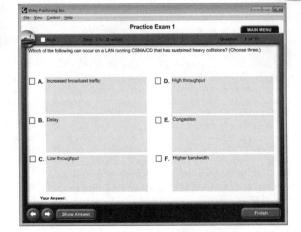

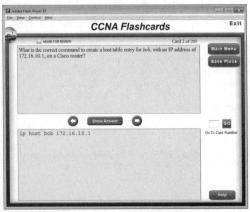

Reinforce your understanding of key concepts with these electronic flashcards!

- Contains over 200 flashcard questions.
- Quiz yourself anytime, anywhere.

Use Glossary for instant reference.

- Glossary of Key Terms for instant reference.

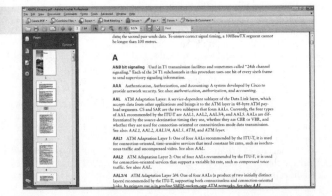